Therapy Culture

Therapy Culture explores the powerful influence of therapeutic imperative in Anglo-American societies. In recent decades virtually every sphere of life has become subject to a new emotional culture. Professor Furedi suggests that the recent cultural turn towards the realm of the emotions coincides with a radical redefinition of personhood. Increasingly, vulnerability is presented as the defining feature of people's psychology. Terms like people 'at risk', 'scarred for life' or 'emotional damage' evoke a unique sense of powerlessness. Furedi questions the widely accepted thesis that the therapeutic turn represents an enlightened shift towards emotions. He claims that therapeutic culture is primarily about imposing a new conformity through the management of people's emotions. Through framing the problem of everyday life through the prism of emotions, therapeutic culture incites people to feel powerless and ill. Drawing on developments in popular culture, political and social life, Furedi provides a path-breaking analysis of the therapeutic turn.

Frank Furedi is Professor of Sociology at the University of Kent, Canterbury. His books include *Paranoid Parenting* and *Culture of Fear*.

Therapy Culture

Cultivating vulnerability in an uncertain age

Frank Furedi

Taylor & Francis Group

LONDON AND NEW YORK

First published 2004
by Routledge
11 New Fetter Lane, London EC4P 4EE

Simultaneously published in the USA and Canada
by Routledge
29 West 35th Street, New York, NY 10001

Reprinted 2004

Routledge is an imprint of the Taylor & Francis Group

Typeset in Times New Roman by
Keystroke, Jacaranda Lodge, Wolverhampton
Printed and bound in Great Britain by
TJ International Ltd, Padstow, Cornwall

British Library Cataloguing in Publication Data
A catalogue record for this book is available from the British Library

Library of Congress Cataloging in Publication Data
Furedi, Frank, 1947–
    Therapeutic culture : cultivating vulnerability in an uncertain age / Frank
Furedi.
        p. cm.
Includes bibliographical references and index.
1. Social psychology. 2. Emotions—Social aspects. 3. Psychotherapy—
Social aspects. 4. Social problems—Psychological aspects. I. Title.
    HM1033.F87 2003
    302—dc21
2003007201

ISBN 0–415–32160–3 (hbk)
ISBN 0–415–32159–X (pbk)

Contents

Figures

Acknowledgements

This book owes a great debt of gratitude to my friends, colleagues and students. They have provided me with a unique opportunity to test out my ideas and to benefit from their insights. During the course of exploring and thinking about therapeutic culture, I was able to profit from the exchange of views with a number of individuals carrying out research in related areas. In Britain, the work of Derek Summerfield, Simon Wessely, David Wainwright, Ralph Fevre and Michael Fitzpatrick has been very important for the development of my arguments. In the US, the work of James Nolan and Joel Best helped clarify some key issues that relate to this text. The participants of a small symposium on *Therapeutic Culture Wars*, held at Boston University in March 2001, had a huge impact on my thoughts on this subject. I am particularly grateful to Vanessa Pupavac and Eleanor Lee for their inspiring comments and criticism. Through discussing therapeutic culture we have become collaborators in the genuine sense of the term. This book is dedicated to my late father Laszlo for trying to teach me to question everything.

Introduction

These days, we live in a culture that takes emotions very seriously. In fact it takes them so seriously that virtually every challenge or misfortune that confronts people is represented as a direct threat to their emotional well-being. Everyday disappointments – rejection, failure, being overlooked – are regarded as risks to our self-esteem. When people are described or describe themselves as vulnerable, the reference is usually to the state of their emotion. Those who are represented as damaged are assumed to be emotionally scarred. People who have 'issues' or who need to 'share' are viewed as preoccupied with the realm of feelings. The language of emotionalism pervades popular culture, the world of politics, the workplace, schools and universities and everyday life.

The significance that contemporary culture attaches to making sense of the world through the prism of emotion is shown by the way that therapeutic language and practices have expanded into everyday life. Children as young as 9 and 10 talk about feeling 'stressed out'. Recently, the American Girl Scouts produced a 'stressless badge', embroidered with a swinging hammock. Troop 459 in Sunnyvale, California has organised a stress clinic for third-grade Brownies. Meanwhile, pupils at St Silas Primary School in Liverpool in England are being offered aromatherapy, foot and hand massages, as well as lavender-soaked tissues to help reduce stress and aggression.[1] Children's behaviour is increasingly portrayed through a psychological label. They are often diagnosed as depressed or traumatised. And while there is still a debate about the validity of the diagnosis of school phobia, virtually any energetic or disruptive child could acquire the label of 'attention deficit hyperactivity disorder'. Between 1990 and 1995, the United States has seen a doubling in the number of children diagnosed with attention deficit disorder. Experts claim that as many as 2 million American children may have ADHD.[2]

The vocabulary of therapeutics no longer refers to unusual problems or exotic states of mind. Terms like stress, anxiety, addiction, compulsion, trauma, negative emotions, healing, syndrome, mid-life crisis or counselling refer to the normal episodes of daily life. They have also become part of our cultural imagination. Most viewers did not think it was bizarre when Tony Soprano, head of America's favourite television gangster family, went to see psychiatrist Dr Jennifer Melfi. Even the hard men of the Mafia appear to make sense of their lives through the idiom provided by America's therapeutic culture. 'I was seeing a therapist myself about a year ago', hardened mobster Paulie Walnuts tells Tony on one show. 'I had some issues', he informs his Mafia boss.

Nor is the new language of therapy confined to describing the state of emotion of the individual. In the US, an urban renewal project is described as a 'confidence-building programme' designed to 'heal America's cities'. The atmosphere during the aftermath of 11 September was often represented as a 'time of national trauma'. It was claimed that the US was a 'nation in distress'. 'New York seeks closure' was how some observers reported the mood in October 2001. Leading US sociologist Neil Smelser argues that the events of 9/11 have inflicted a 'cultural trauma' on America.[3] Similar sentiments were echoed in Australia after the bombing of a nightclub on the island of Bali led to the loss of lives of its citizens. Australia was described as a 'nation in trauma'. In the same way, a year after the assassination of Israeli Prime Minister Rabin, the country was depicted as 'a nation in post-trauma' by a reporter.[4] During the summer of 2002, it was reported that the 'traumatised' English community of Soham was 'seeking closure' after trying to come terms with the tragic killing of two young girls in their midst.

Healing and closure 'were the two most frequently uttered words in the news coverage following Timothy McVeigh's conviction by a Denver jury of eleven counts of murder and conspiracy for the 1995 bombing of the federal building in Oklahoma City', reports *The Nation*.[5] Although terms like healing and closure resembles the moral search for solace, they are essentially psycho-medical concepts. Thus the concept of healing like that of bereavement is frequently represented as a process with its symptoms and clearly definable phases. According to a study of the impact of this tragedy on the people of Oklahoma City, there was 'the unspoken message' that the grieving process should proceed along the lines dictated by therapeutic knowledge.[6]

The tendency to reinterpret not just troublesome but also normal experience through the medium of an emotional script can be see through the phenomenal expansion of psychological labels and therapeutic terms. According to one study the term 'syndrome' was entirely absent from the pages of American law journals during the 1950s, 1960s and 1970s. Yet by 1985, the word 'syndrome' appeared in 86 articles, in 1988 in 114 articles and by 1990 in 146 articles. In one month alone in 1993, more than 1,000 articles in periodicals and newspapers used the term.[7] In Britain, the growth of a therapeutic vocabulary is equally striking. Words that were virtually unknown and unheard by the public in the 1970s would be recognised by most people by the early 1990s. Even in the 1980s, people had never heard of terms like generalised anxiety disorder (being worried), social anxiety disorder (being shy), social phobia (being really shy), or free-floating anxiety (not knowing what you are worried about).

Take the word 'self-esteem'. Today, a low level of self-esteem is associated with a variety of emotional difficulties that are said to cause a range of social problems from crime to teenage pregnancy. Most people have become exposed to discussions of self-esteem through the media, school, health service or place of work. Yet until recently, not only was a lack of self-esteem not perceived as a problem, the term itself had no therapeutic connotations. In the seventeenth century, it referred to a sense of independence, self-judgement or self-will. In the eighteenth and nineteenth century its meaning was modified to refer to the act of self-knowledge. Indeed as late as 1989, *The Oxford English Dictionary* defines it as 'favourable appreciation or opinion of oneself' and makes no reference to its link with problems of the emotion.[8] In contrast today, low self-esteem is one of the most overused diagnoses for the problem of the human condition. A Factiva search of 300 UK newspapers in 1980 did not find a single reference to the term self-esteem (Figure 1). It found three citations in 1986. By 1990, this figure rose to 103. A decade later, in 2000, there were a staggering 3,328 references to 'self-esteem'.

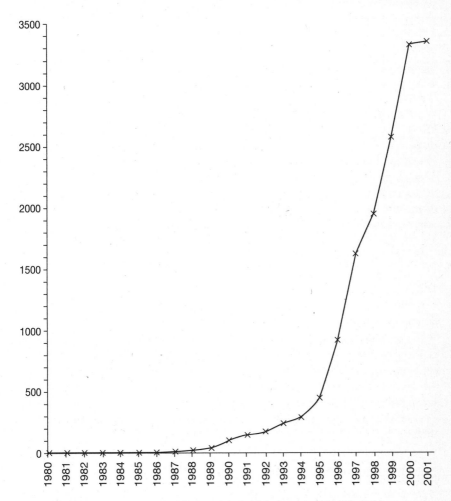

Figure 1 Citations of the term 'self-esteem' in British newspapers 1980–2001.

Source: Factiva.[9]

So widespread are deliberations about self-esteem that it is easy to overlook the fact that the problems associated with it are of relatively recent invention. The transformation of self-esteem into a widely used figure of speech reflects a wider pattern, whereby psychological terms become part of the language of everyday life. So today, trauma means little more than people's response to an unpleasant situation. A Factiva search of British newspapers shows a phenomenal increase in the usage of this word by journalists in articles (Figure 2).

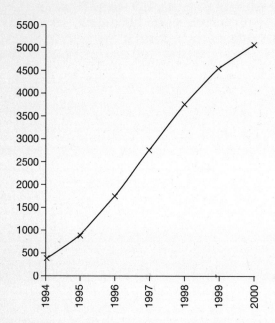

Figure 2 Citations of the word 'trauma' in British newspapers 1994–2000.
Source: Factiva.

A Factiva search also indicates a similar pattern of increase in the usage of words like stress, syndrome or counselling (Figures 3–5).

The expanding usage of the idiom of therapeutics is not simply of linguistic interest. The changing form of language communicates new cultural attitudes and expectations. In particular, the language expresses what one study on the rise of the 'myth of self-esteem' has characterised as the 'current ascendancy of feelings and well-being in the culture as a whole'.[10] This turn towards emotionalism represents one of the most significant developments in contemporary western culture.[11]

The emotional deficit

A closer inspection of therapeutic culture indicates that it speaks not so much about emotion as about the problem of emotional deficit. The concern with people's self-esteem is with its low level. Low self-esteem is invariably interpreted and

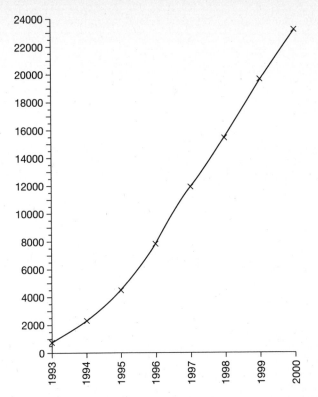

Figure 3 Citations of the word 'stress' in British newspapers 1993–2000.

Source: Factiva.

understood as an invisible disease that undermines people's ability to control their lives. The belief that individuals and society suffer from an emotional deficit informs discussions of the subject of emotional intelligence and emotional literacy. The conviction that people cannot emotionally cope with a growing range of encounters, experiences and relationships informs the way that therapeutic culture makes sense of the human condition.

The perception of emotional deficit is underwritten by an intense sense of emotional vulnerability. As a result, society is in the process of drawing up a radically new definition of what constitutes the human condition. Many experiences that have hitherto been interpreted as a normal part of life have been redefined as damaging to people's emotions. People, particularly children, are said to be prone to a bewildering variety of conditions and psychological illnesses, such as depression or stress-related diseases. Invariably, the public is told that more and more people are afflicted with these emotional injuries. For example, it is frequently claimed that the number of children suffering from depression is rising and that this is likely to lead to a growing incidence of this disease amongst adults in the future. According to one account, in the US 'psychological depression is a greater scourge than poverty'. Moreover, its impact on society is growing all the time.

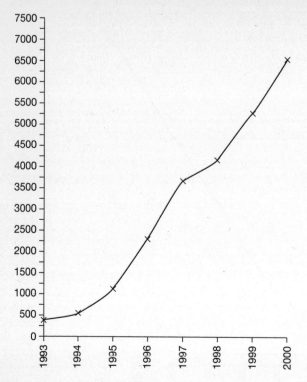

Figure 4 Citations of the word 'syndrome' in British newspapers 1993–2000.
Source: Factiva.

Terrence Real, author of *I Don't Want To Talk About It: Overcoming the Secret Legacy of Male Depression*, contends that since the beginning of the twentieth century 'each generation has doubled its susceptibility to depression'.[12]

One Canadian researcher reported that he found that the younger the respondent, the greater the reported prevalence of depression. 'Not only are today's children likely to be unhappier than their predecessors, but without some dramatic change in their life course, they will be less well-equipped for the task of creating a better Canada for the children of future generations', argues Professor Gus Thompson of the University of Alberta.[13] Thompson believes that this problem is due to the fact that children in Canada have been subjected to more childhood trauma over recent decades than their predecessors. However, it is difficult to imagine that Canada has become a more traumatic society during the past 20 years. One of the central arguments of this book is that what has changed is the cultural imagination of trauma. Today we fear that individuals lack the resilience to deal with feelings of isolation, disappointment and failure. Through pathologising negative emotional responses to the pressures of life, contemporary culture unwittingly encourages people to feel traumatised and depressed by experiences hitherto regarded as routine.

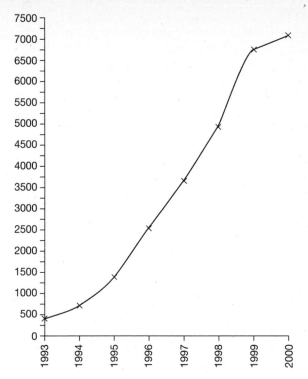

Figure 5 Citations of the word 'counselling' in British newspapers 1993–2000.
Source: Factiva.

There is little doubt that there has been a massive increase in the rate of depression. Amongst those born around the First World War, the lifetime prevalence of depression was about 1 per cent. This rate rose to 5 per cent amongst those born around the Second World War and jumped massively to between 10 and 15 per cent amongst those born in the 1960s. American psychologist Martin Seligman believes that this epidemic of depression is due to the difficulty that people have in dealing with disappointment and failure. 'By blunting warranted sadness, warranted anxiety, it created children at high risk for unwarranted depression', he writes.[14] The discourse of emotional deficit pathologises bad feelings and turns an expanding variety of experiences into sites where emotional survival becomes an issue. This is a perspective that acts to persuade people to regard themselves as ill.

The profound sense of emotional vulnerability is the product of tendency to objectify the uncertainties of life and to recast them in the amplified form of risk. As we argue in Chapter 6, 'The self at risk', through objectifying uncertainty into risks beyond individual control a sense of powerlessness and helplessness is cultivated. The objectification of human experience into the grammar of risks has the potential of turning every new encounter into a test of emotional resilience. It encourages the sense of emotional vulnerability and the adoption of the language of emotional deficit. The flip side of risk consciousness is powerlessness. This is a consciousness that is shaped through the internalisation of the narrative of emotional deficit.

The language of emotional deficit pervades education and illustrates the interplay between risk and powerlessness in what is a basic institution of society. There is a continuous stream of reports that suggest that teachers, school principals and students are in a constant state of anxiety and stress. As the Australian education-alist Dr Catherine Scott argues, her country's system of education appears to be so gripped by an atmosphere of fear that school principals were 'stressed' by the behaviour of their students. In the UK, it is claimed that university academics face an epidemic of stress-related illness and that their students are increasingly suffering mental health problems.[15] One survey stated that 53 per cent of UK university students had 'anxiety at a pathological level' and the British Association for Counselling and Psychotherapy (BACP) argues that one in ten student seeking university counselling is 'already suicidal'.[16] Some researchers in the US argue that schools play an important role 'in laying the groundwork for depression'.[17] In the UK school exams have been criticised on the grounds that they create stress and other illnesses among children. According to one survey, more than half of all 7-year-old children 'suffer from exam stress'. In some schools, children as young as ten are being offered hypnosis to help boost their exam performance.[18]

The transformation of the experience of school into a regime of high risk has as its premise the belief that virtually any event represents a potential threat to a child's emotional well-being. The complex emotional tensions that are integral to the process of growing up are now often defined as stressful events with which children cannot be expected to cope. Concern with children's stress has led some schools to train young students in 'anger management' skills. A project in inner-city Birmingham has been mounted to help secondary school pupils learn to deal with their emotions. This project offers an anger management course taught by a psychotherapist, who encourages secondary school pupils to release their aggression through role-play and exercises, such as punching pillows.[19] And, it seems, it is never too early to start. Pupils as young as 4 are offered counselling as part of a pilot project to tackle childhood trauma at ten primary schools in Peterless, Easington. One organisation, Befrienders International, offers lessons to pupils, as young as 6, on how to cope with the stresses of modern life. Chris Bale, the director of this initiative, hopes that such lessons will help pupils in nursery and primary schools to deal with 'crises later in life and, as result, reduce the suicide rate'.[20] It appears that the therapeutic profession is determined to protect children's emotions from virtually any form of challenging experience. In September 2000, it was announced that telephone help-lines were being set up for children stressed by starting secondary school. These help-lines were complemented by numerous counselling schemes designed to help pupils to make the transition from primary to secondary education. The promoters of the help-line believe that 'mental health work' should be integrated into teaching to help children cope with the pressure of secondary education.[21]

Therapeutic intervention

If children as young as 4 are seen to be legitimate targets for therapeutic intervention, it is not surprising to hear of a growing demand for expanding such services for babies. In the US, infant mental health has become an established professional specialism. Advocates of this specialism in the US and the UK argue for the initiation of a mental health service for babies – a 'service designed to prevent early psychological damage from occurring by strengthening the bond between babies at risk and their main carer, usually the mother'.[22] The belief that there is a deficit of the elementary emotional attributes required for childrearing and that therefore third-party therapeutic intervention is called for in the parent and child relationship is a widely held assumption of parenting 'experts'.[23]

Indeed, every stage in the life course – from birth to death – is portrayed as representing such grave risks as to require counselling and other forms of intervention. Giving birth is represented as emotionally traumatic and it is argued that postbirth stress effects at least one in four mothers. At the other end of the life spectrum, grief is no longer depicted as a pain to be endured, but as a process that is best dealt with through therapeutic support. Contemporary society transmits the belief that problems of the emotion ought not be faced by people on their own. Therapeutic intervention and counselling is continually offered to individuals facing unexpected or difficult or challenging or unpleasant encounters. English football fans were surprised to find out that the German police employed stress counsellors to diffuse potential flashpoints during a World Cup qualifier in Munich.[24] One company has launched a pet insurance package that provides counselling and psychotherapy for people whose pets have died.[25]

Therapists have assumed the role of relationship experts and have succeeded in establishing a demand for their services in virtually every institutional setting. In the 1960s, around 14 per cent of the American public had received some form of psychological counselling at least once in their lives. By 1995, nearly half the population had experienced some form of therapeutic intervention. And it is estimated that by the turn of the century, this figure had edged up to encompass nearly 80 per cent of the American public.[26] It is claimed that during any given week, 15 million Americans will attend one of about 500,000 support group meetings.[27] The 1999 Surgeon General's Report on Mental Health stated that 50 million Americans develop mental health disorders each year.[28] Therapy is sometime depicted as an American eccentricity. However, the impact of therapeutic intervention on British society is no less significant.

Since the 1980s – when counselling became one of Britain's little growth industry – the number of people practising talking cures has grown steadily.[29] Even sections of the counselling profession are concerned by the routinisation of the demand for therapeutic intervention. The psychotherapist Nick Totton has described counselling training as a 'pyramid selling scheme', which has created a 'huge increase in clients'. 'The only way to get therapy and counselling paid for . . . is to get the state and other institutions to pay for it', argues Totton.[30] Evidently, the counselling professions have proved successful in creating a thriving market for its services.

It is now assumed that people facing an unusual event are likely to need or at least likely to benefit from counselling. Take the case of the disbanding of Cleveland County Council in 1995. Although none of the employees faced redundancy – they were to be reassigned to a reorganised local authority – bereavement counselling was offered to council workers to help them overcome any sense of loss they might experience. The employees were warned that the experience could be like the death of a 'friend or a loved one'. Staff were told to expect symptoms, such as loss of libido, mood swings, eating disorders and panic attacks. The council employed 18 counsellors to help employees identify signs of stress and to 'tap into their inner strengths'.[31]

The authority of counselling rests on its ability to give meaning to experience in a world strongly wedded to a therapeutic ethos. According to Nolan, this authority is based on a new priestly class, mainly psychiatrists and psychologists 'who can understand and can decipher the emotivist language emanating from the authoritative self'. Nolan believes that the religious custodians of the old moral order have been replaced by medical and psychiatric authority.[32] Certainly, the self-consciously therapeutic professions play an important role in constructing the idiom of an emotionally oriented moral universe. The staggering growth in the numbers of psychologists, counsellors, therapists and social workers confirms the power of the therapeutic imperative. As Nolan noted,

> The monumental increase in the psychologization of modern life is also evident in the fact that there are more therapists than librarians, fire-fighters, or mail carriers in the United States, and twice as many therapists as dentists or pharmacists. Only police and lawyers outnumber counsellors, but only by a ratio of less than two to one in both instances.[33]

During the years between 1970 and 1995, the number of mental health professionals quadrupled.[34] A similar pattern is evident in Britain. Government has institutionalised counselling throughout the NHS, at all levels of education and the penal system. When the National Lottery handed out money for health projects, 25 per cent went to advice and counselling schemes, compared to 5 or 6 per cent for research charities. During the past decade, the number of members of the British Association for Counselling has more than tripled. It was 4,500 in 1989, rising to 16,000 in 1999. The number of psychotherapists on the UKCP Register of Psychotherapists increased from 3,500 in 1997 to 5,500 in 1999. According to one estimate, half a million people work full- and part-time as counsellors.[35] The pervasive influence of counselling is shown by research carried out by Counselling, Advice, Mediation, Psychotherapy, Advocacy Guidance (CAMP). It mapped the number of counselling encounters taking place in Britain in February 1999 and concluded that 1,231,000 such events took place that month.[36]

Therapeutic intervention is not simply confined to the relationship of the therapist and the client. Such interventions characterise all contemporary organisations and institutions in Britain. The assimilation of the therapeutic ethos and practices by a variety of professions and institutions – teachers, lawyers and social workers –

has been well documented. 'The management of subjectivity has become a central task for the modern organisation', notes Nikolas Rose in his comprehensive survey of the development of the institutionalisation of therapeutic culture in Britain.[37]

The past two decades has seen a discernible expansion in the influence of therapeutic activism in private business. The shake-out of British industry in the 1980s saw the acceptance of the idea that people who lost their jobs were likely to face trauma, thus creating a demand for redundancy counsellors. Soon, these counsellors were not only managing those about to be made unemployed, but were also providing stress therapy to managers to help them handle making others redundant.[38] Since the 1980s, counselling has become incorporated into the normal routine of personnel management. A growing group of British blue chip companies, such as the leisure group Whitbread and Cable and Wireless, have taken steps to provide therapy as part of the employee's contract. Such companies are not merely buying in counselling services, but are also training managers to use counselling skills as part of their work.[39] Within the field of human resource management, the therapeutic approach has come to inform a growing range of practices. The Institute of Personnel and Development in London runs courses on emotional intelligence for executives and actively crusades for the adoption of therapeutic practices in business.[40] A study carried out by the Department of Employment reported that British 'employees are more likely to be offered stress counselling (49 per cent) to help with the effects of the long-hours culture than be offered assistance with their basic childcare needs'.[41]

The expansion of therapeutic intervention into all areas of society has been remarkable. Even institutions which explicitly depend on the spirit of stoicism and sacrifice, such as the military, police and emergency services are now plagued with problems of the emotion. It is often claimed that police and emergency personnel are particularly susceptible to stress-related illnesses, including post-traumatic stress disorder (PTSD). The very conduct of war is regularly portrayed through the language of mental illness. A recent book on war by Chris Hedges, a foreign correspondent for the *New York Times*, describes war as a form of drug, 'often a lethal addiction'. 'Once we begin to take war's heady narcotic, it creates an addiction that slowly lowers us to the moral depravity of all addicts', he writes.[42] If fighting wars is publicly represented in such pathological terms it is not surprising to discover that many soldiers regard their experience of combat as a risk to their mental health. Every major conflict appears to be followed by its own syndrome. The Gulf War syndrome has been followed by the Balkans syndrome, Kosovo syndrome, Chechen syndrome and Intifada syndrome. There is talk of an emerging Afghan syndrome. Concern with the state of emotion of personnel has led the US military to institutionalise therapeutic practices and adopt a therapeutic language. The once feared obstacle course has been renamed 'the confidence course' and a programme entitled 'Caring for others' has been made mandatory for all officers.[43] Lawyers, who are suing the British Ministry of Defence on behalf of soldiers who claim that they were not prepared for the psychiatric injuries of war, claim that their clients are 'facing an occupation which carries psychological and psychiatric risks at the most extreme end of the spectrum'.[44] Many leading officers involved with the police and the military find it difficult to reconcile the role of these services with the turn towards a therapeutic ethos. Chief Superintendent Brian MacKenzie of the British Police Superintendents Association has expressed concern about the force's 'unfortunate dependency on counsellors and social workers' and takes the view that police officers are becoming too soft to do the job.[45]

The therapeutic system of meaning

Therapeutic culture provides a script through which emotional deficits 'make their way into the cultural vernacular' and become available for 'the construction of everyday reality'.[46] From birth, to marriage and parenting, through to bereavement, people's experience is interpreted through the medium of the therapeutic ethos. Numerous studies of this subject have noted that conventional moral meanings attached to concepts such as guilt and responsibility lose their salience in circumstances where the therapeutic ethos gains influence. The sociologist James Nolan writes of the emergence of 'guiltless justice' in his study of the American Drug Court Movement. He writes that, 'inasmuch as the therapeutically defined ideals of illness and of self-esteem assume a more central place in the adjucative process, the notion of guilt is made increasingly less relevant'.[47] The 'reigning paradigm of moral understanding' is 'therapeutic to the core' argues an American study of this subject.[48] As a result, the attempt to gain meaning of new experiences and developments is often pursued through the prism of therapeutics. Even major catastrophes and unusual momentous events are made sense of through their impact on people's mental state and emotions. There has been an emphasis on perceiving an attack on a nation as an assault on society's collective and individual mental health.

The response to the destruction of the World Trade Center in September 2001 illustrates how the therapeutic imagination informed the subsequent interpretation of this tragedy. Of course, commentators warned about the devastating destructive capacity of weapons of mass destruction and raised concerns about America's physical security. However, an important stress was placed on the mental health consequences of this episode and the pain and the hurt that was the legacy of 9/11 was frequently depicted in terms of their impact on emotions. Grief and bereavement were presented as a process that had discernible common features affecting everyone. It was stated as a matter of common sense that grief led to clearly recognised conditions that were treatable by trained professionals. Descriptions of the grief process were frequently transmitted through the media and specialist publications. These outlets often provided a 'do-it-yourself diagnostic tool kit' through which people could make sense of their pain.[49]

Within hours of this terrible event, the potential for great psychological damage to a population represented as traumatised was circulated as a matter of incontrovertible fact. From the outset, therapeutic activists and health professionals predicted that millions of Americans would suffer trauma and long-term emotional injury. A survey carried out in the days after the attack found that 90 per cent of American adults reported a substantial level of at least one symptom of stress.[50]

Within hours of the event, numerous advocacy organisations published information leaflets that provided recovery tips for traumatised individuals and outlined how people in different circumstances were likely to react. Particular emphasis was placed on providing information for helping children cope with the event. Numerous internet sites were established to deal with the psychological impact of 9/11 on children.[51]

The guidance offered to the public was underwritten by the conviction that most Americans required some form of therapeutic instruction to come to terms with the tragedy. This literature was informed by the assumption that intervention on an unprecedented scale would be necessary to deal with the psychological consequences of 9/11. Experts continually published reports that indicated that significant sections of the population were likely to suffer long-term psychological injury. 'Tens of thousands of public-school children in New York City are experiencing chronic nightmares, fear of public places, severe anxiety and other mental health problems months after the World Trade Center attack', argued a study published 10 months after the event.[52] Some reports suggested that even those who thought they were over their trauma faced reminders that brought back bad memories and anxiety.[53]

The expectation of long-term emotional damage was invariably presented as a matter of fact – part of a cultural script for framing public reaction. Reports outlining grave emotional injuries also transmitted expectations of how people were likely to respond. 'While the fear and anxiety that swept the country after the September 11 attacks have subsided for most Americans, hundreds of thousands continue to suffer psychological wounds from that day, according to national mental health experts', reported a staff writer for the *Washington Post*.[54] Experts frequently cited the experience of the Oklahoma City bombing, and pointed out that there the rate of PTSD among survivors and rescuers was 34 per cent. Projections based on the high prevalence of PTSD amongst the Oklahoma City survivors suggested that the dimension of the mental health problems facing the post-9/11 American population would be massive. It was also argued – ostensibly based on the experience of Oklahoma – that 'it may take months for the families and friends of victims to pass through the shock and denial stages, adopt coping strategies and behaviors and address the consequences of those behaviors'.[55] Even if people appeared to have weathered the shock, the road to recovery would stretch way into the indefinite future was the implication of this prognosis. 'The American Red Cross is still in Oklahoma City, and people are still coming for help 6 years later', noted one report.[56]

During the year following 9/11, therapeutic experts continually insisted that the mental health consequence of the event would be enormous. One study published in September 2002 estimated that more than 500,000 people in the New York metropolitan area would have developed PTSD as a direct result of the attacks.[57] However, the expectation of a massive jump in the number of psychologically damaged people demanding mental health services did not materialise. 'I expected to see much higher rates of utilization', wrote Joseph Boscarino, a researcher with the New York Academy of Medicine. Boscarino stated that most of the patients he saw who were affected by September 11 had a history of mental instability.[58] Nevertheless, the relatively small take-up rate of mental health services did not deter therapeutic activists from demanding more resources for expanding their projects. Paradoxically, experts could claim that the very small interest in their services was itself a symptom of the serious scale of the problem. It was stated that 'in many cases, people who develop the most serious emotional difficulties delay seeking help for months or years'.[59] The popular media representation of trauma contained the implication of a life sentence. As we shall note in the chapter on the diminished self, the perspective of being emotionally scarred for life is underwritten by radically new ideas about the working of human subjectivity.

Survivors of the Oklahoma City bombing were frequently featured as experts who could be relied on to instruct the public of what kind of reactions to expect. One mother, who lost her 4-year-old daughter and served as a Red Cross volunteer in New York, drew on her experience to outline the grief response, 'at first you're in this catatonic state, where you can't even function' and sometimes 'you can't even cry, you're so numb from pain'.[60] The idea of 'delayed grief', that severe symptoms could manifest themselves in years to come, was a powerful theme in the emotional script circulated through the media. It underlined the conviction that the events of 9/11 had left people with long-term emotional damage.

The emotional script communicated was one that also sought to create a sense of unity around the common experience of vulnerability. 'Neighbors must support neighbors in the wake of devastating terrorist attacks', argued an ad-hoc group of crime victim assistance organisations a day after the attack.[61] The National Association of School Psychologists issued an extensive guideline 'Memorials/ Activities/Rituals Following Traumatic Events – Suggestions For Schools'. The guidelines asserted that memorials and related activities 'serve an important function in the healing process for both students and staff'. It added that a 'significant purpose of a memorial activity is to bring people together in order to express feelings and concerns together – to reduce feelings of isolation and vulnerability'.[62] Another guide, presented in the form of a questions and answers, advised people to 'pull together'.[63] A survivor of the Oklahoma City bombing reminded New Yorkers that 'her healing came through working on the memorial'. She wrote that 'it was like a group therapy session'.[64]

The post-September 11 exhortations to mobilise collective grief to create memorials represents an important departure from previous norms of memoralisation. It followed the pattern established in Oklahoma City, where the so-called memorial process 'was consciously designed to be therapeutic: to help the community engage the traumatic impact of the bombing'.[65] Such an orientation towards remembrance reflects a powerful shift away from the more traditional affirmation of communal purpose. It represents an important shift towards encouraging people to find meaning through their individual selves. This move from a bereaved community to a community of bereaved expresses the individualising imperative at work in society. As Linenthal's study of Oklahoma City indicates, gaining meaning through memorialisation provides a way to 'stake one's claim to visible presence in the culture'. Bereavement becomes not so much an act of remembrance about the dead, but a therapeutic statement about the survivor. That is why there was such strong pressure to include not only the names of the dead, but also those of the survivors in the Oklahoma City memorial.[66] Therapeutic memoralisation aims to give recognition to the individual self. As we note in Chapters 5, the institutionalisation of the politics of recognition has become a key development in contemporary society.

The therapeutic imagination played an important role in framing the sense of loss and disorientation experienced by the American people. Typically, it sought to represent this reaction in psychomedical terms. Through this language, therapeutic activists sought to provide meaning to an event that appeared beyond comprehension. The American Psychological Association self-consciously embraced this. 'Psychologists can and should build their resilience to help patients and clients effectively during this unprecedented period of American history', the APA declared. It added that 'patients and clients across the country will rely on psychologists to help process the personal meaning of the events that already have taken place and will continue to occur'.[67] Healing through giving meaning through a diagnosis was a strategy adopted by a variety of institutions. At various times sports people, musicians, artists and others claimed that their professional activities could contribute to healing the nation. Phillipe de Montbello, director of the New York Metropolitan Museum, stated that 'people who haven't had the heart yet to go back to work have been coming here for a sense of serenity and the intercession of other people, rubbing shoulders in a kind of womb of culture'. He added that hospitals are there to fix the body and 'we're hear to fix the soul'.[68]

The therapeutic world-view not only influenced the public, it also shaped the way that opinion-makers and officials made sense of events. Dealing with the problem of mental health was a cause that received the automatic support of the political class. It was also a cause that could readily mobilise financial support. In an unusual and unprecedented gesture, the American Red Cross and the September 11 Fund undertook to underwrite the expense of extended mental health treatment for people directly affected by the attacks of 9/11. This initiative intended to pay for psychiatric help, drug or alcohol treatment, psychotropic medications and hospital care of an estimated 150,000 families.[69] At a time when disputes about the allocation of resources to other forms of health and social services dominated the political landscape, the consensus around mental health support stands out as unique. The importance attached to providing public access for psychiatric support illustrates the significance that therapeutic culture attaches to damage caused to the emotion.

The powerful influence of therapeutic culture over the way that September 11 was experienced is highlighted by the fact that it was so rarely contested.[70] A small minority of mental health professionals were critical of the powerful tendency to medicalise people's normal reaction to a major disaster. A letter published by a group of psychologists a week after 9/11 was particularly worried about the mounting of aggressive mental health interventions in disaster situations. The group was concerned about the widespread labelling of people's stress reactions as a type of illness. 'Instead of people saying that it is common to have bad dreams or trouble sleeping when we are stressed, they say the reactions are "signs of PTSD" or that people have "PTSD"', objected Gerald Rosen, one of the signatories of the letter.[71]

One consequence of the representation of the impact of 9/11 through the medium of psychology was to one-sidedly exaggerate the vulnerability of the public. Through conceptualising the problem as that of the impact of terror on the public, the role assigned to people becomes a passive one. 'What will happen to the national psyche if the country is attacked again', asks one report.[72] The therapeutic world view dictates that the answer will be a psychological one – 34 per cent will develop PTSD, etc. However, such a narrow focus on mental health overlooks the possibility that through a sense of common purpose, unity or a commitment to fight, the so-called national psyche may alter and gain purpose and definition. Experience suggests that the impact on the national psyche of sudden military attacks, such as the bombing of Pearl Harbor, the Blitz, terrorist attacks in London and suicide bombers in Jerusalem are mediated through cultural and political influences and institutions. Such violence need not simply traumatise its targets. It can provoke a determination to fight or stimulate the construction of a community around a common cause. It is worth recalling that at the outbreak of the Second World War it was widely expected that one of the outcomes of the conflict would be an increase in the number of mental patients. And although arrangements were made to receive the expected flood of civilian mental patients, there was no increase in their numbers. Studies have reported a similar pattern from experiences as varied as the conflict in Northern Ireland and the Spanish Civil War. As Bracken argues, 'there is good evidence that wartime suffering and trauma is not inevitably associated with increased morbidity'. In these instances, an increased sense of solidarity and community provided people with a sense of meaning through which they could make sense of the experience of adversity.[73] Whether people feel traumatised and if they do, how they experience it, depends at least in part on how they interpret that experience. One of the contributions of therapeutic culture is to encourage individuals to make sense of dramatic episodes through mental health terms. The influence of this approach may dispose people to react to major events, like 9/11, as potential trauma victims rather than as concerned citizens.

The therapeutic response to September 11 highlights many of the trends that are evident during the course of less publicised tragedies and adverse episodes. In Britain, the consequences of recent flood disasters and the recent outbreak of foot and mouth disease were portrayed in similar mental health terms. The response to the tragic murder of two 10-year-old girls – Holly Wells and Jessica Chapman – in the Cambridgeshire village of Soham in August 2002, bore all the hallmarks of therapeutic culture. Counselling services and a special help line were swiftly organised by the local authorities and the community was actively encouraged to participate in memorial activities. In the UK, the words 'counselling is being offered' conveys a sense that something exceptionally serious has happened.

A system of meaning for our time

The ascendancy of therapeutic culture cannot be charted with precision and exactitude. Changing cultural values and expectations evolve gradually. They develop alongside traditional norms and often merge with them to redefine their meanings. Studies of American and British societies indicate that the therapeutic sensibility has a long history. Eva Moskowitz in her book *In Therapy We Trust: America's Obsession with Self-Fullfillment* starts her story in the mid-nineteenth century. Rose's study of this development in the UK shows that during the interwar period the therapeutic ethos had gained influence over officials, policy-makers and business managers. Throughout the Second World War and the establishment of the Welfare State there were considerable opportunities for the institutionalisation of therapeutic practices.[74]

But although public interest in therapeutics coincides with the rise of modernity, it remained confined to clearly defined areas of life. Despite the expanding influence of psychology in the twentieth century, until the 1960s it was merely one of many (and by no means the most influential) strands of influence on western culture. It is when therapeutics begins to influence and arguably dominate the public's system of meaning that it can be said to have emerged as a serious cultural force. Today, with the rise of the confessional mode, the blurring of the line between the private and the public and the powerful affirmation for emotionalism, there is little doubt that it has become a formidable cultural force. Its power is demonstrated through its influence over popular culture. That the therapeutic code can overwhelm other more traditional codes of meaning is strikingly illustrated in the *Sopranos*. Tony's abandonment of the traditional Mafia code of silence for the confessional medium of therapy is represented as a predictable attempt to catch up with the times. Exploring and engaging with the inner-self has become an important constituent of contemporary identity.

In a pioneering study of the rise of therapeutic culture, Philip Rieff observed that 'each culture is its own order of therapy'.[75] What distinguishes circumstances today from past therapeutic regimes is that the system of therapy is not confined to a distinct and functionally specific role, it has merged with wider cultural institutions and has an impact on all institutions of society. As we shall see, the therapeutic ethos has a significant impact on education, the system of justice, provision of welfare services, political life and medicine. It appears to have colonised all the professions and institutions of society. The invasion of the therapeutic ethos into other professions and forms of authority is particularly striking in relation to its former competitor – religious institutions. Recently, the Archbishop of Canterbury has claimed that therapy was replacing Christianity in western countries. According to Archbishop Carey, 'Christ the Saviour' is becoming 'Christ the counsellor'.[76] Priests are increasingly encouraged to adopt counselling skills. Gradually, the theologian has assumed the role of a therapist. Organisations that have sought to harness therapeutic expertise for the work of the Church inevitably assume a secular orientation. The Westminster Pastoral Foundation, for example, which was established by a Methodist minister in the early 1970s in order to combine the insights offered by counselling, psychotherapy and Christianity, has weakened its religious connection. Its director, Dr Tim Woolmer, states that nevertheless they are still interested in 'wider religious questions such as: why are we here and what's it all about'.[77] This subordination of religious doctrine to concern with people's existential quest reflects a wider shift towards an orientation towards a preoccupation with the self. A study of 'seeker churches' in the US argues that their ability to attract new recruits is based on its ability to tap into the therapeutic understanding of Americans.[78]

The colonisation of the sphere of religion by therapeutic authority is manifest in relation to the way society engages with the phenomenon of death. Tony Walter's important exploration into this subject suggests that the experience of bereavement has changed away from the external mourning behaviour of previous times towards 'grief process' played out within the bereaved inner psyche.[79] This displacement of the externally focused spiritual towards the psychological is highlighted by the example of CRUSE, the UK's leading bereavement agency. This organisation, which was founded by Quakers in 1959, had become by the 1990s 'an entirely secular organisation in which counselling technique and a kind heart are seen as sufficient'.[80]

Even in the US, where therapeutic culture first acquired influence, the powerful impact that it has on everyday life is a relatively recent development. Allan Horwitz, who carried out research on outpatients seeking help at a community mental health centre in the early 1970s recalled that 'from the vantage point of the early 1970s, it was impossible to predict that the general disturbances of living that troubled these outpatients would soon metamorphose into specific psychiatric diseases that afflict the clients of mental health professionals today'.[81] Looking back on his data from the 1970s, Horwitz was struck by the relative absence of psychiatric labelling of the outpatients. 'In retrospect, what seems remarkable about these data is the insignificant role psychiatric diagnoses played in characterizing the kinds of difficulties this group faced', he concluded.[82]

The triumph of therapeutic culture is most striking in Britain, a society that was formerly associated with reserve, understatement and reticence. During the 1960s and 1970s, stoic Britain was frequently contrasted with the let-it-all-hang-out ethos of the US. But after the unprecedented display of public emotionalism over the death of Princess Diana in 1997, it is difficult to sustain the myth that Britain is the land of the stiff upper lip. Since this event, the powerful influence of therapeutic culture on British society has been widely acknowledged. 'The age of British reserve is over', concluded one comparative study of national emotional attitudes. It stated that the British are brasher than the French or the Germans, but not as extrovert as Mexicans or Israelis.[83] Leading social commentators not only acknowledge this development, but also tend to welcome it as a distinctive feature of a more caring and more expressive New Britain. According to a commentator in the *The Guardian*, the focus of British culture has shifted from the 'life of the mind' to the 'life of the heart'. She claims that 'rationality has been downgraded, emotion rules' and boasts that since 'women are better at emoting', they have men 'particularly those over the age of 45 brought up on strict stoicism' on the run.[84]

The belief that we lack the emotional resources to cope with disappointment and adverse circumstances is a relatively recent development. Such perceptions of vulnerability stand in sharp contrast to the way people viewed their engagement with adversity in previous decades. It is easy to forget that the promiscuous application of therapeutic diagnosis to describe the condition of people confronting misfortune is a product of the past decade or so. Today, every minor tragedy has become a site for the intervention of trauma counsellors and therapeutic professionals. Counselling the bereaved, their relatives and friends has become mandatory. Commentators continually allude to hidden psychological damage that is likely to incapacitate people for some considerable time, if not for ever.

Until the 1980s, the British cultural script regarding personhood invoked notions of 'stoicism, understatement, the stiff upper lip and of fortitude (e.g. bulldog tenacity which popular memory associates with the nations experience during the Second World War)'.[85] Although, as with all cultural constructs, the notion of British fortitude represented an idealised version of human behaviour, it helped frame the interpretation of everyday life, including the experience of adversity. Take the case of one of the most devastating industrial tragedies in post-war Britain: the Aberfan disaster of 1966. Despite the horror of a village school engulfed by a coal-tip slide, nobody demanded compensation for their trauma or their psychological distress. The relatives of the 116 children and 28 adults who died during this tragedy, took the view that they did not want to pursue prosecution because that would be to 'bow to vengeance'. The surviving children resumed their education a fortnight after the tragedy 'so that their minds may be taken off the disaster'. A year after this disaster, Mary Essex, a family and child psychologist from the University of Wales, noted that the surviving children seemed normal and adjusted. *The Times* observed that 'the villagers had done admirably in rehabilitating themselves with very little help'.[86] Today, such a response to a major disaster would be unthinkable. There would be an automatic assumption that every survivor in the area was deeply traumatised and inevitably scarred for life. Sending young pupils back to school so soon after a tragedy would be scorned as bad practice. The very attempt by the community to cope through self-help would be denounced as misguided, since such victims could not be expected to deal with such problems on their own.

A recently published book on Aberfan is genuinely perturbed by the stoicism of the survivors of this strategy. It documents how people perceived offers of psychological help in negative terms and bemoans the fact that the local consultant psychiatrist found it difficult to get people to realise they needed help. 'The stigma of seeking psychological help was stronger in the 1960s than today', conclude the authors. The authors are delighted that since the subsequent invention of post-traumatic stress disorder, authorities are likely to respond to such a disaster with clearly focused therapeutic policies.[87]

Since the 1990s the history of Aberfan is being rewritten in line with today's therapeutic ethos. Researchers are busy helping survivors to reinterpret their experiences through the language of trauma. A collection of recently conducted interviews of Aberfan survivors suggests that, retrospectively, people have discovered past traumas. A survivor who has authored a recollection of this disaster echoes this sentiment, when she remarked that 'one crucial area where I feel we were badly let down in Aberfan was in the lack of proper counselling'.[88] Such is the power of present-day sensitivity to emotional injury that past events can only make sense through the language of trauma. Instead of exploring the resilience of this Welsh mining community, commentators are far more likely to treat the survivors as hidden victims whose emotional needs were ignored by a callous officialdom.

The stoic response to the tragedy at Aberfan was by no means exceptional. The public presentation of the 1952 and 1953 flood disaster that led to death of 164 people provides a useful case study. The press coverage was mainly informational rather than emotional. Although the Queen 'sent sympathy to relatives', there was none of the emoting that one associates with the media coverage of contemporary disasters.[89] Even the funeral of the flood victims was described dispassionately without the use of therapeutic categories. The funeral of the thirteen people who died at Lynmouth was portrayed in the following terms: 'it was a poignant occasion that brought to the little cemetery groups of mourning relatives – sturdy Devon folk who bore their sorrow with fortitude'.[90] Today, formerly sturdy Devon folk would be presented as vulnerable, traumatised and emotionally damaged individuals.

Concern with emotional vulnerability and long-term psychological trauma is also conspicuously absent in the presentation of the 1950s floods. 'Again our people have displayed their characteristic courage', stated Clement Attlee, former prime minister and leader of the Labour Party. He added that 'there have been moving stories of heroism on the part of men, women and children'.[91] Survivors, traumatised victims and emotionally damaged communities were absent in this scenario. Significantly, the event was interpreted through the grand narrative of religion, rather than a self-oriented psychology. The Archbishop of Canterbury claimed that the 'disaster had a kind of majestic honesty about it'. He believed that 'it was part of the eternal conflict which man waged against the forces of nature and which was the condition of man's existence' and that the 'tragedy sprang from those elementary conditions which Divine Providence set for mankind to work out its own salvation'.[92] Today, such comments would be regarded with incomprehension by society.

This is clear when we compare the response of the 1950s with the representation of the floods that wreaked havoc in Britain in 2000. Newspaper headlines proclaimed that Britain was in a state of crisis and facing a major natural disaster. Although the floods caused considerable damage and led to the indirect loss of four lives, it was a relatively minor disaster compared to previous experiences. Yet, the flood was experienced as a traumatic experience with far-reaching consequences to people's emotional health. Significantly, the health threat posed by the flood was often presented in psychological rather than physical terms. 'The long-term effects of flooding on psychological health may perhaps be even more important than illness or injury', warned an editorial in the *British Medical Journal*. It added that 'for most people the emotional trauma continues long after the water has receded'. It pointed out that 'making repairs, cleaning up, and dealing with insurance claims can be stressful' and warned that 'if there is a lack of support during the recovery process, stress levels may increase further'.[93] This emphasis on the emotional vulnerability of flood victims is a recurrent theme in contemporary British culture.

Today, the belief that emotional vulnerability defines the human condition is so strong that it is easy to imagine that the reaction of people to disappointment and adversity is similar to ours. As a result there is a veritable industry of rewriting history in line with current therapeutic imagination. Many scholars find it difficult to believe that people in the past actually experienced adversity with bravery and fortitude. As with the case of Aberfan, history is being reinterpreted according to the standpoint of the therapeutic imagination. So, for example, according to a survey carried out by a psychologist in 1997, 750,000 British women are still suffering from the stress and trauma of the Second World War. The psychologist Melinda Waugh calls these women the 'forgotten generation', and states that it is 'possible that children of the women bore the psychological scars of post-traumatic stress disorder'. All this speculation was based on extrapolation from a survey involving 100 women.[94] As the following chapters will make clear, the discovery of undisclosed mental health problems in the past says more about the contemporary preoccupation with the inner world of the self than with what happened in previous centuries.

The book

Accounts of therapeutic culture often associate this phenomenon with the selfish or at least self-centred quest for self-fulfilment, individual choice or satisfaction, self-expression, expressive individualism and emotionalism. Such critics point to its downside and present it as constituting a culture of narcissism, selfishness or irresponsibility. While some of these characterisations contain useful insights, they overlook what maybe some of the most important features of the therapeutic outlook. This book suggests that the therapeutic imperative is not so much towards the realisation of self-fulfilment as the promotion of self-limitation. It posits the self in distinctly fragile and feeble form and insists that the management of life requires the continuous intervention of therapeutic expertise. The elevated concern with the self is underpinned by anxiety and apprehension, rather than a positive vision realising the human potential. Therapeutic culture has helped construct a diminished sense of self that characteristically suffers from an emotional deficit and possesses a permanent consciousness of vulnerability. Its main legacy so far is the cultivation of a unique sense of vulnerability.

The most significant feature of therapeutic culture is not so much the promotion but the distancing of the self from others. In this it consistently crystallises the contemporary mood of individuation. Therapeutic culture both reflects and promotes the trend towards fragmentation and alienation. But it also does much more than that. As we note in Chapter 3, it actually seeks to legitimise the trends towards fragmentation. It does this by systematically stigmatising informal relations of dependence. That is why the greatest hostility of therapeutic culture is reserved for the sphere of informal relations. Indeed, as we shall argue, the disorganisation of the private sphere is probably the main accomplishment of therapeutic culture.

Therapeutic culture is often characterised as a retreat to the inner world of the self. In fact the orientation to the self has the paradoxical effect of opening up the sphere of private life to therapeutic management. Consequently, the management of the self has become part of the business of government and other institutions. The potentially authoritarian implications of this will be discussed in the final chapters of the book.

A few words about the meaning of therapeutic culture. The ascendancy of therapeutic culture should not be confused with the growing influence that therapy exercises over people's lives. In this book we are interested in therapy as a cultural phenomenon rather than as a clinical technique. As the sociologist Robert Bellah put it, it is 'a way of thinking rather than as a way of curing psychic disorder'.[95] A culture becomes therapeutic when this form of thinking expands from informing the relationship between the individual and therapist to shaping public perceptions about a variety of issues. At that point it ceases to be a clinical technique and becomes an instrument for the management of subjectivity.

A culture encompasses a system of beliefs about the meaning of life and offers a vocabulary through which we can make sense of an individual's relationship to society. Cultural representations of this relationship are underpinned by perceptions of what constitutes the individual. Every culture offers a statement about human nature and insights into the potential and limitations of human action. Therapeutic culture today offers a distinct view about the nature of human beings. It tends to regard people's emotional state as peculiarly problematic and at the same time as defining their identity. As a result, therapeutic culture regards the management of emotion as the most effective way of guiding individual and collective behaviour.

Therapeutic culture should not be equated with the totality of western culture. In day-to-day life people are confronted with what sociologists Peter Berger and Thomas Luckmann characterised as a cacophony of competing cultural claims.[96] Individuals are asked to respect the authority of the state, compete against their business rivals, exercise responsibility or reflect on their selves. As Hewitt contends, cultures contain 'several sets of beliefs about motivation, each one operating within a specific sphere of activity and thought to explain and justify actions taken within it'.[97] A capitalist about to fire an inefficient employee makes sense of the act through the cultural logic of the market. But the employer is also responsive to other cultural trends and when the dismissed worker is also offered counselling, the influence of the therapeutic ethos becomes evident. Therapeutic culture does, therefore, provide a system of meaning and symbols through which people experience and make sense of the world. Arguably it offers a web of meaning that is distinctive to contemporary times. Although in competition with other currents, therapeutic culture has acquired a powerful influence over the conduct of individual behaviour. It has no monopoly over the way society gains meaning over life, but it is arguably the most important signifier of meaning for the everyday life of the individual. Explaining why it has become so important is one of the purposes of this book.

People adopt an active and selective engagement with their culture. As Ann Swidler argues, 'in all societies people make choices about what cultural meanings to accept and how to interpret them'. And not only do people adopt cultural perspectives selectively, when they 'appropriate cultural materials, they adapt them to their own purposes'.[98] Cultural norms sanction certain form of behaviour and stigmatise others. As we shall see in the following chapters, therapeutic culture provides a script through which individuals develop a distinct understanding of their selves and of their relationship with others. People also read from other scripts but when it comes to making sense of who they are, therapeutics exercises a formidable impact on their lives. Since this self-perception has a significant effect on behaviour, therapeutic culture influences social and political action. The chapter on therapeutic politics indicates why this culture can provide a focus for mobilisation.

Throughout the book, the terms therapeutic culture, therapeutic ethos and therapeutics are used interchangeably to avoid repetition. I have refrained from defining this ethos because it is still in the process of becoming. Superficially, its attempt to give meaning and guidance resembles the way religions, civic codes and ideologies have operated in the past. However, it is far too diffuse and incoherent to earn the designation of ideology or religion. Its appeal may well be its reluctance to try to answer the hard questions previously reflected on by ideologies, religions and humanist thought.

1　The culture of emotionalism

Trying to make sense of the problems that confront us in a complex modern society is a challenge fraught with difficulty. Many of the important forces that shape our lives – globalisation, the workings of the market, political and cultural institutions – have an abstract, almost invisible, character. Consequently, most of the time we are not aware of the forces that mould our behaviour and influence the decisions we take. Not surprisingly, we tend to believe that 'our actions and feelings are derived from something inside ourselves'.[1] So we often attribute our actions and choices to the state of our emotions – to such 'facts' as that we are 'in denial' or 'stressed' or 'burnt out' or going through a 'mid-life crisis'. This view of human behaviour is based on widely held assumptions that 'create a picture of meaning as something produced within an individual's mind; this is held to be something internal, private and solitary'.[2]

Today, the conviction that our experiences are the outcome of personal choices is fuelled by a heightened sense of individuation. In an age of hypermobility and the fragmentation of communities and social networks, people's lives have acquired an intensely atomised character. The German sociologist Ulrich Beck writes of the 'isolation of individuals within homogeneous social groups'.[3] As a result, our ability to perceive the many things that we share and to grasp the wider social forces that influence our decisions is compromised by the experience of isolation. In such circumstances finding meaning in our experience is fraught with difficulty. Isolation also encourages individuals to interpret the difficulty they have in making sense of their lives as the product of their internal life, rather than as a statement about the inability of society to provide people with a common web of meaning. In such circumstances, the distress that emerges from social conditions can be experienced as a problem of the self. Increasingly, we tend to think of social problems as emotional ones.

Recasting social problems as emotional ones

Today, western culture makes sense of the experience of social isolation through interpreting behaviour through the highly individualised idiom of therapeutic discourse. Our culture has fostered a climate where the internal world of the individual has become the site where the problems of society are raised and where it is perceived they need to be resolved. This shift of focus from the social to the internal life of the individual has also led to a reorientation of intellectual life towards a preoccupation with the self. Since the self is defined through feelings, the state of emotion is often represented as the key determinant of both individual and collective behaviour. Social problems are frequently recast as individual ones that have no direct connection to the social realm.

One of the consequences of this decline in the sociological imagination is a growing tendency to redefine public issues as the private problem of the individual. This mood is vividly captured through the individualised idiom of therapy. Through the language of psychology, therapeutic culture frames the way that problems are perceived. 'The result is that social problems are increasingly perceived in terms of psychological dispositions: as personal inadequacies, guilt feelings, anxieties, conflicts and neuroses', concludes Beck.[4] As David Smail, a British clinical psychologist, argues, the language of therapy helps to construct a common sense that regards feelings and behaviour as the outcome of 'interior causation'.[5] Everyday common sense instructs us to regard feelings and behaviour as the product of passions that come from inside ourselves. As Bracken suggests, contemporary human subjectivity is understood as the 'source of everything'.[6]

Of course, understanding the self and the internal life of the individual is important for comprehending individual behaviour and the wider life of the community. However, a one-dimensional preoccupation with the self often leads to overlooking the social and cultural foundations of individual identity. This approach leads to a novel and specific representation of the self – one that the American sociologist John Rice has characterised as an 'asocial self'.[7] From the standpoint of the asocial self what matters is its internal life. The significance of social and cultural influence is discounted in favour of a narrow psychological deliberation of personal emotions. In previous periods of modern life, important intellectual trends tended to attach little significance to the individual self in their explanations of society. A crude economic or social determinism had little room for the individual subject. For example, a bewildering variety of human action – why people joined clubs, why women had small families or why a particular group hated foreign people – was explained as the outcome of economic circumstances. But yesterday's economic and social determinism has been overtaken by a new and far cruder variety of determinism – that of 'emotional determinism'. The state of our emotion is now represented as the cause of many of the problems faced by contemporary society. The way we feel about ourselves – our self-esteem – has become an important explanatory tool for making sense of the world.

Low self-esteem is now associated with many of the ills that afflict society. Policy-makers, media commentators and experts regularly demand that action should be taken to raise the self-esteem of school children, teenagers, parents, the elderly, the homeless, the mentally ill, delinquents, the unemployed, those suffering racism, and lone parents, to name but a few of the groups experiencing this problem. Moreover, as we note in Chapter 8, the self-esteem deficit is often presented as a condition that transcends the individual and afflicts entire generations and communities.

From the standpoint of emotional determinism, the individual is perceived as the source of the problems facing society. This doctrine perceives the individual as one who is afflicted by a general state of emotional deficit. In the past, the cultural elites castigated the lower orders for being irrational and not in control of their emotions. Refined and delicate emotions were associated with the more elevated and educated sections of society. According to today's cultural script, no-one is immune from the problem of emotional deficit. Aristocrats like Princess Diana, Mafia mobster Tony Soprano as well as the ordinary folk who are just trying to get on with life, are all suitable candidates for the couch.

Both in Britain and the US, explanations oriented towards the emotions are now used to make sense of problems that in the past were illuminated through socio-economic or philosophical analysis. 'Problems that were once considered political, economic, or educational are today found to be psychological', notes Eva Moskowitz in her important study of the history of therapeutic culture in the US.[8] Moskowitz notes that America's 'obsession with feelings' in the 1970s helped establish an environment where social problems tended to be framed from a psychological perspective. This trend was particularly evident in relation to the problem of racial oppression, where increasingly the consequence of discrimination was interpreted in therapeutic terms. According to this approach, those who suffered from racism suffered permanent damage to their personality. In effect they became damaged people. In turn, Elisabeth Lasch-Quinn has noted that the cure for the damaged personality requires therapeutics leading to an emphasis on managing attitudes and away from tackling the question of equality.[9]

In Britain, too, there is a growing tendency to psychologise the problem of racism. Whereas in the past critics of racism emphasised the salience of economic inequality, discrimination and violence, today there is a tendency to adopt the therapeutic language of victimisation. A recent study conducted by the Joseph Rowntree Foundation focused on the 'devastating stress' suffered by victims of racial harassment. The report self-consciously sought to win public sympathy for victims of racism by focusing on the therapeutic card. Its focus was on the 'anger, stress, depression, sleepless nights' of the respondents of this survey.[10] Racism itself has been recast as a semiconscious psychological process. The influential Macpherson Report, published in 1999, helped codify feelings and emotions into law. Sir William Macpherson, the author of this report, defined institutional racism as a problem of the mind. In his definition of institutional racism, Macpherson declared that it 'can be seen or detected in processes, attitudes and behaviour which amount to discrimination through unwitting prejudice, ignorance, thoughtlessness and racial stereotyping which disadvantage minority ethnic people'. The key word here is 'unwitting'; an unconscious response driven by unregulated and untamed emotions.

The tendency to perceive the failures of institutions and of society in terms of their impact on individual emotions is not confined to the issue of racism. When *The Guardian* newspaper published a major report on the crisis in Britain's education system, its emphasis was on the emotional damage suffered by poor children, rather than on their social conditions or the failure of the system of education: 'Poverty does its worst damage with the emotions of those who live with it'.[11] It seems that society is far more comfortable in dealing with poverty as a mental health problem than as a social issue. This approach is supported by a widely held premise that adverse circumstances, even relatively banal ones are stress-inducing and cause trauma and various forms of mental illness.

In Britain, the shift of focus from problems rooted in the social realm to emotional turmoil began in the 1970s, but acquired a significant momentum in the 1980s. During the economic upheavals of the early 1980s, even radical critics of society began to emphasise the mental health consequences of free-market capitalism. As they grappled with a growing mood of disenchantment with trade union militancy and redistributionist politics, many activists became drawn towards protesting about the mental health consequences of inequalities. Numerous studies indicting the destructive mental health outcomes of unemployment and job insecurity were published during this period. One report, published in 1980, predicted that 50,000 people will have died by 1984 as a result of stress caused by unemployment.[12] Studies proclaiming the negative mental health impact of un-employment converged with wider cultural influences to replace a socio-economic critique of capitalism with a therapeutic one. 'It is now possible to show empirically that the unfettered free market is bad for the nation's mental health', declared a critic of the Conservative government in *The New Statesman*. He added that a 'substantial and growing part of the population is suffering psychologically from government policies'.[13]

The prevailing cultural climate provided a fertile terrain for the growth of thera-peutic critique of capitalism. Its orientation towards psychological damage caused by systemic forces was one that could readily be accomodated by the individualistic temper of the 1980s. Even the Thatcher government was happy to absorb forms of therapeutic management into its schemes targeting the unemployed. Resources devoted to the counselling of the unemployed were systematically expanded in the 1980s. The cumulative effect of these trends was to individualise protest and encourage what Beck characterises as the 'individual therapeutic ways of handling problems'.[14]

Problems of the emotions are not just represented as the inexorable outcome of problems, such as poverty, racism, poor parenting and domestic violence. Emotional dysfunctions are, in turn, frequently depicted as the cause of virtually every form of social breakdown. According to the outlook of emotional deter-minism, unprocessed and unmanaged emotions are the cause of the ills that afflict society. This deterministic outlook is widely promoted by advocates of the idea of emotional intelligence. Proponents of the doctrine of emotional intelligence believe that lack of self-awareness and a reluctance to acknowledge one's true feelings are responsible for both individual distress and the problems facing society. They claim that people who are emotionally illiterate are potentially destructive personalities, who bear responsibility for many of the ills facing society. This transformation of social and cultural problems into psychological ones is most eloquently expressed in Daniel Goleman's bestseller, *Emotional Intelligence: Why It Can Matter More than IQ*. Goleman takes the view that society faces a 'collective emotional crisis'.

He sees a 'growing calamity in our shared emotional life', which is expressed in marital violence, child abuse, rising juvenile delinquency and the growing incidence of depression and post-traumatic stress. The problems associated with emotional illiteracy are alarming according to Goleman. The shooting of classmates by American schoolchildren, teenage pregnancy, bullying, drug abuse and mental illness are some of the consequences of the public's refusal to attend to its emotional needs. The solution offered by Goleman is more emotional education, which provides strategies for managing emotions and recognising feelings.[15]

British advocates of emotional literacy claim that the origins of 'violence and inequality' can 'in part be found in the childhood experience of avoidant individuals whose feelings have been brushed aside and thus not treated as "equal", in the sense of having their emotions respected'.[16] Emotional determinism is mobilised to account for the problem of the environment. According to Antidote, an organisation devoted to raising the emotional literacy of the British people, 'fear of loss, fear of the unknown and fear of someone else having more than us renders us blind to the obvious direction the natural world is heading'. Antidote claims that our 'anger' drives us to 'ignore this reality'. Antidote indicts society for wasting 'much of its precious resource: the energy and creativity of its people'. It claims that this unhappy state of affairs is a 'consequence of our reluctance to acknowledge that feelings influence almost everything we do'.[17]

Violence between nations and wars are also attributed an emotional causation. It is claimed that 'trauma', especially when unprocessed and 'congealed over generations', fuels outbursts of violence. 'Long-term deep-set and unconscious trauma can do much to explain, for example, why September 11 happened; why Orangemen are still marching; why young Palestinians are killing themselves in suicide bombings', writes the head of an advocacy group devoted to providing therapeutic training to journalists.[18] The belief that international conflict arises from trauma-induced psychological and social dysfunctionalism has influenced the thinking of organisations involved in the field of humanitarian aid. A UNICEF briefing document noted in 1994 that, 'the world has only just begun to realise that left untreated, the psychological wounds of war can be most damaging, as children grow up unable to function normally, often driven to perpetuate the violence they have experienced'.[19] As Vanessa Pupavac observed in her studies of post-conflict strategies, increasingly, 'many international documents refer to the "rehabilitation of post-conflict societies", rather than their reconstruction'.[20]

The refusal to acknowledge or process one's feelings is also depicted as the cause of the Middle East conflict. Not even Saddam Hussein is exempt from gaining a therapeutic diagnosis. Whilst the West put pressure on the Iraqi regime to reveal its weapons of mass destruction, Saddam was frequently characterised by the media as 'in denial'. One American political psychologist, Dr Jerrold Post, stated that 'it all goes back to his mother's womb'. According to Post, Saddam's mother 'both tried to commit suicide and to have an abortion'. This experience 'wounded his self-esteem', creating a condition known as 'the wounded self'. Another account contends that Saddam was so shamed by his humble origins that it left him 'pathologically incapable in later life of trusting anyone'.[21]

The belief that 'it all goes back to the womb' is the axial principle of emotional determinism. This argument is based on the premise that the early emotional experience of a child will determine and define behaviour in later years. It is claimed that the emotional damage suffered by children can constitute a life sentence. Many observers contend that 'invisible scars' inflicted on the psyche never heal and damage the victim for life. Unlike physical acts, which have a beginning and an end and are specific in nature, the realm of emotions knows no boundaries. According to this intensely deterministic model, children who experience distress become traumatised and carry the scars of this episode with them into adulthood. It is claimed that the trauma suffered by such young adults can dispose them towards acts of violent behaviour. Childhood trauma is represented as the point of departure for the destructive behaviour of adults. This deterministic world-view has been used to explain the violent conflict in Afghanistan. According to one account, a significant majority of children in Kabul have been traumatised through the impact of the culture of violence on their lives. 'While such events can lead to considerable psychological trauma and distress, they may also inure a young mind to violence', argues an advocate of emotional determinism. The consequences of childhood trauma are elaborated in the following terms:

> The average Taliban and Northern Alliance soldiers are a product of the same cycle of social upheaval experienced from early childhood. Ignorance, isolation, and a daily ritual of violence greatly temper their vision of the world. This 'lost generation' is likely to breed many more unless action is taken to bring the cycle of violence to an end.[22]

The idea that violence breeds violence has proven to be so attractive that it has become something of a cultural myth. Yet there is considerable evidence to suggest that people deal with the experience of violence in diverse ways. And as one critic of emotional determinism argues, 'ultimately, it is the economic, educational and sociocultural rebuilding of worlds, allied to questions of equity and justice, which above all will determine the long-term well-being of millions of child survivors worldwide'.[23]

The idea of a causal link between trauma and violence has been systematically elaborated in the cycles of abuse model of family literature. Although the validity of this hypothesis is highly contested, the belief that abuse begets trauma which in turn leads to abuse has acquired the status of a truism. During the 1990s, the term trauma was expanded into an interpretative device for making sense of any form of painful event.[24] Traumatic experience has been converted into an all-purpose explanation for numerous forms of crime and antisocial behaviour.

Emotional causation also dominates the contemporary presentation of crime. Ideas about crime reflect public fear and anxiety and the sensibility of a culture towards the threats it faces. Since the 1980s, there has been a major transformation in the public presentation of crime. In the early 1980s, anxieties about law and order were focused on violent public crime. Drug wars, gangs and especially the mugger symbolised the danger of crime at that time. Those offering a diagnosis of this problem blamed greed or deprivation and a variety of socio-economic causes, such as poverty, poor parenting, failure of authority and education. Although violent public crime still excites the imagination, contemporary culture seems much more fascinated by emotionally perverted individuals, who are far more driven by their inner urges, rather than the desire for economic gain. The criminals that excite the cultural imagination are the serial killer, the child abductor, the sexual predator and the stalker. These are monsters who are driven by unimaginable emotional urges. Many of the crimes that define our times are the product of violent or abusive relationships and of destructive individual behaviour. Some of the high profile crimes of the emotion include hate crime, domestic violence, child abuse, date rape, bullying and school violence, road rage and stalking. None of these recently constructed crimes is inspired by the motive of economic gain. These crimes are depicted as the outcome of human pathology and are not influenced by economic calculation. This shift from the motif of social causation or economic greed to that of a destructive personality indicates the influence of emotional determinism on contemporary representations of crime. And since emotions are seen as the root of so many of society's misfortunes, they have become the subject of intense cultural concern.

Ambiguities about emotion

The widespread influence of emotional determinism represents an important statement about the human condition. It advances a view of the world where emotions dominate life and cause most of the problems that confront us. That is why the development of emotional determinism should not be interpreted as signifying the unreserved embrace of emotions. To be sure, promoters of the shift of cultural focus from the 'life of the mind' to the 'life of the heart' celebrate public emoting as evidence of a more intelligent and sensitive society.[25] But although outwardly therapeutic culture heaps praise on the public display of feeling, it also wants to restrain those emotions that are a source of many of society's ills. Therapeutic culture is deeply ambiguous about emotion.

Therapeutic culture promotes not simply emotionalism but emotionalism in an intensely individualised form. This understanding of emotion is alien to cultures where the experience of pain or of joy is not a private matter, but a response to matters that affect an entire community. When he was released from jail, Nelson Mandela was surprised by the number of questions from western commentators directed at his private feelings and psychology.[26] Such questioning would have also made little sense in western societies in the past, where the process of feeling was bound up with wider communal responses to events. It is worth noting that not so long ago, during the Second World War, the individual experience of distress and violence were mediated through the cultural coping resources of communities. Painful experiences were made sense of as part of a community's system of meaning rather than as symptoms of an individual emotional problem.

In an age where emotionalism has acquired a formidable cultural status, it is important to remember that society is selective about which emotions it embraces and which it rejects. Emotions that assist the project of self-fulfilment tend to be presented in a positive light, whilst those feelings that bind the individual to others are regarded with suspicion. This tendency to both celebrate and fear emotions is consistently displayed through the therapeutic language that is used to account for the world of feeling.

Emotion is both an object of cultural veneration, but also of medicalisation. Emotions, especially strong ones, are systematically treated as pathologies and addictions that require therapeutic intervention. So anger is frequently represented as a symptom of an illness, such as an addiction. Some claim that it is the most powerful emotional addiction. Recently invented conditions such as 'road rage', 'computer rage', 'trolley rage', 'golf rage' or 'air rage' indicate that the emotion of anger can swiftly transform itself into an illness. The therapeutic lobby claims that the solution to this emotional addiction is the application of stress or anger-management techniques. It appears that therapeutic intervention is always the conclusion implicit in the story transmitted through contemporary culture's emotional script. The need for the therapeutic management of feeling indicates that the significance that western culture attaches to domain of the emotion is fuelled by the perception that it constitutes a serious problem.

Emotions are frequently classified into those that are positive (joy, happiness, contentment) and those that are negative (fear, anger, sadness, hate). One of the most distinct features of our emotional script is its celebration of happiness and contentment. From this perspective, positive emotions are those that make the individual happy. In contrast, negative emotions 'can be described as any feeling which causes you to be miserable and sad'.[27] The feeling of contentment is increasingly seen as the defining feature of individual health. 'Wellness' has been transformed into a health goal in line with the World Health Organization's 1946 redefinition of health as a 'state of complete physical, mental and social well-being, not merely the absence of disease or infirmity'. The emphasis which our emotional script attaches to feeling good about oneself is a distinct feature of contemporary culture. It is underpinned by an outlook that regards the individual self as the central focus of social, moral and cultural preoccupation. As one advocate of self-oriented positive emotions argues, 'the possible benefits of positive emotions seem particularly undervalued in cultures' that 'endorse the protestant ethic, which casts hard work and self discipline as virtues and leisure and pleasure as sinful'.[28] Since feeling good is regarded as a state of virtue, forms of behaviour that distract the individual from attending to the needs of the self are frequently devalued. Consequently, traditionally held virtues such as hard work, sacrifice, altruism and commitment are frequently represented as antithetical to the quest of the individual for the feeling of happiness.

To be able to privilege immediate happiness over other emotional states depends on it being oriented inward. Even happiness can become problematic if its realisation depends on others. Frances Wilks, author of *Intelligent Emotion: How To Succeed Through Transforming Your Feelings*, prefers the goal of 'cultivation of joy' to that of happiness. She prefers the state of joy because it is triggered by feelings from within whereas happiness requires a favourable 'outward state of affairs'. Wilks claims that it is unrealistic to expect to achieve fulfilment through 'people and things', through 'outer-directed' activity. Instead, people should settle for the compensation provided by momentary pleasures experienced in the 'inner-directed' process of self-discovery and self-expression.[29]

Feelings that distract individuals from their own needs tend to be defined as negative ones. Many emotions are depicted as negative precisely because they disorient the individual from the search for self-fulfilment. According to Dr Thomas Yarnell, a clinical psychologist, 'as long as you hold a negative emotion about someone, you are emotionally, tied to that person'. Such emotions are deprecated because they tie an individual to another person or to an ideal or to a cause that transcends the self. What makes an emotion negative has little to do with any of its intrinsic quality. An emotion is negative because it 'ties' an individual to another person. Yarnell argues 'when you love someone, you are tied to them', when 'you are angry at someone or afraid of them, you are also tied to them', and concludes, 'being tied to them keeps you from growing and moving on emotionally'.[30]

Yarnell's warning about the binding character of love reflects contemporary society's ambiguity about commitment. Although love remains a cultural ideal, the powerful emotions associated with this feeling are often portrayed as harmful to the self. Paradoxically, although love is portrayed as the supreme source of self-fulfilment, it is also depicted as potentially harmful because it threatens to subordinate the self to another. That is why passionate feelings of love towards another person are often perceived as destructive and dangerous. Anne Wilson Schaef in her bestseller, *Escape From Intimacy*, uses labels such as 'sexual addiction', 'romance addiction', 'relationship addiction' to stigmatise passionate feelings towards others.[31] Intense love towards another is regularly criticised for distracting individuals from fulfilling their own needs and from pursuing their self-interest. Since the 1980s, numerous advice books have been written to warn the public about the risks of 'loving too much'. Books such as *Women Who Love Too Much, When Parents Love Too Much* or *For People Who Love Their Cats Too Much* caution people from allowing their passion for others to overtake their lives. Love is often denounced as a risky delusion and people are advised not to trust the language of the heart. The UK academic Wendy Langford argues in her book, *Revolutions of the Heart*, that romantic love damages women.[32] And too much love is said to lead to the many psychological illnesses associated with 'co-dependency'. So it is claimed that 'parents who love too much' produce dysfunctional people who are over-reliant on the approval of others.[33] It is also alleged that individuals who crave intimacy are not in touch with their own needs and literally love too much and suffer from the psychological dysfunction of sex addiction.

Contemporary hesitancy towards the emotion of love reveals an ambiguity towards feelings that transcend the individual self. Unlike contentment, which is unambiguously represented as a positive emotion, feelings that transcend the individual self is often depicted as a potentially troublesome feeling. The problematisation of the emotion of love has little to do with love as such. It is fuelled by an emotional script that regards all feelings that are directed at objects external to the self with mistrust. Consequently, individuals who are emotionally caught up in causes external to themselves, such as making a spouse happy, caring for sick parents, or working hard (especially for a cause), are also often regarded as dominated by negative emotions. It has been suggested that people who have too much faith may be suffering from religious addiction. Father Leo Booth in his book *When God Becomes A Drug* warns of becoming 'addicted to the certainty, sureness or sense of security that our faith provides'. John Bradshaw, one of the leading advocates of the American co-dependence movement, has produced a self-help video entitled *Religious Addiction*. 'These tapes describe how co-dependency can set up for religious addiction, and how extrinsic religion fosters co-dependency', notes the blurb advertising the video.[34]

Probably the most stigmatised negative emotion today is that of guilt. 'Guilt, once considered unpleasant, but instructive, has become so dangerous as to be avoided if at all possible', notes a study on American emotional culture.[35] According to previous cultural norms, the feeling of guilt indicated that an individual was in touch with the moral expectations that prevailed. Since through the feeling of guilt an individual acknowledged expectations of right and wrong, the emotion was regarded as an important element in the process of socialisation. Today, guilt is regarded as a pathology, since through this emotion an individual subordinates the self to external demands. The feeling of guilt not only makes individuals unhappy, it also diverts emotional energy towards attending to demands imposed by wider society instead of cultivating the self. According to contemporary therapeutic culture, the emotion of guilt is responsible for the development of behavioural problems and personality disorders. Anglo-American parenting advice on discipline, for example, is now based on the belief that anything which makes children feel guilty should be avoided.

Emotions as objects of management

One of the most curious features of the culture of emotionalism with its acclamation of 'emotional intelligence', 'emotional literacy', 'emotional openness', 'getting in touch with yourself' or 'expressing yourself' is its suspicion of the human capacity to feel. Therapeutic culture is highly ambivalent about how to value emotion. Today's self-consciously open display of emotion in Anglo-American societies is frequently applauded by the cultural elites. The ability to display spontaneous and natural feelings is frequently cited with approval. Yet, at the same time, therapeutic culture instructs the public to be wary of raw unprocessed emotions. Contemporary culture does not simply applaud emotions it also demands that strong feelings be curbed and moderated. This paradox was noted in Leslie Irvine's study of American emotional culture. She observed that 'in the American emotional culture, beliefs glorify spontaneous, "natural" feelings, even while norms sanction most displays of strong emotion'.[36] Her research into the workings of co-dependency groups suggests that although members are exhorted to get in touch with their emotions, what is really demanded is that they 'control the intensity' of their feeling.[37] Ambiguity towards emotions is grounded in the belief that they are the source of so many of society's problems. That is why emotions are frequently represented as objects to be managed.

Acknowledging emotions constitutes the prelude to managing them. This process of 'cultural cooling' invites individuals to moderate their feelings in line with today's emotional script. As Hochschild argues, today's relationship advice proposes 'cooler' emotional strategies towards one's lover than in the past.[38] The voyage of self-discovery with its promise of open and authentic experience exists uncomfortably alongside the exigencies of therapeutic management. The demand for emotional conformity negates the project of the open-ended project of self-discovery.

Nor is the management of emotion a project that can be left to the individual. Individuals get in touch with their emotion not simply through their own effort, but through accessing therapeutic support. Despite the orientation of therapeutic culture towards the self, the management of emotions is seen as far too important to be left to the efforts of ordinary people. That is why the appeal to 'attend to your emotional needs' often masks a call for therapeutic intervention. In practice, 'attending to your emotional needs' means being prepared to seek therapeutic support. In fact, therapeutic professionals frequently use terms like 'exploring your emotions' as a euphemism for seeking help. So one British university counselling service describes its services as 'about exploring our feelings and learning to accept their reality'.[39] Increasingly, emotional well-being is associated with the willingness to seek help.

Many professionals dealing with purported cases of co-dependency and addiction vociferously warn against victims trying to deal with their conditions themselves. Some therapists dismiss individual attempts to overcome addiction and other problems as futile expressions of a 'perfectionist complex'. 'Admit that you're sick and you're welcome to the recovering persons fold; dispute it and you're "in denial"', is how Kaminer described the attitude of many therapists.[40] Avoiding professional treatment serves as proof of the gravity of the problem facing the victim. Therapeutic professionals describe denial as the avoidance of the pain of acknowledging a problem and of taking action to seek help.[41]

Forms of behaviour that run counter to help-seeking are often castigated as symptoms of emotional illiteracy. Despite its celebration of the self, our therapeutic culture is hostile to behaviour patterns that demonstrate self-reliance and self-control. One expression of this hostility is the stigmatisation of stereotypical masculine behaviour, particularly the aspiration for self-control, which is seen as a ludicrous attempt to deny genuine emotion. 'We have learned to go it alone and to do without the help of others', complains a male academic advocate of emotionalism. He also objects to an ethos, where men 'learn in diverse ways to minimise hurt and pain and to take pride in this as a sign of our strength', since it 'makes it very difficult for us to accept our vulnerability, as an integral part of our male identity'. The apparent inability of masculinity to acquiesce to weakness is presented as a fatal flaw in the male psyche.[42] Self-control and the aspiration for individual autonomy are viewed as psychologically destructive impulses. The therapeutic profession continually decries the tendency of young boys to aspire to autonomy. According to two British psychologists – Dan Kindlon and Michael Thompson – 'stereotypical ideas about masculine toughness deny a boy his emotions and rob him of the chance to develop the full range of emotional resources'.[43]

Boys are routinely castigated for their emotional illiteracy. It appears that 'regardless of age, most boys are ill-prepared for the challenges along the road to becoming an emotionally healthy adult'.[44] The pathology of masculinity prevents boys from acquiring the 'subtleties of emotional language'. The therapist Roger Horrocks argues that the outward appearance of male rationality and coldness is symptomatic of a 'male malaise', a kind of 'male autism'.[45] The refusal to openly acknowledge complex emotions is depicted as not merely a disease of the person, but as a powerful harmful force with damaging consequences for the whole of society. This opinion is held by a significant body of commentators and social scientists. As MacInnes notes, 'male "instrumentalism" is increasingly seen as central to the dynamics of modern society, and contrasted with the virtues of feminine expressiveness'. He adds that there is 'an astonishing consensus which urges men to abandon what is imagined to be traditional masculinity in order to get in touch with their feelings and develop their emotional articulacy'.[46]

The aspiration for control, which runs counter to the ethos of help-seeking, is often interpreted as especially damaging to the emotional well-being of men. One ethnographic study of skydivers concludes that men tend to develop a distorted sense of their ability to control 'fateful circumstances'. Critics of what cultural feminist (female and male) academics call 'hegemonic masculinity' go a step further and claim that risk-taking men who value control are not only deluding themselves, but are in reality also losing control over their lives by not attending to their emotional needs. They contend that the failure to disclose vulnerability, ensures that men become incapable of handling emotional problems maturely.[47] Invariably, the aspiration for control is portrayed in pathological terms as a delusion with damaging consequences. This medicalisation of masculinity has become an accomplished fact in the field of health promotion. One study condemns 'high masculinity' for its refusal to ask for help and claims that it is a 'significant predictor of poor health practices'.[48] According to the advocates of new health screening programmes, men find it much easier to talk about sport and beer than about, for example, testicular abnormalities.

Men who act like women are clearly preferred to women who act like men. According to the emotionally correct hierarchy of virtuous behaviour, feminine women come out on top. Feminine men beat masculine women for second place. And, of course, masculine, 'macho' men come last. This hierarchy informs the attitude of many health professionals. According to one study, masculinity signals poor health practices. In contrast, 'feminine characteristics' are linked with 'health promoting behaviour'. The emphasis here is not on gender, but on behaviour. The study argues that 'highly feminine men' exhibit the greatest concern about their health and that, irrespective of sex, those with a feminine orientation are more likely to 'maintain good health habits'. From the perspective of therapeutic culture, the preoccupation with personal health and the willingness to seek help represent the foundation for emotional maturity. That is why so much resources are devoted to cultivating dependence on the professional experts.[49]

Individuals who are not inclined to adopt help-seeking behaviour face considerable pressure to fall in line with prevailing cultural expectations. An example of this was seen in reaction to the tragic bombing in Oklahoma in 1995. The 'grief industry' invaded the city and within a short space of time this tragic event was 'translated into an official or authoritative language of suffering by "trauma" experts'. And although some family members of the victims 'resented the overwhelming presence of the grief industry', the psychological interpretation of the experience came to define the event.[50] The relentless pressure to experience a tragic event according to a pre-given emotional script ensures that the public internalises help-seeking behaviour.

The promotion of help-seeking behaviour was also systematically promoted in the British countryside at the end of the 1990s, reaching a climax during the outbreak of the epidemic of foot-and-mouth disease in 2001. The traditional image of the hardy, self-sufficient British farmer was gradually transformed into one who is overwhelmed by the trauma of grief. It all began back in 1999, when mental health campaigners began to publicise the claim that farmers were twice as likely to kill themselves as men of the same age in other occupations. The focus on suicide in the farming community swiftly gained nationwide publicity. Commentators in the media were quick to point out that British farmers were particularly prone to suicide because of their reserved, stoic and self-sufficient outlook. Unlike their urban cousins, farmers found it 'difficult' to ask for help and lacked the 'emotional skills' to handle difficult circumstances. The mental health charity Rural Minds explained that 'farmers don't like asking for help', since by the nature of their work they are a 'pretty solitary bunch'. The issue of rural suicide continued to be publicised and in October 2000 The Rural Stress Information Network, promoted as the 'listening ear for stressed farmers', was set up in partnership with the Ministry of Agriculture, Fisheries and Food. By the time the recent epidemic of foot-and-mouth disease broke out, the counselling industry was well prepared to deal with the therapeutic needs of the countryside. Within weeks of the outbreak of this disease, mental health experts were predicting a rise in suicide and an outbreak of post-traumatic stress disorder in rural Britain.

Mental health campaigners perceive the farming community as a challenge to be conquered and regarded the outbreak of the foot-and-mouth epidemic as an opportunity to re-educate the emotionally illiterate farmer. Campaigners took a barely concealed delight in highlighting the psychological problem of farmers. 'We are talking about basically self-sufficient people who have to rely on their own resources for much of their life and work', noted Sue Barker of the mental health charity Mind, before adding that sometimes 'their own resources are not enough'. Campaigners adopted something of a missionary zeal in using every opportunity to highlight the emotional plight of farmers. In February 2001, the Rural Stress Information Service reported a 10-fold increase in the number of calls made to its help-line. According to Caroline Davis, director of this organisation, many farmers were 'breaking down in tears on the telephone'. 'Part of what motivates them to call is the publicity about high suicide rates', added Davis. Unable to resist the temptation of conquering the countryside, the Depression Alliance announced that it, too, was offering counselling and support to farmers facing pressure due to the foot-and-mouth crisis. By April 2001, the image of the grieving farmer had come to dominate media representations of the crisis in the countryside. The virtue of therapeutic help-seeking had become institutionalised in rural Britain.[51]

The act of acknowledging one's feelings and, by implication, an openness to seeking help is culturally represented as virtuous behaviour. In contrast, the reluctance to acknowledge the problem of the emotion and the refusal to seek help is regarded as an act responsible for both individual distress and many of the problems facing society. Help-seeking has acquired positive moral connotations akin to the act of acknowledging guilt in more traditional cultural settings. Within the criminal justice system, offenders who accept help and undertake some form of therapy are frequently rewarded for their positive behaviour. Kathleen Lowney's study of American television talk shows indicates how the virtue of seeking of help is refracted in popular culture. She notes that 'guests are chided until they agree to enter therapy or go to a 12-step program or some other support group'.[52]

Openness to the therapeutic management of one's emotion encourages the public display of feeling. The recent growth of the phenomenon of public emoting has been widely commented upon, but it is often misinterpreted as representing the celebration of the display of intense raw emotion. In fact, the public display of emotion has become a ritual of collective help-seeking that creates a supportive environment for its management. Through the display of emotionalism, therapeutic culture transmits clear signals about the conduct of everyday life.

Feeling in public

The acknowledgement of emotional pain acquires meaning through its public display. This act of disclosure involves the act of communication with others. It requires the naming emotional pain – 'I am an addict' – at least to a therapist and preferably to a support group. This therapeutic act of acknowledgment has become culturally esteemed through the positive valuation extended to the act of reflecting on feelings in public. As a result, public figures are regularly judged by the way they feel rather than by their deed or the outcome of their action.

The significance attached to public emotionalism was vividly confirmed during the events surrounding Princess Diana's funeral. In line with the ethos of emotionalism, sections of the cultural elite were particularly vitriolic against members of the royal family who did not wish to share their inner pain. The media took it upon themselves to instruct Queen Elizabeth and Prince Charles on the form of grieving the public expected from them. The desire to mourn in private and in accordance with one's individual feeling was pathologised and denounced as cold and inhuman.

Prince Charles was hysterically lectured for not putting his arm around his boys in public. One leading British journalist, Susan Moore, accused him of emotional illiteracy, while a psychologist wrote in a daily paper that the absence of visible touching between Charles and his sons was an 'act of child abuse'. Increasingly, popular culture transmits the message that individuals who grieve and feel privately are not behaving appropriately. A. Scott Berg, the author of a biography of Charles Lindbergh, told the press that a lot of 'Lindbergh's behaviour took my breath away'. Why? Because it appears that Lindbergh was 'capable of astonishing cold-ness to his family'. The shocked biographer stated with an accusatory ring, that Lindbergh 'could not express his grief over his son's kidnapping and death and insisted that his wife cry in private'.[53] That Prince Charles or Lindbergh may be just as able to grieve as the emotionally unrestrained is simply not entertained by critics who are dismissive of private emotion. This celebration of public feeling seems to have acquired the status of a religious doctrine and is now widely promoted in all walks of life. A poster, widely displayed inside the walls of the University of London Union, advertising one of a number of help-lines, put it clearly: 'THE STIFF UPPER LIP WENT OUT IN THE FORTIES'. This indictment of the stiff upper lift is driven by the conviction that open display of emotion is good for you and it is OK to ask for help. The promotion of emotional intelligence and of emotional literacy is symptomatic of this important shift in values.

Has all this exhortation to feel in public made people more self-aware? Self-awareness is an objective that mature adults aspire to achieve. To know oneself is an important quality associated with maturity and conscious reflection. Knowing oneself exists in a dynamic relationship with knowing others since it is through a conscious reflection on relationships and experiences that the important insights are gained. But acknowledging one's emotions and feelings need not mean worshipping or becoming obsessed with them. Indeed, if the search for self-knowledge becomes an end in itself, little insight will be gained. That is why, although there are more people seeing therapists and counsellors than ever before, self-knowledge has not been conspicuously on the increase. The search for the real self has merely intensified society's preoccupation for feeling and emotion. But searching for the self may not be the best strategy for understanding it. The self is not lost, waiting to be discovered. Self-knowledge and an awareness of who we are is the outcome of a conscious reflection on our experience of interaction with others.

Of course, the search for the self has a long and honourable tradition in the history of the modern imagination. During the past two centuries, numerous thinkers have expressed a sense of revulsion against the demands of economic survival and social routine. The sociologist Arlie Hochschild believes that a common response to what she calls the 'commercial distortion of the managed heart' has been the search for the 'real self'. According to writers concerned with the problem of human alienation, the rules and regulations of a capitalist society force people to behave in ways which contradict their real selves. Those concerned with the authenticity of the real self tend to regard socially acceptable forms of human behaviour as in some sense violating the real feelings and emotions of the individual. As Hochschild remarked, this perception has led to greater virtue being attached to what is 'natural' or 'spontaneous'. She adds that the high regard for 'natural feeling' is symptomatic of a sentiment which believes that spontaneity and emotion is a 'scarce and precious' resource.[54] One manifestation of this celebration of spontaneous feeling is the growing popularisation of psychological therapies, especially those that stress the need to get in touch with your spontaneous feeling and the real you.

There can be little doubt that in any modern society there will be an aspiration for authenticity. Social fragmentation and fluidity, individuation and change constantly throw up questions like 'who am I?' and 'where do I belong?' In such circumstances there is a considerable temptation to go beyond self-reflection and to regard one's feeling as the only genuine source of authenticity. Moreover, in a world where everything appears as fluid and ephemeral, the belief that there is a stable innate self offers a degree of comfort to otherwise anxious individuals. The 'true self', with all its passion and emotions, tends to become the focus for the uncertain imagination. The belief that spontaneous and natural emotions can only be defiled by the demands of society for self-control, autonomy and reason often follows from this outlook. That is why modern culture has continually celebrated the genuine, natural and spontaneous emotion.

But it is necessary to insist that the classical search for authenticity has little to do with the contemporary pressure to feel in public. At times, the search for authenticity expressed a critical reflection on certain dehumanising practices in society. Today's demand for emotional literacy does not emanate from any rebellious impulse. It is the world-view that demands emotional conformity. As the sociologist Mestrovic noted, today it is the opinion-makers who tell us how to feel.[55] One need only add that they not only tell us how to feel, they also insist that it is mandatory for us to get in touch with our feelings. There is now a veritable industry – Mestrovic has called it the authenticity industry – oriented towards helping people to get in touch with their feelings. This industry, working to a therapeutic formula, is mainly devoted to training people to adopt certain forms of behaviour. The contrast between people struggling to understand themselves and the training manuals of the authenticity industry is a striking one. To take one example. A leaflet advertising a manual entitled *Achieving Emotional Literacy: A Personal Program to Increase Your Emotional Intelligence*, by Claude Steiner, announces:

> Dr Claude Steiner has taught emotional literacy to groups and individuals for twenty years. Now in this step-by-step audiobook, Dr Steiner tells you how to increase literacy. You will hear Dr Steiner's clear and systematic response to the emotional blocks that hold us back. he will tell you how to:
>
> - Reverse the dangerous self-destructive patterns that can rule a person's life
> - Open your heart and mind to honest and effective communication
> - Survey the emotional landscape
> - Take responsibility for your emotional life.[56]

Books, videos and courses on emotional literacy resemble those on keep-fit, dieting and sex. They offer emotion by rote learning and have little to do with spontaneity or authenticity. It is emotional conformity on demand – through easily digestible sound bites.

The rise of the confessional

Claims about the value of public disclosure of emotion have been so thoroughly assimilated into popular culture that its therapeutic significance is rarely contested. The very validation of individual feeling requires that it should be disclosed, preferably in public. That is why feeling and emotion have lost so much of their private character. Paradoxically, therapeutic culture's absorption with the internal life of the self has led to its apparent opposite – the steady erosion of the sphere of private life.

The erosion of the boundary that separates the private from the public is one of the significant accomplishments of therapeutic culture. By now everyone is used to seeing television celebrities telling the world about their illness, addiction, sex lives and personal hurts. One of the themes promoted through confessional television is that in order to heal, emotionally injured individuals need to let go of 'private wound by sharing them with others'.[57] The act of 'sharing' – that is turning private troubles into public stories – strongly resonates with current cultural norms. 'Popular therapies have demonized silence and stoicism, promoting the belief that healthy people talk about themselves', writes Wendy Kaminer, an American social critic.[58]

Individuals who have lost a loved one through tragic circumstances have found the invitation to share it through the media difficult to resist. Often, society's appetite for sharing in someone's private grief has been welcomed by individuals who believe that talking to the public about their pain is an effective form of therapy. Jayne Zito, whose husband was killed by a mentally ill assailant, recalled that she had a 'huge need to go on talking'. She set up the Zito Trust since 'there seemed to be very limited areas in which I could talk about how I felt, and it was crucial to work through that'.[59] The idea of therapeutic campaigning to work through personal problems is widely endorsed. Colin Parry, whose young son Timothy was tragically killed by an IRA bomb blast in Warrington, became a public figure often consulted about the management of the political situation in Northern Ireland. Colin Parry regarded the media as a form of personal therapy. Parry has argued that if it had not been for the opportunity provided by the media to talk about his personal grief, life would have been 'unbearable'. 'Colin needed the media as his therapy', noted Parry's wife, Wendy.[60]

Some social commentators have been disparaging about the emergence of the public confessional style in Anglo-American societies. The rise of reality TV and self-disclosure television – Oprah Winfrey, Geraldo, Ricki Lake – exemplifies the mass transmission of streams of emotion. Yet, thrash TV, along with its more elevated literary cousin, the new genre of self-revelatory biography, mirrors new cultural norms about notions of intimacy and private space. It seems that everybody wants to talk or write about themselves. As Peele noted, first-person accounts of drunken careers, so called drunkalogues, have long been staples of the American literary scene.[61] During the 1970s and 1980s the publishing of this genre of addict confessions took off. Examples of this genre are Jill Robinson's *Bed Time Story*, Barbara Gordon's *I'm Dancing as Fast as I Can* and the multi-authored *Courage to Change*. Since the late 1980s there has been a steady stream of celebrity books about drug and alcohol problems. Books by actress Carrie Fisher, the footballers Thomas Henderson and Lawrence Taylor and musicians Judy Collins and Graham Nash discuss at length their emotional problems. While the cultured 'literati' of Britain might object to the tackier talk shows imported from the US, many of them have followed closely the weekly diaries written in the broadsheet newspapers by more distinguished individuals about their diseases and other tragedies.

In the 1990s, confessional autobiographies and semifictional accounts expanded beyond the usual 'I was an addict' stories and adopted themes that were far more private than before. American and British novelists have taken to writing disguised memoirs that revel in family dysfunction and offer dramatic accounts of incest and other forms of child abuse. Alongside psychologists, well-known writers such as Tracy Thompson and Elisabeth Wurtzel have produced a stream of first-person accounts of their mood disorders. Confessional accounts of a variety of mental problems vie for shelf space with anthologies of patients' testimonies about their depression. What the American critic Laura Miller has characterised as the 'illness memoir' became one of the most distinct literary genres of the late 1990s. Authors of illness memoirs relive their diseases, syndromes and addictions. In minute detail they inform their readers of their most intimate experience of their sickness. Elizabeth Wurtzel's *Prozac Nation*, Lowell Handler's *Twitch and Shout: A Touretter's Tale*, Marya Hornbacher's *Wasted: A Memoir of Anorexia and Bulimia*, Emily Colas' *Just Checking: Scenes from the Life of an Obsessive–Compulsive* are some of the highlights of the American diseased victim literature. In Britain, Ben Watt's, *Patient*, a highly acclaimed account of his own debilitating illness, indicated that the illness memoir is alive and well in Britain. Cultural critic Andrew Calcutt's prediction, that memoirs of addictions, cancer, post-natal depression and a variety of other afflictions are likely to turn into a growth area in British publishing, has been vindicated by the experience of the past few years.[62]

It is not just well-known celebrities and authors who publicise their personal problems and dysfunctions through the medium of a memoir. Back in 1996, James Atlas, editor of the *New York Times Magazine*, counted more than 200 confessional memoirs published in the US during the previous year. As evidence of more books to come, he cited *First Love* by Marion Winik, a tale of a Jewish Harvard-bound poet from New Jersey and her marriage to a gay working-class Italian hairdresser doomed to die of AIDS, and former Princeton Professor Michael Ryan's *Secret Life*, which tells how he had sex with his dog.[63] The marketing of intimacy is most eloquently expressed in Catherine Texier's *Breakup: The End of a Love Story*. Published in 1998, *Breakup* recounts in minute detail the collapse of Texier's marriage. It is not simply a rant against her husband, but a chronicle of jealousy, pain and humiliation. Although, it ends on a note of triumph – she kicks out her husband – it is a classical victim confessional, where the happy ending is that of emotional survival.

The vast scale of the publishing of intimate revelations indicates that the popularity of sharing private troubles must represent some important developments within society. The demand for disclosure and the obsession to talk about one's feeling are strongly supported by the value system of therapeutic culture. Disclosure represents the point of departure in the act of seeking help – an act of virtue in therapeutic culture. Help-seeking also constitutes the precondition for the management of people's emotion. That is why there are such strong cultural pressures on the individual to 'acknowledge pain' and 'share'.

Disclosure and confession preferably through therapy relieves the burden of responsibility and it also offers a route to public acceptance and acclaim. Sports stars who drink or take drugs invariably face denunciation from the media. When British footballer Paul Gascoigne was exposed in a newspaper as a binge drinker and cigarette smoker, he faced the full wrath of the media. He was treated as a public outcast until he acknowledged that he had a 'problem' and checked into a clinic. By acknowledging his problem, Gascoigne performed a mandatory ritual which was necessary for his re-entry into the moral community. In contrast, sports stars who refuse to undergo therapy are treated with suspicion. In Britain, Eric Cantona, the Manchester United football star, was vilified because he refused to apologise publicly for getting into a fight with a hostile fan. Likewise, American reviewers were highly critical of the basketball player Kareem Abdul-Jabbar, who admitted in his 1983 autobiography, *Giant Steps*, to using drugs in college. The reviewers resented his refusal to humiliate himself and play the victim card. As Peele noted in an ironical vein, if Kareem Abdul Jabbar had 'lost control, become addicted, and then been suspended from basketball while he entered treatment, he could have become a role model for our children'.[64]

Celebrities in sport need to acknowledge their weakness in public before they can be considered as suitable role models. In Britain, the football players Paul Merson and Tony Adams received the applause of the media for bravely and publicly acknowledging their addiction. Paul Merson is the role model's role model. After admitting to his addiction to cocaine, gambling and lager, he gave a display of his vulnerability by crying at a press conference. He dutifully repeated the performance when, at another press conference, he cried again. This time, not for himself, but for his vulnerable ex-club mate Paul Gascoigne. Tony Adams, former captain of the England national side, has also earned the respect of the media after he disclosed his alcohol problem to the public. During the summer of 1998, Adams published his autobiography *Addicted*, which provides vivid details of his drunken debauchery, including admissions of wetting the bed. Some of the wags who suggested that he is now probably more respected for his addiction than his football appear to be vindicated as Adams has become the paradigmatic victim-hero in British sports.

The public exposure of inner pain can count on the affirmation and support of today's culture. In some cases the expectation of a positive response to the claim of emotional survival is manipulated by those seeking acclaim. Highly successful authors delicately let slip that they have a background of emotional distress. A high profile interview in *The Guardian* with British writer Amy Jenkins dwelt at length on how her life had been 'falling apart' six years previously. 'I got into clubbing and drugging and really mad unsuitable boyfriends and things got quite scary, out of control', Jenkins told the interviewer. Which is probably why she was paid £600,000 for two novels that she has not even written.[65]

The celebration of personal troubles and dysfunctions symbolises the way in which therapeutic society represents the human experience. From this perspective, self-destructive behaviour is no longer regarded as exceptional, but quite normal. Not only is there no shame attached to such episodes, they have become important cultural signifiers of people in positions of influence. And the ability to survive potentially destructive experiences like drug abuse or a psychological syndrome has been reinterpreted as an act of bravery worthy of our applause. Consequently, more and more people identify themselves through their addiction, syndrome or physical illness. As Laura Miller remarked, 'in a world where unadulterated heroism is harder and harder to define, let alone accomplish, the syndrome memoir turns simple survival into a triumph'.[65] The moral authority attached to the public display of private troubles led David Godwin, a top British literary agent, to remark that 'illness has become hip'. Illness as a fashion statement is emblematic of a cultural outlook that attaches so much significance to emotional survival.

However, the opportunistic routinisation of the confessional should not obscure the far more important aspect of reality – which is that society itself creates and rewards the tendency to erode the line between the private and the public. By upholding the act of seeking help, society continually demands the public exposure of pain. No longer is it just church leaders who encourage people to talk about their feelings. Therapeutic culture continually demands public contrition. From this perspective, claims for privacy represents a refusal to accept the etiquette of emotional correctness. And by treating emotion and feelings as the defining feature of individual identity, the private sphere has become a legitimate area for public scrutiny. This process of opening up relations of intimacy to therapeutic intervention, as we shall see in Chapter 4, has been paralleled by a tendency to devalue the private world.

2 The politics of emotion

Individual emotions and experience have acquired an unprecedented significance in public life. Increasingly, television news reporters want to know how a politician feels rather than what he or she has done. There is a new brand of so-called 'engaged reportage' that seeks to transform major events into bite-size stories about people's emotion. One critique of this brand of confessional journalism has warned that the 'danger of this outlook of "engaged reportage" is that news subjects become more counselled by reporters than scrutinised'.[1] The colonisation of public life by hitherto private emotions has had a major impact on contemporary political style. There is a growing tendency for public figures to adopt an emoting style in their presentation of themselves. They demonstrate their humanity by revelling to the world details of their broken family, alcoholic mothers, abusive fathers or the tragic afflictions of their children. Revelations of private hurt and suffering are likely to receive the full attention and approval of the media.

Politicians have always been in the business of managing emotions. Some of the most important calls to arms sought to harness the depth of people's feelings to a cause. 'I have nothing to offer but blood, toil, tears and sweat', stated Winston Churchill in his first statement as British prime minister. Churchill's speech revealed little about his personal emotion – it was devoted to inspiring the feelings of others. This call for sacrifice had very little to do with how Churchill felt, but about what had to be done. This is not surprising, since until recently the manifestation of personal emotion was seen as inconsistent with the exercise of political authority and leadership. Crying was perceived as unprofessional, an indication that an official was not in control of the situation. Back in 1972, the presidential candidate Senator Edmund Muskie had to abandon his ambition because he was seen to cry. Three decades later, in the aftermath of 9/11, the approval rating of George W. Bush rose after the American public saw a few salty tears in his eyes.

Until recently, politicians were regarded as public officials whose private lives were just that – private. Most of the time the public was unaware of the personal tragedies and personal problems that afflicted their leaders. The wheelchair-bound American President Franklin Delano Roosevelt, who lost the use of a leg to polio, hid his disability from the public. In contrast today, the private troubles and grief of leaders are often regarded as matters of utmost public concern. The happiness shown by British Chancellor Gordon Brown after the birth of his baby girl, followed by the grief felt for her tragic death, was interpreted in minute detail by the media. It was favourably represented by sections of the media as proof of this inscrutable politician's humanity. According to one journalist, 'the public has seen the human side of the chancellor and their view of him has been transformed'. The journalist added that the 'warmth that flowed towards Brown once he lost the uptight rictus grin of the politician, and replaced it with the open face of the thrilled father, points to what seems like a reliable rule of politics: that voters want their leaders to be just like them'.[2] Whilst it is far from evident whether voters want their leaders to be like themselves, it is clear that there are strong cultural pressures on politicians to demonstrate that they too have normal feelings and suffer from the usual range of human problems. Politicians and public figures are under great pressure to discuss and reveal aspects of their hitherto private emotional life. It is claimed that without making such a gesture, a public figure will fail to come across as human or approachable.

The breach in the border between the public and the private is closely linked to the trend for reassessing all social relationships in emotional and psychological terms. This chapter reviews the tendency to frame public dialogue through the language of therapeutics. It also considers one of the relatively unnoticed, but important features of our time: the coincidence of a high level of social disengagement with the ascendancy of therapeutic politics.

The changing status of emotions in public life

Emotions have always been on public display and have been a constant feature of social life. Every culture promotes and celebrates certain emotions. A culture transmits clear signals about how people are expected to feel in public. In previous times expressions of joy were sanctioned during moments of national triumph or the marriage of a royal prince. Feelings of awe and reverence were expected in response to rituals and symbols deemed sacred. Back in the nineteenth century, the ruling elites sought to cultivate positive emotional attachments towards symbols of authority to facilitate the maintenance of social order. The constitutional expert Walter Bagehot promoted the centrality of emotion, particularly the sentiment which bound the masses to the symbols of the monarchy.[3] The sentiment of patriotism was also routinely praised, as was the dislike, even hatred, of the enemy. But although certain forms of feeling in public were culturally validated, the political elites tended to be deeply ambivalent about the public display of emotions. Emotions could be legitimately displayed as long as there was not too much of it. Take the case of nationalism. In the past, the Anglo-American elites denounced the populist nationalism of other societies for its manifestation of extreme passion, unrestrained feeling and irrationality. J.A. Hobson, in his classic work *Imperialism: A Study*, warned against the 'chief perils and disturbances associated with the aggressive nationalism of today'. Harold Laski, a leading Labour intellectual, warned in the 1930s that the 'excesses' of nationalism 'will destroy civilisation' unless curbed.[4] From the standpoint of Hobson and Laski, it was the strength of feeling provoked by nationalism that constituted the problem. Nationalism was acceptable if it was felt in moderation. Hence British nationalism was praised on the ground that it was understated and seldom provoked strong passions. According to one account, Britain's confidence in its power 'may have bred in us an unconscious kind of nationalism, one that seldom needed to assert or even to know itself'.[5] Feelings of nationalism that were dignified and moderate enjoyed the approval of the British political establishment.

A nationalism that did not have to 'assert or even to know itself' was one that lacked passion and strong emotions. As long as patriotism did not unleash any powerful emotions amongst the masses, it was acceptable from the point of view of the political elites. However, the elites were uncomfortable with the political passions and emotions that stirred the urban masses. In Britain, prominent Liberal figures such as J.A. Hobson were taken aback by the outburst of jingoism at the outbreak of the Boer War. Hobson's book *The Psychology of Jingoism* provided a powerful statement of the elite's suspicion towards the mind of the crowd. Hobson observed, 'a coarse patriotism fed by the widest rumours and the most violent appeals to hate and the animal lust of blood, passes by quick contagion through the crowded life of cities, and recommends itself everywhere by the satisfaction it affords to sensational cravings'.[6]

In the late nineteenth century, the French crowd psychologist Gustave Le Bon provided one of the most influential elite accounts of the threat posed by public emotions. According to Le Bon and his colleagues, the mind of the crowd was influenced by savage and irrational impulses. He believed that its destructive emotions would vanquish reason and represented a threat to society. Le Bon wrote:

> It is not even necessary to descend so low as primitive beings to obtain an insight into the utter powerlessness of reasoning when it has to fight against sentiment. Let us merely call to mind how tenacious, for centuries long, have been religious superstitions in contradiction with the simplest logic.[7]

The apprehension of the political elites towards the mentality of the crowd was driven by the assumption that its emotions could be manipulated towards destructive ends by demagogues. These paternalistic assumptions were forcefully argued by the American commentator Walter Lippman in his classic 1992 study, *Public Opinion*. Lippman declared that the proportion of the electorate which is 'absolutely illiterate' is much larger than one would suspect and that these people who are 'mentally children or barbarians' are natural targets of manipulators. The belief that the public was dominated by infantile emotions was widespread in the social science literature of the interwar period. Often it conveyed the patronising assumption that public opinion does not know what is in its best interests. As one American sociologist noted in 1919, 'public opinion is often very cruel to those who struggle most unselfishly for the public welfare'.[8]

The tendency to regard public opinion as the prisoner of irrationality informed the attitude of the elite towards the public display of emotion throughout most of the twentieth century. Officials and opinion-makers were particularly worried about the capacity of radical ideologies to generate too much political emotion.

The passion and anger of protestors on the streets were regarded as the antithesis of reasoned and enlightened democratic process. And it was generally assumed that once mobilised, irrational emotionalism could vanquish the forces of rationality. That is why the widely respected economist Joseph Schumpeter argued for the need to limit access to public affairs. Schumpeter believed that 'utilitarian reason' was simply no match for the extra-rational determinants of conduct'.[9] He feared that people were likely to be swayed by their emotion and ignore the interests of society. Schumpeter's fears were widely shared by the political establishment, on both sides of the Atlantic. Consequently, the institutions of socialisation and the media sought to cultivate an ethos of emotional restraint. Public displays of emotion were discouraged unless they were channelled through traditional rituals and symbols. Indeed, one of the tasks assumed by governments was to monitor public opinion so as to ensure that the emotional life of society was confined within acceptable boundaries.

Ambivalence toward the public display of emotion by the Anglo-American political elites was founded upon an inclination to regard the lower classes as morally inferior people. This assumption directly informed their attitude to the public life of emotions. Elite apprehensions about public emotions were linked to the belief that the mental outlook of the 'lower classes' was distorted by its brutal upbringing. It was claimed that the emotional outlook of the working class created a propensity to adopt antidemocratic and authoritarian causes. The comments of the American social scientist Seymour Martin Lipset, a leading voice on this subject during the Cold War, is paradigmatic in this respect: 'to sum up, the lower-class individual is likely to have been exposed to punishment, lack of love, and a general atmosphere of tension and aggression since early childhood – all experiences which tend to produce deep-rooted hostilities expressed by ethnic prejudice, political authoritarianism, and chiliastic transvaluational religion'.[10] These early variants of today's cycle of abuse theories portrayed the lower classes as composed of psychologically damaged individuals who could not be relied on to affirm democratic values. The contrast drawn between the emotionally refined middle classes and the emotionally illiterate working classes was forcefully drawn by Hans Eysenck, a well-known British psychologist. Eysenck claimed that 'middle-class Conservatives are more tender-minded than working-class Conservatives; middle-class Liberals more tender-minded than working-class Liberals; middle-class Socialists more tender-minded than working-class Socialists and even middle-class Communists are more tender-minded than working-class Communists'.[11]

Keeping emotions out of politics was dictated by the recognition that in a polarised environment, anger and resentment could provoke instability and social unrest. Today the political situation is radically different. The political passions that were associated with twentieth-century revolutions and social strife appear exhausted. With the decline of ideologically driven social movements and of political polarisation, passion appears to be conspicuously absent in the public sphere. Political enthusiasms rarely engage the public imagination and the spectre of emotional crowds heading for the barricades has given way to that of public tedium and disengagement. With the erosion of social support for ideologies, emotions that were once directed towards transforming society have become disconnected from political life. The decoupling of passion from politics was already anticipated in the 1960s by the American sociologist Daniel Bell in his classic work *The End of Ideology*. Although Bell celebrated the apparent defeat of ideology, his book also mourned the passing of political passion. He warned that 'the young intellectual is unhappy because the "middle way" is for the middle aged, not for him; it is without passion and is deadening'.[12] If anything, the experience of recent decades goes even beyond Bell's prediction. It is not simply the 'young intellectual' who is turned-off – virtually the entire electorate has become estranged from political life.

The decoupling of passion from political life has encouraged the depoliticisation of emotions. In a sense, emotions have been made safe in the west. A powerful illustration of this trend was provided by the anti-war demonstration in London on 15 February 2003. With more than three-quarters of a million people protesting against the threat of a war against Iraq, this was by far the largest public mobilisation in modern British history. Yet, it was also one of the quietest and most restrained manifestations of public concern. According to one account of the mood of the demonstration, 'this groundswell of emotion doesn't generate anger – there wasn't much in evidence on Saturday – so much as stubborn resistance'.[13] The emotion that does not generate anger is one that has probably become distanced from belief, conviction, purpose and passion.

The sentiments of anger, resentment and hate continue to fuel the actions of many anti-western groups and movements. However, such sentiments are rarely expressed or mobilised within western societies. Trade unions are far more likely to organise anger management courses for their members than to incite them to feelings of resentment and class hate. Through its depoliticisation, emotions such as anger and hate have been reconfigured as the therapeutic concept of rage. The term rage not only medicalises the feeling of anger – it also individualises it. Rage is the product of something that comes from within the self. It is something that can be suffered in silence and in isolation from others. At the same time it is a concept that represents a critique of the self. To be in rage or to be enraged is a sign of individual weakness and though the reasons for it are sometimes understandable, it is the fault of the out-of-control individual. In the individualised form of rage, manifestations of anger are denuded of their social character and represented as individual character failings. The air-raged passenger is given treatment for air rage, but the conditions – flight cancellations, hassles at the airport, patronising treatment by staff – which may have influenced the outburst of anger is missed out of the equation.

Emotion has not only been disassociated from politics, its relationship to many of the traditional institutions, rituals and symbols that sustained it in the past has weakened. Take the feeling of patriotism. Periodically, in the aftermath of a major event that impacts on the psyche of the nation – 9/11 in the US, 2002 football world cup in the UK – a rise in the sentiment of patriotism is predicted only to be followed by the acknowledgement that little had changed.[14] Since the manifestation of public emotion is frequently not linked to traditional collective symbols it has acquired an arbitrary and unpredictable character. Depoliticised and individualised, public emotions often acquire an intensely personal focus. Public empathy with kidnapped children, hatred for paedophiles, obsessive fascination with the lives of celebrities, sorrow for those who have lost their lives are expressed through a variety of makeshift new rituals, such as the wearing of ribbons and the construction of spontaneous shrines.

With the decline of strong ideological or intellectual commitment, the public display of emotions is far less likely to be perceived as threatening. Consequently, the traditional elite suspicion of public emotionalism has become far more muted than in previous times. Because public emotionalism is rarely experienced as a problem, today's cultural and political elites have become less concerned, even positive, about its display. Once the public sphere has become depoliticised, emotionalism is less likely to be perceived as a source of instability. That is one reason why there has been so little elite opposition to the growth of therapeutic culture. On the contrary, the therapeutic management of public emotion is often deployed to tackle dissatisfaction and anxiety. Dana Cloud has observed the effective way in which US television news played an important role during the Persian Gulf War 'by rearticulating political outrage as personal anxiety'. She noted how news oriented towards the support of families of military personnel focused on questions like how people were 'coping with the war' to forge a sense of emotional unity. As one television correspondent cited by Cloud noted, 'on the home front, the Persian Gulf is a war of emotions'.[15]

Whereas in the past the public display of emotionalism was frequently stig-matised as the irrational act of deficient people, today it is often praised as an expression of maturity and openness. Numerous advocacy groups and academics plead the case of expanding the role of emotions in public life.[16] Indeed, the more that society accommodates to a therapeutic sensibility, the more it is encouraged to go further still. At a time when therapeutics dominates cultural life, zealous crusaders complain that Britain is still not emotional enough. The denunciation of Britain as 'culture of emotional inhibition' by Ian Robertson, a Cambridge neuropsychologist, is illustrative of the standpoint of the therapeutic crusade. He remarks that:

> As a nation we are mistrustful – nay scared – of emotion. We like to sneer at these self-indulgent Americans and continental Europeans with their unseemly emotional outbursts. Our stiff-upper-cortex bullies the emotional centres of the brain in the limbic system into cowed obeisance, the result being a nation of emotional cripples.[17]

As far as therapeutic activists are concerned, Britain remains in a state of emotional illiteracy.

Take the British think tank Antidote. The aim of Antidote is to integrate the insights of psychology into political and public life. It seeks to advocate policies that tend to 'foster emotional attitudes tending to support the development of more cohesive societies'.[18] One of its stated goals is the creation of an emotional and social index, which would gather information about the emotional consequences of policies. Recently it has published a manifesto that touches on virtually every area of public policy.[19] Associates of Antidote are intensely interested in promoting the institutionalisation of the therapeutic ethos and in transforming the vocabulary of politics. A recently published book by Andrew Samuels, one of the founders of Antidote, explicitly argues for this agenda. He contends that policy committees and government commissions should have a 'psychotherapist sitting on them as part of a spectrum of experts'. The book argues for a national emotional audit and for the creation of a range of institutions, such as an emotional and spiritual justice commission 'that would monitor the effects on psychological and spiritual health of all policy proposals'.[20] As we shall see, politicians and government officials are more than willing to accommodate to this call for the politics of emotionalism.

It would be inaccurate to characterise the consolidation of the influence of therapeutic ethos on public life as a turn to emotion. Emotions, including outbursts of popular resentment, have always been part of public life. For its part, ruling elites have never been indifferent to the emotional life of the public. The management of the public mood has always been a task of government. What has changed is that in its individuated form, the management of emotion involves intervening in areas hitherto regarded as private. Consequently, the line that separates the private from public has become blurred. 'Private emotion' now seems inconsistent with the therapeutic ethos of our time. People are expected to express emotions that hitherto might have been confined to the private sphere. According to one account, 'caution has been reconceptualised as inhibition, and diffidence as withholding'.[21] Whilst private emotions go public, public life itself has become emptied of its content. The shift from politics to the personal in public life is the corollary of the individualisation of the private sphere.

Managerialism with an emotional face

Changing elite attitudes towards emotionalism go hand in hand with the depoliticisation of public life. Bell warned back in the 1960s that the decline of ideology threatened to deprive political life of any real content. He believed that the loss of meaning in politics would disorient the young generation of intellectuals.[22] As he predicted, the pragmatic managerialism that now goes by the name of politics lacks the capacity to inspire the electorate's imagination. The displacement of politics by managerialism has fostered a climate where conflict between parties and politicians are regarded as boring and irrelevant by a significant section of the electorate. The main beneficiary of this decline in the political imagination has been the therapeutic ethos. Almost three decades ago, the relationship between political disengagement and the expanding influence of therapeutic culture became visible. At the time Lasch went even so far as to argue that 'the therapeutic outlook threatens to displace politics'.[23] Since the 1970s the process identified by Halmos in the UK and Lasch in the US has become more consolidated. As we shall see, politics has not so much been displaced by therapeutics, but has been transformed by it. Conventional politics has adopted a therapeutic sensibility and often treats the public as clients rather than citizens.

At a time when people have lost interest in conventional politics, politicians are continually searching for new ways of interacting with the public. That is why professional politicians have been so quick to assimilate the therapeutic ethos. Politicians have come to recognise that their political, ideological and moral links with the electorate are characteristically fragile. Traditional forms of party politics, political values and identities have little purchase on an evidently disenchanted public. Popular mistrust of authority is confirmed by the growing alienation of people from the system of elections. American-style voting apathy has become a fact of life in the new Europe, where a significant proportion of the electorate believes that voting is a waste of time.

Increasingly, every election threatens to become an embarrassing reminder of the political wasteland that we inhabit. Apathy is no longer an adequate term of description for the steady erosion of the public's involvement in the political life of the United States. Since 1960, voter participation has steadily declined in almost every presidential election. Overall, the percentage of the electorate voting in presidential elections declined from 62.5 per cent in 1960 to 50.1 per cent in 1988. During the election in 1996, only 49 per cent of the voting age population bothered to cast their ballots – the lowest turn out since 1924. The election in 2000 continued this pattern, with only about 50 per cent of registered voters participating. The alienation of the public from the political process is particularly striking in relation to the election of 2000. Unlike the election of 1996, where the outcome was seen to be a foregone conclusion, the contest in 2000 was the most open for decades. Yet the number of Americans who voted was roughly the same as in 1996. According to the Committee for the Study of the American Electorate, 'the cumulative effect of voter disengagement during the past 30 years is that today, 25 million Americans who used to vote no longer do so'.[24] Yet, voter participation in presidential elections appears positively high compared to the ballots cast for candidates running for a seat in the House of Representatives. These have averaged around 35 per cent in the 1990s.

In the aftermath of 9/11, media pundits speculated that this tragic event and the growth of a sense of patriotism which ensued might increase political participation. However, it soon became evident that not even such a major event could disrupt the pre-existing pattern of disengagement. The first 18 primaries prior to 5 July 2002 saw 'not just low turnout, but record low turnout – with only 8 per cent of Democrats and 7 per cent of Republicans going to the polls'.[25]

Nor can European commentators feel smug about the political illiteracy of the American electorate. A leader in *The Guardian* entitled 'Don't yawn for Europe. Apathy must not win the elections', written prior to the June 1999 elections, indicated that public disenchantment with political life is no longer confined to the other side of the Atlantic. In Britain, the facts speak for themselves. It is worth recalling that in 1997, New Labour was backed by only 31 per cent of those qualified to vote. Voter turnout at this election was the lowest since 1945. 'The 1997 general election excited less interest than any other in living memory' concluded the authors of a Nuffield College study of this event. Even the highly hyped public relations campaign surrounding devolution in Scotland and Wales failed to engage the public's interest. Voter participation in these 'history-making' elections in 1999 indicated that the public regarded it as yet another stage-managed event. The majority of the Welsh electorate chose the less than history-making option of staying at home. Only 46 per cent of them bothered to vote. In Scotland a high profile media campaign designed to promote voter participation led to a 59 per cent turnout. And on the same day, polling booths in England were literally empty. Only 29 per cent of registered voters turned out for the 6 May local elections. The June 1999 UK elections to the European Parliament represented an all time record low. Only 23 per cent turned out to vote. In one polling station in Sunderland, only 15 people turned up out of the 1,000 entitled to vote. In comparison to the general election of 2001, that of 1997 looked positively exciting. Throughout the 2001 election campaign, apathy emerged as the dominant issue under debate. The turnout was an all-time low of 59 per cent at the 7 June 2001 general election.

The steady decline of voter participation is directly linked to a much wider process at work. Lack of participation provides a clear index of disillusionment and public mistrust in the existing political system. Surveys of American public attitudes indicate that approval of the government has steadily declined in recent decades. Whereas in 1958 over 75 per cent of the American people trusted their government to do the right thing, only 28.2 per cent could express a similar sentiment in 1990. Since the beginning of this decade trust in politicians has continued to decline. The 1996 *In a State of Disunion* survey conducted by the Gallup organisation found that 64 per cent of the respondents had little or no confidence that government officials tell the truth.

A major study carried out by the Brookings Institution in May 2002 found that not even the wave of patriotism that followed in the aftermath of 9/11 translated into a durable growth of trust in the US government. This survey showed that, whereas in July 2001 only 29 per cent of Americans expressed a positive regard for their government, in the aftermath of the events of 11 September, this figure almost doubled to 57 per cent. However, by May 2002, the public trust in federal government had fallen back to almost pre-9/11 figures. Although it stood at 40 per cent, experts felt the opportunity for the reforging of a relationship of trust had probably passed.[26]

Surveys in Europe point to a similar pattern. Studies carried out in the European Union indicate that around 45 per cent of the population is dissatisfied with the 'way that democracy works'. In Britain, surveys reveal a high level of public cynicism towards politicians. A Gallup poll conducted in April 1995 concluded that the opinion of most towards Members of Parliament was 'low' or 'very low'. A decade previously only a third had adopted this view. According to another survey, carried out in 1994, only 24 per cent of the population believed that the British government places the national interest above their party interests.[27] Politicians consistently come at the bottom of the list of professions that the public trusts. A survey published by the ICM in June 1999 found that only 10 per cent of the respondents stated that they trust politicians a great deal, 65 per cent a little, and 25 per cent indicated, not at all.[28] A study carried out by the BBC in February 2002 indicated that many people under the age of 45 were disillusioned with politics and regarded politicians as 'crooks', 'liars' and a 'waste of time'.[29]

During the 1990s, the erosion of public trust was reflected in a national mood of suspicion towards the political system itself. What emerged was a brand of antipolitics, a cyclical dismissal of the elected politician and an obsession with sleaze and corruption in Westminster and Washington. The Clinton era was one of permanent scandal. Controversy surrounded the manner of Bush's election, only to be followed by a series of corporate scandals that culminated with the collapse of Enron. New Labour success in portraying the Conservatives as a party of sleaze was crucial to its electoral success of 1997. In turn, the New Labour government soon discovered that it too was not immune to the politics of the scandal. Within months of being elected, the New Labour government was hit by a spate of minor scandals involving Labour MPs and ministers. The issue of sleaze continued to haunt the government as successive ministers were forced to hand in their resignation in 1998. The furore that surrounded 'Cheriegate' in December 2002 – despite the absence of any allegation that the Prime Minister's wife had done anything illegal – indicates that cynicism towards government is a permanent feature of life.

The exhaustion of political life has little to do with political corruption, inept political leaders or insensitive bureaucracies. What has changed during the past two decades is the very meaning of politics itself. At the beginning of the last century, political life was dominated by radically different alternatives. Competing political philosophies offered contrasting visions of a good society. Conflict between these ideologies was often fierce and sometimes provoked violent clashes and even revolutions. 'Left' and 'Right' were no mere labels. In a fundamental sense, they endowed individuals with an identity that said something very important about how they regarded their lives. Ardent advocates of revolutionary change clashed with fervent defenders of the capitalist system. Their competing views about society dominated the conduct of everyday politics.

The beginning of the twenty-first century offers a radically different political landscape. Politics today has little in common with the passions and conflicts that have shaped people's commitments and hatreds over the past century. There is no longer room for either the ardent defender of the free market faith, or the robust advocate of revolutionary transformation. It would be wrong to conclude that politics has become simply more moderate. Politics has gone into early retirement. The end-of-century ethos continually emphasises problems which are not susceptible to human intervention.

Theories of globalisation continually stress the inability of people and of their nation states to deal with forces which are beyond their control. The big issues of our time – the impending environmental catastrophe, threats to our health, killer bugs, weapons of mass destruction – are presented as perils that stand above politics. It is widely believed that the world is out of control and that there is little that human beings can do to master these developments or influence their destiny.

Deprived of choice and options, humanity is forced to acquiesce to a world-view which Margaret Thatcher aptly described as TINA – There is No Alternative.

And if indeed there is no alternative, politics can have little meaning. Without alternatives, debate becomes empty posturing about trivial matters. Politicians are forced to inflate relatively banal proposals to the level of a major policy innovation. This is the age of 'micropolitics'. Politics has adopted the language of technocracy and presents itself through a depoliticised language of managerialism. Politicians now promise to 'deliver'. They carefully 'cost' proposals and offer 'value for money'. Policies are no longer good – they are 'evidence-based'. Policies are rarely generated by a world-view – they are derived from 'best practice'.

The growth of a managerial political style has gone hand in hand with a shift from politics to the personal. Personalities and individual behaviour dominate the presentation of contemporary politics. As public life has become emptied of its content, private and personal preoccupations have been projected into the public sphere. Consequently, passions that were once stirred by ideological differences are far more likely to be engaged by individual misbehaviour, private troubles and personality conflicts. The private lives of politicians excites greater interest than the way they handle their public office. In Britain it is widely noted that the reality TV show *Big Brother* 'arouses passions that politics can no longer stir'.[30] In the US, plans are afoot to launch a television programme entitled *American Candidate*. The aim of this programme is to use the reality TV format to pick a 'people's candidate' from its contestants. With so many people turned off managerial politics, is it any surprise that politicians are turning to reality television producers to learn how to engage with an otherwise disinterested public.

Therapeutic participation

Although emotions have become depoliticised they still represent an important instrument of mobilisation. But having been decoupled from ideologies and collective interests, the public display of emotions tends to have an individuated character. Such mobilisations serve as a form of therapy for the expression of individual feeling. In a highly fragmented and individualised world, individual grievances can be temporarily shared through a common expression of emotion. At a time when the public finds it difficult to articulate a clear political view, the act of displaying emotion with others is interpreted as a very genuine and important statement. Public manifestation of emotionalism is often favourably contrasted to what is perceived as the estranged artificial world of politics.

Not surprisingly, participation in acts of emotional solidarity is valued for its own sake. Participation in these acts of mourning represents a form of publicly sanctioned therapy that suggests that involvement is good in itself. The Italian sociologist Alberto Melucci claims that one of the distinct features of contemporary social movements is that people's participation within movements is no longer a means to an end: 'Participation in collective action is seen to have no value for the individual unless it provides a direct response to personal needs'.[31] Such participants are making a personal statement about their feeling. However, in the very act of feeling in the company of others, individuals become at least temporarily part of an emotional community.

Some of the largest mobilisations in Europe during the 1990s have been influenced by this trend of expressing 'personal needs'. The mass demonstrations in Spain, in July 1997, to mourn the murder of Miguel Angel Blanco by ETA, manifested a strange emotional dynamic. At times the crowd exuded a sense of intensity as if something tragic was just about to happen. At other times, a sense of anticipation – not unlike at pop festivals – helped create a feeling of exhilaration. Demonstrators told interviewers that they were not sure why they were there and some suggested that they too felt like victims. This reaction was self-consciously cultivated by the crowd with the gesture of placing their hands at the back of their heads in the posture of surrendering prisoners.

But probably the most important manifestation of the politics of emotion was the Belgian White March of 1996. This, the largest display of public solidarity in the history of Belgium and the subsequent growth of the White Movement underlines the strength of the politics of emotion. What began as an act of solidarity with the murdered child victims of a depraved serial killer soon turned into a condemnation of the entire Belgian political system. While politicians lost some of their authority, that of King Albert gained in strength. Why? Because unlike the politicians, Albert was quick to display his emotions on television. And if opinion polls are anything to go by, the public positively responded to such displays of human frailty.

The most easily recognised symbol of the politics of emotion is the wearing of a ribbon. It is difficult to say when it all started. The fashion for wearing yellow ribbons was first visible during the imprisonment of the American diplomatic hostages in Tehran in 1980. People wore their ribbons so that they too could be part of the experience. In more recent times, red ribbons have been worn by people who identify with the victims of AIDS. Yellow ribbons were again worn by well-wishers of soldiers going off to fight Saddam. Black ribbons were worn by anti-ETA campaigners in Spain in July and pink ribbons have been distributed by breast cancer charities in the United States. Supporters of Louise Woodward, a British nanny accused of killing an infant in her care by an American court, also distributed ribbons. It symbolises awareness of a community of feeling. The wearing of a ribbon represents a personal statement. 'I am aware' and 'I empathise' are the key sentiments associated with ribbon wearing.

One of the defining features of therapeutic politics is that it combines political disengagement with public outbursts of emotionalism. These two features appear to be inversely proportional to one another. It is worth noting that some of the most significant public manifestations of collective emotion have coincided with a widespread suspicion of the political process. Belgium is paradigmatic in this respect. According to the Belgian sociologist Marc Hooghe, there is a 'total lack of patriotism' amongst his country's population. He believes that a 'severe loss of confidence in the political system' explains why the White Movement was so suspicious of Belgium's political institutions. A series of surveys of the participants of the White March carried out by Benoit Rihoux and Stefaan Walgrave indicate an intense level of popular mistrust for political parties. Clearly, many Belgians regarded themselves as the victims, rather than as participants of their political system.

Popular mistrust of authority is most strikingly confirmed in the widespread circulation of rumours which indict existing authority. In Belgium it was widely believed that the people who committed the horrendous crimes were protected by leading officials and politicians. The public reaction to the infamous Alcacer case – the sexual violation and murder of three teenage girls in Spain – also revealed a deeply held mistrust of authority. Opinion polls indicated that there was widespread support for the view that the Guardia Civil was implicated in the case and that the girls were killed for the purpose of making snuff videos. In the same vein, it was widely rumoured in parts of Britain that Princess Diana was killed by an officially sanctioned assassin in order to prevent her marrying a Muslim.

The corollary of such rumours of mistrust is an intense sense of alienation and powerlessness. It is well worth noting that the icon of the politics of emotion is the victim. Public grief for Diana was inspired by her high profile as Britain's best-known sufferer. The reaction of the public to events in Belgium was similar. Surveys indicate that participants on the White March took the streets because they emotionally identified with the victims. Public identification with the cult of vulnerability represents a sense of shared experience of suffering. The common bond is that of suffering and everyone who wears a ribbon can participate the same drama of public grief. Through a collective display of emotion, an otherwise fragmented society achieves a temporary moment of unity.

But the politics of emotion is not just merely a symptom of alienation and powerlessness. To a considerable extent it also expresses the problem of legitimacy experienced by a variety of political systems. At a time when collective reactions are rare, these expressions of suffering solidarity are just about the only manifestation of national unity being offered, and the politicians and the media have exploited them for all they are worth. It is difficult to avoid the conclusion that, with British people feeling so fragmented, the ritual of grieving provides one of the few experiences that create a sense of belonging. The huge anti-ETA mobilisation in July 1998 was probably the most important all-Spanish event of recent years. For a brief moment, regional differences between Catalonia, Euskadi, Andalusia, etc., was put aside for a brief act of collective solidarity.

In Belgium, there was a clear attempt to translate the White March into a national myth. King Albert in his televised Christmas message represented this experience as proof that Belgian was a good society. He emphasised the new hope brought by the march and how it 'impressed the whole world by its strength and dignity'. 'It prompts every one of us to take responsibility for finding solutions to society's numerous problems', stated Albert. A similar point was echoed by the political class of Britain. Leading politicians pointed to the public reaction to Diana's death and declared that here was Britain at its best.

Since public displays of solidarity are so rare, everyone is reluctant to look too closely at the community built around suffering. But there is something sad about a society that can only experience solidarity through common mourning. What is truly tragic is that even critical observers are reluctant to ask the question of what kind of society needs tragic deaths to gain a common public emotional reaction. The spirit of solidarity must be very weak if extraordinary tragedies are needed to bring a common response to the surface. However, at a time when little else stirs the passion, the mobilising potential of emotionalism stands out as unique. It promises to connect with an otherwise alienated public. 'What the political establishment has to contend with is the failure of liberal democracies to inspire a kind of political emotion – which underpinned commitment, and the willing sacrifice of individual self-interest for the collective', writes one observer.[32] That is why every tragedy or funeral tends to be regarded as a rare opportunity to renew a sense of community. The Church of England organised a poster campaign to increase attendance, designed to tap into the public outpouring of grief for Diana. The poster depicted a pile of floral tributes and cuddly toys and handwritten messages and carried the slogan 'If All This Started You Thinking, Carry On At Church This Easter'. The Reverend Robert Ellis, an organiser of this campaign, stated that in 'recent years we have witnessed the collective outpouring of grief' and 'we wanted to harness that feeling, and through this campaign, to point people towards the next step'.[33]

The therapeutic political style

The managerial style of politics lacks the capacity to engage the interests of the electorate. Politicians are continually looking for ways to 'reconnect' with the public. In Britain, politicians have even consulted Peter Bazalgette, the creator of the successful reality television programme, *Big Brother*, to advise them how to connect with the voters, particularly young people. Bazalgette claims that the reason why young people were more likely to vote for a contestant on *Big Brother* than for a political candidate is because 'they are emotionally engaged by the programme'.[34] This is a message that clearly resonates with the political class since they have adopted a clear orientation towards the public's emotion.

Professional politicians and their advisors are intensely sensitive to their isolation from their electorate. Not surprisingly they are continually searching for new ways of strengthening their links with the public. In an era of depoliticisation, the orientation towards public emotion is regarded as an important way of getting round people's indifference to politics. That is why politicians often tend to act as if they are not politicians – but outsiders, regular people who have the same problems as the rest of us.

Throughout the western world, politicians have begun to look for new forms of legitimisation. Such a search needs to engage with a highly individuated electorate that has distanced itself from traditional values and indeed from any commonly held beliefs and ideologies. Public concern with the problem of the self creates a climate where a therapeutic sensibility informs the perception of social problems. As a result, the therapeutic ethos has provided an obvious focus for the energies of the political classes. The American sociologist James Nolan argues that US politicians concerned with mobilising popular support have attempted to extend their influence through harnessing the influence of therapeutic consciousness.[35]

Politicians have sought to adopt a therapeutic political style in order to connect with the mood of the times. Politicians vent their private feelings and inform their public about their personal problems and their dysfunctions. From the standpoint of the politics of the confessional, what matters most is how you feel rather than what you stand for. As Wendy Kaminer reports, 'presidential candidates are regaling us with stories of their personal odysseys, as if the nation were one large support group'. Kaminer notes how both Al Gore and Bill Clinton specialised in telling the world about their personal growth stories.[36] Increasingly, politicians eschew the image of the powerful leader and flaunt their vulnerability. Jean Corston, a former chairman of the Parliamentary Labour Party claimed that Members of Parliament required counselling to stop them becoming depressives. 'I do think there's an argument for counselling provision which is in no way stigmatised and which could be confidential', stated Corston.[37] Far from being stigmatised, the act of seeking help is represented as an act of bravery.

Through publicly acknowledging their vulnerability, politicians transmit the message, that 'like you I feel pain'. The public display of strong emotion is best represented through the act of fighting off tears. Such gestures convey the image of a genuine person acting truthfully. Ex-senator Bob Kerrey was choked up and 'close to tears' when he confessed his previously undisclosed role in the killing of more than a dozen Vietnamese civilians. 'I was so ashamed, I wanted to die', stated Kerrey in April 2001.[38] For other leading figures – especially those discredited through a scandal – the public confessional serves to lighten the burden of responsibility. And going into therapy represents a statement of political virtue. That is why Ron Davies, a Labour MP who resigned after a sex scandal in 1998, made a public announcement in June 1999 that he had begun a course of psychiatric treatment for what he described as his 'darker side'. He blamed his condition on a 'troubled, violent, emotional dysfunctional childhood'.[39]

This political style has been perfected by the Clinton administration, successfully copied by New Labour and increasingly emulated on the Continent. Nolan suggests that the therapeutic rhetoric employed by Clinton during the 1992 election marked a major shift in the prevailing political discourse. At the time it was widely reported that both the Clintons and the Gores were involved in counselling. And both Clinton and his running mate, Al Gore, talked publicly about their marital problems, issues related to Roger Clinton's drug addiction and his stepfather's alcoholism. Since 1992 Clinton has never stopped talking about his feelings and his personal failures. And when he tells the world 'I feel your pain', Clinton's sense of inner vulnerability becomes exposed for the world to see. Hillary Clinton has affirmed her partner's damaged psyche and during the Lewinsky affair, she presented her husband as an 'abused' child. 'He was so young, barely four, when he was scarred by abuse that he can't even take it out and look at it', she stated.[40]

According to Nolan, the triumph of therapeutic rhetoric was most conspicuously demonstrated during the 1996 political conventions of the Republican and Democratic Parties. Elizabeth Dole's emotional tribute to her husband at the

Republican convention in San Diego was more than matched by Gore's sob story about his sister's death from lung cancer at the Democratic convention in Chicago.[41] Since then, Gore's wife Tipper has shared with the American public her own struggle with depression. And Elizabeth Dole's husband, Bob, has thought it important to inform American society about his erectile dysfunction. 'Now even button-downed Bob Dole has been crying on the campaign trail', noted an observer, before adding that 'when he mentions either his war experience or his tough childhood in Kansas, he chokes up, reassuring his audience that he is, indeed human, one of them'.[42]

During the presidential campaign of 2000, both contenders – George W. Bush and Al Gore – made time to appear on the Oprah Winfrey show. Bush demonstrated his humanity by crying on the show. According to one account, 'talking about when his wife Laura became toxaemic while carrying their twins, his eyes became wet and continued to glisten even after the following commercial break'.[43]

George W. Bush's eyes filled with tears when he took the oath of office as the newly inaugurated President of the US, indicating that the politics of emotionalism enjoys bipartisan consensus. In the aftermath of the tragedy of 9/11, Bush's sense of emotional anguish was on open display. He appeared visibly shaken on the day of the attack and on the days following he seemed to be trying to avoid tears.[44]

Blair's New Labour has drawn heavily on the Clinton experience. The 1996 Labour Party convention demonstrated that therapeutic politics had arrived in Britain big time. The high point of this conference was the speech made by Ann Pearston, the main public figure of the Dunblane-based Snowdrop campaign against gun ownership. Evoking memories about this recent tragedy, Pearston succeeded in stunning the conference into silence. Delegates wept openly as Pearston recounted the details of the tragedy. Her speech was followed by an enthusiastic standing ovation. And Tony Blair led the conference in a minute's silence to mourn the Dunblane victims. This was political theatre at its best. Carefully orchestrated – Pearston's speech was patiently rehearsed by New Labour spin doctors – it demonstrated the power of political emotionalism. Indeed, it was the only memorable moment of the conference. It is worth recalling that the Tories had declined to accept Pearston's offer to address their conference. Their ineptitude in engaging with the politics of emotion may in part explain their subsequent defeat at the polls and their current exile in the political wilderness.

During the year leading up to New Labour's 1997 election victory, there were clear signs that the party had opted for the politics of emotionalism. Joy Johnson, one of Labour's leading spin doctors, resigned from her post in 1996, on the grounds that she did not want a job that was primarily about 'selecting "real people" with emotional stories to tell'.[45] At the October 1996 party conference, Blair demonstrated what she meant when during his speech he made an emotional 'off-the-cuff' tribute to his 73-year-old father Leo. Blair also recalled the funeral of a leading union leader, Sam McCluskie. He remarked that a family member gave him a strip of red ribbon belonging to McCluskie, a keepsake that the Labour leader still treasured. Such tearful demonstrations of emotion are emblematic of the new style of therapeutic politics. Even when commenting on major events of historic significance, Blair cannot resist the temptation to emote. 'This isn't a time for sound bites', he remarked just before the signing of the Northern Ireland agreement, before adding 'but you know, I feel that the hand of history is really on our shoulder, I really do'.

Therapeutic politics eschews matters of policy and principle and attempts to establish a point of contact in the domain of the emotion with an otherwise estranged electorate. The most effective practitioner of this art in Britain was the former Secretary of State for Northern Ireland, Mo Mowlam. Mowlam not only exuded ordinaries, she affected a persona of intense warmth who routinely embraced members of the public in front of the camera. Her public struggle with a serious illness demonstrated that she is no stranger to pain and suffering. She had also survived childhood living with an alcoholic father in what she described as a 'dysfunctional family'. With such qualifications, it is not surprising that until recently she was the most popular member of the New Labour government. What counts are the public gestures of being down to earth, warm and emotional rather than the quality of ideas, strategic thought or leadership. The emphasis on these gestures was clearly brought out in a report that contrasted a warm Mowlam with her aloof predecessor:

> Dr Mowlam . . . came into the job of Northern Ireland Secretary only 2 years and 5 months ago. She breezed into Belfast one morning in May 1997, and politics hasn't been the same since. On that day she glad-handed her way along city-centre Belfast, having a chat here, offering a big hug there, taking a bite out of someone's apple, being extravagant with her kisses. This, coming after the patrician aloofness of her predecessor, Sir Patrick Mayhew, was refreshing and almost shocking. 'Well done, Mo, I hope you kick the politicians into shape here', a Catholic man told her. That indeed was part of her purpose. With her informal behaviour, her fondness for risqué jokes, her profligate use of the vernacular, nationalists generally warmed to her. Unionists, though, much more strait-laced, often found her a difficult character. She was 'unladylike', some complained.[46]

The ability to forge an emotional bond with the public has become the principal virtue of therapeutic politics. That is why those with political ambition need to cultivate a therapeutic style.

The therapeutic style of politics requires public figures to exploit their personality traits. The constant demand for emotional reaction means that politicians have little scope for privacy. The media encourages politicians to reveal their personal selves. They are rewarded for coming across as accessible, humorous and very human. Not surprisingly, spin doctors have realised 'that how something is said can be as important and compelling as what is said'.[47]

The political idiom of emotionalism is characteristically expressed through personal statements about feelings and moods. Nolan points out how President Clinton regularly employs the phrase 'I feel good about . . .' to justify his action and policies.[48] This shift in rhetoric from standing up for what is 'right' to upholding what one feels good about signifies the incorporation of emotionalism into the heart of political decision-making. A similar shift is also evident in the British political scene, where the Blair regime has become wedded to the politics of emotion. When accused of acting improperly over the Ecclestone affair in November 1997 – one of New Labour's scandals – Blair admitted that he was 'hurt and upset'. Blair often insists that he feels the pain or understands the problems faced by sections of the public facing adversity.

The ascendancy of the therapeutic political style means that public figures are increasingly assessed in relation to their emotional skills. According to Fraser Seitel, a communication consultant, Rudy Giuliani, the former mayor of New York, was an effective leader during the immediate aftermath of 9/11 because of his communication skills. 'As hard-nosed as he is, Rudy Giuliani has no trouble expressing emotion', writes Seitel. Giuliani's 'hesitant, heart-rending' acknowledgment of lost friends is contrasted favourably with President Bush, who was 'at first stiff and formal in the face of calamity'. However, Seibel praises Bush for showing himself 'to be much more human' a few days later, 'particularly when he momentarily broke down in an impromptu Oval Office press conference'.[49] In Britain, too, politicians are graded on their emotional skills. Since the Irish peace process, the Nationalist leadership has won praise for adopting the therapeutic style. Sinn Fein leader Gerry Adams has repeatedly apologised for the pain and hurt caused by the Republican movement, while constantly reminding others that the nationalist community has suffered too. Adams even borrowed Bill Clinton's election slogan, 'I feel your pain'. Unionist politicians who stand out for resisting the adoption of therapeutics face the disapproval of Britain's cultural elite. David Trimble, the leader of the Ulster Unionists, has been described as an enigma for eschewing 'emotion' and talk of 'personal transformation'.[50]

The institutionalisation of therapeutic politics

In today's climate, the practice of individual therapy is seen as indistinguishable from the measures that are required for the 'healing' of society. When Blair or Clinton indicate that 'I feel your pain', they are offering empathy through assuming the role of the politician–therapist. Public institutions have also adopted this orientation towards the management of emotion.

The management of emotion and of personal relationships has become a key concern of the institution of the state. Rose has noted that the 'personal and subjective capacities of citizens have been incorporated into the scope and aspirations of public powers'. The internal lives of British people 'now enters into the calculations of political forces about the state of the nation and the problems facing the country about priorities and policies'.[51] Since the 1980s there has been a rapid acceleration of the assimilation of therapeutic objectives and practices by public authority. The current New Labour government is a robust and self-conscious promoter of this approach. As Arnar Arnason notes, 'it is telling that technologies similar to those employed by counselling have now become part and parcel of the way in which the current British Government governs its people'.

Arnason believes that the government's obsession with focus groups and other instruments designed to gauge public opinion represents a quest to 'gain unfettered access to people's subjectivity'.[52]

The core institutions of the British state have started to internalise the ideology of emotionalism. In August 1999, the Civil Service College announced that it was to offer courses in emotional intelligence in order to improve the capacity of senior civil servants to relate to their political masters. Roy Howells, the tutor in charge of the new courses, indicated that the programme was designed to bring out 'the soft skills' in civil servants. Civil servants seeking a fast track to promotion are to be encouraged to 'develop their emotional side and to stop macho posturing'.[53] Similar courses have been initiated in a variety of other government services.

Many of New Labour's distinctive policies target people's emotions and offer counselling and therapy as part of its programme. This approach has gained prominence in the field of education policy. There is now a manifest tendency for school pupil's socialisation to take the form of emotional training. It is worth noting that a British government advisory group on 'Education for Citizenship and the Teaching of Democracy in Schools' considers self-esteem as an important core skill.[54] The Department of Education's guiding statement on 'Sex and Relationship' education instructs schools to undertake the task of building pupil's self-esteem. Schools are advised to prepare young people to have 'the confidence and self-esteem to value themselves and others'. A similar approach informs the pedagogic perspective of the Scottish Executive. Its national guidelines insists that if pupils lack self-esteem, they are 'unlikely to make progress in classroom learning'. Accordingly, Scottish schools offer special focus programmes which attempt to develop children's emotional skills. The most widely used technique is 'circle time' in which 'pupils sit in a circle and say something about their own feelings on a special issue'. They may be asked to complete a sentence beginning 'I feel happy when' or 'I feel sad when'. This technique is often linked to the realisation of the objective of emotional intelligence, 'that is, the ability to understand and manage one's own emotion'.[55]

Although, the development of emotional education within the national curriculum is still at an early stage, some local authorities have already adopted a self-consciously therapeutic approach. In 1998, the Southampton Educational Authority took a decision to assign emotional intelligence the same level of importance as 'ordinary' literacy. Southampton teachers are encouraged to 'take time and stare' in order to understand their own emotions so that they can help develop the emotional literacy of their pupils.[56] A variety of government-sponsored pilot projects aim to assess whether therapeutic techniques can be used effectively as teaching tools. One project, which involves four secondary and two primary schools in east London, presents itself as 'an experiment to see whether psychotherapeutic techniques can help children do better in class'. The first phase of this project involves the carrying out of an 'emotional literacy audit' in each school. Once problem areas have been identified, an action plan will be devised, leading to initiatives like anger management schemes and meditation sessions.[57]

Another project, based in Lambeth, 'Supporting Parents on Kids Education', is run by Stephen Scott, a child psychiatrist. This 3-year project aims to give children a good start by developing their self-esteem. The project also aims to involve the children's parents in a therapeutic relationship in order to show them how to parent.[58]

The role of therapy has acquired an important dimension in New Labour's social policy towards the unemployed. The practice of counselling the unemployed was adopted during the Thatcher era, albeit in a hesitant and unsystematic manner. Since the election of the Blair government in 1997, this approach has become a key component of welfare policy. The Gateway programme, which is designed to assist the government's project of modernising the welfare state, offers guidance and counselling. In September 1998, it was reported that officials of the Department of Social Security were expected to switch their role from that of an officer to that of a counsellor. 'The ability of civil servants to switch from paper-bound administrators to flesh-and-blood counsellors is one of the New Deal's most crucial aspects', argued one analysis of this development.[59]

The government has encouraged the use of therapeutic techniques to manage the problems posed by homeless people. The government's 'Rough Sleepers Unit' has adopted an outlook that defines the homeless as vulnerable people who require mental health services. In Scotland, Edinburgh City Council has adopted the policy of providing homeless women with lessons in aromatherapy and in using scented oils to combat stress.[60] Local authorities appear to have strong faith in the power of therapy. In August 2001, it decided to offer traffic wardens stress management sessions, including shamanic meditation which uses drumming, to counter the effects of abuse on Edinburgh's streets.[61]

Therapeutic intervention in family life in order to alter parenting practices and to curb antisocial behaviour has become one of the defining features of New Labour social policy. The management of interpersonal relationships by therapeutic experts appears as the government's answer to the problem of family life. Many public figures are still hesitant about pursuing policies that would in effect transform the citizen into a patient. 'Government's have to be very careful in devising policies that affect our most intimate relationships', warns the government's consultation document 'Supporting Families'.[62] Despite its rhetoric about exercising care, 'Supporting Families' encroaches into areas that directly affect intimate aspects of family life. It outlines the intention of government to initiate a programme for helping people to prepare for marriage and lays the foundation for the systematic management of family relations.[63] One key objective of this approach is to transform parents into clients of therapeutic experts. Jack Straw, the former Home Secretary, has stated that the culture of parenting needs to be changed so that 'seeking advice and help is seen not as failure but the action of concerned and responsible parents'.[64]

Failed parents are the targets of 'parenting orders', a new scheme enacted by the Blair government to deal with fathers and mothers whose children fail to turn up in school. The core requirement of a parenting order is that 'the parent attends counselling or guidance sessions' as specified by the courts.[65] This approach has been anticipated by numerous local pilot projects that have experimented with the treatment model for dealing with antisocial families. For example, the Dundee Family Project, launched in 1996, has sought to deal with antisocial tenants on local authority housing estates through the provision of family therapy. In order to avoid permanent eviction, problem families are sent to a residential unit, where they live for an average of 9 months. These families have to agree to a 'personally challenging supervisory regime', including three visits per day. During the course of their residence, the families are offered modules on domestic and anger management, addiction counselling and parent/child therapy.[66]

The application of the treatment model is most deeply entrenched within the British criminal justice system. Treatment programmes for certain types of offenders, e.g. sex offenders, have been in place for some time. The Sex Offender Treatment Programme, started in 1991, is based on getting a sex offender to publicly acknowledge his need to change. Such offenders are offered eighty 2-hour therapy sessions in which therapists use the cognitive-behavioural approach.[67] In recent years, the treatment approach has been extended and now assumes an important role within the Home Office's plan to devise a policy of a 'seamless sentence'. The stated aim of former Home Secretary Straw was to oblige more offenders leaving prison to be electronically tagged. Such offenders would also be forced to attend courses in anger management, drug and alcohol addiction or sex therapy.[68] These initiatives are heavily indebted to policy innovations in the US. In the criminal justice system, the American Drug Court Movement provides a paradigmatic example of the institutionalisation of the therapeutic ethos.[69]

Northern Ireland is an important testing ground for the institutionalisation of therapeutic politics. Throughout the peace process, the British government has sought to endow its initiatives with legitimacy through establishing a point of contact with the victims of the Irish war. In November 1997, the government established a Victims Commission, which published its report shortly after the signing of the Good Friday Agreement, in April 1998. The report, entitled 'We Will Remember Them', written by Sir Kenneth Bloomfield, Northern Ireland Victims Commissioner, is fully inspired by the therapeutic ethos. The report proposed the establishment of a post of a 'champion' for victims and their support groups, greater advice and counselling and high priority for the treatment of pain and trauma. The Secretary of State for Northern Ireland quickly announced that the government would appoint a 'minister for victims', who will be there 'to understand and listen'. One of the first initiatives to be announced by Adam Ingram, the newly appointed 'Minister for Victims', was the allocation of £700,000 to establish a trauma unit in Belfast for young people and families affected by the troubles.[70] In turn, Tony Blair announced a grant of several million pounds to underwrite 'comprehensive and effective counselling initiatives'.

The politicisation of emotion has emerged as an important motif in contemporary political life. Intrusion into the world people's feeling has become institutionalised under the present system of evolving therapeutic governance. There is very little opposition to this trend and hardly any concern with the potentially authoritarian implications of a system of government that is in the business of telling people how to feel. In a depoliticised environment, concern with people's emotion is frequently seen as a symptom of enlightened thinking. The implications of this development for people's private life will be explored in the next chapter.

3 Targeting privacy and informal relations

A private or self-contained emotional style is unlikely to appeal to a culture which applauds the very public display of emotionalism. But therapeutic culture is not only uncomfortable with a self-contained emotional style – it is also deeply suspicious of feelings that are expressed outside the public gaze. The legitimacy enjoyed by the open display of emotions is rarely extended to the individual management of feeling in the private sphere. Although therapeutic culture promotes the ideology of self-help, it has little time for the self-contained variety of emotion management. Invariably, self-help turns out to be the idea of helping yourself through seeking help and support. Strong pressures directed against the individual management of feeling are underpinned by a cultural climate which fosters suspicion about private behaviour. Since it is mainly because of what goes on in the private sphere, that emotions become a problem there are strong pressures to open it up to public scrutiny. The contemporary therapeutic imagination is haunted by the belief that damage to the emotions is systematically inflicted on the individual within the family and during the course of day-to-day interpersonal relations. Consequently, therapeutic culture conveys a strong sense of unease towards the private sphere. At times this unease turns into hostility toward the informal world of private life.

The sordid secrets of private life

That the therapeutic cultural sensibility conveys negative signals towards private life is, at first sight, puzzling. Contemporary therapeutics is focused on the self and often promotes the idea of individual self-discovery. Moreover, therapy presents itself as a private matter conducted in isolation from public scrutiny. Yet, therapeutic culture is intensely public and at times intolerant of those who prefer to keep their personal feelings, just that, personal. As already noted, the classical virtue of stoicism is frequently dismissed as an obstacle to self-healing, self-discovery. Privacy and intimacy have little value to an outlook which validates the self through public display of emotion. Consequently, the project of self-restraint is often dismissed with derision and scorn. The striving for self-control is increasingly ridiculed as a dishonest attempt to cover up a variety of pathologies.

Stripping away the protection of privacy is one way of forcing individuals to confront their 'delusion' of self-control. The media treats privacy as a condition to be breached and turned it into an entertainment format. Millions of people watch *Big Brother* or *Survivor* as they are drawn into the intimate personal details of the contestants. In Britain, more than 12 million viewers watched the final episode of the survivor show, *I'm a Celebrity, Get Me out of Here* in September 2002. Reality television encourages the contestants to continually expose their emotions to the viewing public. Contestants who emote deeply and reveal intimate details of their personal troubles are customarily applauded for being 'brave', 'honest' and 'strong'. Invariably, professional counsellors and therapists are on hand to interpret the meaning of the emotions on display to the wider public.

Outwardly, the right to privacy is still upheld as a cherished cultural norm. But the disapproval of the right to privacy is implicit to the value system of therapeutic culture. A shift in attitude towards the private sphere is continually nourished on the terrain of therapeutic culture. This development is most visible in the way that intrusion into the private lives of public figures has become an acceptable fact of life. This development became institutionalised during the Clinton presidency. From the moment he was elected, every aspect of his private life became a subject of media scrutiny. His golf game was scrutinised, his eating habits were ridiculed and the public was informed that his penis had 'distinguishing characteristics'. During the investigation of his affair with Monica Lewinsky, the independent counsel's 453-page report about his sexual escapades were put on the Internet. Although the worldwide exposure of Clinton's personal life represents an extreme manifestation of the erosion of privacy, it is symptomatic of a trend that affects everyone in society.

How public figures feel has become an important question in societies wedded to a therapeutic ethos. Through radio and television the emotional orientation of the public figures defines an event. 'Capturing a sob, seeing tears flow down cheeks, looking into the eyes of the interviewee during tight camera shots merged as critical features of the message and, in some cases, the most important part of the report', writes Davis Altheide in his stimulating study of media news in the US.[1] This preoccupation with public figures' feelings has inexorably led to more and more intrusive questions being posed about their personal lives.

This invasive sentiment is actively communicated through popular culture. The 'secret lives' approach of the new breed of biographers and film directors is based on the premise that they have the right to inspect every detail of their subject's private life. In some cases, biographers have used medical records and psychiatrist's notes and tapes to reconstruct the life of their deceased subject. The psychiatrist who released his notes to the biographer of the poet Anne Sexton claimed that 'sharing her most intimate thoughts and feelings for the benefit of others was not only her expressed purpose and desire, but the purpose for which she lived'. He added that 'privacy was of no concern to her'.[2] Privacy is of little concern to Elizabeth Wurtzel, who has made a literary reputation out of recounting her bout of depression. Wurtzel takes the view that we need the confessional mode because the 'privacy we guard so desperately is also the aloneness we want punctured so badly'.[3] Nor is anyone's privacy of very much concern to scores of biographers who believe that they have moral authority to occupy and almost treat as their own someone else's internal life.

Just over a decade ago, the American critic Joyce Carole Oates, borrowing a phrase from Freud, called this new genre of writing 'pathography'. Oates noted that pathographers focused on 'dysfunction and disaster, illnesses and pitfalls, failed marriages and failed careers, alcoholism and breakdowns and outrageous conduct'. One question posed by Oates was how did this genre emerge? She noted that although raw malevolence was sometimes the guiding motive, there had to be other influences at work.[4] Probably the most important development that accounts for the emergence of the 1990s pathography has been the discrediting of the idea of the inviolate private sphere. Once upheld as the site for the conduct of a life of virtue, private life is now more likely to be associated with repression, family violence and toxic relationships.

A culture which places so much premium on emotional vulnerability finds little time for the claims of the hero. Exceptional achievement and acts of bravery are no longer sufficient to earn the individual the title of a hero. There is a destructive cultural compulsion to expose the claim of heroism to the scrutiny of a psychological investigation. The obsession with the private lives of historic figures and major personalities pervades contemporary literature and popular culture. The focus on private life is driven by the desire to show that in reality the great are no better and probably worse than everyone else. This trend is particularly evident in the literary genre of biographical writing. Whereas in the past biographies tended to uncritically celebrate the achievements of their subject, today the objective seems to be to uncritically destroy their reputation. The old-fashioned hagiography has been replaced by a taste for literary gossip of people's sex life. As the literary critic Michiko Kakutani observed, 'formerly we used to canonise our heroes', but the 'modern method is to vulgarise them'. Kakutani believes that biography has become a blood sport oriented towards mercilessly debunking its subject.[5]

There is, of course, nothing intrinsically objectionable about biographers dwelling on the emotional and psychological side of their subject. Freud's study of Leonardo Da Vinci is a classic investigation of the internal life of a major figure. But, as he said, his aim was not to 'drag the sublime into the dust' but to make a 'great man's achievements intelligible'.[6] Contemporary biographers are often driven by a more destructive agenda. Leading poets, such as Robert Frost and Ted Hughes, are literally tried by their biographers and found guilty. Ellis Amburn's biography of Jack Kerouac is typically titled *The Hidden Life of Jack Kerouac*. The author has no literary purpose for probing into Kerouac's life. Instead, Amburn is keen to present Kerouac as a fundamentally dishonest man, destroyed by drink and fame, who was also a homophobic homosexual, an antisemite and a racist. In *Rage and Fire*, the feminist biography of Louise Colet, the author portrays Flaubert as a narrow-minded, mendacious sexist practitioner of 'fetishism, sadomasochism and masturbation'. Michael Sheldon's biography of the author Graham Greene, entitled *The Man Within*, is particularly fascinated by his subject's interest in anal sex. Mitchell Leaska's *Granite and Rainbow: The Hidden Life of Virginia Woolf* argues that Woolf's incestuous childhood longings for her father made her a guilt-ridden neurotic women in later life. And Scott Bergs's *Lindbergh* exposes this hero as a thoroughly malicious and unpleasant man. The well-known British right-wing critic Paul Johnson uses his study, *Intellectuals*, to savage the personal reputations of left-wing and radical figures. Karl Marx's failure to bathe and Rousseau's callous behaviour towards his children are offered as evidence of the corrupt mind of the radical intelligentsia.

Contemporary biographies which seek to devour their subjects are sometimes justified on the ground that their dark secrets tell us more about them than their public deeds. Biographers often reduce the achievements of well-known public heroes to a psychological response to some hurt or humiliation. It is often implied that it is the experience of emotional turmoil which drives many to look for public recognition for their achievement. It was in this vein that one television programme suggested that it was Lord Mountbatten's reaction to his wife's infidelity which drove him to succeed as a military hero. The psychologising of human achievement probably says more about the biographer than the state of mind of the subject. This compulsion to debunk the public hero expresses a profound hostility towards the aspiration to greatness. Their subtext is a health warning against embracing the heroic figure. From this perspective, heroes are most likely to be sad and dysfunctional people whose achievements are driven by dark and destructive motives.

Film-makers and television directors are also fascinated by the dark sides of heroes. In Britain, a recent series of documentaries entitled *Secret Lives*, on Channel 4, went to great pains to inform the viewer that the heroic male image of Hollywood icons, like Errol Flynn, was just a cover for real-life sad, inadequate or sick individuals. The programme devoted to Robert Baden-Powell, the founder of the Boy Scout movement, presented a sad and pathetic figure who was thoroughly confused about his sexuality. This hero of the British Empire was presented as an immature homosexual with strong sadistic tendencies. People like Walt Disney, Freud and Enid Blyton were depicted as dishonest, racist child abusers. According to *Secret Lives*, Marie Stopes, a leading pioneer in the field of reproductive rights, had a terrible sex life and was a thoroughly inadequate mother. And Second World War pilot hero Douglas Bader was bad tempered, rude and dishonest. He lied about the number of planes he shot down and put other people's lives at risk. So obsessed are British programme-makers with yet again revealing the negative side of their subject matter, that they even produced a documentary on the dark side of the old Carry On comedy films.

For today's cultural elite, heroism has become a distinctly unfashionable, even offensive, trait. They can just about put up with a deeply flawed and vulnerable hero, but find the strident, self-sufficient and self-confident variety to be somewhat anachronistic. The symbol of the end-of-the-century anti-hero is Captain O'Grady, the American pilot shot down during the war in Bosnia. After he was shot down, O'Grady managed to bail out of his aircraft and hid to evade Serb troops on the ground. 'Can I have a tissue please?', he asked as he cried during a press conference celebrating his rescue. 'Everyone is saying "you're a hero, you're a hero", but all

I was, was a scared little bunny rabbit trying to survive', he informed the media. Although other pilots were scathing about O'Grady's failure to follow basic procedure, the media celebrated this tearful military hero. O'Grady neatly fitted the role because there was nothing exceptional about his character. Whereas in the past, heroes were celebrated for saving other people, O'Grady needed only to save himself. As the uncertain, rather ordinary emotional casualty of military conflict, O'Grady personified the values of therapeutic culture.

Although philosophers and social theorists have long debated the relationship between the private and the public sphere and often clashed about which they preferred, it is only in the 1980s that an overwhelming consensus emerged against traditional attachments to private life. In the past, even radical thinkers who regarded family life as stultifying still believed that a private life was essential for the moral development of people.[7] By the 1970s, the private sphere, particularly family life, had acquired overtly negative connotations amongst intellectuals and other opinion-makers. Within a decade, such negative sentiments towards private life had spread way beyond the confines of academia. The revision of social attitudes towards the private sphere has gone hand in hand with the emergence of a new consensus that regarded family life as *the* source of individual emotional distress. This shift in attitudes represents probably the single most important alteration to the value system of western societies in the past two decades.

Many conservative thinkers have mistakenly attributed the decline of the values and practices associated with privacy to the conscious sabotage of the family by 1960s intellectuals. In fact, the mood of distrust towards the private sphere is the product of the very same cultural influences that inform today's emotional script. One of the charges levelled against the private sphere is that it makes people emotionally ill. According to this scenario, emotionally disoriented individuals threaten to become a danger to their intimates as they vent their passions against those closest to them. As a result, the private sphere is regularly depicted as an institution of abuse. There has been an important mutation in the public perception of privacy. Once regarded as a safe refuge from the demands of everyday life, it is now more likely to be represented as a source of emotional distress.

Contemporary culture still retains a resilient strain of respect for privacy and family life. But important influences that shape popular culture continually seek to 'expose' the harmful effects of these institutions. Terms like the 'dark side' of the family invoke a sense of dread about private and invisible relations. Victimologists have been in the forefront of a clamour to allow more public scrutiny of private life. Feminist thinkers have mounted a trenchant critique of privacy. Many feminists argue that in the private sphere women are rendered invisible, their work becomes unrecognised and therefore devalued and their lives becomes subject to male violence. Catherine MacKinnon has insisted that for 'women, the private is the distinct sphere of intimate violation and abuse, neither free nor particularly personal'.[8] The association of intimacy with violation has been further developed in the vast and ever-growing literature on family violence.

The view that the private sphere is an intensely dangerous place, particularly for women and children, has acquired the character of an incontrovertible truth in academia. Even mainstream contributions on the subject stress the violent features of family life. According to one authoritative account:

> What is new and surprising is that the American family and the American home are perhaps as or more violent than any other single American institution or setting (with the exception of the military, and only then in time of war). Americans run the greatest risk of assault, physical injury, and even murder in their own homes by members of their own families.[9]

Other, more radical accounts go even further and imply that the private sphere masks the conflict of interest between parents and their children from public view. Bob Franklin, a British campaigner for children's rights, claims that high profile cases of child abuse have 'exploded the myth of the family as an institution which offered its members security and safety'. He is delighted that now the public perceives the family as a 'potentially dangerous arena'.[10]

As I argue elsewhere, professional attitudes towards parents convey a barely concealed attitude of contempt.[11] Advocacy groups continually publish reports and surveys which demonstrate the inability of parents to respond to the emotional needs of their children. One such survey completed in 1998, commissioned by Prevent Child Abuse America, claimed that 37 per cent of American parents reported insulting or swearing at their children within the past 12 months, 50 per cent had neglected their children's emotional needs and 6 per cent had hit or tried to hit their children.[12] The message communicated by this survey was unambiguously clear: parents cannot be trusted to attend to the emotional needs of their children.

The shift in cultural perceptions of family life are reflected in the contemporary social science literature, where it is virtually impossible to find any systematic defence of privacy and family life.[13] The general approach adopted by most contributions on the subject is to privilege the public over the private on the ground that terrible things occur under the cloak of privacy. It is often suggested that the problem is not the erosion of privacy but that public authority does not intervene enough to protect the vulnerable casualties of family life. The argument that only an ever-vigilant public institution can protect children from adult predators is one of the most frequently repeated objections against the claim for the autonomy of the private sphere.[14]

Forms of emotion that characterise intimate family relationships are often dismissed with a health warning. It is claimed that individuals 'can be easily trapped inside affective unions'. Women in particular risk becoming enslaved to their maternal roles. Even the emotion of love directed towards a child is suspect since 'relying on love alone to secure the well-being of children shows a misguided and perilous optimism'.[15] That is why it is argued that the right to privacy 'on the part of parents can seriously collude with the perpetration of very serious harm to children'.[16] The premise of the field of therapists specialising in dealing with co-dependency is that 'families develop rules to hide their secrets, their embarrassments, and their black sheep from outsiders. The children learn and internalise these rules in order to please their parents and later in adult life re-enact the same script.'[17]

The tendency to depict privacy as a 'cloak' or a 'sham' is based on the premise that toxic emotions dominate family life. It assumes that left to their own devices and away from public view, people tend to be dominated by destructive emotions. Men in particular are condemned for using the privilege of privacy to terrorise women and children. This unflattering representation of intimate relationships constitutes a warning of imminent victimisation. From this standpoint, privacy can have no redeeming features. On the contrary, for some, particularly cultural feminists, intimacy by definition represents a relation of violence. From the standpoint of therapeutic culture, the opening up of the private sphere to the regulation of public opinion is therefore a desirable outcome.

There is little doubt that private life can be violent and degrading in certain instances. Privacy can provide a hiding place for the exercise of destructive behaviour. But these negative aspects of private life do not provide a coherent argument for eradicating the private sphere any more than the prevalence of street crime do for the elimination of the domain of the public. The casual dismissal of the private sphere represents a disturbingly cavalier attitude towards one of the most important sites of human experience. The separation of the public and private spheres has been essential for the emergence of the modern individual. The aspiration for autonomy and identity cannot be entirely resolved in the public sphere. The private sphere not only has the potential for providing space for reflection, but also for the development of personality. Intimate relationships require privacy if they are not to disintegrate under the pressure of public scrutiny. Whatever the distortions of the private sphere, it provides a site for the potential development of intimacy and self-expression and self-exploration. Such qualities, which are part of the make-up of the publicly responsible individual, cannot survive intact if transferred to the public arena. Ideas, emotions and passions expressed to an intimate soulmate become something different when disclosed to a public audience. As the philosopher Hannah Arendt argued, love is 'killed or rather extinguished, the moment it is displayed in public'.[18] If there are problems with the organisation of private life than it is the problems that need to be challenged and not privacy itself.

And the surprising degradation of the public

Ironically, the devaluation of the private sphere does not mean a commitment to the positive development of the public one. The demonisation of the private sphere goes hand in hand with the decline of an ethos of public responsibility. The attitude of therapeutic culture towards the private and public sphere is a contradictory one. Calls for sharing emotions coexist with the sacralisation of self-absorption. There is now a fertile cultural terrain for the growth of self-absorption. Contemporary culture continually promotes the ideal of fulfilling your own needs and the primacy of expressing yourself. Therapeutic advocacy groups like Antidote welcome the fact that in end-of-the-century Britain, 'politics has become a form of self-expression'.[19] The idea that politics is about fulfilling yourself relegates wider public attachments to a secondary role. Feeling good becomes an end in itself – and the individual relationship to a wider moral or political framework threatens to become an insignificant side issue. Questions of right and wrong become arbitrary matters to a devotee of the cult of feeling. Instead of right and wrong, there are only different ways of feeling about the world. Therapeutic morality 'focuses our attention on the private life, blinding us to the larger, public good', writes Eva Moskowitz in her study *In Therapy We Trust: America's Obsession With Self-Fulfilment*.[20]

The orientation to the self is legitimised by the pedagogy of self-esteem and emotionalism. According to Nolan, the goal of raising the self-esteem of school children is often promoted on the ground that it enhances their sense of responsibility. But the concept of responsibility advocated by emotional educators has little to do with any notion of public good. 'Its point of reference, like self-esteem, is to the self, rather than to the common good', writes Nolan. One of the main reason given 'for fulfilling one's duties' is that doing so will raise one's self-esteem.[21] This redefinition of responsibility as responsibility to oneself helps provide emotionalism with moral meaning.

According to the therapeutic profession, the prerequisite to emotional literacy is the ability to be in touch with yourself and to feel good about yourself. That is why self-absorption is rarely seen as narcissistic, but as an instrument for raising awareness. New psychological therapies consciously encourage this predilection for self-monitoring. The popularity of primal therapies, such as rebirthing and past-life therapy, vividly confirm the narcissistic turn of society. The codependence movement in the US encourages the adult children of alcoholics and other addicts towards the goal of personal recovery. Co-dependents are advised to 'embrace the child within you' and to see the world through the eyes of an infant. All these therapies are oriented towards discovering something in the individual's past in order to recapture feelings or the ability to feel. As Arthur Janov, the well-known populariser of primal therapy, has argued, his approach is a way of 'recapturing feelings'.[22] For such a self-referential orientation there can be no cause or belief that transcends the affirmation of the self. The language of 'my pains', 'my anger', 'my hurt' and 'my feelings' informs the newly 'aware' product of mass therapy.

Therapeutic ethos places a premium on what it characterises as 'awareness'. To be aware is one of the defining features of therapeutic ethos. But awareness to what end? The statement 'I am aware' is really meant as an object-free proposition. Awareness exists in a state of indifference to the public world at large and implies a state of enlightenment about one's emotion. In so far as it means anything more than a rhetorical device it relates only to the self. It is easy to confuse the celebration of the self as representing a positive turn towards privacy. However, it is important to realise that the therapeutically constructed self is one that is unencumbered by the obligations that are demanded by intimates in the private sphere. That is why the affirmation of the therapeutic self represents an estrangement not only from public life, but also the private sphere. From the standpoint of therapeutic advocates, the relationship that really counts is to the self itself. In some accounts, intimacy is redefined as a relationship that one has with one self.[23]

It is the erosion of the distinction between the two spheres, rather then the celebration of the public, that characterises our era. Therapeutic culture is not a forceful advocate of the public ideal. The declining moral significance attached to public activity is vividly illustrated by the rise of the politics of biography. Politicians are increasingly judged on their character and the scandal has become a significant subject of public debate. The private life of politicians is deemed to be a public issue and personal troubles are interpreted as a defining statement of a politician's worth. Controversial politicians like Bill Clinton in the US or Peter Mandelson in Britain are criticised less for their political views then for the how they conduct their personal affairs. As we note in Chapter 2, public apathy is the flip side of therapeutic politics.

Gradually, the debate and exploration of important public issues has given way to an almost pornographic fascination with the private problems of public figures. As the sociologist Zygmunt Bauman observes, increasingly public interest is 'reduced to curiosity about the private lives of public figures, and the art of public life is narrowed to the public display of private affairs and public confessions of private sentiments'. And he adds that public issues 'which resist such reduction become all but incomprehensible'.[24]

Therapeutic culture feels ill at ease with those who have won authority on the basis of their achievements and their public act. Public achievements and even exceptional deeds are now subject to a highly intrusive public scrutiny. Investigations of people's private lives – often posthumously by biographers and journalists – ensure that no-one can escape unscathed. The inspection of intimate details will invariably uncover skeletons in the cupboard and ensure that no-one's reputation for great public works will survive intact. The compulsive drive to deconstruct private lives, to 'unmask', 'uncover' embarrassing episodes reflects a tendency to downgrade public issues in favour of dwelling on personal troubles. The medium of television continually encourages the public's obsession with private troubles. This approach is not confined to so-called thrash TV. Take, for example, the leaflet circulated to potential guests for the programme *What Now*, shown on the prestigious British channel BBC1 (see p. 75).

Inciting individuals to 'share' their personal problems with millions of viewers is the entertainment formula of a culture where disclosures of individual troubles masquerade as a public service. 'Sharing problems' has assumed the character of a civic virtue which we affirm with the words 'thanks for sharing'. Indeed, contemporary ideals of community seek to achieve a sense of unity through the sharing of private thoughts.

Often, the sharing of emotions is self-consciously pursued as a focus for civic mobilisation. 'One of art's vital functions in society is to provide a common language to share deeply intimate feelings of grief and sorrow', argued Peter Hewitt, Chief Executive of the Arts Council of England. He added, 'art provides a bridge to coax the private and intimate out into a shared, public setting'. From the standpoint of therapeutic management, 'coaxing' the private and intimate

---

TV Show Needs You

Is your relationship getting you down?

Are you having trouble at work?

Are your kids driving you mad?

Are you finding it hard to communicate with your parents?

Are your neighbours a nightmare?

Is your sexuality an issue?

Do you think you might be gay?

Whatever your problem we'd like to hear from you.
What Now is BBC1's new TV programme featuring you, and a panel on
hand to give advice about your dilemma.

Remember . . . a problem bared is a problem shared.

---

feelings into the public arena may seem an act of civic virtue. But the growth of
public emotionalism can only distract society from reflecting on the challenge
of how to go about deliberating on the public good.

Contemporary cultural norms towards the relationship between the private
and the public are inconsistent, diffuse and often confusing. The self is celebrated
but at the same time privacy is frequently treated as something to be exposed. The
sharing of emotions in public is actively promoted, while in apparent contradiction,
individuals are counselled to look after their needs. To make sense of these
apparently conflicting demands requires that we take a close look at shifting cultural
attitudes towards the conduct of personal relationships.

Targeting informal relations

One of the distinctive features of therapeutic culture is a deep-seated aversion
towards family and informal relations. This attitude is not surprising since one of
the justifications for the therapeutic relationship is the claim that problems of the
emotion stem from family-based pathologies, which cannot be solved through ties
of kinship and friendship. The very justification for a distinct therapeutic profession
is that it is able to provide a relationship that takes individuals out of their informal
networks. As the sociologist Talcott Parsons explained, 'I take it that the important
feature of the development of psychiatry for the present purposes is the emergence
of a professional role which is structurally differentiated and hence in a sense
segregated from that of parent or spouse in the family, but which is adapted to the
task of dealing with problems of the personality of the individual which root in

the family, but which, cannot be effectively dealt with simply as a function ascribed to familial roles'. For Parsons, one of the merits of the therapeutic process was that it could exercise the leverage 'necessary for getting out of vicious circles of involvement with familial problems which are often both symptoms and determinants of psychopathological conditions'.[25]

The correlation between individual distress and family pathology can provide useful insights into the management of mental health problems. However, over the decades this insight has been gradually transformed into a dogma where the cause of mental illness is invariably located within the orbit of family conflict. By the 1960s, the focus of radical therapies became the 'communicative interaction of the family'.[26] As a result an unmediated and direct causal relationship between the family and mental health problems was forged. With the ascendancy of therapeutic culture, the claim that the cause of psychological problems was to be found within the family was gradually transformed into the assertion that intimate family relations were a toxic threat to the individual. As Susan Smith notes in her study *Survivor Psychology*, by the mid-1980s, the idea that the family was a 'toxic vehicle for transmitting dysfunctionality' had gained considerable influence within American popular culture. A clear manifestation of this development was that society 'became increasingly desensitised to pathological labelling' and that the language of public personalities and celebrities became riddled with therapeutic jargon.[27]

Susan Forward, author of *Toxic Parenting* captures therapeutic culture's aversion towards informal relations. She regards the effects of bad parenting as akin to 'invisible weeds that invaded your life in ways you never dreamed of'. Parents who transmit invisible poisonous substances to pollute their vulnerable offspring personify evil in the contemporary cultural imagination. As Forward noted,

> As I searched for a phrase to describe the common ground that these harmful parents share, the word that kept running through my mind was toxic. Like a chemical toxin, the emotional damage inflicted by these parents spreads through the child's being, and as the child grows, so does the pain. What better word than toxic to describe parents who inflict ongoing trauma, abuse, and denigration on their children.[28]

The association of family interaction and the polluting and defilement of the emotions has been turned into a new genre of books and films that dwell on the theme of tormented childhood. Dave Pelzer's best-sellers, *A Child Called It* and *The Lost Boy* vividly capture this morbid fascination with toxic relationships.

According to the contemporary therapeutic sensibility, it is not just the relationship between parent and child that is potentially toxic to the individual self. Every close relationship of dependence can be a cause of debilitating emotional injury. The toxic metaphor has been extended to describe love relations, friendships and relations at work. The title of the first chapter of Harriet Braiker's *Lethal Lovers and Poisonous People: How to Protect Your Health from Relationships That Make You Sick*, sums up the book's attitude to relationships: 'Warning: This relationship may be harmful to your health'.[29] Florence Isaacs' *Toxic Friends/True*

Friends expands the use of the toxic metaphor to the domain of friendship.[30] And *Toxic Emotions at Work* by Peter Frost uses the metaphor to account the emotional distress cause by relations at work.[31] The well-known psycho-mystic Deepak Chopra warns against contaminating your body with toxic emotions. It is worth noting that toxic emotions are not just simply used as a synonym for negative emotions. The term 'toxic emotion' contains the assumption of being dependent on another person. Detoxification involves breaking free from a relation of dependency. 'Relinquish your need for external approval', counsels Deepak Chopra. Why? Because, 'you alone are the judge of your worth; and your goal is to discover infinite worth in yourself, no matter what anyone else thinks'.[32] The advocacy of the goal of breaking free from needing the approval of others is not confined to a handful of pop-psychologists. Advice columns in newspapers, women's magazines and publications targeting parents and teens continually echo the call for weakening relations of dependence.

From the 1960s onwards, advice columns in Britain and the United States began to advocate the expression of emotion. Amal Treacher's study of *Woman* magazine indicates that whereas in the 1950s columnists counselled readers to control their emotions, by the 1970s they encouraged the pouring out of emotions. This shift in approach towards the expression of emotion was paralleled by a change in attitude towards the self. In the 1950s, the magazine sought to promote the idea of putting others before the self and pleasing other people. 'The sin was to brood and dwell on one's self', writes Treacher. By the 1970s, and certainly the 1980s, the reader was advised to reclaim their self. Alongside the call to embrace the self was a significant change of attitude towards the conduct of relationships. The demand of putting the self before another led to the representation of dependency as a form of sickness. Treacher argues that this pathologisation of dependence in advice columns reflects wider cultural forces. 'From popular psychological texts to many political discourses, dependency is seen as the new evil, something which is toxic, poisonous, a tough weed, and the killer of people's spirit', states Treacher.[33]

The codependence and recovery movements continually indict relations of dependence for the emotional pain suffered by addicted individuals. The guiding principle of the recovery movement is that unhealthy relationships are the direct cause of addiction and other emotional dysfunctions. 'Unhealthy relationships – those that thwart individuals from being the best they can be – are even more harmful than the physical effects of addiction', writes Lowney in her study of the recovery movement.[34]

In the therapeutic world-view, strong relations of dependence come with a health warning. Such dependence is presented as a precursor of a one of a number of newly invented addictions to emotions. An advice columnist in *Lesbian News* informs the reader, 'if you let your relationship meet all your needs you may suck it dry and become totally addicted to your partner'.[35] Intense feelings that were once described as passionate love are now stigmatised as a form of relationship addiction. Many of the symptoms associated with this disease are feelings that can be regarded as a normal manifestation of passionate love. Nancy Joy Carroll in her *The Love Handbook for Singles* offers a list of 'Danger signs of romantic addiction'. These include:

- Having a compulsive drive for love to the point that a relationship is based on need rather than choice.
- Spending considerable time thinking about another person; giving excessive time and attention to him or her.
- Wanting a partner to prove love in unrealistic ways; expecting a partner to fulfil all of one's needs.
- Feeling devastated when a relationship ends.[36]

There is, of course, nothing new about warning individuals against the unrealistic expectation in romantic attachments. What distinguishes the diagnosis of co-dependency is that the desire for passionate love, the exhilaration of intimacy, as well as the painful disappointment of losing an intimate partner, have been recast as symptoms of a disease.

Robin Norwood's book *Women Who Love Too Much*, which sold more than three million copies in North America after its 1985 publication, established 'codependency' and 'relationship addiction' as a fact of life in therapeutic culture. According to Norwood, women entered unhealthy relationships not through choice, but through addiction. The belief that emotionally addicted women end up in abusive relationships has become one of the dogmas of our time. A well-known British psychologist, Oliver James, contends that 'female victims of abuse are far more likely to marry abusers'.[37] Relationship addiction is a disease that thrives within the structure of the family and can be passed on from one member to another. 'Most authorities in the field believe that being molested as a child sets up individuals themselves to be sexual addicts and molesters', notes Anne Wilson Schaef.[38] The American National Mental Health Association claims that co-dependency is a 'learned behavior that can be passed down from one generation to another'. It is learned 'by watching and imitating other family members who display this type of behavior'.[39]

In line with the growing aversion against family and informal relationships, the meaning of the term addiction and codependency has expanded to account for a puzzling number of experiences. Advocates of the disease of emotional addiction claim that the pathology of codependency was 'discovered' as a result of studying interpersonal relationships in families of alcoholics in the 1980s. Initially, the term 'codependent' was a term used to describe partners in chemical dependency, persons living with or in a relationship with an addicted person. Within a short period of time, 'the term was broadened to describe any codependent person from any dysfunctional family'.[40] As a result, codependence has become a diagnosis that can be applied to virtually any relationship of dependence.

Literally any manifestation of love, friendship and loyalty can be labelled a form of addictive behaviour. The British-based PROMIS Recovery Centre asserts that acts formerly regarded as forms of altruistic behaviour should be diagnosed as the addiction of 'compulsive helping'. Compulsive helpers disregard their own needs and feelings and focus on helping another person.[41] According to this definition, individuals who make great sacrifices to care for elderly parents or relatives or who devote their energy to helping others may well suffer from compulsive helping. Putting others first or at least not placing one's individual needs before a relationship could be a symptom of yet another addiction.

Addictions of the emotion target the desire of individuals for intense relationships. The website of Robert Burnley, a 'spiritual teacher, codependence counsellor, grief therapist, author', states that 'as long as we believe that we have to have the other in our life to be happy, we are really just an addict trying to protect our supply – using another person as our drug of choice'.[42]

Responsibility and loyalty are still upheld as public virtues, but in practice these ideals are compromised by the exhortation to put the self before the other. Consequently, the ideal of responsibility to another and the sentiment of sociability and loyalty can now be characterised as symptoms of relationship addiction. The very idea that a relationship of dependency can be the root cause of emotional addiction represents a deeply pessimistic statement about the informal world of private life. It is but a prelude to the conclusion that people cannot be expected to conduct personal relationships without professional support. A study of problem pages in women's magazine by Mary Louise Ho states that in 1980, 97 out of 138 letters meet with the recommendation to seek professional help.[43]

Throughout human history people have known that emotional involvement with another can be painful and cause distress. Emotions and passions bound up with sexuality have always been treated as both troublesome and as potentially threatening to the prevailing moral order. Sexual passion was traditionally portrayed as destructive because it threatened to subvert the conventional boundaries of social life. In contrast today, passion itself is decried because of its potential for damaging the emotional self. Consequently, sex is often construed as a fertile source for emotional damage. These apprehensions have fused with the more traditional puritanical ethos around a moral outlook which regards sexual activity as risky and damaging to the emotion. The traditional indictment of recreational sex as immoral has been transformed into a therapeutic health warning about the peril that such passions represent to the emotion. Often, sex is decried on the ground that it is bad for your health and your emotion. Nineteenth-century moralising about how sex saps the individual's vitality is recycled in a therapeutic discourse about how it destabilises the emotions. Young girls are advised to say 'No' on the grounds that sexual activity threatens to lower their self-esteem. A recent campaign launched by the Health Education Board for Scotland was devoted to raising the awareness of teenagers about the 'emotional dangers of having first sex at too early an age'. It warned teenagers of 'sex trauma' and the problems which sex could cause in later life through anguish and regret.[44]

In contrast to previous times, therapeutic moralising is not simply directed at sex. It is primarily concerned about emotional involvement through sex and other forms of intimate relationships. The representation of sex as a form of addiction represents a major inflation of this concept. As one of the most important sites for emotional investment, sex bears upon every aspect of human behaviour.

However, unlike cigarettes, alcohol, or drugs, sex is not a thing but a relationship. As Levine and Troiden write in their critique of the myth of sex addiction, 'sex is an experience, not a substance'.[45] And once this experience becomes medicalised, there is no reason why people should not become addicted to friendship or human warmth.

Previous moral codes sought to control sexual activity to prevent transgressions of the moral order. Today's therapeutic world-view seeks to justify the need to manage all forms of informal relationships. Such an orientation towards private life could not thrive if it did not reflect the temper of our times. As Christopher Lasch noted, therapeutic culture is characterised by a 'thorough-going disenchantment with personal relations'.[46] Treacher echoes this point, 'underpinning much of the thinking about dependency is the view that it is crucial to be independent and self-reliant, because if you rely on others they will inevitably let you down'.[47] The targeting of informal relationships preys on this disenchantment. It feeds on prevailing anxieties towards relationships and strengthens the public's fears towards them. Its practical effects is to diminish our sense of dependency on others. As our dependence on informal relations diminishes so our subservience to the professional grows. The weakening of informal relations is proportional to the growing power of therapeutic ones. The erosion of our sense of dependence on others does not enhance individual independence.[48] It merely leads to the replacement of one form of dependence by another. Of course informal relations of dependence still play an important role in our lives, but it now competes with a new kind of dependency on professional support or advice.

Criminalising interpersonal relationships

In Chapter 1 it was noted that contemporary crime is increasingly understood as a form of behaviour motivated by destructive emotions. These crimes of the emotion are frequently ones that are committed in the sphere of interpersonal relations. In recent years, crime is increasingly perceived as what people do to their acquaintances, colleagues and family members. There has also been a shift of emphasis away from public street crime to the threats faced by people in the private sphere. This reorientation towards crimes committed by the familiar, even intimate, predator has encouraged an important development in the system of criminal justice – a disposition to criminalise interpersonal relations. Many of the recent high profile crimes – domestic violence, child abuse, rape, date rape, different forms of harassment, bullying – evoke the risks attached to the conduct of interpersonal relationships.

They all point to the potentially dangerous quality of personal relations and offer a health warning about becoming too trusting towards others. The message that is conveyed through this process is that no one can be trusted, especially not someone who is already close to you. The British domestic abuse charity, Refuge, warned women not to be swept off their feet by a slick Romeo on Valentine's day since their lover could be a violent predator. Refuge warned that men who use attentiveness and charm are merely manipulating women before subjecting them to violence.[49] By rebranding the ordinary, banal and routine human relationships as potentially victimising, society has sent a signal that we must all be on guard against one another. Institutionalised mistrust of interpersonal relationship often leads to its criminalisation.

A growing sense of unease towards the informal sphere has shaped the way that individuals perceive the risks that confront them. Trusting those closest to us is frequently called into question by warnings about the danger of dependency. The very manner in which trust relations are experienced has undergone important modifications. In the past, mistrust has tended to be oriented towards specific groups – foreigners, criminals, political opponents – who were deemed to be different to anyone else. Criminals and other suspicious characters were seen as threats to people's lives precisely because they were different to the normal law-abiding section of the population. Such targets of suspicion were disliked because they represented a threat to society's institutions and to people's economic security. Today, mistrust is no longer confined to strangers who are different to us. There is increasing suspicion towards individuals with whom we have personal encounters and such relations are often characterised as potentially threatening.

As noted previously, family life, once idealised as a haven from a heartless world, is now widely depicted as a site of domestic violence and abuse. Child protection professionals and press commentators are continually warning about the dangers that children face from their 'normal' parents. In turn, the normalisation of child abuse has led to claims that literally everyone within a family is at risk from everyone else. A constant theme of family violence literature is that 'every' child is potentially at risk and that every men is a latent wife batterer. Nor do children and women exhaust the possible targets of family violence. The invention of the term 'elder abuse' indicates that victimisation is a fact of family life from cradle to the grave. Even the relationship between children and siblings has been problematised by a leading American expert on family violence. According to David Finkelhor, sibling abuse is the most 'common kind of victimisation' facing children. Finkelhor argues that such assaults affect 80 per cent of children in some form. He uses the term 'pandemic victimisation' to underline the frequency of this form of child abuse.[50] This warning has been echoed in Britain by reports which suggest that a small child is as likely to be killed by a brother or a sister as by a stranger.[51]

It is the pathologisation of the private sphere that invites the construction of interpersonal problems such as that of sibling abuse. Through recasting everyday conflict between siblings into the language of abuse, advocates of this problem turn a routine experience into a source of emotional distress. A study authored by Carol Wilson and Mary Ellen Fromouth is concerned that although childhood sibling abuse is common, most adults 'don't remember it that way'. The underlying objective of the study is to change adult perceptions of sibling rivalry and turn it into a relation of abuse.[52] Through reinterpreting routine forms of sibling conflict into a form of domestic violence, advocacy research can claim dramatic rates of prevalence. Dr Vernon Wiehe, professor of social work at the University of Kentucky and author of *Perilous Rivalry: When Siblings Become Abusive*, states that as many as 53 out of every 100 children abuse a brother or sister. Moral entre-preneurs attempting to raise public 'awareness' of this issue argue that 'emotional abuse is present in all forms of sibling abuse'. They suggest that survivors of sibling abuse often display signs of PTSD, complex post-traumatic disorder and dissociative identity disorder.[53] That sibling relations can be treated as an important source of emotional illness indicates that every type of personal relationship has become the subject of cultural contestation.

If victimisation within the family is pandemic then quite clearly we are entitled to mistrust even those closest to us. The focus of anxiety can no longer be the alien stranger or criminal, but our closest family relations, neighbours, friends, lovers and workmates. Such an attitude towards everyday life represents an important redefinition of the way people are expected to relate to those closest to them physically and emotionally. In the past people feared the state and the powers that be. Today, mistrust is more likely to be attached towards other individuals in both informal and more formal institutional settings. It is the closed door that hides family relations from public scrutiny rather than bureaucratic secrecy that evokes powerful anxieties in popular culture.

The closed door symbolises suspicion towards private encounters. The title of a classic account of family violence, *Behind Closed Doors: Violence in the American Family* (1980), articulates the mistrust in fundamental private encounters. Suspicion regarding what is likely to happen behind the closed door has become an important motif in contemporary culture. One American artist, Justine Nuaman Greif, exhibited a three-panelled folding screen piercing entitled 'Behind closed doors'. According to one review of this work:

> At first glance, the screen seems to depict Everytown USA, some of the homes are modest; some of the homes and gardens are opulent; all of them seem to be a portrait of tranquillity. It is not until the visitors pull down the faces of each home and read the correlated messages that they are confronted with the realisation of what happens behind closed doors. Justine Nauman Greif has created a powerful means of reminding us that each time we retreat to the sanctuary of our own safe environments, we cannot forget the thousands of victims in our own communities who are fighting for their lives behind closed doors.[54]

Raising 'awareness' about the danger presented by the closed door is emblematic of the lack of trust that society feels towards private one-to-one relations.

Conclusion

Therapeutic culture's aversion to the private sphere is underpinned by its goal of managing and ultimately, policing people's emotions. Its call for emotional openness is confined to how people feel in public. The feelings that people have towards one another in private are treated as ones that require not openness, but careful processing. This double standard exercised towards the display of feeling is motivated by the belief people cannot be left to themselves to sort out the emotional issues that emerge during the course of their personal relations. This pessimistic perspective towards the capacity of people to conduct their personal affairs actually contributes to the diminishing of people's emotional life. The often repeated assertion that society has become more open to tolerating displays of emotion is, in practice, negated by its call to restrain the way we feel towards our intimates.

The private sphere provides an important arena for feelings that most people find difficult, even impossible to display in public. What endows privacy with a unique quality is that it is the only site for the constitution of intimate relationships. Privacy is necessary for the formation of intimate relationships since it allows people to reveal themselves through emotions and feelings to friends, family members and lovers. Such displays of emotion are intimate precisely because they are withheld from the rest of the world. Through such unpoliced disclosures some of our most life-defining relationships are forged. Such a spontaneous display of emotion cannot be readily assimilated and managed. They do not readily conform to the demands of therapeutic management. That is why there are strong pressures to formalise relationships that are primarily conducted informally. As Bellah noted, therapeutics 'etches the social contract into our intimacy'.[55]

The etching of the contract into relations of intimacy means that the 'contractual structure of economic and bureaucratic world' is becoming 'the ideological model of personal life'.[56] However, the introduction of contractual norms into the realm of interpersonal relationships can only contribute to the disorganisation of the private sphere. A contract which is based on the premise of a conflict of interest inevitably undermines people's capacity to honestly display their entire range of feelings.

Nor does the disorganisation of informal relations in private encourage the flourishing of the public sphere. The disorganisation of the private sphere does not merely impact on private life. It also discourages the formation of relations of dependence amongst friends and work colleagues. Suspicion and mistrust towards others – what Lasch has described as a 'war of all against all' – afflicts the conduct of public affairs.[57] The growth of litigation and conflict between colleagues in the workplace confirms Lasch's pessimistic prognosis.

Advocates of the therapeutic ethos contend that emotional honesty and literacy helps forge a sense of connectedness to others. They believe that through acknowledging our emotion, a greater public understanding of the problems facing us can be gained and that conflict and violence may be reduced. 'Emotional literacy involves becoming aware of our own inner experience, so as the better to understand other people and through them to experience a sense of connection to the wider community', declares an advocacy group in its call for a manifesto for an emotionally literate society.[58] Sadly, such a laudable aim is unlikely to become the outcome of the growth of therapeutic sensibility. On the contrary, the orientation of therapeutic ethos to the self fosters a climate of petty squabbles and resentment and a sense of estrangement from the public sphere.

4   How did we get here?

Many of the trends discussed so far – the growth of emotional determinism, the rise of public emotional culture and the stigmatisation of private, informal relations – are relatively recent developments. As we noted previously, it was in the 1980s that therapeutic culture came to exercise a dominant influence over society. Before the 1980s, terms like syndrome, self-esteem, PTSD, sex addiction and counselling had not yet entered the public vocabulary. Of course, therapeutic culture did not just appear from nowhere. Its dramatic take-off in the 1980s was preceded by the century-long expansion of the influence of psychology. Historical accounts of this development point out that by the end of the nineteenth century there was a significant interest in this new profession's claim to provide a science of the mind. During the first half of the twentieth century, the prestige of the psychoanalytic tradition grew steadily. Experimental psychology, psychometrics and behaviourism made great forward strides during this period. Increasingly, the professional management of emotion was accepted as a crucial task by both the private and public sector. By the 1950s, and certainly by the 1960s, therapeutics had become a significant feature of Anglo-American mainstream culture.

The early manifestations of therapeutic culture were noted by a number of prescient observers. Writing in the late 1950s, Barbara Wootton, a well-known British social scientist, observed that over 'large areas the psychiatrist, along with his psychiatrically-oriented satellites, has now usurped the place once occupied by the social reformer and the administrator, if not indeed the judge'.[1] Her views were echoed across the Atlantic a few years later when Thomas Szasz drew attention to the emergence of a 'therapeutic state' in the US.[2] When the sociologist Peter Berger wrote in 1965 that 'psychoanalysis has become part of the American scene', he could be sure that his audience would treat his statement as a matter of fact. Berger observed that psychoanalysis had become a cultural phenomenon that influenced the American legal system, religion, literature and popular culture. He claimed that at least three areas of everyday life – sexuality, marriage and child-rearing – had been 'significantly' affected by it.[3] During the same year, Paul Halmos published the first systematic investigation of the impact of this phenomenon on British society and concluded that its influence is 'in a process of rapid growth'.[4] A year later the American sociologist Philip Rieff announced *The Triumph of the Therapeutic*. Discussion of the growing impact of the therapeutic ethos was not confined to the Anglo-American world. Serge Moscovici in France and Thomas Luckmann in Germany testified to the impact of this trend in Continental Europe.[5]

These pioneering critics of the influence of therapeutics on culture were exploring a trend still at a relatively early stage of development. Although Rieff gave his book the provocative title *The Triumph of the Therapeutic*, the phenomenon he was discussing still had a relatively modest impact on society. In the 1960s, therapeutic sensibility had not become a dominant feature of culture. It had a significant influence on officials, opinion-makers and sections of the middle class, but it had not yet become one of the defining features of everyday life. So what transformed therapeutic sensibility into a powerful if not dominant cultural force? This development is in part an outcome of significant changes to the pattern and conduct of personal relations during the last quarter of the twentieth century. The taken-for-granted dimension of relations between people has diminished in significance. As a result of the decline of shared meaning, uncertainty has a disproportionate impact on the conduct of human relations. In such circumstances professionals have considerable latitude to mediate such relations. The discernible tendency towards the professionalisation of daily life has had a formidable impact on the conduct of personal relations. In recent decades everyday life has become increasingly professionalised. Professionals now instruct the public about how to conduct their relationships, how to parent, how to deal with problems at home and at work and how to grieve. It is not simply the wife of the British Prime Minister who employs a 'lifestyle guru' to help her shop and dress.

Professional intervention has encouraged a process whereby relationships between people have become increasingly formalised and codified. The formalisation of relationships is particularly striking inside institutions – workplace, schools, universities – where codes of conduct regulate relations between people. Not surprisingly, this tendency has been at the expense of the informal ties that bind people together. Increasingly, the individual's link to a wider network of informal relations has diminished in significance. And, although these trends have been evident for some time, they have gained considerable momentum during the 1980s. This period, which saw a widespread disenchantment with public life and the erosion of the prevailing system of meaning, opened up new areas of personal life to therapeutic intervention and have contributed to the disorganisation of the private sphere. In turn, a disorganised private sphere creates further demand for professional intervention. Various explanations have been put forward to account for the rise of therapeutic culture. The decline of tradition, the decline of religion and the decline of politics are some of the key themes in contributions on this subject. This chapter will assess the relevance of these explanations and will put forward an explanation for the ascendancy of therapeutic culture.

The decline of tradition

Pioneering cultural analysts based in the US, such as Phillip Rieff, Peter Berger, Christopher Lasch and Richard Sennett, explained the rise of therapeutic culture by emphasising the erosion of social solidarity and of communal norms, and the weakening of the influence of traditional authority on the conduct of everyday life. They believed that these processes led to the fragmentation of social life and construction of an intensely individualised private existence.[6]

Tradition represents the institutionalisation of the authority of the past. Drawing upon the collective memory of the past and the institutions that embody it, tradition provides a model for action and readily understandable identities for the individual. Since the beginning of modernity, tradition has always been a source of concern. Once change becomes a normal feature of society, the relationship between the past and the present undergoes a transformation. In such circumstances, the force of tradition is weakened and its capacity to provide the standard for human conduct is weakened. The cumulative effect of this tendency towards detraditionalisation is to alter the relationship between the individual and external authority. According to one account, the decline of tradition leads to a shift of authority from without to within.[7] The weakening grip of tradition creates anxiety about the lack of clarity about the conduct of life. It also provides the individual with considerable potential to exercise authority in circumstances where the effectiveness of tradition has declined.

The decline of tradition has had significant implications for culture. Cultural shifts are reflected in human behaviour and in the way that individuals perceive their relations with others and with their community. The decline of tradition can be interpreted as the erosion of a system of meaning through which people make sense of their lives. Such a system of meaning not only links people to an accepted way of doing things, it also helps situate the self within a wider sense of purpose. It has been suggested that the decline of tradition fosters a disengagement from a wider communal purpose leading to a more self-oriented pattern of behaviour. According to this analysis, the method of social control usually exercised through demands affirmed by a moral consensus would give way to a more individualised management of personal troubles.[8] The decline of tradition is associated with the growth of anxiety and a sense of uncertainty. It is claimed that uncertainty about the rules and norms governing life create a demand for interest in psychological answers. It is argued that for those left in an 'enduring position of personal and moral uncertainty', the 'psychotherapeutic ideology offers a substitute certitude' and suggests that moral solidarity is recreated in the form of 'psychological solidarity'.[9]

In recent decades, this line of argument has been developed by sociologists, who believe that we live in a risk society. According to leading British sociologist Anthony Giddens, the intensification of uncertainty and risk has led to the emergence of a reflexive project of the self. As a result, therapy comes to be used as an instrument of self-conscious planning of the life course in conditions that continually generate uncertainty. In circumstances where little can be taken for granted – inadequate information and minimal predictability prevails.[10] The main contribution of theorists of risk society is to link the erosion of tradition and taken-for-granted relationships and practices to the disorganisation of individual identity. Giddens argues that the expansion of psychological syndromes is the product of a 'post-traditional order', one where a sense of continuity has become eroded and where individuals are 'obliged to negotiate life-style options'. Giddens' emphasis on the link between the erosion of a system of common belief and the disorganisation of self-identity takes the argument about the impact of the erosion of tradition a step further.[11]

The weakening of tradition does not simply influence the prevailing moral order, it also ceases to provide a focus for communal unity. This decline of communal solidarity helps accelerate the process of individualisation. As individuals become displaced from their communities the ties that bound them together diminish in significance leading to social isolation and the rise of social isolation. For the isolated self, both private life and personal relationship is problematic. Ernest Gellner speculated that the material struggle for survival of former times has been replaced by a personal struggle for 'attention and acceptance'. People embrace therapy because 'analysis is one of the few times you get complete attention'.[12] He also believes that these trends gain momentum as society becomes more prosperous. 'Modern life in affluent societies, though accompanied by a sense of secure material well-being, is notoriously riddled with other anxieties – anxieties which were not wholly absent in the past, but which those who lived in physically less comfortable ages could not afford to place at the very centre of their attention', writes Gellner.[13]

An exploration of the theme of the decline of tradition helps situate the demand for new ways of making sense of the world. However, on its own it cannot account for the rise of contemporary therapeutic culture. Arguments that emphasise the weakening of tradition and associate the rise of the therapeutic with the changing cultural requirements of modernity have an excessively timeless character. Since industrialisation, the declining influence of traditional beliefs has often been experienced as a crisis of morality and community.[14] It is worth noting that the problem of tradition has been a focus of widespread anxiety since the early nineteenth century. Laments about the 'lack of respect' accorded to some traditional value or institution recurs time and again in public debates during the past century. However, the significance of the therapeutic imperative has only become a subject of serious discussion since the 1960s, and its transformation into one of the defining influences on culture is an even more recent development.[15]

Until recently the problem of tradition has been contained by the rise of ideologies and collective visions that could inspire significant sections of society. As a result, the fragmentary tendencies that developed through individualisation of everyday life and the growing preoccupation of the self were tempered by a wider sense of collective identity. Ideals and values that were external to the self could motivate and gain the commitment of individuals. It was not so long ago that millions were prepared to make sacrifices to advance a variety of causes. Even in the US – where the influence of ideologies was relatively feeble – the belief that one ought to make sacrifices for a higher cause influenced the public imagination.

Society's relationship to tradition is continually shaped and reshaped by experience. In every period views about the past and the salience of tradition are mediated through culture and social experience. It is not the loss of tradition in general, but the specific role assigned to it in contemporary society that may help illuminate the powerful influence of the therapeutic ethos. One of the distinguishing features of our time is the frail character of cultural and institutional affirmation for tradition. Governments still attempt to affirm a sense of common tradition through the celebration of past events and the waving of the flag. But these displays of traditional symbolism have a relatively superficial and feeble character. This tendency is particularly striking in Britain, where a so-called modernising government using the language of the 'New Britain' seeks to self-consciously distance the nation from its past. In the US, traditional symbols such as the flag have a greater significance in public life. However, the so-called traditions associated with the American way of life are frequently compromised by the estrangement of the public from them. Debates thrown up by the recent 'culture wars' indicate that the authority of the past has become much weakened in recent decades. Lack of consensus around moral norms and the contestation for cultural authority is no less evident in the US than in the UK.

The estrangement of authority from tradition coincides with the expansion of interest in the past. Superficially, society's obsession with the past – royal jubilees, Second World War commemorations, pop histories on television, widespread consumption of nostalgia – appears to call into question the claim that tradition-based authority has undergone a process of marginalisation. Although such initiatives reflect an aspiration to retain a link with past, they rarely constitute more than a form of public entertainment.

Public advocates of tradition are conspicuous by their lack of social weight and marginality. Their isolation from the managers of public opinion stands in sharp contrast to the experience of previous times. Until recently, ruling elites have sought to invest their authority with the force of traditional values. Even as it was diminishing in its significance, tradition was systematically assigned positive qualities. Indeed, tradition and authority were linked together in the imagination of the ruling elites. It is only in recent times that traditional morality has, so to speak, lost the moral high ground. Although it survives, it does so in a defensive form and amongst the least influential sections of society. The so-called opinion-makers in politics, the media and academia are wholly distanced from it. Indeed, the most dynamic and influential sections of the elite have opted for a distinctly antitraditional cultural style.

In the past, tradition tended to be ignored, rather than explicitly rejected. Today, many traditional values have been recast in negative terms. Key traditional institutions like the family are denounced as the site of domestic violence and abuse. Patriotism is often represented as discriminatory and noninclusive. The term 'loyalty' is often coupled with words like 'blind' or 'mindless'. Heroism is often mocked or dismissed as implausible. A new genre of popular culture is devoted to exposing the 'secret lives' of past heroes in order to reveal their many flaws. Paternalistic, hierarchical, elitist and exclusive are some of the terms used to castigate traditional institutions.

Probably the most significant development that accounts for the negative attitudes towards tradition today has been the attempt of the elites to divest their authority from it. It is difficult to imagine how profound cultural changes, such as the wholesale rejection of tradition and the embrace of therapeutics, can take place without at least the acquiescence of the elites. According to Rieff, the triumph of the therapeutic is inextricably linked to the crisis of authority. Back in the 1960s, Rieff diagnosed that the ruling elites were suffering from a failure of nerve. He declared that 'the death of culture begins when its normative institutions fail to communicate ideals in ways that remain inwardly compelling, first of all to the cultural elites themselves'. A lack of self-belief enhanced by a profound sense of disorientation undermined the capacity of the American political elite to transmit its narrative of cultural traditions. 'Many spokesmen for our established normative institutions are aware of their failure and yet remain powerless to generate in themselves the necessary unwitting part of their culture that merits the name of faith', decried Rieff.[16] Rieff claimed that not only did the elites cease being supportive, they also became critical of traditional culture as a 'moral demand system'. This rejection of tradition, he believed, represented a cultural revolution with far-reaching consequences.[17]

Of course, individuals and groups still appeal to the claim of tradition and many of their critics often believe that they represent a formidable obstacle to the realisation of their 'nontraditional project'. Liberal observers often warn about the power of the so-called religious right and the forces of conservatism. However, experience shows that recent attempts to 'go back to basics', or to reaffirm 'family values', or 'just say No' invariably have a minimal impact on cultural life. On the contrary, institutions like the church are far more likely to rid themselves of its traditional image and embrace the more individualistic orientation of therapeutics.

The decline of religion and of shared moral norms

The early sociological accounts of the rise of therapeutic culture focused on the insecurities created by the erosion of social solidarity, the fragmentation of everyday life and the diminishing significance attached to traditional moral codes. The therapeutic ethos was often represented as filling a social need created by the decline of organised religion and traditional morality. It was argued that the fragmentation of a moral consensus has forced individuals to look for their own system of meaning. Without a socially accepted moral compass to help people negotiate the problems they face, ambiguity and confusion surrounds the question of how to make sense of existence. The weakening of shared values fragments this quest for meaning. This fragmentation of the search for meaning privatises it and lends it an individualised character. Therapeutics promises to provide answers to the individual's quest for the meaning of life. That is why the confusions that surround important life events can create a demand for psychological answers. Therapeutics is oriented to the experience of the atomised individuals and tries to give meaning to the experience of isolated alienation. Studies of the impact of therapeutic culture on the way we mourn regard the psychological turn as a response to the need to find a replacement for religion.[18] 'Why has psychology become so dominant', asks the sociologist James Hunter. He writes, 'with theology in all its forms discredited as a public language, psychology has offered a seemingly neutral way to understand and cultivate the best qualities of the human personality'.[19]

The inability of religious morality to compete with the scientific claims of medicine and psychology is also regarded by many as an important cause of the therapeutic revolution. Wootton explained the rise of the therapeutic ethos as the result of the rising prestige of medicine and psychiatry that precipitated a shift in the boundary that separates medical from moral problems. She saw the struggle between the 'rival empires of medicine and morality' as the contemporary equivalent of the 'nineteenth-century battle between scientific and religious explanations of cosmic events or terrestrial evolution'.[20] Only this time the battle is confined for the allegiance of the individual soul. North adopted a similar approach. 'The professional has become almost the only readily listened-to arbiter in controversies that are essentially over moral issues', he noted.[21]

Peter Berger has offered an interesting variant to the decline of religion thesis. According to Berger the decline of religion is inextricably linked with the privatisation of individual identity. Berger claims that individuals increasingly lead a dichotomised existence, whereby they derive meaning through their activity in the private rather than public sphere. In such circumstances, public morality and religion ceases to resonate with the individual quest for private identity. Berger believes that 'institutionalised psychologism overcomes dichotomised life'. Moreover, it 'is capable of doing just what institutionalised religion would like to do and is increasingly unable to do – to accompany the individual in both sectors of his dichotomised life'.[22] Following this line of approach, Nolan notes that that 'the therapeutic ethic, as such, is uniquely constituted to relieve this dichotomised modern condition, or at least to make it less cognitively dissonant'.[23] According to this analysis, the therapeutic ethos provides a cultural script that binds the quest for private identity to a wider publicly acknowledged view of life.

The 'disenchantment' of the world that follows in the wake of the erosion of traditional authority and morality is another theme stressed in the discussion on the decline of religion. The concept of disenchantment, originally developed by the renowned German sociologist Max Weber, pointed to a development whereby the process of rationalisation undermines the spiritual, magical and religious influences over society, thereby depriving life of meaning.[24] It is suggested that for people trying to make sense of their life, disenchantment creates an intense need to comprehend subjective experience. Therapeutic ideology promises to re-enchant subjective experience. It endows the individual's emotional life with special meaning. By promising to provide unique insight into the individual's internal life, therapeutic offers to bring people in touch with their 'true' selves. Through validating the self, the ideology of emotionalism helps reconstruct a form of spirituality where the individual becomes the focus of attention. That is why New Age religions and other cults which stress the values of self-expression, self-knowledge and self-discovery are so fashionable in an individuated cultural climate. One of the most striking expression of this trend is the angel fad in the US. Numerous books and television programmes are devoted to stories about angels who watch over us. These are our own angels who exist to watch over us and help validate ourselves.

Classically, religion sought to make sense of the subjective inner experience of the individual through a vocabulary shared with others in the community. In this way it helped made sense of life and helped temper the impact of harsh reality. Without a clear story about the human purpose, the process of economic rationalisation appears to subordinate life to powerful forces beyond individual control. That is why the affirmation of subjective experience often takes the form of an emotional reaction to rationalisation. Deborah Lupton links the appeal of emotionalism to this reaction against regulation and instrumentalism. She writes that in contrast to the instrumentalist imperative of public life, the 'intensity of lived emotions, such as love, fear and anger, provide a depth of experience – they make us aware that we are alive, and underline our humanity'.[25]

Although therapeutics promises to make sense of the individual's quest for meaning, it has little in common with religion. It can be argued that the most important contribution of religion to social life is not its explanation of life, but its ability to provide a web of meaning for the community as a whole. Religion provides a focus for communal cohesion and for acting collectively. In contrast, therapeutics provides a script for the self. As we noted previously, unlike religion, the therapeutic ethos posits no values higher than the self. Nor does it offer a worldview through which people can collectively share meaning. Instead of offering an alternative to religion, it attempts to avoid the problem of how people can be bound to a shared view of the world by offering individuated solace. As Nolan noted, therapeutic culture offers 'the moral reference points to which individuals appeal in order to navigate their way through social life'.[26] But it does so, not by providing guidance for the attainment of solidarity, but by endowing the experience of lack of solidarity with purpose. In effect, the therapeutic ethos represents an accommodation to moral disorientation and the weakening of solidarity through celebrating the cultivation of the self as an end in itself.

Religion has not only declined, but also it has been forced to internalise important elements of therapeutic culture. This development was explicitly acknowledged by the former Archbishop of Canterbury, George Carey, when he complained that 'Christ the Saviour' was becoming 'Christ the counsellor' in watered-down sermons'. In the US, the therapeutic approach has been self-consciously adopted by different faith communities and organisations like the American Association of Pastoral Counselors promote themselves as a mental health service.[27] However, the decline and transformation of religion is a factor but not the cause of the ascendancy of therapeutic culture. The rise of secularism and the decline of religion has been widely noted during the past two centuries. Apprehensions about the decline of religion and the weakening appeal of moral codes have haunted the western imagination for almost two centuries. A sense of loss, and the recognition that there was nothing to replace the old certitudes, became a central motif in western thought in the twentieth century. In the past 'the death of God' was not linked to the valorisation of emotion, but to the growing significance attached to science and reason. In the twentieth century, the rise of the new ideologies of communism, socialism and fascism were represented as meeting the need created by the decline of religion. By the time that therapeutics emerged as a significant cultural force religion had been in decline for some time.

The association of the decline of religion with new systems of meaning fails to explain why people embrace different types of world-view in different historical periods. The scientific world-view appeals to rationality and reason. Ideologies, such as communism and socialism, attempt to recast solidarity on a secular foundation. In contrast, therapeutic culture rejects both the ethos of rationality proclaimed by science and the orientation towards the collective promoted by twentieth-century ideologies. This highly individualised and emotivist therapeutic culture is only one possible outcome of the decline of traditional religion.

The demise of politics

The therapeutic ethos represents not so much an alternative to religion as the political ideologies that reflected, questioned, defended specific social, moral, political and economic institutional interests and commitments in modern times. Since the rise of secularism the role of religion as a constituent element of modern governance has been relatively insignificant. Most of the nineteenth and twentieth centuries were a period when ideological competition influenced the actions of both the defenders and the opponents of the status quo. That is why it is the declining significance of ideology that has such enormous impact on today's political landscape. This development has been widely commented upon.[28] There is a general consensus that the decline of social engagement is associated with a shift of focus towards the individualisation of political life. The importance attached to individual concerns and personal issues can be seen as a development that closely parallels the decline of ideology. Since the 1980s the theme of political disaffection has been overshadowed by the pursuit of personal troubles.

The close association between the demise of politics and the rise of therapeutics was noted by some of the pioneering studies discussed in the previous section. Paul Halmos explicitly linked the rise of therapeutics to the demise of politics. He wrote that the decline of interest in politics is 'both an outcome of the spread of counselling activities, and a favourable social context for their further spreading'. Halmos took the view that this development directly influenced the intellectual mood of his time. 'The social science of the "political era" was a predominantly political social science, and one that much helped to stress political priorities; contemporary social science is small group oriented, and stresses therapeutic action', he concluded.[29] In the late 1970s, Christopher Lasch offered a trenchant critique of what he saw as the growth of narcissistic politics. 'Having displaced religion as the organising framework of American culture, the therapeutic outlook threatens to displace politics as well, the last refuge of ideology', he observed. Lasch believed that this demise of politics fostered a cultural climate where the state bureaucracy could transform 'collective grievances into personal problems amenable to therapeutic intervention'.[30]

It is tempting to interpret the transformation of collective grievances into personal problems as the outcome of elite initiative. Some of the radical critics of the therapeutic imperative regard it as driven by a political strategy in a self-conscious manner. Dana Cloud claims that the therapeutic can be understood as a 'set of politically motivated instrumental discourses that can be described, explained in their political contexts, and evaluated'.[31] From this perspective the therapeutic can be seen as a 'political strategy of contemporary capitalism' for containing dissent through the discourse of individual or family responsibility.[32] So is this a case of Big Brother brainwashing the masses? Cloud seeks to avoid a conspiracy theory-type explanation and insists that 'therapeutic discourses are not the product of an elite cabal set on controlling the minds of the duped masses'.[33] Nevertheless, many radical critics of therapeutics believe that its was the conscious promotion of this ethos, in particular by the political right in the 1980s that accounts for its influence.

The view that therapy provides a vehicle through which Reaganite and Thatcherite ideas of individual responsibility can be communicated has been advanced by some critics of free-market capitalism. Heelas suggests that advocates of enterprise culture have sought to cultivate ideas of selfhood that promoted right wing ideas of self-interest.[34] Janice Russell claims that the celebration of individual autonomy by British Tories is 'startlingly similar to the ethical justification and principles of counselling, particularly those espoused by the "client-centred" approach'.[35] Joanna Moncrief, a British advocate of mental patients' rights, states that medicalisation 'diverts attention away from the political and environmental factors that can make modern life so difficult and distressing'. She, too, takes the view that the growth of therapeutic culture represents an attempt to divert attention from the destructive impact of economic liberalisation in the 1980s and 1990s.[36] Tana Dineen's study of the North American 'psychology industry' also associates the growth of therapeutics with the climate created by the 'conservative, right-facing, self-serving form of Reaganomics'.[37] This manipulative dimension of therapeutic practices has also been stressed by American scholars, who claim that it has been used to gain social control through individualising responsibility. It is also claimed that therapeutic ethos has been used to foster an individualised identity through the celebration of consumption.[38]

As we noted in Chapter 2, there is little doubt that the management of subjectivity represents an important feature of contemporary politics. At various times, psychology has been 'used' to reconcile people to their insecure existence in industry and during war. However, the instrumental use of the therapeutic by political interests does not account for its expanding influence over social life. Individual agents and political actors do not have the power to transform culture and individual subjectivity. Politicians have always sought to shape mass psychology. Since the turn of the twentieth century there have been numerous attempts made to manage public opinion.[39] So there is nothing new about the deployment of psychology for the management of public opinion. The questions that needs to be answered is why has this strategy acquired such a prominent role within contemporary political culture and why does it appears to resonate with the outlook of today's public?

To take one example – the counselling of the unemployed. Back in the early

1980s, the Thatcher regime supported local initiatives which offered counselling to those who were or were about to be thrown out of work. Many commentators identified these schemes as a cynical attempt to contain and defuse the reaction of the unemployed through getting them to accommodate to their precarious existence. Government energy was far more devoted towards helping the jobless 'cope' with the 'predicament of unemployment' than with creating new jobs.[40] At the time, critical comments about the schemes were widely heard. Many counsellors confided that the unemployed were not interested in their help. Yet by the late 1980s and 1990s, such counselling initiatives had become widely institutionalised and frequently sought by people, insecure abut their relationship to the labour market. Today, it is the trade unions and not the 'capitalists' who are the most vociferous advocates for the provision of therapeutic support in the workplace in Britain and the US.[41] It has been noted that in the US, most employees using the therapeutic services offered through the Employee Assistance Programmes are self-referrals, rather than supervisor referrals. Although this scheme has often been presented as a devious attempt to control labour, its embrace by workers raises the question of whether it 'can be classified as a means of corporate social control'.[42] There are a variety of reasons that account for this explosion in the demand for counselling in the workplace. One important influence was the impact of the decline of ideology on the workplace and on trade unionism. As we noted elsewhere, the internalisation of the therapeutic ethos by unions coincided with this development. Paradoxically it is not so much a right-wing strategy but therapeutic trade unionism that accounts for transforming the problem of job loss into one of psychosocial transition.[43]

Despite the attempt by radical scholars to link it to a distinct economic or class interest, the therapeutic ethos provides a cultural script with which a diverse range of motives can be expressed. Indeed, emotionalism and the language of therapy is as much if not more extensively deployed by opponents of the status quo than by the political elites. Cloud's study provides a detailed account of the pervasive influence of emotionalism on dissident movements. She writes that in the US since 1968, 'therapy has become an increasingly persuasive alternative to political action from below'.[44] This view is shared by Lupton, who has remarked that rage has become a central construct through which the lives of the marginalised is defined – indeed the reaction to anything can be presented through rage form.[45] Mass mobilisation of protest movements often adopt a therapeutic vocabulary for expressing their grievances. As Eva Moscowitz's account of 1960s American radical protest indicates, 'the social movements of this turbulent era relied heavily on the authority of psychological experts and the tenets of the therapeutic gospel'.[46] To understand this development it is necessary to examine how the changes discussed in this chapter have influenced people's personal and everyday life.

Of course, the therapeutic turn enjoys considerable institutional support and corresponds to the individuated orientation adopted by modern state bureaucracies. Policy-making is increasingly engaged with developing institutional response to individual grievances. But while the institutionalised individualist style of policy-making may shape the public's relationship to the state it cannot be held responsible for the prevailing therapeutic sensibility. To understand this development it is necessary to look at other factors that shape the therapeutic imagination.

Social control

One reason why political authority has embraced therapeutics is because it helps governments forge points of contact with an otherwise fragmented public. The reorientation of public institutions toward the individual also provides authorities with a potentially important instrument of social control. The idea that therapy functions as a mechanism of social control was systematically elaborated in the post-war era by Talcott Parsons. According to Parsons, therapy not only gave access to individuals, but it could also subject them to influences that could not be exerted through other forms of interaction.[47] Normal forms of institutional interventions often leave individual subjectivity untouched. In contrast, therapeutic intervention can by-pass the resistance of the individual and can influence the internal life of people. Unlike other authorities charged with the maintenance of social control – officials, religious leaders, teachers – therapists are not charged with maintaining the moral order. Rather than judge, therapists empathise with the individual's predicament and can establish a relation of 'permissiveness' with the patient.[48] Through a relation of permissiveness – what today would be called being nonjudgemental – therapists are able to gain a priviliged access to people's subjectivity. Therapists are also able to reward compliance through rewarding individuals with a diagnosis.[49]

Through a diagnosis, therapists are able to assign the status of being sick to a patient. Parsons' concept of the 'sick role' provides interesting insights into the mechanics of therapeutics as a form of social control. The sick role exempts individuals from having to behave in accordance with prevailing social and moral expectations, since 'being ill cannot ordinarily be conceived to be the fault of the sick person' and 'illness can justify certain exemptions from normal expectations of performance'.[50] In return for gaining these exemptions, sick individuals are expected to define their condition as undesirable and aberrant, and to do everything possible to get well. Parsons saw the sick role as a temporary one, during which the therapist could establish an important emotional connection with the patient based on the exercise of detached empathy. During this relationship, the therapist's diagnosis of illness shapes the way the individual understands his or her condition. Since definitions of illness are informed by prevailing cultural norms and expectations, the assignment of the sick role contains the potential for motivating the reintegration of the patient into the wider social system.

From the Parsonian perspective, the therapeutic relationship enacts the dialectic of temporary separation and reintegration of the individual into the social system. Insights into the effectiveness of permissive empathy as an instrument of social control have been validated by experiments carried out in the field of industrial relations. Therapeutic forms of social control were innovated in industry in order to raise the efficiency of labour. Several industrial experiments carried out in Britain and the US indicated that if workers received professional attention and recognition and felt that someone cared about their workplace experience, output and productivity would increase. The development of therapeutic techniques in industry by the American psychologist Elton Mayo during the interwar period was based on studies carried out at the Western Electric Company's Hawthorne Works. Through this experiment, the researchers discovered that their interviews unexpectedly provided them access to the emotional life of the workforce. As Peter Miller notes, 'nondirected and neutral questions, with the interviewer listening rather than talking, allowed the person the possibility of revealing his/her genuine feelings and grievances'. This technique 'had the advantage of providing access to those dimensions of industrial life hitherto obscured, and in itself supplied a rudimentary therapeutics', adds Miller.[51] Not surprisingly, providing employees with an opportunity to air grievances has become an important feature of human resource management. And the nondirected interview in its diverse form has become an important tool of management control.

Parsons' idea of permissive therapeutics is but a variant of the nondirected interview. Through the provision of calculated empathy and recognition of the individual's distress, permissive therapeutics offers a relationship or a point of contact to the otherwise estranged individual. But it does so at a price. By recognising the authority of the therapist the individual accepts a relationship of dependence – and acquiescence to this subordinate status becomes a way of life. Unlike forms of social control which are based on the threat of repression, permissive therapy works in an indirect manner. Therapeutic culture 'attempts to control and exploit hostile impulses toward the social order, as well as other anti-institutional and anticultural impulses, not through repressive controls but by means of tolerant remission on the assumption that many impulses are less harmful than they first appear, while others may be made safe through controlled, cathartic releases', observes Woolfolk.[52]

The exercise of social control through permissive therapeutics has become increasingly significant in recent times. It plays a prominent role in contemporary political culture and informs the contemporary style of government. With the demise of politics, it has been necessary to reconstitute authority based on ideology on a new foundation. As we discuss in Chapter 8, the institutionalisation of therapeutic practices by the state attempts to bypass the general problem of legitimacy by reconnecting with the public as individuals.

Parsons took the view that the exercise of social control through permissive therapeutics would be effective as long as there prevailed an 'institutionalised consensus' with respect to 'what constitutes "moral integrity" in our society'. He believed that such a consensus existed, since without it 'the degree of stability which our society has shown could not be understood'.[53] This, integrative social control model of therapy rests on the assumption that moral consensus prevails in society. While this may have been so during the height of the Cold War, this assumption can no longer be taken for granted. In the last three decades there have been important cultural changes that undermine the assumption of a consensus on what constitutes 'moral integrity' in society. The weakening of a moral consensus is strikingly reflected in debates about the meaning of illness and health.

Consequently, the line that divides health from illness has become increasingly blurred.

Parsons assumed that the therapeutic relationship is underpinned by a shared 'positive valuation of health and the negative valuation of illness between therapeutic agent and sick persons'.[54] Yet today, definitions of illness are highly contested and a negative valuation of illness is itself a subject of controversy. Being ill can now constitute a defining feature of an individual's identity. 'For some, the patient career may be a permanent way of life, with a self-supporting network of friends, activities, doctors and treatments', writes Elaine Showalter.[55] Identities associated with illness are often cast in a positive light. Some individuals positively value being deaf or blind. One study of women's experience with fibromyalgia claims that the illness can create intimacy and kinship. It suggests that this experience 'provides one with an opportunity to recognise oneself'. Another study of cancer-related identity speculates about how this illness can be a 'potentially positive experience'.[56] The valorisation of the 'positive' features of illness calls into question of original conceptualisation of the sick role. According to its original formulation, the sick role is conceptualised as a temporary episode. However, if as today, the sick role is experienced as an affirmation of identity, it is likely to assume a more durable character. Terms like 'cancer survivor' and 'recovering alcoholic' testify to a growing tendency to represent illness as constituting a long-term influence on identity.

Changing attitudes towards illness and identity are symptomatic of a growing tendency to embrace the sick role. In Britain and the US, the institutionalisation of permissive therapeutics has led to the extension of the experiences that now warrant exemptions from normal standards of accountability.[57] It has fostered a climate that is hospitable to the continuous widening of the definition of illness, particularly of psychological illness. The legitimisation of permissiveness within the therapeutic relationship has created the potential for its expansion into other spheres of life. It contributes to the displacement or transformation of prevailing moral forms. Paradoxically, the permissive and nonjudgemental and affirming qualities of therapeutics have become the defining features of the prevailing cultural sensibility. This development is well documented in Alan Wolfe's study of what middle-class Americans think about political, cultural and social issues. They 'are reluctant to pass judgement on how other people act and think', writes Wolfe, before suggesting that 'Thou shalt not judge' has become the Eleventh Commandment of middle-class Americans.[58]

The relationship between permissive therapeutics and the prevailing normative order is one of permanent tension. Once permissiveness is granted to some individuals some of the time, it becomes difficult to contain other demands for exemption from the prevailing normative order. As Lasch concluded, 'inappropriately extended beyond the consulting room . . . therapeutic morality encourages a permanent suspension of the moral sense'.[59] People who are sick cannot be expected to exercise critical judgement or to accept moral responsibility for their action. And when this attitude is extended 'beyond the consulting room' it becomes not simply a treatment for the ill, but a guide for individual behaviour. That is why the promoters of therapeutic culture regard therapy as not only necessary to cure the ill, but as indispensable to the conduct of healthy relationship and normal life. 'Therapy is too good to be limited to the sick', wrote two American psychologists, Erving and Miriam Polster in 1973.[60] The normalisation of therapy has important implications for understanding the social significance of the sick role. It blurs the line that divides the state illness from that of being well and potentially provides everyone with access to exemptions from the prevailing normative order.

Can therapeutics still assist the maintenance of social control when permissiveness is normalised and the meaning of the sick role becomes the subject of debate? The institutionalisation of permissive therapeutics has the contradictory effect of undermining the wider normative order whilst re-establishing order on the basis of containing the wider aspirations of the citizen. The paradox of a feeble moral consensus coexisting with a submissive public is the inevitable consequence of the exercise of this form of control. In adopting the sick role, individuals accept that their capacity to function is impaired and that therefore their ability to exercise individual autonomy is significantly compromised. Despite its disruptive effect, the normalisation of illness promotes a sense of subservience to the professional.

The professionalisation of everyday life

The development of modern society has had a profound impact on the conduct of everyday life. Unlike in a traditional setting, the modern individual's attachment to others is distinctly fragile and provisional. People's obligations and expectations of one another is often ambiguous and confusing. The continued thinning of communal ties helps foster a sense of depersonalisation. This fragmentation of social experience means that knowledge about the conduct of life is no longer transmitted automatically by a community to its members. Numerous sociologists have pointed out that individuals are increasingly forced to make their way without the supportive network provided by family, community, religion and the various informal and formal organisations associated with the world work.[61] People's isolation from a supportive institutional fabric raises important questions about how individuals gain insight and guidance regarding their behaviour and relations with others.

One of the characteristic features of modern times is that the decline of taken-for-granted ways of doing things has encouraged the perception that individuals are not able to manage important aspects of their life without professional guidance. The conduct of routine forms of social interaction are frequently represented as difficult and complicated. That is why child-rearing can be treated as a science and why we often talk about parenting skills, social skills, communication skills and relationship skills. The belief that the conduct of everyday encounters requires special skills has created an opportunity for the 'expert' to colonise the realm of personal relations.[62] This professionalisation of everyday life has been a distinct trend from the outset of modernity. But since the 1960s, the expansion of the professionalisation of personal problems has accelerated at a breathtaking pace. Ever since professionals declared in the late nineteenth century that the task of child-rearing and parenting required their input, they have systematically expanded the range of personal issues that demands expert knowledge. Today, professionals give guidance on marriage and other intimate relationships. Every aspect of life from birth through to school and career to mourning has been subjected to professional counselling. We live in an age of personal trainers, mentors and facilitators. This process of professionalisation contains an important therapeutic dimension. Relationship expertise is self-consciously oriented towards the management of the 'client's' feelings.

The growth of the 'professional complex', as Talcott Parsons characterised the ascendancy of the relationship expert, was widely noted during the mid-twentieth century. Peter Berger drew attention to the way in which this development in America led the development of what he called 'the counselling and testing complex'.[63] Since the 1960s, when ideas about the professional complex were elaborated and discussed, there has been a massive increase in its size and influence. Today, this complex resembles the character of an industry. As one British mental health professional notes, 'there is a veritable trauma industry comprising experts, lawyers, claimants and other interested parties; it is a kind of social movement trading on the authority of medical pronouncements'.[64] In the US, the development of the professionalisation of everyday life is equally expansive. Tana Dineen writes of the 'psychological industry' in the US that has successfully infused 'psychology into the human experience'.[65]

Until relatively recently, the professionalisation of everyday life was contained by the belief that the problems of the private sphere were best left to the informal solutions worked out by people in their communities. Although the claim that the expert knew best was rarely contested, the helping professions had far less opportunity to colonise private life than today. The so-called helping professions were free to encroach into the life of people living on the edge of society. But until the 1960s, professionals had little opportunity to encroach into the private world of 'normal', especially middle-class people. This was an age where many were genuinely shocked by the arrogant claim of the professional to believe that they knew best.

The growth of relationship expertise was not simply an outcome of the activities of new professionals. It reflects important cultural changes that have encouraged the problematisation of human relationships and of individual experience. One important development that has boosted the power of the professional is a socio-cultural process that sociologists characterise as that of medicalisation. Medicalisation describes a process through which the problems of everyday life are treated as medical ones, usually in terms of illnesses, disorders or syndromes. The process of medicalisation is not confined to diagnosing problems linked to the body. In cultural terms it involves exporting the ideas of illness and disease beyond the body to make sense of conditions and experiences that are distinctly cultural and social. One of the most important ways in which medicalisation has evolved during the second half of the twentieth century has been through 'discovering' diseases that are nonphysical and are to do with emotional problems. Increasingly, psychological problems to do with stress, rage, trauma, low self-esteem or addiction provide a medical label for interpreting virtually every human experience. Strictly speaking, the process that we are describing can be more accurately expressed as that of psychologisation, rather than medicalisation. However, given the wide usage of the latter, we shall use it to describe the process through which personal problems are recast as medical or psychological conditions.

The process of medicalisation has been inseparable from that of professionalisation. As James Chriss writes, 'professional organisations whether organised around medicine, law, business, social science, or the burgeoning array of helping professions – always seek to expand the range of objects and phenomena to which their members' expertise may arguably be applied'.[66] This expansive dynamic is in part driven by economic expedience and by the opportunities created by the modern state. As Dineen argues, the psychology industry is 'first and foremost a business, intent on selling its services and expanding its market'.[67] Since the nineteenth century, professionals have been remarkably successful in creating a demand for their services. Lasch claims that 'the new professions themselves invented many of the needs they claimed to satisfy'. He adds that 'they played on public fears of disorder and disease, adopted a deliberately mystifying jargon, ridiculed popular traditions of self-help as backward and unscientific, and in this way created or intensified (not without opposition) a demand for their own services'.[68] However, the pursuit of professional self-interest cannot, on its own, account for the all pervasive tendency to medicalise social experience. As Hochchild notes 'the significance of the growth of new therapies cannot be dismissed by the argument that they are simply a way of extending jobs in the service sector by creating new needs'. The question remains, 'why these needs'.[69]

But above all, the demand for medicalisation is generated by cultural changes that inflate the sense of individuation and of powerlessness. These changes – the thinning out of community attachments, the decline of systems of moral meaning – have been reinforced in the 1980s by the demise of politics and social solidarity. The individuation of social experience has heightened the sense of personal vulnerability creating further opportunities for the market to encroach into the realm of social experience. According to the British psychologist David Smail, 'there was a positive explosion in the expansion of the therapy and counselling industry in Britain'. This explosion was made possible by an all-pervasive cultural tendency to redefine personal difficulty as a pathology requiring professional management. Smail notes that as part of this process 'the market was extended in several new directions and "counselling" – previously considered a minority practice of doubtful validity – suddenly became the self-evident necessary antidote to occasions of distress which up till then people had just had to muddle through as best they could'. Smail gives the examples of disaster counselling and the development of the concept of post-traumatic stress disorder as examples of the 'extension of the frontiers of the market into previously noncommercial territory of ordinary social intercourse'.[70]

The experience of the 1980s represents a distinct phase in the history of medicalisation. Throughout the past two centuries there have been numerous struggles against attempts to medicalise certain forms of behaviour and people.

During the 1960s, the anti-psychiatry movement was in the forefront of questioning various claims that defined people as mentally ill. In the 1970s, the campaign against the diseasing of same sex relationships succeeded in demedicalising homo-sexuality. Until the 1980s, the medicalisation of women's experiences, particularly in the domain of reproduction, was fiercely contested. Feminist and other critics challenged the medicalisation of childbirth and of abortion. In contrast, today leading feminist voices such as Naomi Wolf are in the forefront of promoting the medicalisation of childbirth through popularising the diagnosis of post-natal depression. 'Postpartum depression affects 400,000 mothers per year in the USA', argues Wolf.[71] Recent attempts to medicalise female behaviour – premenstrual syndrome, battered women's syndrome, new mother's syndrome – are now rarely challenged.

Since the 1980s, opposition to medicalisation has been minimal. This period has also seen an unprecedented level of the medicalisation of social experience. This is the era of dyslexia, sex addiction, attention deficit disorder, social phobia and codependency. Increasingly, it is not professional bodies but grass-roots campaigners who are in the forefront of demanding a medical label to describe their condition. Organisations demanding recognition for ME or fibromyalgia are highly critical of doctors who are reluctant to recognise their claim for a medical label. Campaigners promoting the cause of Gulf War syndrome reject as an insult the suggestion that they are not suffering from a physically based illness. Advocacy groups promoting medical recognition of chronic fatigue syndrome have sought to raise money to finance 'the discovery of diagnostic markers and treatments that would legitimise and indeed, medicalise the constellation of symptoms they experience'.[72]

The readiness with which the pathologisation of human behaviour is embraced indicates that the medicalisation of life has become an accomplished fact. New opportunities exist for the professionalisation of human behaviour and in turn professional intervention creates a greater demand for medicalising the problems of day-to-day living. The provision of counselling advice – no matter how sound and commonsensical – further diminishes the capacity of people to negotiate the problems they encounter. The problem is not that professional advice is always misguided, but that it short-circuits the process through which people can learn how to deal with problems through their own experience. Intuition and insight gained from personal experience is continually compromised by professional knowledge. This has the unintentional consequence of estranging people from their own feelings and instincts since such reactions require the affirmation of the expert. In such circumstances people's capacity to handle relationships and to have confidence in their relationships diminishes further.[73] This only creates new opportunities for professional intervention in everyday life.

Professional intervention unleashes a process whereby the dependency of the individual on the expert becomes increasingly more systematic. The mediation of experience by the professional has the effect of distancing people from one another, thereby fragmenting the network of relationships still further. Although the process of fragmentation is bound up with the process of modernity, its professionally mediated form is a relatively recent development. Moreover, the mediation of experience through the professional alters the very character of human relationships. The mediation of experience undermines the organic links that sustain relationships. The problem is removed from its real-life context and is reconstituted as an object of professional management. As mediators of experience, professionals cannot help but alter the relationship between people. Couples who carry out intimate communication with their counsellor end up communicating to one another in a different way. Parents who are discovering their children's problems through discussions with the expert become distracted from the developing forms of communication with their children that is the outcome of spontaneous interaction. Interdependence between people vies with dependence on the professional, thereby complicating the conduct of relationships. Almost semiconsciously, therapeutics targets the relation of dependence between people. Such an approach is most strikingly manifested in the ethos of the codependence movement. This is a movement that seeks to stigmatise relationships on the ground that dependence on others is akin to a disease.[74]

Probably the most significant legacy of professionalisation is that it encourages the formalisation of relationships. A seminal study carried out by Robert Bellah and his colleagues draws attention to the way in which therapeutic attitudes distance American people from their 'social roles, relations and practices'. Instead of friends, neighbours, elders and the many informal roles that have no name, we have peers, mentors, appraisers, life-style gurus, personal trainers and a whole army of counsellors. Even intimate relationships have become subject to the influence of contract-like procedures. Bellah is not so much concerned about the danger of professional domination of personal life. He fears 'that too much of the purely contractual structure of economic and bureaucratic world is becoming an ideological model for personal life'. He concludes that 'the prevalence of contractual intimacy and procedural co-operation, carried over from boardroom to bedroom and back again, is what threatens to obscure the ideals of both personal virtue and public good'.[75] Previously, we noted that the process of rationalisation leading to the disenchantment of the world creates a demand for meaning, to which therapeutics provides a possible answer. It is the ability of therapy to reinterpret social experience into personal meaning that motivates many to seek professional support. However, the attempt to contain the psychic effects of rationalisation through therapy has the perverse consequence of expanding rationalisation into the domain of intimate relationships. Through the professionalisation of everyday life, formal procedures are introduced into the realm of personal relations. The formalisation of relationships imports ideas of self-interest, calculation and mistrust into the realm of intimacy. Its effect is to render relationships impersonal – thereby creating an even greater demand for the promise of a personalised remedy offered by therapeutics.

Conclusion: the disorganisation of the private sphere

According to Ellen Herman, the idea that therapy was useful for everyone gained momentum in the US, because 'it meshed easily with cultural trends that made therapeutic help appear acceptable, even inviting, to ordinary people'.[76] Today, the normalisation of therapy is an accomplished fact. According to the American Psychological Association, by 1995, 46 per cent of the population had seen a mental health professional. Some have predicted that soon 80 per cent of the American population will be users of mental health services.[77]

Recent social and cultural trends have intensified the perception that individuals lack the capacity to control their lives. Through the normalisation of the sick role, therapeutics provides an explanation for this problem of control – we are sick and therefore unfit to manage our affairs. It also offers the promise of understanding and support. However, the very normalisation of the sick role disempowers people further still. The erosion of the line that separates the ill from the well raises fundamental questions about the ideal of human self-determination. Contemporary culture answers these questions by stating that everyone needs help and everyone needs support. That is why ideals of independence and self-sufficiency have given way to a culturally sanctioned state of dependency. 'As therapeutic points of view and practice gain general acceptance, more and more people find themselves disqualified, in effect, from the performance of adult responsibilities and become dependent on some form of medical authority', writes Lasch.[78]

The therapeutic imperative is a cultural response to an estranged world that is highly fragmented. But therapeutics is not a simple reflection of the state of fragmentation. Through accommodating to the process of individuation it contains an inherent tendency towards intensifying the erosion of the personal bonds that link people to one another. Whilst therapeutics seeks to encourage the dependence of the individual on the professional, it is uncompromisingly hostile to the relations of dependence that bind people together. Therapeutics creates a demand for itself by continually compromising the informal networks of support that people rely on to negotiate the challenges of daily life. As noted in our discussion of therapeutic culture, it turns help-seeking into an act of virtue.

One of the direct consequences of the professionalisation of relationships is to diminish our sense of dependency on one another. Professional intervention not only complicates relationships but undermines the ability of people to communicate and interact with one another. This is not an accidental outcome of the therapeutic imperative. Contemporary therapeutic culture is distinctly hostile to the informal networks that bind people together. The ideology of contemporary therapeutics explicitly targets everyday informal networks. So-called liberation therapy in the US and the antipsychiatry movement in the UK is often critical of culture and society for rendering people ill. However, a closer inspection of their doctrine indicates that what they really object to is not society as such but family and interpersonal relations. As Russell Jacoby argues, radical therapy 'often confuses interpersonal, family and social analysis'. Radical therapists often see the problem as the 'communicative interaction of the family' rather than that of wider social processes.[79]

Rice's analysis of liberation therapy in the US shows a direct parallel with Jacoby's critique of the British antipsychiatry movement. Rice notes that despite liberation therapy's critique of culture, its real focus is the informal relations of dependency between people. He writes that the 'brunt of liberation therapy's anti-institutionalism has been borne by those largely informal institutions – such as friendship, courtship, intimate relations, family, community – that stand between and mediate the relationship between the individual and the abstract and exceedingly powerful state and economy'.[80] The hostility of therapeutics towards informal relations is most developed in the doctrine of codependency. From the standpoint of this doctrine, love, passion and mutual dependence are regarded as pathological conditions that require an invasive therapeutic intervention.

The pessimistic representation of interpersonal relations is reflected in the changing focus of therapy. Not all forms of therapy incite the individual to view the human condition and personal relations as inherently destructive. In the past, some schools of therapy adopted an optimistic view of the future and believed that their techniques could help realise the potential for human emancipation. However, with the consolidation of therapeutic culture this optimistic orientation has become dissipated. 'Rather than focusing on human potential', notes Moskowitz, promoters of therapy today tend to focus on 'psychological vulnerabilities'.[81] Although individual therapists sometimes make extravagant claims about the effectiveness of their product, therapeutic culture is distinctly modest about the claims it makes. Therapies tend to be promoted on the ground that they help people to cope and to come to terms with their condition. Such relatively modest claims stand in contrast to the way that therapy was promoted in the past. Throughout most of the twentieth century, therapy was promoted as both a cure and as an instrument for the construction of a happy society. It was advertised as a positive way of exploring and expanding the individual's personality. Throughout the 1960s and 1970s, an optimistic view of human potential guided therapeutic ideas. It was often presented as a way of realising 'personal growth'. However, by the 1980s, this optimism had evaporated and instead of 'focusing on human potential, promoters of the therapeutic gospel focused on psychological vulnerabilites'.[82]

From the perspective of today's therapeutic ethos, therapy is much more an instrument of survival than a means through which enlightenment can be gained. Individuals are not so much cured as placed in a state of recovery. Recovering alcoholics and sex addicts and their codependants are represented as survivors of problems that threaten to compromise their emotional well-being for the rest of their lives. As a result, the need for some form of therapy, counselling or support may be a never-ending one.

The combined effect of the professionalisation of relationships and its targeting of informal networks is the disorganisation of people's private lives. Therapeutics spreads mistrust about the experience of intimacy and, as the sociologist Ann Swidler indicates, it 'also redefines the ideal love relationship'. Swidler notes that 'therapy becomes the model for a good relationship, so that what truly loving spouses or partners do for each other is much akin to what therapists do for their clients'.[83]

The disorganisation of the private sphere has important implications for the exercise of selfhood. The distancing of the self from a wider informal network threatens to deprive the individual from an organic source of support. This problematisation of interpersonal relations diminishes the expectation that stable bonds, organic to an individual's experience can be forged. In lowering the individual's expectations towards relationship, therapeutic culture helps foster the perception of the self – as uniquely vulnerable and weak. As Gergen argues, 'once people understand their actions in terms of mental deficits, they are sensitised to the problematic potential in all their activities, the ways in which they are infected or diminished' and adds 'the sense of enfeeblement becomes complete'.[84]

Although the broad social changes that have led to individuation and the fragmentation of social experience provide the terrain on which therapeutics thrives, it does not by itself lead to the construction of the dimished self. Nor is the recent expansion of the demand for therapy a direct consequence of the process of individuation. The loss of meaning and stable framework of guidance provided by tradition need not be experienced merely as a process of disorientation and confusion. It also offers people new choices for making decisions about how to conduct their lives. There is no iron law of history that forces people confronting uncertainty to comply with the demands of the professional. It is the disorganisation of the private sphere brought about through the targeting of informal networks that creates the conditions for the sense of enfeeblement. Without the insulation of a network of interpersonal relations, the individual stands exposed to the pressures of the world and experiences the condition of the self as indeed that of vulnerability. This sense of vulnerability, which is the defining feature of the contemporary self, will be investigated in the next two chapters.

5   The diminished self

Therapeutic culture presents itself as the harbinger of a new era of individual choice, autonomy, self-knowledge and self-awareness. 'The idea that individuals are at least potentially, in charge of their own fate lies at the very heart of therapeutic philosophy', writes David Smail.[1] The language of therapeutics continually endorses the project of self-realisation and holds out the promise of individual enlightenment through the exercise of autonomous behaviour. Therapy often justifies itself by claiming to provide the expertise required for the project of self-discovery. Outwardly, at least, therapeutic culture holds out the possibility of self-emancipation and projects an optimistic if not flattering representation of the self.

Supporters of therapeutic culture often acclaim the liberating potential of therapy and the opportunities it provides for the realisation of self-awareness through the exercise of individual choice. This more 'aware' self is often attributed with the power to construct new, more emotionally democratic relationships that are characteristically more enlightened than previous ones. Through learning to 'appropriately express our emotions' we become 'rounded people capable of helping ourselves' and in turn 'we will be better able to help others', writes one advocate of emotional literacy.[2] According to one account, autonomous individuals can now enjoy the 'freedom based on self-knowledge, to choose the partner with whom one can further one's self-realisation, a project to which therapeutic discourse has much to contribute'.[3] This optimistic account of the self is systematically elaborated in the influential writings of the British sociologist Anthony Giddens. Giddens advances the idea of reflexivity – a self-defining process based upon the monitoring of psychological and social information about possible trajectories of life. From this perspective, the reflexive self is able to engage in the project of self-determination through the practice of self-monitoring.[4] The idea that the self is self-determined and can be evaluated against a self-imposed criterion is 'implicit within most styles of counselling and therapy'.[5] This idealised version of the self-determining self is central to the outlook of the so-called human potential movement associated with the theories of Abraham Maslow and Carl Rogers.

The significance assigned to the project of self-reconstruction through self-discovery would suggest that therapeutic culture conveys a powerful image of the self. Some critics have criticised the naively optimistic version of the self proposed by promoters of self-actualisation.[6] However, a closer inspection of therapeutic culture indicates that its account of the self is far from an optimistic one. The image of the self-actualising individual gaining enlightenment through self-reflection and the exercise of autonomous choice is, in practice, contradicted by the fundamental premise of therapeutic culture, which is that the individual self is defined by its vulnerability. As noted previously, contemporary culture valorises the help-seeking self. The very fact that the realisation of the self is predicated on a relationship of dependence on therapeutics, calls into question the quality and meaning of individual autonomy.

A culture, which as we saw previously is so troubled by the workings of the human emotion, is unlikely to display much confidence in the power of the self to cope with the trials of life. The manner in which emotions have been problematised implicitly raises questions about the ability of the individual to deal with disappointment, misfortune, adversity or even the challenge of everyday life. Terms like self-discovery and self-reconstruction describe processes that are not undertaken just by the self. These are projects which are guided by a detailed cultural narrative and often with the guidance of professionals. That is why the project of self-actualisation may turn into 'the pursuit of standardisation of people, rather than a self-determined individuality'.[7] The relation of dependence on professionals compromises the individual self's ability to make choices. Professional intervention can short-circuit the act of self-determination. 'They feel their actions to be outside the realm of choice, inevitable and unchangeable, unless they place themselves – dependently – in professional hands', argues Gergen.[8] The concept of the autonomous self is in reality contradicted by powerful cultural messages about the inability of individuals to handle their emotions without support. As noted in Chapter 8, the very fact that society is so pre-occupied by the low level of self-esteem of its citizens calls into question the image of the omnipotent, self-constructing self. As we shall see, therapeutic culture continually diminishes the sense of individual self and promotes a distinctly feeble version of human subjectivity.

The frequently repeated exhortation to 'acknowledge your emotions' represents a demand to re-evaluate the self's perception of itself – in relation to its past and other people. But unless this act of acknowledgement contains the potential for action that has consequences, it negates the claim that self-consciousness can make a difference. In practice, therapeutic culture helps individuals reconcile themselves to a more 'realistic' and more 'vulnerable' version of the self. The self is presented as constantly subject to grave injury and illness. The insistence that such risks are part of everyday life has the effect of heightening the individual's sense of vulnerability and disposition to illness.

The vulnerable self

It is in fact through the capacity of the individual to manage the challenges of everyday life that insights may be gained into the workings of the self. The verdict of therapeutic culture on this point is unambiguously clear. It casts serious doubts about the capacity of the self to manage new challenges and to cope with adversity. Individuals confronted with the ordinary troubles of life are now routinely advised to seek professional advice and counselling. A change in individual circumstance is often elevated into a problem that requires professional support. Transition counsellors specialise in offering support to individuals embarking on a new phase in their lives. 'The counselling team are fully aware of the importance of managing transition and are here to help you find the way ahead', acclaims the University of Bath counselling service on its website. As illustrations of the kind of transitions that might require professional support, it mentions entering university as a first-year undergraduate, the move of second-year students from campus-based residence to living in town, final-year students returning after being away on placement and newly arrived postgraduate students. 'It could be that feelings of self-confidence are quite threatened by the unfamiliarity of new surroundings and new people', warns the service.[9] Transition counselling was also proposed for hereditary peers to help them face the trauma of losing their seats when the House of Lords was reorganised.[10] Athletes who retire from competition face the 'onset of post-sporting depression' caused by the 'failure to adjust emotionally to life without competition and the built-in adrenaline rush', argues Dr Chris Riddoch, an academic based at Bristol University.[11] And of course they need counselling. Throughout the Anglo-American world, universities report a massive increase in the number of students seeking counselling. For example, both Columbia University and the State University of New York reported a 40 per cent increase in the numbers of students seeking on-campus help for depression and anxiety, as well as schizophrenia, bipolar, obsessive–compulsive and panic disorders in 2002.[12]

The problems of transition facing university students and British aristocrats pale into insignificance compared to those facing the military. Increasingly, new recruits into the American military machine are regarded as emotionally vulnerable people. Recruits are provided with access to CARE counsellors and like students at Bath University are offered counselling about such transition problems as how to deal with loneliness and making friends.[13] Those involved in making the transition from combat to duties in peacetime are deemed to face even greater damaging psychological outcomes. A recent study published by researchers from Yale University calls for transition counselling following exposure to combat on the grounds that this experience 'contributed significantly to the likelihood of current post-traumatic disorder, major depressive disorder, drug and alcohol abuse, unemployment, job loss, separation or divorce, and abuse of a partner or spouse'.[14]

One of the most dramatic manifestations of the perception of human vulnerability is the growing sense of being ill. Even occupations that demand physical resilience and fortitude have been plagued by the growth of illness. In August 2002, it was revealed that more than one in ten of Britain's soldiers were unfit to go into battle. More than 750 sailors attached to the Royal Navy were reported to be suffering from maladies such as sea-sickness in small boats. It was also noted that 2,500 air force personnel were unfit to take to the air.[15] Even the SAS, Britain's elite military unit, appears be afflicted by the plight of emotional injury. In August

2001, it was reported that SAS soldiers were campaigning for resources to set up their own counselling centre in order to reduce the number of suicides and jail sentences involving distressed former troopers. The stress of secret operations was blamed for an escalation of suicides and outbursts of violent rage by former members of this regiment.[16] 'CopShock' is the term used by Allen Kates to describe the experience of trauma suffered by police personnel. He claims that as many as 'one in three cops' may suffer from PTSD.[17] Mental health problem prevalence rates of one in three and one in four is often attributed to different groups of emergency workers.[18] According to a recent study, mental disorders, such as depression and substance-abuse problems, are among the most common illnesses in the US armed services. By 1995, mental disorders had become the second-leading cause of hospitalisation of active military personnel. Studies also showed that military personnel were much more likely to leave the service after treatment for mental health conditions, compared with a physical ailment.[19] In recent years, people who work in emergency services have been represented as individuals who are particularly susceptible to post-traumatic stress because of the nature of their work. Proponents of the condition of emergency service stress claim that emergency personnel face a significant risk of suffering from post-traumatic stress through witnessing the pain of others. In the very act of helping victims of an emergency, people risk becoming traumatised by the pain of others.[20] So police officers who rescued injured fans during the 1989 Hillsborough football disaster have won a battle for compensation for being mentally traumatised whilst carrying out their duties.[21]

It is not simply the experience of combat or shoot-outs with criminals that are perceived to cause serious mental health problems. According to a recently pub-lished report from the World Health Organization, one in four people around the world suffer from mental illness at some point in their lives. WHO also estimates that mental health disorders will become the second most common cause of death and disability by 2020.[22] One mass survey found that one in four British lesbian and gay men sought professional help for mental illness because of their sexuality.[23] Caring for an ill or disabled family member can lead to an emotional health problem. A study supported by the US National Institute on Aging found that women providing care were more likely to suffer from emotional distress than those who did not.[24] Housework, too, makes women depressed. A study conducted by Professor Nanette Mitrie of the University of Glasgow concluded that 'the more housework you do, the more depression you report'.[25] A survey carried out by the British Medical Association indicated that stress caused by excessive workload made 25 per cent of general practitioners want to quit the National Health Service.[26] Over 90 per cent of British school pupils suffer from school-related stress claimed a survey in September 2002.[27] Numerous mental health advocates claim that Christmas causes large numbers of people to feel stressed and anxious. Dr Donald Dossey of an Internet-based 'stress management centre' argues that 90 per cent of the US population suffers from holiday fears and stress around Christmas. 'Bulimia reaches an all-time high over Christmas', says the UK Eating Disorders Centre, 'with people throwing up all the time and some resorting to cutting themselves'.

A survey carried out by the Samaritans charity in Ireland found that 56 per cent of the population felt stressed and/or depressed by the pressures associated with the Christmas and New Year period. 'Holiday stress push many to the edge', warns *The Las Vegas Sun* in its discussion of how depression 'plagues the yuletide season'. Mental health advocates contend that we are experiencing an epidemic of depression – and not just at Christmas. 'Every indication suggests that more people are depressed, more of the time, more severely, and starting earlier in their lives' argues Richard O'Connor, the American author of *Undoing Depression* (1997).[28] Not surprisingly a recent study of American college students found that between 1989 and 2001, the percentage of students treated for depression doubled as did the percentage of suicidal students.[29]

The construction of mental health problems is intimately linked to a cultural perspective that regards most forms of the human experience as the source of emotional distress. The assumption implicit in this representation of the human condition is that psychological survival is the principal issue facing individuals in society. Increasingly emotional well-being is represented as the fundamental problem of health. *The Surgeon General's Report on Mental Health* in 1999 stated that 'among developed nations, including the US, major depression is the leading cause of disability'.[30] The prominence given to mental health is also justified on the ground that physical disease is often caused by emotional distress. In Britain, the 1998 Government green paper *Our Healthier Nation* signalled the reorientation of the NHS from physical health to emotional well-being. The paper defined health in the language of therapeutics as 'being confident and positive and able to cope with the ups and downs of life'.[31] Advocates of this approach claim that 'initiatives which aim to promote physical well-being to the exclusion of mental and social well-being may be doomed to failure'.[32]

It is now common to represent emotional injury to the individual as more damaging than a physical one. Campaigners against domestic violence against men contend that in most cases 'men are more deeply affected by emotional abuse than physical abuse'.[33] It is argued that even relatively insignificant episodes of physical trauma can cause intense psychological damage. According to one account, 'the psychological aspects of trauma may be important even when injury seems trivial'. As a result, 'disability may become greater than might be expected from the severity of the physical injuries'.[34] The belief that relatively routine forms of physical injuries may cause serious psychological damage to the individual often informs the response of health professionals to the management of accidents and disasters.

It is worth noting that until the late 1970s, post-disaster rehabilitation programmes focused on tackling infrastructural and housing problems and on community organisation. It is only since the 1970s that therapeutic intervention has come to play a prominent role in disaster management.[35] During the past decade, it is the psychological damage caused by disasters that has become the focus of attention. This emphasis was clearly evident in the aftermath of 9/11 and the Oklahoma bombing. But this approach also characterises the response to natural disasters, even in circumstances where there is no loss of life and minimal physical injury. So the long-term damage caused by the 1999–2000 floods in Britain tended to be presented through the prism of therapeutics. The *British Medical Journal*'s editorial, 'Flooding and human health; the dangers posed are not always obvious', is paradigmatic of this approach. It stated that the 'long-term effects of flooding on psychological health may perhaps be even more important than illness or injury'. Why? Because 'for most people the emotional trauma continues long after the water has receded'. It added, 'making repairs, cleaning up, and dealing with insurance claims can be stressful' and warned that 'if there is a lack of support during the recovery process, stress levels may increase further'.[36] A year later, a study commissioned by the Environment Agency noted that families whose homes were flooded 3 years previously were still suffering from a variety of illnesses. It reported that some of the people affected suffered from colds, skin problems and upset stomachs. However, these complaints appeared to be relatively minor compared to the psychological damage experienced. According to the study, many were displaying symptoms – increased stress levels, sleep disorder, anxiety – of common mental disorders associated with undergoing a traumatic event.[37]

The concept of psychological damage is informed by a cultural sensibility that regards emotional problems as far more debilitating than hitherto recognised. There is a widely held assumption that once damaged, an injury to the emotion can never be put quite right. Since these are invisible injuries, there is considerable scope for the exercise of the cultural imagination. The title of David Kinchin's book, *Post-Traumatic Stress Disorder: The Invisible Injury*, points to a world of pain beyond the perception of the eye. Terms like 'scarred for life', used to describe the experience of trauma, ominously convey the implication of a life sentence. This sentiment continually informs interpretations of the problems of childhood. Contemporary depictions of childhood send out a powerful message that psychological damage will continue to haunt adulthood. This alarmist account of childhood trauma is not confined to popular culture. Professionals continually bombard parents with warnings about the manifold risks facing the emotional development of their children.[38] Infant mental health has become a respectable professional specialism in the US and the ethos of 'early intervention' has gained influence on both sides of the Atlantic. The promotion of early intervention is guided by research that suggests 'that the most effective time – sometimes the only time – to take action is during babyhood'. It is claimed that after the first 2 years of a child's life it may be too late to prevent children from suffering psychological damage.[39]

One of the most extraordinary developments during the past 25 years has been the acceptance of an ever-widening definition of psychological distress. Recent decades have seen the discovery of an unprecedented number of new types of illnesses. This is the age of traumas, syndromes, disorders and addictions. The diagnosis of PTSD, depression, addiction, chronic fatigue syndrome, attention deficit hyperactivity disorder (ADHD), multiple personality disorder (MPD) are being applied to a wide section of the population. In the early 1970s, MPD was a rare diagnosis – less than a dozen cases in the previous years. By the 1990s, thousands of people were diagnosed as multiples. Alcoholism was initially represented as the disease of the addicted individual. Since the 1980s, the children of alcoholics, their partners and carers are diagnosed as codependent. At the same time, traditional illnesses associated with the emotion, such as depression, have been elaborated and redefined to encompass a far larger constituency of people than hitherto imagined. Once primarily associated with women, depression is now represented as an infirmity that also afflicts children, students and men. Until recently, the diagnosis of ADHD was confined to children. It has now been reinvented as a condition that afflicts adults. This elaboration of the impact of mental disorders is paralleled by the growth in the number of routine experiences that are said to cause psychological damage.

The relationship between the narrative of illness transmitted through therapeutic culture and its impact on people is a dialectical one. The narrative of illness does not simply frame the way people are expected to feel and experience problems – it also constitutes an invitation to infirmity. Take the growing phenomenon of stressed-out children. A recent survey in the UK discovered that children as young as 8 described themselves as 'stressed by relationships and school'. The study found 'unprecedented levels of stress in Britons of all ages; and "worryingly" high levels among children'. Professor Stephen Palmer of City University, who led the study, was 'surprised by the extent of the problem'. He added that, 'if you had asked 8-year-olds about stress 20 years ago, they would have looked blank', whereas 'now they understand the concept and a significant number report experiencing it'.[40] The fact that 20 years ago 8-year-old children would have not understood the meaning of stress, but they do so today, is a testimony to the impact of therapeutic ethos on the popular imagination. The representation of children's lives through the vocabulary of psychology inexorably leads to a situation where young people begin to make sense of their behaviour through it. Through concepts like stress, children become educated to make sense of the problems they experience. Through medicalising children's emotional upheaval, young people are trained to regard troublesome experiences as the source of illness for which help needs to be found.

Adults, like children, are continually invited to make sense of their troubles through the medium of therapeutics. Take the experience of crime. The belief that the impact of crime has a major influence on people's emotional life is a relatively recent one. Back in the 1970s, crime surveys tended to suggest that the impact of most crime on the victim was superficial and of relatively short duration. The first British crime survey indicated that only 2 to 5 per cent of its respondents were still 'very much' or 'quite a lot' affected by their experience of crime.[41] But during the past 25 years, criminologists have adopted a radically different interpretation of the effects of victimisation. Most studies highlight the acute stress, trauma and psychological damage suffered by victims of more serious crime. Paradoxically, those victims who claim that they are all right and do not feel traumatised are often described as being in a state of denial about their true conditions.

Concern with trauma suffered by a victim has been gradually extended to family members, friends and eyewitnesses of the incident of victimisation. Members of a family of the direct victim are often referred to as indirect victims. Victim advocates argue that family members and sometimes friends must be given access to therapeutic services and other resources. People who witness a crime or who are simply aware that something untoward has happened to someone they know are often represented as potential indirect victims. The concept of the indirect victim allows for a tremendous inflation of the numbers who are entitled to claim therapeutic support. This was the outlook that influenced the British government's law reform body, the Law Commission, when it recommended in March 1998 that people who suffer mental illness after witnessing or hearing of a relative's death, even on television or radio should have the right to compensation.[42]

Today's unprecedented cultural sensitivity to the vulnerability of people to emotional injury is underwritten by a distinct outlook about the workings of human subjectivity and personhood. Prevailing attitudes about the state of people's emotions can be understood through the concept of ethnopsychology. 'Every culture contains a set of ideas and beliefs about the nature of human beings, what motivates them to act, the way they perceive the world, how their minds work, and the emotions that are natural to them', writes Hewitt in his description of the concept of ethnopsychology.[43] Ideas about emotion, individual behaviour and vulnerability are underpinned by the particular account that a culture offers about personhood and the human potential. As Derek Summerfield asserts, such accounts embody questions as 'how much or what kind of adversity a person can face and still be "normal"; what is a reasonable risk; when fatalism is appropriate and when a sense of grievance is, what is acceptable behaviour at a time of crisis, including how distress should be expressed, how help should be sought, and whether restitution should be made'.[44]

People's perception of their ability to cope with the problems of life is shaped by the particular account that their culture offers about nature of the human potential. Individuals make sense of their experiences through reflecting on their specific circumstances and in line with the expectations transmitted through prevailing cultural norms. The consciousness of the self is the negotiation of individual experience and cultural norms. People have no inner desire to perceive themselves as ill. However, powerful cultural signals provide the public with a ready-made therapeutic explanation of their troubles. And once the diagnosis of illness is systematically offered as an interpretative guide for making sense of distress, people are far more likely to perceive themselves as ill. Government officials have been shocked to discover that between 1985 and 1996, there has been a 40 per cent increase in the number of British people who consider themselves disabled. According to the survey, amongst the 16–19 age group, the increase is an astounding 155 per cent! The authors of the survey have concluded that the difference between 1985 and 1996 figures 'appear too large to be explained by a real increase in the prevalence of disability' but are at a loss to explain why more and more people are so enthusiastic about embracing the disabled label.[45] The explanation for this trend does not lie in the field of epidemiology, but in the realm of a culture that invites people to classify themselves as infirm. It is important to stress that how people cope with painful encounters is strongly influenced by cultural and historical factors that shape the way people make sense of them. Such cultural factors may increase or reduce the ability of the individual to cope with adverse circumstances. As Wainwright and Calnan point out, today's cultural influences – 'the aggrandisement of victimhood, a lowering of expectations about human competence and agency and an increasing reliance on therapeutic intervention' – amounts to a 'diminution of the self, which accentuates human frailty and vulnerability'.[46] Not surprisingly, feeling ill becomes normal when so much of people's experience is framed from the perspective of vulnerability.

The constant problematisation of human emotion inexorably leads to its recycling in a disease form. And once painful responses are culturally validated in a disease form they will – sooner or later – be experienced as such. The distinct contribution of therapeutic culture's narrative of illness is to establish psychological damage as the most likely outcome of distressful episodes.

The transformation of distress into a condition of emotional injury has as its premise the belief that people are likely to be damaged by unpleasant encounters and the setbacks thrown up by everyday life. Trauma has become an all-purpose term to describe the individual's state of mind in the aftermath of an adverse experience. The portrayal of psychological damage as a long-term affliction flows from a lack of belief in the capacity of people to cope with the experience of misfortune. Distress is not something to be lived, but a condition that requires treatment. The rendering of inner pain into a mental disorder alters the relationship between the individual and the experience of misfortune. According to this version of personhood, the individual lacks the power to deal with the trials of life. The state of vulnerability has become the defining feature of personhood entitling the individual to demand help and support from professional experts. As Lasch notes, the 'dominant conception of personality sees the self as a helpless victim of external circumstances'.[47]

From the standpoint of therapeutic culture, the integrity of the person is threatened through exposure to adversity. As Craib argued, this 'difficulty in accepting depression, despair and conflict – in a word disappointment – as part of life', represents a significant 'inhibition of the self'.[48] The tendency to inflate the problem of emotional vulnerability and to minimise the ability of the person to cope with distressful episodes runs counter to the therapeutic idealisation of the self-determining individual. However, in reality the rhetoric of therapeutic self-determination never granted individuals the right to determine their lives. Self-discovery through a professional intermediary is justified by the assumption that individuals are helpless to confront problems on their own. According to the therapeutic version of personhood, people are not so much the authors, but the victims of their circumstance.

Victims of circumstance

With such high rates of prevalence of illness and damaged emotions, the ideals of therapeutic self-determination are negated by a powerful cultural narrative of human helplessness. At least one leading psychologist – Martin Seligman of the University of Pennsylvania – takes the view that the influence of a narrative that instructs people 'that there is nothing that they can do' actually has the effect of robbing people of their ability to deal with distress. According to Seligman, the epidemic of depression in the US is partly attributable to this 'learned helplessness'. He contends that 'if you have someone who believes they are a victim and there is nothing they can do and they're helpless, you have someone who is set up for depression'.[49]

Therapeutic culture does not merely instruct people to resign themselves to a state of helplessness it also advises the public how to make sense of it. The victim personifies the intense powerlessness of the vulnerable self. This subjectivity is ratified by the belief that our actions are subject to powerful forces outside our control. In the past this sense of powerlessness was explained as a result of socially determined circumstances – due to a collective condition experienced by all. Today, such explanations are far more individualised – they relate to the self's vulnerability to long-term psychological damage caused by parents, lovers, partners and friends.

With emotional vulnerability a principal feature of the human condition, the ideals of self-determination and of resilience assume a marginal role. As the sense of being the author of one's destiny loses cultural support, it has become acceptable to account for failure, mistakes and antisocial behaviour through a diagnosis that absolves individuals of responsibility for their predicament. There are no longer sinners only addictive personalities. Take lust. Those who would have previously been called lustful are now described as 'addicted' to sex and in need of therapy. The American Association on Sexual Problems has estimated that between 10 and 15 per cent of all Americans – around 25 million people – are addicted to sex. Through the confessions of a number of high profile sex addicts – David Duchovny, Michael Douglas – what used to be called promiscuity has acquired a high profile medical label. Friends and former lovers of Bill Clinton have also jumped on the band wagon and assert that he too is the victim of this addiction. Organisations like Sex Addicts Anonymous insist that this condition is very difficult to cure. This point was affirmed in a report, written by US doctor Martha Turner, who claimed that sex addiction is the hardest psychological illness to treat, with high relapse rates and low levels of recovery. So what can you do? 'Your sexual behaviour is out of control and you want to get help' is the advice of Spirit of Recovery, an on-line organisation offering therapeutic advice.

The sentiment that 'helpless people' cannot 'help it' now influences perceptions of misdeeds. It is not simply ordinary people whose misdeeds are seen to be caused by their vulnerability. Politicians and priests are cast in the role of vulnerability in face of temptation. It is the presupposition of such vulnerability that informs the adoption of new codes of practices guiding the behaviour of religious pastors with their flock. The language of church codes synthesises the traditional theme of temptation with 'victim speak' regarding the vulnerability of its priests and parishioners. Church codes do not merely seek to protect the innocent, but also to explain that errant clerics' behaviour is often the outcome of their unique vulnerability.

The report of the Diocese of Oxford claims that 'every person with pastoral responsibility' is 'vulnerable'. It suggests that it precisely those who believe that they are 'unlikely to fall into the temptation to abuse another' who are most vulnerable because 'their guard is lowered'.[50] This perspective situates clerical misbehaviour in the wider context of therapeutic culture. This outlook influenced some participants in the controversy around the US Catholic Church's recent paedophile scandal. According to William Butler, a Boston-based priest accused of sexual abuse, many of his paedophile colleagues were young priests whose 'emotions' were not 'developed'. 'All of a sudden you're cast out into a world and you're still searching for your own understanding of sexuality and intimacy issues', he pleaded.[51] A.W. Sipe, a retired La Jolla, California, psychotherapist and ex-priest, took the view that young priests are 'vulnerable' and that psychological research shows that 'sexual deprivation can lead a person to turn to children'.[52]

That religious figures are prepared to embrace a feeble standard of moral responsibility indicates that no institution remains immune to the influence of therapeutic culture. Until recently, clerics accepted the ideal of subordinating their selves to a higher purpose. These days – at least for some clerics – the focus has shifted to a preoccupation with their own emotional injury. Christian counsellors frequently raise concern about the difficulty that clerics experience in coping with the demands of their ministry. One survey argued that in Britain, 38 per cent of the pastors it interviewed felt 'overwhelmed by pastoral care demands'. The survey noted that of all the problems, concern with stress came top. Most of the problems mentioned focused on 'psychological states (like stress, depression, loneliness and unforgiveness) and on life transitions (like marriage guidance and bereavement)'.[53] In the US, the Southern Baptist Convention has created the Wounded Heroes programmes to deal with the 'toll of depression in their ranks'. The convention estimates that one-third of the staff and clergy of the 62,000 Baptist churches 'suffer from depression because their jobs are so demanding'.[54] The Clergy Consultation Service of the New Jersey-based Kairos Institute provides counselling for ministers and their families.[55]

Disenchanted clerics have reinvented themselves as victims and have set up support groups to promote their cause. They bitterly accuse their former employers for causing psychological damage. The website of BALM – Bullied and Abused Lives in Ministry – A Christian Support group for damaged ministers, international and inter-denominational – literally flaunts the emotional scars of its members. The support group is run by Pauline and Arthur Kennedy, who claim that 'as a result of being bullied, we are no longer engaged in any active ministry'. They add,

We are both suffering psychiatric stress injuries including:

- Post-traumatic stress disorder
- Reactive depression
- Chronic fatigue.

As from 1 January 2002, Arthur is retiring from ministry on to a disability pension.[56]

In the United States, disenchanted religious pastors receive counselling from support groups devoted to helping victims of religious addiction. That religious commitment can be depicted as an addiction indicates that when it comes to handling distress and disappointment, clerics are no less vulnerable than their flock. They too are victims of circumstances beyond their control.

In some instances church officials cannot resist the temptation of evading responsibility for the consequences of clerical abuse by arguing that the perpetrator was himself a victim of such abuse. This was the approach taken by the Catholic Archdiocese of Birmingham when it rejected compensation claims made by victims of a paedophile priest. It argued that Father Eric Taylor, jailed in April 1998 for 7 years after being convicted for 18 assaults on young boys, had been deeply affected by 'deprivations suffered as a prisoner of war'.[57]

Those who suffered at Father Taylor's hands were outraged by the Birmingham Archdiocese's letter and argued that it insulted anyone who fought in the war, since it implied that 'they may turn out to be paedophiles'. Whilst this reaction to the church's attempt to deflect responsibility is understandable, the Birmingham Archdiocese was merely following a route, well established in the secular world. According to conventional wisdom, the victimiser often turns out to be a former victim of a psychologically damaging act of abuse. This was the argument that Ron Davies, the disgraced former British Secretary of State, used to justify his run-in with the police in November 1998. He told Parliament that he was brutally beaten by his father as a child and added, 'we are what we are'. He informed the press that he suffered from a 'compulsive disorder', which was caused by a 'troubled, violent and emotionally dysfunctional childhood'.[58] Hillary Clinton, the USA's former first lady, clearly echoed this sentiment when she informed her interviewer that her husband's philandering was the outcome of the psychological abuse that he suffered as a child. 'He was so young, barely 4, when he was scarred by abuse', she insisted during the summer of 1999. Clearly, if priests like Father Taylor 'can't help it', what can we expect of lay politicians like Clinton or Davies? In the United States, abuse excuses for criminal actions are often used during court proceedings. In some of the most sensational court proceedings, such as the Menendez brothers murder trial in Beverly Hills in 1993 and the Lorena Bobbitt trial in Virginia in 1994, the defence lawyers blamed their clients' behaviour on the emotional injury they suffered, respectively, on battered child syndrome and battered women syndrome.[59]

The linkage drawn between the act of abuse with the previous experience of psychological damage represents a fundamental statement about the contemporary human condition. The outlook that links Father Taylor's sexual assaults of young boys with his prior experience of abuse is based on the thesis that human beings are simply too weak to overcome the effects of their psychic injury and often go on to damage others. From this perspective, emotional damage is represented as both a life sentence and a prelude to further acts of victimisation. Professional experts on abuse continually stress the long-term effects of the experience. It is held to be a life sentence for the victim. This model informs the literature on bullying. Bullying has left 'scars' on the minds of the victims. Little can be done to eradicate this spiritual mutilation. 'Very few children escape the experience of victimisation unaffected', concluded a study of child victims. A similar conclusion was drawn by a study entitled 'Peer rejection places children at immediate, long-term behavioural risk'. It argued that the long-term effects of peer rejection were delinquency, dropping out of school and psychopathology. Writing in the same vein, the authors of a study of adults with a history of child sexual abuse concluded that they are 'severely damaged people', who use the health services much more than other adults. It appears that 'more of them have weight problems, misuse alcohol and drugs and have irritable bowel syndrome'.[60]

The diagnosis of long-term effect of psychological damage has gained respectability from the influential 'cycle of abuse' theories. This model of the intergenerational transmission of violence is one of the uncontested themes of the family violence literature. Those who uphold this thesis see abuse as an intergenerational disease. Abusers were themselves abused when they were children, and their victims will go on to manifest delinquent behaviour. Thus abuse does not end with a victim; it has a life of its own, which is then transmitted to future generations.

Cycle of abuse theories offer a strikingly fatalistic account of the human condition. Its widespread influence is symptomatic of society's pessimism regarding the human potential. At no time since the emergence of modernity has the latitude for human action and control been so strongly denied as today. Influential currents in the therapeutic profession, such as the advocates of codependency, continually affirm the powerlessness of the individual. An important study of the codependency movement argues that from the standpoint of this institution, problems such as 'incest, the various forms of abuse, and criminality are all instances of "unmanageable" behaviour resulting from people's "powerlessness" over their own actions'.[61] This inflation of human powerlessness symbolises a new diminished concept of the self. This model has as its premise the belief that human action is continually subject to powerful forces beyond its control. Such a fatalistic worldview is often conveyed through the proposition that the experience of psychological damage in early childhood directly determines many of the actions of adults for life.

Codependency literature offers an unambiguous variant of the thesis that human identity is the direct outcome of early childhood experience. As Rice, in his study of this movement, notes, proponents of codependency contend that 'childhood experience does not merely shape, but unequivocally determines identity'.[62] The corollary of the importance attached to the childhood experience is a version of adulthood where control and autonomy are conspicuously absent. That is why in contemporary therapeutic literature the line that divides children from adults is difficult to discern. The concept of the adult child is emblematic of this infantilised version of the self. The tendency to collapse the distinction between childhood and adult experience is strikingly manifested in codependency literature. Rice points out that supporters of the codependency movement speak 'of everything that has happened as the inevitable consequence' of their childhood experience. In their language they are 'living the script' created in their childhood.[63]

The notion that adults are merely acting out a script set in motion during their childhood has encouraged people to continually look for clues about their lives in the past. Accordingly, the key to understanding the adult self lies somewhere in childhood or beyond. Primal therapy and past life therapy are oriented towards the extraction of existential meaning through the process of moral archaeology. Contemporary society accords unusual insights to the recovery of memory, and the recovered memory movement never fails to discover acts injurious to the psyche, which are said to account for the adult's predicament.[64] Consequently, in contemporary culture, self-identity is based less and less on what people do and know about themselves than about what they can no longer remember. Hence, the privileged role assigned to therapy for uncovering the lost identity of the self. On it own, a diminished self is seen to be incapable of understanding its inner essence and adults need professional help in their search in their past for unravelling the sources of their present misery.

The importance attached to the character-forming role of childhood and even prechildhood experience is based on a highly deterministic perspective of the human condition. It suggests that people's adult existence is predetermined by their childhood experience. The many experiences we have as adults pale into insignificance compared to an act of abuse we experience as children. As in a Greek tragedy, through our life we simply realise our fate. People are encouraged to see themselves as victims of family life, rather than as self-determining agents. This renunciation of self-determination coincides with a dramatic reconceptualisation of the adult self. It is a weak or diminished self, which is explicitly disassociated from many of the historically idealised characteristics linked to adulthood: moral autonomy, maturity and responsibility. As one critic of this movement comments, codependency literature 'depersonalises the responsibility for pathologic behaviour'.[65]

The codependence model offers only an extreme variant of how therapeutic culture conceptualises the relationship between the individual and society. Whether the self is presented as diseased, abused, weak or just vulnerable, it can do little to reverse the destructive consequences of psychological damage, particularly when they occur in childhood. This fatalistic premise of the irreversibility of damaged childhood has acquired the status of a religious truth. To challenge this premise is to risk accusations of sacrilege. And yet the cycle of abuse thesis is open to serious interrogation. The view that violence breeds violence is based on retrospective studies. Such studies often depend on comparing aggressive and nonaggressive adolescents and men to see if those who are aggressive were more likely to be abused when they were young. There are many problems with such studies. The status that one assigns to recollection is one area of contention. How and what people remember is influenced by their predicament.

Another fundamental weakness of cycle of violence studies is the causal relationship drawn between the experience of childhood abuse and the subsequent act of adult abuse. Is this a direct causal relationship? Was this experience of violence the cause of subsequent adult violent behaviour or are there other influences that shaped the response? To abstract one variable – abuse – and construct a direct lineage with future acts of abuse is to ignore a variety of social phenomena that influences human behaviour. A review of longitudinal studies of the outcomes of child abuse by Joan Kaufman and Edward Zigler found that more than 70 per cent of all abused children did not mistreat their offspring. 'Hardly an inevitable "cycle"', commented the psychologist Carol Tavris.[66]

The thesis of long-term damage of child abuse was also tested in a study by Bruce Rind and Philip Tromovitch. Rind and Tromovitch's study raises important questions about the consensus which causally links child sexual abuse to long-term psychological maladjustment. They have concluded that only a small proportion of such cases are permanently harmed and that a 'substantially greater proportion of females than males perceive harm from these experiences'. At the very least, such differential responses to the experience of abuse raises important questions about its causal connection with long-term harm. Rind and Tromovitch note the tendency of sex abuse researchers to exaggerate the harmful consequences of the experience.[67] It is also possible that this tendency is premised on the prior assumption about the irreversibility of emotional damage. This is an assumption which is spontaneously generated by a society obsessed about the diseased character of the self. The cycle of abuse thesis gives a new definition to powerlessness. Unlike traditional notions of harm, it is no longer seen as a one-off act. The damage caused by abuse lingers on in the body and the psyche of the victim. Moreover, the effects are so significant as to influence virtually every aspect of life of the survivor. Addictions, eating disorders and phobias are manifestations of this life sentence.

It is worth noting that the cycle of abuse thesis was constructed on the basis of speculation rather than empirical research. Hacking's study of the politics of memory notes that this a priori assumption was initially heavily qualified in the first papers on the subject. But soon the bold statement 'abused as a child, abusive as a parent' acquired widespread currency. The swift transformation of speculative opinion into a 'scientific truth' was supported by the contention that it is the childhood experience which forms the adult. Hacking also believes that this view was also strengthened by the opportunism of abusive parents who 'profess having been abused as a child' since 'that explains and thereby mitigates the behaviour'.[68] But above all, it is society's affirmation for the idea of the toxic effects of psychological damage that has helped transform a cultural prejudice into a rarely contested truth.

The fetish of addiction

Throughout history, sceptics have raised questions about the scope for human potential. However, today such scepticism is not confined to small groups of critics but dominates intellectual and cultural life. The intensely fatalistic interpretation of the human condition projects a highly deterministic vision of individual life. One unfortunate consequence of this view is the proclivity to belittle the possibility of people being able to take control over their lives. As a result, in many areas of life, human behaviour is seen to have little to do with conscious choice. Emotional determinism acquires its most striking cultural manifestation in the addict. Through the concept of addiction, therapeutic culture makes sense of its feeble version of the self. The compulsive behaviour of the addict extends the idea that people cannot help but act out the script assigned to them in childhood.

The consciousness of powerlessness acquires cultural meaning through the fetish of addiction. Compulsive behaviour is frequently interpreted as both proof of prior emotional injury and as warning of future offences. One leading victimologist explicitly links acts of victimisation to addictive behaviour on the fatalistic premise that today's offenders are yesterday's victims.[69] The addictive personality represents a crystallisation of powerlessness. It is a personality that is driven towards actions over which little control can be exercised. Addiction plays the role of a cultural fetish through which society makes sense of diverse forms of behaviour. In attributing so much of human behaviour to this fetish, therapeutic culture demeans the potential for human action.

The fetishisation of human behaviour through addiction involves the alienation of the self from the consequences of its action. The world-view represented through addiction encourages people to regard personal problems as having an existence outside their selves, rooted in some medical condition. Like a disease that infects an individual, addiction is a harm that befalls them. The intensity of dysfunctional behaviour resulting from addiction are attributed to the strength of the disease. The person simply cannot help it. It is worth noting that, fortunately, this negation of the human subjectivity also flies in the face of everyday experience. As one critic of the narrative of addiction points out, 'people regularly quit smoking, cut back drinking, lose weight, improve their health, create healthy love relationships, raise strong and happy children and contribute to communities and combat wrong – all without expert interventions'.[70]

In previous times, addiction was linked almost entirely to physical dependency on alcohol or drugs. Addictions were related to carefully defined biologically based cravings. The term 'physical dependency' suggested that a particular compulsive habit was driven by forces independent of individual control. Today, the variety of biological factors allegedly causing compulsive behaviour has expanded dramatically. But more significantly, the meaning of addiction itself has changed. Most of the recently discovered addictions – Internet addiction syndrome, compulsive gambling, workaholism, compulsive shopping disorder, sex addiction, codependence – have no basis in biology. These are addictions of the emotion – the medical label 'impulse-control disorder' is increasingly used by psychiatrists to describe what they regard as compulsive addictions.

Society has become so hooked on addiction because it has lost the ability to imagine people who can behave in ways which they can act as authors of their destiny. The pervasive consciousness of vulnerability, discussed previously, has fostered a climate where people are not expected to exercise control over significant aspects of their lives. This essentially self-limiting outlook is continually drawn towards a fatalistic interpretation of behaviour. Society's embrace of addiction represents an abandonment of a standard of accountability usually associated with the Enlightenment concept of human choice. The self-determining individual was always an idealised representation of existence, but it provided a standard for understanding human behaviour. Today, the ideal of the self-determining individual has given way to a more modest interpretation of subjectivity and the pathology of addiction provides a new standard for illuminating behaviour.

The inability of individuals to control their lives assumes the character of a self-evident truth in the narrative of addiction. It is almost as if it is expected that people are potentially the slaves of very new innovation. Every new innovation brings fears of a new breed of addicts. No sooner was the National Lottery launched in the UK than experts were warning of a nation hooked on gambling. 'Britain is producing a generation hooked on the lottery and fruit machines', warned the front page of the *Daily Mail*.[71] The compulsive mobile phone user and the obsessive cake eater are joined every month by a new cohort of addicts. Even working out in the gym is no longer seen as unequivocally healthy and worthy of encouragement. Recently, American psychologists have decided that men who compulsively work out are in fact suffering from 'muscle dysmorphia'. And women who spend too much time in the gym are labelled 'exercise addicts'. 'We treat exercise addicts no differently from any other addicts', notes Andrew Vincent, the addictions treatment programme manager at the Priory Hospital in Sturt, Surrey. Vincent adds, 'they would be in group therapy with alcoholics, drug addicts, shopping addicts and all kinds of other addicts, because it boils down to the same thing – a way of avoiding emotional pain and events'.[72]

The medicalisation of bad habits has important consequences for the way that society judges behaviour. It is difficult to hold people to account if they suffer from one of a number of impulse-control disorders. On the contrary, rather than being condemned for their behaviour, such addicts are represented as victims of circumstances beyond their control and therefore worthy of our sympathy. New categories of addiction validate the claim that the individuals who suffer from these conditions are not responsible for their behaviour. Such a diagnosis directly calls into question an ethic of responsibility and, as Downs argues, they 'unnecessarily compromise the presumption of individual responsibility upon which legal and equal citizenship rest'.[73]

The assumption of powerlessness is central to the newly reconfigured self. The discourse of addiction and victimisation is focused on survival rather than on the drive to realise potential. The defining feature of the addict becomes his or her passive side. Thus, the subject is continually distanced from the 'problem' and individual action has only a minimal role in shaping life. Not surprisingly, the significance of motive and character are constantly diminished. This is a misanthropic view of the world which undermines elementary notions of individual autonomy. The new knowledge is dubious about people's ability to cope with the problems of everyday life. It seems that people's attempts to cope with the demands of life are doomed to fail. Terms like 'on their own' or 'coping alone' serve as health warnings against the attempt to deal with personal and emotional problems. The inadequacy of the individual is often contrasted with the special skills and resources which many encounters are presumed to demand. The variety of encounters and experiences which are said to overwhelm the individual has increased enormously in recent decades. Even some of the most elementary adult roles such as parenting have been redefined as skills requiring professional support. From this perspective, the attempt to assume a degree of control of one's life becomes a pathetic gesture, for people need help and not independence.

The tendency to regard compulsive behaviour as a relatively normal form of human conduct is a relatively recent development. Back in 1980, an important sociological contribution on this subject observed, 'the concept of compulsive behaviour suggests helplessness and loss of control that is itself an unflattering self-portrait to which many object, better to be thought a sinner, but responsible for myself, than to be the victim of the fates'.[74] Today, the negative cultural representation of compulsive behaviour has been substantially modified, if not entirely normalised. The addiction to sex of Hollywood actors such as Michael Douglas, David Duchovny, Don Johnson or Rob Lowe has not diminished the appeal of these stars. More significantly, there is virtually no moral stigma attached to compulsive behaviour. Addictions are the handiwork of mothers and fathers with poor parenting skills. 'The big empty place that leads to addiction usually starts forming at birth', writes Charlotte Kasl, an American psychologist and healer.[75]

Addiction is often portrayed as a normal problem of existence that afflicts every section of society. Celebrity addicts – Kate Moss, Princess Diana, Kurt Cobain – symbolise the fate that almost no-one can evade. The cultural association of glamour with addiction – heroin chic – signals the message that the state of vulnerability is the norm. In popular culture, the acknowledgement by the addict that he or she has a problem that they cannot manage is often represented as an act of bravery and honesty. Many therapeutic entrepreneurs affirm this sentiment and add that without this act of bravery they simply cannot help the addict.

The representation of the acknowledgement of powerlessness as an act of defiance is culturally shaped by the values that prevail in society. Such an act represents a prelude to a treatment based on the rewriting the narrative of the self. Through the categorical admission of impotence, past events are redefined through the metaphor of an external disease. From this standpoint the problems of the addict are crystallised – but they are crystallised as the inexorable outcome of conditions not of the addict's making. Consequently, powerlessness becomes not merely an episode in one's biography, but the defining condition. From this fatalistic perspective, treatment acquires a passive even fatalistic character. Addicts are told that they will never be completely cured. Moreover, instead of inspiring people to confront their problem through action they are offered the ritual of rewriting their past. There is little scope for changing oneself in a treatment based on the premise that one can never completely overcome addiction, only minimise its significance. For the so-called recovering addict, addiction still remains a defining feature of identity.

Contemporary definitions of addiction elevate the issue of powerlessness in order to underline the claim that no-one can overcome their addiction on their own. Many professionals dealing with codependency and addiction vociferously warn against victims trying to deal with their conditions themselves. Some therapists dismiss individual attempts to overcome addiction and other problems as futile expressions of a 'perfectionist complex'. Avoiding professional treatment serves as proof of the gravity of the problem facing the victim.

According to our cultural script, the role assigned to addicts is to acknowledge that they lack the power to overcome their condition. An acknowledgement of this state of impotence is the point of departure for most therapies offering treatment.

The first step in the well-known 12-step therapy innovated by Alcoholics Anonymous exhorts addicts to admit that they are 'powerless over alcohol' and that they have lost control over managing their lives. Other addiction groups also demand that individuals acknowledge that they are powerless in the face of their addiction. Through this narrative of powerlessness, individuals are expected to come to terms with their diminished selves

The socialisation of the passive subject

The normalisation of addiction has as its premise a radically fatalistic view of the process of socialisation. Addiction, which was once represented as exceptional and rare, is frequently depicted as normal. According to the British advocacy group Action on Addiction, 'almost every one of us has either experienced some form of addiction or knows someone who has'. 'In fact, over one in three adults suffer from some form of addiction', it claims.[76] An American expert on sex addiction believes that 'most women have struggled at some time with various aspects of sexually addictive or sexually codependent behaviour'.[77] With so much of human behaviour catalogued under these labels it becomes evident that far from being an exceptional experience, society itself is inherently addictive. For many writers, human dysfunctions, compulsive behaviour and acts of abuse are products of a society that is inherently addictive. A leading American victimologist argues that 'ours is an addictive society because, in many ways we are taught to depend on large institutions for our ideas, our morality, even our survival'.[78] The term 'addictive society' is a powerful rhetorical device that helps to naturalise human frailty. But it is a rhetorical device rather than a tool of analysis since the alleged connection between what is essentially an act of socialisation and the affliction of an addiction is usually just asserted. It is also ironic that the rhetoric of blaming society for creating dependency is adopted by precisely those people who encourage people to become dependent on therapy. Therapists who continually warn addicts about the dangers of looking for a cure on their own certainly cannot be accused of fostering the spirit of independence.

The contemporary narrative of addiction regards this condition as the direct product of socialisation. This crude model of socialisation, which extinguishes any notion of individual choice, goes way beyond classical sociological theories of society. Classical social theorists – for example, Marx and Weber – have long recognised the important influence of society on shaping individual identity. Other thinkers, like Freud, George Herbert Mead and John Dewey, have claimed that the demands of culture often constrain the self and have a decisive impact on the forging of the identity of the individual. However, these thinkers did not offer a fatalistic formula that denied the potential for individual choice or self-determination. They emphasised the element of interaction where individuals could exercise a degree of individual choice, though often in circumstances not of their own making. From this classical perspective, the self is both the product and producer of social reality. In recent times, this model of interaction has given way to an outlook where the individual is one-sidedly presented as a mere social product, whose action is almost never the outcome of choice, but of compulsion.

In many accounts, the argument that society and culture negates the striving of the self and transforms individuals into addictive personalities is presented in a rhetorical manner. Anne Wilson Schaef's *When Society Becomes An Addict* uses the term as a metaphor for accounting for all forms of social distress. The British commentator Helen Wilkinson points to the work ethic as one of the causes of an 'addictive culture of workaholism'. In the same way, the psychologist Oliver James, claims that abusive parents create children who suffer from what he calls 'emotional addictions'.[79] Neither the work ethic nor abusive parents are recent developments and these theories do little to explain why addiction should become so prevalent in contemporary society. There is considerable evidence that forms of behaviour that are today labelled as addictions – such as drunkenness – were viewed in a different light in the past. Although in colonial America alcohol consumption was higher than today, drinking was informally regulated by the local community and not considered to be a disease. 'When drunkenness did occur, it was the individual, rather than the alcohol, which was seen as the problem', observes Nolan.[80] Moral and medical views of drinking alcohol are bound up with changing cultural norms. The representation of alcoholism as a disease inflicted on the individual by society is influenced by a highly atomised view of the individual self. It is remarkable that the country with the highest per capita alcohol consumption in Europe (Luxembourg) has so few AA groups that it does not bother to list them in any national registries. France consumes the second highest amount of alcohol and only lists seven AA groups per million population. By contrast, the country with the lowest per capita alcohol consumption in Europe (Iceland) has by far the highest density of AA groups (784 per million population).

A more sophisticated version of the addictive society thesis is offered by Anthony Giddens, who claims that the expansion of addiction is the product of a 'post-traditional order'; one where a sense of continuity has become eroded and where individuals are 'obliged to negotiate life-style option'. Giddens is right to emphasise the relationship between the erosion of a system of common belief and the disorganisation of self-identity and its unpredictable impact on behaviour.[81] But whether these changes directly foster a climate of addiction is far from evident. However, the disorganisation of self-identity does help to intensify the sense of individuals vulnerability and powerlessness. Therapeutic culture both reflects and intensifies the disorganisation of self-identity. Through the suspicion it directs towards relations of dependency it encourages the estrangement of individual from a wider network of support. A self directly exposed to external pressure experiences important aspects of life as if it is under siege. The sense of powerlessness that results from the disorganisation of identity creates the condition where a palpable sense of being out of control can be experienced as compulsive behaviour.

The narrative of the addictive society provides an intellectual framework for representing diminished subjectivity. Through situating the roots of addiction within the structures of society, compulsive behaviour becomes normalised. However, through normalising addiction, such narratives provide a one-sidedly passive account of human nature: one that is intensely sceptical about the principal of individual self-determination. This tendency is most pronounced within codependence therapy, where, as Rice points out, it is claimed that mainstream culture is an 'addictive system' that mass produces an 'addictive personality'.[82] In codependence theory, the problems of existence is seamlessly transformed into addictions. This outcome is achieved through the annihilation of any element of self-determination and through the reduction of behaviour to the acting out of a cultural script. The concept of an addictive society is a metaphor of powerlessness that has little to do with a theory of society as such. Typically, it offers little in the way of an analysis of social trends and of changes that have encroached upon the space available for individual autonomy. The concept of the addictive society is actually a metaphor, signifying impotence.

It would be wrong to interpret the concept of an addictive society as a new variant of social determinism. Theories of social determinism have been mobilised in the past to argue that since people are products of society, they cannot be blamed for their actions. There have been many attempts by defence lawyers to try to exonerate the actions of their client by arguing that society is to blame for it. The metaphor of the addictive society represents a statement about individual consciousness and behaviour. It is a statement of individual pathology that masquerades as a critique of society. Society is fatalistically represented as the source of individual pathology but no constructive alternative is proposed to alleviate the condition of addiction. Why? Because, in essence, proponents of the addictive society thesis have very little to say about society. The term 'society' is confusingly used to describe what is actually the domain of interpersonal relations. The content of this critique of society amounts to little more than the condemnation of human pathologies rooted in dysfunctional parenting and destructive relationships. From this perspective, unhealthy relationships 'are even more harmful than the physical effects of addiction'.[83]

Instead of acting as a source of support and strength, human relationships are represented as diminishing the power of the self. Advocates of the fetish of addiction represent personal relationships as the cause of compulsive behaviour. 'How many functional families do you know', demands Anne Wilson Schaef, before asking 'how many perfect families have bit the dust as new information about addictions and codependency has come into common currency?'[84] These rhetorical questions are designed to ridicule the idea of a 'perfect family'. Suspicion towards the conduct of family life is promoted as a more sensible approach towards relations of intimacy. Estranging the self from others is offered as a cure to the disease of existence.

6   The self at risk

The sense of powerlessness assigned to the contemporary self is unprecedented in the age of modernity. The emphasis placed on human vulnerability dooms people to the role of helpless victims of circumstance. This deflation in the status of human subjectivity coincides with the inflation of the threat that external circumstances represent to the integrity of the individual self. 'Psychological trauma is an affliction of the powerless', writes Judith Lewis Herman, before noting that 'it was once believed that such events were uncommon'.[1] Herman's suggestion that traumatic events that incapacitate the individual are more common than previously thought resonates with the therapeutic sensibility. The metaphor of trauma clearly captures the way that therapeutic culture conceptualises the relationship between the self and external reality. The external world is conceptualised as an object over which people can have little control. Through this objectification of social reality people are recast into a powerless role. 'At the moment of trauma, the victim is rendered helpless by overwhelming force', notes Herman.[2] In this scenario, the counterposition of the helpless self to the overwhelming force of the external world helps validate the proposition that people lack the power to make a difference. Today's tendency to interpret events through the prism of trauma serves to cultivate a profound sense fatalism in the public imagination. As Linenthal recorded in his survey of the way that the Oklahoma bombing was internalised by people, the 'traumatic vision' of the event strongly influenced the public's reaction. This 'traumatic vision' revealed a self that was 'intrinsically weak, passive seemingly helpless amid the onslaughts of traumatic events', notes Linenthal.[3]

Therapeutic culture transforms the trauma and profound sense of helplessness recounted by Linenthal into an objective mental health condition. However, a community's sense of helplessness can more usefully be understood as the sentiment of disorientation caused by the difficulty of giving meaning to adverse experience. As Bracken suggests, 'vulnerability with regard to meaningfulness may not simply be the result of trauma but might, in some way, be a predisposing factor for the development of problems after such events'.[4] There is considerable evidence to suggest that communities who possess a robust system of meaning are able to deal remarkably well with disasters and violent conflict. 'Social disintegration increases traumatic stress, while a strong sense of community, like political commitment, enhances the resilience of individuals in the face of danger', writes Vanessa Pupavac. Pupavac drew on research carried out in different war-torn parts of the world to argue that people's response to violent episodes can be influenced by community strength, moral and ideological commitments.[5]

Pupavac's work is reinforced by Derek Summerfield, who has worked extensively with refugees and conflict-ridden communities in different part of the world. In a series of monographs, Summerfield has argued that cultural factors, such as the prevailing system of meaning, play a crucial role in influencing how people cope with their suffering. The impact of violent disruption and mass destruction on how people experience their pain is not reducible to the intensity of the experience. According to Summerfield, 'psychological trauma is not like physical trauma: people do not passively register the impact of external forces (unlike, say, a leg hit by a bullet) but engage with them in an active and problem-solving way'. He adds that 'suffering arises from, and is resolved in, a social context'.[6]

Social context also influences how the self is expected to negotiate unexpected and painful experience. Since the rise of modernity, the exercise of human subjectivity has been associated with the potential for altering and transforming external reality. Even the experience of pain is mediated through the exercise of subjectivity; through the act of perception, cognition and reflection. Instead of posing external reality as an unalterable objective force bearing down on a passive subject, the Enlightenment tradition suggested that human beings had the potential to shape that reality. With the rise of therapeutic culture this activist sense of the subject has given way to one that is distinctly passive.

At risk – the objectification of the self

Through the vocabulary of therapeutics, the sense of powerlessness is cultivated as part of the normal state of being. 'The effects of traumatic stress on individuals, organisations, communities, and nations are of substantial and increasing concern in the present world climate', argues the Maryland-based Center for the Study of Traumatic Stress. According to this organisation, nearly 17 million people in the US are exposed annually to trauma and disaster.[7] When it comes to unusual or distressing situations, the assumption that people cannot cope on their own informs the work of the trauma industry. Critics of 'trauma tourism' argue that therapeutic professionals may be 'overhelping' when they intervene to assist fire fighters facing occupational stress. Gist and Woodall warn that they 'may ultimately disempower those they purport most to aid by depriving them, to greater or lesser degrees, of the very essence of resilient resolution – the sense of personal mastery that flows from standing to threat and challenge and prevailing under duress'.[8] Lise Simonson, psychological support officer with the International Federation of Red Cross and Red Crescent Societies, is critical of the 'tendency to label any kind of "distress" as trauma', since it may 'encourage people to develop a passive victim identity that hampers recovery'.[9] This point is echoed in an impressive review carried out by Simon Wessely and his colleagues. Their review suggests that PTSD counselling or debriefing may actually produce worse outcomes by unwittingly eroding people's resilience and coping strategies.[10] However, reservations made about the routine characterisation of distressful events as traumatic goes against the grain of therapeutic ethos.

The positing of people as victims of circumstances reflects western cultural sensibilities towards the uncertainties confronting twenty-first century society. These uncertainties are conveyed through a therapeutic discourse of trauma, anxiety and stress. However, therapeutics does not simply reflect uncertainties; as we noted previously, it also cultivates a distinct orientation towards the world. It sensitises people to regard a growing range of their experiences as victimising and as traumatising. As noted previously, the cornerstone of the therapeutic ethos is the belief that the defining feature of personhood is its vulnerability. 'Whereas earlier psychiatry assumed the general resilience of population and sought to diagnose individual susceptibility to psychological breakdown', argues Vanessa Pupavac, the current diagnosis of PTSD 'assumes universal vulnerability'.[11] Victimising and traumatic episodes used to be associated with unusual and often extreme events, such as wars and violent crime. Today, the unusual has become the norm. As Lasch noted in his discussion of what he terms the 'survivalist' outlook, 'everyday life has begun to pattern itself on the survival strategies forced on those exposed to extreme adversity'.[12] The rare attempt to endow the survivalist outlook with positive potential invariably expresses the mood of low expectations. Anthony Giddens attempts to retrieve a crumb of comfort when he states that 'someone who concentrates on surviving in personal relations, as in other spheres of life, cannot be said to have abandoned all autonomy over his or her life's circumstances'. He adds that 'even if only in a somewhat negative sense, the individual clearly seeks active mastery: to survive is to be able in a determined way to ride out the trials of life and overcome them'.[13] The idealisation of the project of 'riding out the trials of life' indicates how far society has moved from the modernist vision of people assuming control over their affairs and transforming their lives.

Increasingly, the survivalist outlook projects every conceivable experience as a 'trial of life' that raises the issue of survival. Consequently, coping with relatively banal, unexceptional episodes is now represented as an act of survival. There are over a thousand different self-help books in print with the word 'surviving' contained in their title. Titles like *Crazy Time: Surviving Divorce and Building a New Life*, *Surviving an Affair*, *The Girl's Guide to Surviving a Break Up*, *Surviving Motherhood* signal the need for survival strategies for dealing with personal relationships. Titles such as *Surviving Complaints Against Counsellors and Psychotherapists* indicate that even the therapeutic profession has its own self-help survival books. The term surviving is sometimes used in a light-hearted jocular manner – *The Go-Girl Guide: Surviving Your 20s with Savvy, Soul and Style*. However, the very fact that it is used in this way indicates that such titles are attempting to tap into society's reservoir of survivalist consciousness.

The vulnerability and impotence of the individual stands in sharp contrast to the formidable powers that therapeutic culture attributes to the everyday circumstances that people face. From the standpoint of the therapeutic scenario, the individual self stands exposed to forces that threaten to overwhelm it and wreak emotional damage on it. The self-determining or history-making role of people is all but abolished in this representation of the relationship between humanity and the process of change. Through the constant amplification of the risks facing humanity even the limited exercise of individual choice becomes restricted by the harsh regime of uncertainty. Those who uphold this objectified representation of risk and uncertainty are also pessimistic about the ability of the self to engage with it. Accordingly, Beck remarks that 'faced with the opaque and contradictory character of modern society, the self-focused individual is hardly in a position to take the unavoidable decisions in a rational and responsible manner, that is, with reference to the possible circumstances'.[14]

The model of human vulnerability and powerlessness transmitted through therapeutics coincides with a far wider tendency to dismiss the potential for people exercising control over their lives. The narrative of emotional vulnerability coexists with powerful ideas that call into question people's capacity to assume a measure of control over their affairs. Social commentators regularly declare that we live in the era of the 'death of the subject', 'the death of the author' or the decline of agency. Such pessimistic accounts of the human potential inform both intellectual and cultural life in the west. The survivalist outlook alluded to by Lasch is not simply fuelled by a preoccupation with the vulnerability of the self, but also by the conviction that the world has become an intensely dangerous place beyond the control of humanity. Western society is continually haunted by the expectation of crisis and catastrophe. Environmental disasters, weapons of mass destruction, 'technology gone mad' are just some the concerns that have helped to fashion a permanent sense of crisis. It is difficult to disagree with the statement that 'contemporary social thought has become dominated, if not obsessed by the idea of crisis'.[15]

The relationship between emotional vulnerability and the wider global threats to human existence is most clearly represented through the concept of being 'at risk'. The conceptualisation of being 'at risk' is a relatively recent innovation that is bound up with the crisis thinking of the 1980s. Its entry into the vernacular coincides with the ascendancy of therapeutic culture. The concept of being at risk encapsulates an outlook which is dramatically different from the classical notion of taking a risk. The formulation, to take a risk, contains the assumption that individuals can both exercise choice and choose to explore and experiment. Taking a risk has as its premise active subjects whose actions have the potential to realise positive outcomes and to alter their circumstance. In contrast, the concept of being at risk reverses the previous relationship between human beings and experience. To be at risk assigns to the person a passive and dependent role. To be at risk is no longer about what you do – it is about who you are. It is an acknowledgement of powerlessness – at least in relation to that risk. Increasingly, someone defined as being at risk is seen to exist in a permanent condition of vulnerability. It objectifies the vulnerability of the self. This trend acquires its most striking expression through the widely used expression 'at risk child'. Although rarely defined, the term 'at risk child' evokes the sense of permanent vulnerability. At risk has become a fixed attribute of individuals.

Being at risk implies the autonomy of the dangers that people face. It also reverses the idea of the autonomous subject acting on the world so that it is the objectified self that is acted upon. Instead of the dynamic of interaction and transformation, both the individual at risk and the conditions of existence are objectified. Risk is rarely conceptualised as an activity bound up with choice. It is generally represented as a force that exists independent of the people confronted by it. Once risk is seen to exist in its own right and is therefore only minimally subject to human intervention, the only possible role for a person is to avoid or to minimise a pre-existing risk. In this scenario, the risks are the active agents and people at risk are cast in the role of passivity. The diminution of the human agency that is implicit in the 'at risk' concept acquires clear definition in contemporary therapeutic ideas about the powerless self. Contemporary consciousness of being at risk – that is, existing in a state of powerlessness – gains shape and definition through therapeutic culture's focus on emotional vulnerability. People who are at risk or people confronting risky situations do not simply face physical harm. Increasingly, it is the element of psychological distress that dominates deliberations surrounding anxieties about risks. As outlined previously, often it is the psychological and not the physical damage suffered during the course of a natural disaster that appears to define the problem. 'When a natural disaster occurs, we do a great job of getting medical services, food and shelter', maintains University of South Florida professor Michael Rank. However, he notes that 'we ignore the emotional aspects' and argues that 'We need to pay attention to emotions and psychological state of mind and state of heart of the trauma victim'.[16]

It has been noted that the intensity of public anxiety about environmental and toxic disasters is underpinned by a profound sense of powerlessness and vulnerability. Of course, feelings of helplessness and vulnerability are common in moments of crisis. But as Kai Erikson argues in his influential work on 'Toxic Reckoning', these insecurities 'can broaden into something more ominous, for survivors of severe disasters can experience not just vulnerability but a feeling of having lost immunity to misfortune, a feeling that something terrible is bound to happen'.[17] This feeling of unbounded vulnerability is interwoven with the sense of being at risk. Kai Erikson appears to believe that this sense of unbounded vulnerability is the product of the unique dread inspired by toxic disasters. But is it? In numerous other nontoxic incidents and disasters, the claim is often made that the victims feel that they have lost their immunity to misfortune. In the aftermath of the earthquake that devastated El Salvador in January 2001, some emergency experts claimed that because natural disasters occur frequently in this part of the world, 'people are unable to recover fully' and suffer from a sense of permanent emotional vulnerability.[18] The same diagnosis was repeated time and again during rural Britain's foot-and-mouth crisis. According to one account, 'farmers have been left "broken men" by the foot-and-mouth crisis'. One farmer told the press, 'I am very sorry to say that a lot of farmers are never going to recover from this and the psychological wounds will never heal'.[19]

And it is not simply in response to natural disaster that the sense of unbounded vulnerability kicks in. In our previous discussion of toxic relationship, it was noted that the emotional damage suffered contained the implication of a life sentence. In fact it is not so much the dread generated by anxiety about a specific toxic danger but the wider sense of being powerless or at risk that frames perceptions of unbounded vulnerability. That is why the child at risk is no less a personification of unbounded vulnerability than the victim of an earthquake.

Therapeutic culture is not responsible for the development of contemporary apprehensions about risk. The problems that western society have in managing uncertainty and the prevailing mood of scepticism concerning the status of the human subject are the outcome of historic and social influences that are discussed elsewhere.[20] Therapeutic cultural trends are not so much the cause, but the reflection of present-day apprehensions regarding uncertainty. In turn, through recasting these responses through readily understandable ideas about emotional vulnerability, therapeutic culture serves as a filter through which the wider mood of uncertainty acquires an individual form. In this way, the wider problems bound up with uncertainty are reinterpreted and experienced as risks to the emotional health of the individual. Through the individualisation of social experience, people do come to feel more vulnerable or at risk and come to approximate the subjectivity assigned to them by therapeutic culture.

The process of individuation is by no means a novel phenomenon. The break-up of communities and old forms of solidarities, the decline of organised religion, geographical mobility and urbanisation are all-important elements in the development of modern society. However, today's individuation is not merely more of the same. In the past, the erosion of institutions took place in conditions where new forms of solidarities were created. Moreover, the private sphere and network of informal relations managed to evolve and even thrive. However, as noted previously, today even the private sphere has become the target of suspicion and relations of dependence are culturally reviled. In such circumstances, the process of individuation enhances the sense of vulnerability. Many people are literally on their own. Through social isolation many of the wider problems facing communities are internalised as individual issues facing the self.

The fearful subject

Therapeutic culture's version of the diminished self is part of a wider reaction to the promise of modernity. Strong antimodernist sentiments question the ideal of human progress. In its most systematic form, this scepticism has turned into an antihumanist world view that is cynical about the potential that men and women possess for influencing their destiny. This belittling of the human potential has as its premise the belief that the attempt by humans to control their destiny is not only unrealistic, but also very dangerous. This disenchantment with modernity is linked to a vision of society where humans play a minor, undistinguished role.

The tendency to denigrate the idea of self-determination reflects a potent mood of disenchantment towards the experience of human progress during the past century. Not only is the ideal of individual self-determination regarded with scepticism, contemporary culture provides little support for the idea of societal self-determination. Both individually and collectively, people are assumed to lack the capacity to assume control over societal forces. Currently influential theories of risk society portray a semi-conscious humanity that is desperately attempting to take control of the forces – mainly destructive – that it has created. According to this model, powerless human agents who confront powerful forces have no choice but to engage in an exercise of damage limitation. Ulrich Beck echoes this point in his *Risk Society*: 'basically, one is no longer concerned with attaining something "good", but rather with preventing the worst'.[21] This motif of fear driving people's response to social experience is justified on the ground that the risks we see today are unbounded. This perception of risk is rooted in the sense of unbounded vulnerability transmitted through therapeutic culture. The world does become more dangerous when the self is perceived to be uniquely powerless and vulnerable. The relationship between the therapeutically constructed subject and the uncertain world is mediated through a consciousness of risk permeated by fear.

In a sense, the growth of risk consciousness and of the perception of emotional vulnerability is proportional to the diminished role assigned to human subjectivity. The claim of powerlessness is frequently justified through calling into question the power for human reasoning. Critics of the Enlightenment, science and human progress have always questioned the capacity for human reasoning. In the nineteenth century such antihumanist critics claimed that 'irrational' and 'unconscious' forces are often more powerful than that of reason.[22] Disappointment with the development of modern capitalism often leads to the questioning of reason. During the 1980s this trend has acquired significant momentum. The tendency to limit the application of reason has become a dominant feature of western intellectual life. The sociologist Jeffrey Alexander writes of the 'omnipresence of irrationality'. According to Alexander, reason 'has been experienced as a hollow shell, progress as inconceivable, and often actually undesirable'.[23]

One reason why rationality is sometimes represented as undesirable is because it is often held responsible for many of the ills confronting society. In some cases, the Enlightenment and its vision of progress and rationality are held responsible for mass destruction, the rise of totalitarianism or the Holocaust. The association of science and technology with frightening and dreadful outcomes has become commonplace in both intellectual and cultural life. Films frequently depict arrogant scientists 'playing God', who end up inadvertently unleashing powers of mass destruction. Such attitudes towards the development of science and knowledge are not confined to the sphere of popular culture. Many of the leading authorities on the sociology of risk associate its development with the advance of knowledge. They argue that many of the uncertainties and anxieties that we face are the result of the growth of human knowledge.[24] In turn, growing uncertainty deprives individuals from making meaningful choices. As Zizek points out, 'the freedom of decision enjoyed by the subject of the "risk society" is not the freedom of someone who can freely choose his destiny, but the anxiety provoking freedom of someone who is constantly compelled to make decisions without being aware of their consequences'.[25]

It is a paradox that at a time when there is so much talk of freedom of choice, that freedom is so often experienced as frightening. Disappointment with the legacy

of the Enlightenment and with the track record of social and political experimentation has made society extremely cautious in its relationship to uncertainty.
Consequently, we lack a web of meaning through which people can make sense
of uncertainty and change. As a result, the individual often experiences freedom
as disorienting and emotionally painful. The very fact that individuals can so
easily be emotionally damaged and that the impact of this damage can be so debilitating means that people are entitled to fear a growing range of social experience.
According to an authoritative review of the field of sociology of emotion,
'subjective experiences are influenced not only by a society's emotion vocabulary,
but by cultural beliefs about emotions'.[26] The experience of risk and of fear
confirms this diagnosis.

Fears, which are an expression of psychic vulnerability, are often misleadingly
seen as the product of a world that faces unprecedented dangers. Numerous claim-
makers – environmentalists, health professionals, crime experts, counsellors, etc.
– continually insist that the world is becoming more and more dangerous. However,
simple logic suggests that it is unlikely that so much of life has become more risky
and dangerous. Public perceptions of new risks and dangers are rooted in the sense
of powerlessness circulated through therapeutic culture. This emotional script helps
frame perceptions independent of any risk – invariably they tend to overwhelm
any objective calculation of risk.

Increasingly, people's feelings about the status of particular risks tends
to influence – sometimes decisively – the subsequent definition of those risks.
Recently, there have been numerous investigations into claims that the pollution
of the environment has caused cancer clusters in particular communities. Despite
the absence of any scientific evidence, such investigations have been launched
because people 'feel' that they are threatened by pollution. This was the case in
the investigation into childhood cancer in Toms River, New Jersey, in 1996.
Although officials believed that the number of childhood cancers in the area was
not 'statistically meaningful' they sought to respond to community concern by
launching an investigation. Activists and parents were certain that their community
was being polluted since that was what their gut feeling told them. 'In my heart
and in my mind, I have no question – now, it's up to the scientists to use logic and
common sense to get at the truth', argued Linda Gillick, chairwoman of a local
community group, and the mother of a cancer victim.[27] In this case the truth arrived
at through feeling overrides the scepticism of science. Science is not entirely
dismissed – it is simply assigned the role of validating pre-existing feeling.

The diminished sense of self is continually validated through the prevailing
perception of risk. As a result it is sufficient to feel at risk to be at risk. The very
perception of psychological vulnerability can cause damage to the emotions and
therefore to feel at risk is to be at risk. The way that therapeutic culture frames
the sense of self ensures that it genuinely feels at risk. In this way the powerlessness of the therapeutically constructed self, refracted through the perception of
being at risk of some external harm, itself becomes a source of fear and anxiety.
This process is misunderstood in the literature on risk where public anxieties are
interpreted as a response to externally generated factors. This was an approach

taken by the report of the expert panel of the Workshop on the Psychological Response to Hazardous Substances written for the US Department of Health. The report took the view that it was the uncertainty produced by the invisible character of toxic contamination that accounted for the anxiety of people living near hazardous waste sites. It observed that unlike the 'damage and injuries caused by a natural disaster, many toxic substances are invisible to the senses', and that this invisibility 'results in feelings of uncertainty'. Moreover, 'the lag time between exposure and the appearance of a chronic disease related to the exposure' means that health outcomes are 'uncertain' and 'leave people with a loss of control'. It concluded that the 'two areas where people have the most difficulty coping are with uncertainty and loss of control'.[28] That loss of control and uncertainty can contribute to a state of stress and anxiety is not in doubt. However, as our exploration of contemporary ethnopsychology suggests, the sense of powerlessness and of vulnerability are pre-given attributes of contemporary subjectivity that are quite independent of any specific risk of toxic or any other contamination. Uncertainty and powerlessness are not simply the outcome of an engagement with a specific risk. Such sentiments are systematically transmitted through popular culture.

The invisibility of risks to health can be understood as a metaphor through which the self attempts to make sense of uncertainty. The use of the metaphor of invisibility appeals to our imagination to look beyond the realm of physical perception. One of the symptoms of emotional vulnerability and of emotional injury are long-lasting invisible scars. Trauma itself is often presented as an invisible injury. *Invisible Trauma: The Psychosocial Effects of Invisible Environmental Contaminants*, the title of a well-known text on the subject, clearly links the psychological to the environmental through the metaphor of invisibility.[29] Nor is the term 'toxic' confined to physical dangers. Toxic relations and toxic families summon up the image of a world where people pollute – not just the environment, but also each other. That is why the many anxieties expressed about the risks involved in personal relationships have the same structure and dynamic as those which prevail in the controversies that surround the environment and technology. They too are invisible. Indeed, one of the concerns raised about the private sphere is that it hides all manner of destructive behaviour and that the behaviour of family members is invisible to others.

Through toxic dangers, the sense of emotional vulnerability acquires a powerful definition. Edelstein has argued that toxic as opposed to natural disasters are more psychological: 'the "facts" of toxic disaster are often unclear, making the "perception" of the disaster central to its effects'.[30] Through the influence of therapeutic culture such perceptions are likely to exacerbate the pre-existing subjectivity of powerlessness and dispose many to psychosocial effects. As Bartholomew and Wessely note, sociogenic illness has a long history.[31] But what distinguishes circumstances today is that in contrast to previous times there is a cultural climate that strongly supports claims of psychosocial distress. Indeed, the very perception of risk by itself can be deemed as psychologically damaging. As Burgess argues, 'while the affliction of unexplained or untreatable illness seems to have always disposed people to be concerned about unknown dangers from their surroundings, intellectual support for such fears is more recent'.[32]

The 'self at risk' is a construction of cultural norms that regard people's fear as itself a source of risk. From this perspective, the evaluation of risk assumes a one-sidedly psychological dimension so that feelings of anxiety and powerlessness become constituent elements of the definition of risk. Of course, the evaluation of risk always has a psychological dimension. 'Risk assessment is inherently subjective and represents a blending of science and judgement with important psychological, social, cultural, and political factors', writes Paul Slovic in an influential review of the subject.[33] But although an intrinsically subjective act, it is only in recent times that feelings and emotions have come to assume such an important direct role in the assessment of risk. The sense of emotional vulnerability frames risk perception. How uncertainty and powerlessness have become a constituent part of evaluating risks can be seen in response to the controversy that surrounds the risk of cell phone technology. Back in 1996, the insurance company Swiss Re published an interesting report entitled *Electrosmog – A Phantom Risk*. This study, authored by Christian Brauner, stated that the insurance industry faced a greater danger from a potential explosion of claims made against the mobile phone industry than hitherto expected. Brauner argued that this threat had little to do with the incalculably small health risks, but with the incalculably great risk of sociopolitical change. The report predicted that changing social values could result in scientific findings being evaluated differently in the future than in the past. With the growing sense of fear regarding uncertainty and the validation of the condition of being at risk, scientific findings are indeed evaluated differently. In particular, scientific findings now compete with the public's feelings in the cultural representation of risk.

Brauner's prescient account of the politics of risk is based on a useful distinction between EMF health risk and EMF liability risk. Regardless of whether mobile phones constitute a health risk, cultural mistrust of new technology may turn it into a liability risk. To put it bluntly, if society wants to treat electromagnetic fields as a cause of illness, they will be deemed a cause of illness. The report pointed to the influence of social and cultural factors in the calculation of risks. Since the publication of this report, growing concern with emotional injury and vulnerability has led to a more therapeutic orientation towards the calculation of risk.[34] As a result, the perception that mobile phones are dangerous is itself seen as a potential health problem. In New Zealand, the psychologist Ivan Beale, a leading anti-phone mast campaigner, has argued that courts should not rely simply on physical evidence when making a ruling on the siting of these towers. According to Beale, phone masts can constitute a health risk even without the actual occurrence of any harmful exposure to radiation. 'When exposure is invisible as is the case with electromagnetic fields, the mere possibility of exposure is threat enough to produce fear', leading to illness, he wrote.[35]

Beale takes the view that the very existence of an 'unacceptable risk' is sufficient to create mental and physical health problems. And with so many aspects of change interpreted as unacceptable and with the fear of change so pervasive, cell phones or any other new technology is liable to be evaluated as a health risk. In Britain, the government-sponsored report of the Independent Expert Group on Mobile Phones adopted Beale's approach and, in part, justified its stance on the ground that people's well-being can be compromised if their worry about the risks posed by radiation from phone masts is ignored. The report took the view that if the public feels excluded from decision-making about the siting of phone masts, the resultant frustration 'has negative effects on people's health and well-being'.[36] From a strict biomedical perspective, this redefinition of frustration as a health risk makes little sense. However, as a statement about the therapeutic sensibility of our time it affirms the conviction that if the subject feels at risk, it is at risk.

Risky relationships

From the previous discussion it should be evident that diminished subjectivity expresses itself in a powerful consciousness of risk. This consciousness of risk is as powerful in regard to human relations as they are in relation to new technology and the environment. It is worth noting that the concept of at risk is most con-sistently used to depict the dangers confronting vulnerable children from adults. But ideas of risk pervade all forms of relationship that demand the management of emotion. A recent study of romantic relationships in North America concluded that people 'are increasingly motivated by the need to alleviate expanding levels of perceived risks associated with interpersonal love relationships and mate selection'.[37] The risk of emotional injury is not confined to the relation of love. Emotional damage may be the outcome of personal encounters in virtually any setting. Emotional damage is invariably presented as an assault on self-esteem. It is perpetually claimed that those who have faced such an assault are likely to lose their self-confidence, suffer from anxiety and find it difficult to sustain close personal relations. The term 'emotional abuse' is sometimes used to convey the sense that even insensitive remarks and criticisms can unwittingly cause damage to the other person.

An NSPCC guide for protecting children in sporting activities from abuse defines emotional abuse in terms which in the past would have been characterised as putting children under pressure. It states that emotional abuse includes situations 'where parents or coaches subject children to constant criticism, bullying or un-realistic pressure to perform to high expectations'.[38] According to child protection guidelines used in Britain, emotional abuse can refer to virtually every parental failing, from 'failure to meet a child's need for affection' to being so 'over protective and possessive' that they prevent their children from experiencing 'normal social contact or normal physical activity'.[39] Anything that has the potential for making another person unhappy can be redefined as an assault on the emotion. Nor is this approach restricted to children. Since fragile emotion has become defined as rooted in existence, the line that divides mature adults from highly impressionable children has become indistinct. Most policy statements on harassment at American and British institutions of higher education warn that personal harassment can directly lead to stress, depression and/or physical illness. So what is this act of personal harassment that can cause such negative outcomes?

Most policy statements prefer a loose definition that includes conduct that is 'inappropriate' or 'unacceptable'. It is behaviour that is interpreted as 'offensive or intimidating' by the recipient. Harassment can also be either 'deliberate or unintentional'. When such a wide range of acts – clumsy gesture, bad practical joke, outburst of resentment – becomes causally linked to psychological illness, then fundamental forms of human interaction acquire a menacing complexion.

Widely accepted definitions of harassment, stalking and bullying insist that these acts are determined by the victim's feelings rather than by the intention of the person who has caused the offence. Many companies have adopted policies on bullying and harassment, which allows the recipient to determine whether he or she has been injured. For example, the leading retailer, Marks and Spencer's policy states that individuals 'have different levels of sensitivity and it is up to the recipient to decide whether they are experiencing behaviours unacceptable to them'. [40] As the notion of unacceptable behaviour is typically left rather vague the range of individual acts that it can encompass becomes infinite. It is the individual's emotion rather than any objectively defined criteria that ultimately define an act or an experience as harmful. This subjective interpretation of what constitutes a harmful act indicates that the heightened sense of injury that pervades contemporary society relates principally to harms that violate the emotion.

Since emotional pain is defined so broadly, it is not surprising that it should become a normal experience of life. It is difficult to imagine any important aspect of life which is not potentially risky. During the past decade or so, sex has been redefined as an essentially victimising experience with potentially destructive consequences for the emotion. The American psychologist Paul Okami persuasively argues that during the late 1970s and the 1980s there was a noticeable shift from the relatively benign representation of sex. 'Sexual aggression, abuse, and harassment became topics of concern for a great many professional and popular writers, as did the medical and social consequences of sexually transmitted diseases', notes Okami. He further observes that 'high levels of sexual activity and unusual sexual practices became pathologised in diagnoses such as "sex addiction" and "sexual compulsivity".'[41] To substantiate this thesis, Okami points to the greater interest in the negative aspects of human sexuality, which can be seen in a review of listings in *Psychological Abstracts*. In 1969, there were no index categories for 'sexual abuse', 'sex offenders', 'sexual harassment', 'rape incest', 'sexual sadism' or 'paedophilia'. All these acts were subsumed under the category 'sexual deviations', which contained 65 entries. However, by 1989 all the above index categories were added to *Psychological Abstracts* and in that edition there were over 400 articles dealing with sexual aggression, crime and intergenerational sex. There was a 20-fold increase in listings between 1969 and 1989 according to Okami.[42] These trends are clearly reflected in popular culture where the themes of abuse, sexual violence, stalking and serial sex crime constitute the staple diet of contemporary fiction and television.

Probably the most extreme manifestation of risk consciousness is the growing tendency to transform relations at work into a source of disease. Like sex, relations at work have also been recast as a threatening experience. The place of work is often presented as a central site for emotional injury. In 1998, the British TUC claimed that 5 million people had been bullied at work. The TUC figure of 5 million has been subsequently presented as a statement of fact by numerous organisations involved in the field of human resource management.[43] Such claims – rarely put to question – lend weight to the impression that work represents a major risk to people. Typically, the problems cited are bound up with the employee's emotional life rather than the traditional economically driven acts of exploitation. The big workplace issues – harassment, bullying, stress – all touch upon the mental state of the victims.

In Britain, the trade union movement has been in the forefront of the promotion of the therapeutic ethos in the workplace. Successive union initiatives have claimed that bullying, harassment and stress are rampant in the workplace. If their reports are even half accurate, then the experience of victimisation has become the norm for most British workers. Reports commissioned by unions claim that something like 30–38 per cent of workers have been bullied. A study of union representatives in 1997 suggested that 66 per cent had either witnessed or experienced bullying. A survey published by the Manufacturing, Science and Finance Union (MSF) reported that 30 per cent of its activists thought that bullying was a serious problem at their workplace and that it had got worse during the past 5 years. And 72 per cent stated that their employer had bullied employees. The National Association of Schoolmasters Union of Women Teachers published a report in 1996 that claimed that 72 per cent of their members were either subject to bullying or had witnessed it. A TUC-sponsored report claims that 75 per cent of the respondents who had witnessed or experienced bullying said it affected their physical or mental health. 'Stress, depression and lowered self-esteem were the most common complaints', according to the TUC.[44]

A closer inspection of the claim that the workplace has become traumatised by an epidemic of bullying indicates that what is under discussion is what used to be called office politics, assertive management and the compulsion to get the job done. Workplace bullying covers a multitude of sins. Virtually any negative uncivil encounter can and is defined as bullying. Richard V. Denenberg, a supporter of the US-based Campaign Against Workplace Bullying, has noted that bullying encompasses vandalism, gestures, witholding of important information and making faces – 'even smiling the wrong way'. 'It can be very subtle', said Denenberg.[45] Another American expert, the academic Loraleigh Keashley, claims that bullying involves mainly 'subtle types of aggression, including ignoring a person's contributions, flaunting status, pulling rank, making unwanted eye contact and openly belittling individuals'. Keashley contends that psychological aggression in the workplace can have 'devastating effects leading to physical, mental and emotional illness, as well as reduced productivity and increased absenteeism by employees.[46]

The rise of the issue of bullying coincided with the increased recognition accorded to stress as a symptom of a more widespread malaise afflicting the workplace. In the aftermath of the shakeout of British industry, human resources experts emphasised stress and problems of the emotions as the negative outcome of this process. A report published by one employer organisation, The Industrial Society, in 1993 claimed that bosses listed stress, emotional and personal problems as the most important reason for sick leave after colds and 'flu.[47] Three years later, the TUC launched a publicity campaign against 'this new industrial epidemic'. Numerous reports covering education, banking, the health sector, manual public sector workers and telephone companies offered alarming figures, which suggested that 50 to 60 per cent of employees suffered from stress.[48] Antibullying activists were quick to link their cause to the issue of stress. Workplace stress now had an active human cause. It was an emotional injury inflicted by a bully. Psychology professor Cary Cooper has forcefully drawn attention to this causal relationship. He stated that 'bullying is one of the biggest contributory factors' to workplace stress. According to his account, his 'researchers have talked to thousands of people in 70 occupational areas and believe bullying accounts for a third to half of all stress-related illness'.[49]

Trade union reports link the pressure to meet targets to the creation of an environment in which 'intimidation and victimisation are almost unavoidable'.[50] The key focus of trade union activists is the pathologising of workplace stress. Their reports claim a phenomenal rise of workplace stress. An increase in workload combined with a more bullying style of management is held accountable for the prevalence of this disease. For example, a survey carried out in 1995 by the MSF claims that 60 per cent of the respondents suffered from stress due to pressure of work. A UNISON report indicated that 87 per cent of nurses believed that their stress levels had increased over the preceding years, 60 per cent of union members at Barclays Bank had found their job more stressful then previously and 22.7 per cent had received treatment for a stress-related illness which they blamed on work. Another union study in 1996 indicated that manual workers were more stressed than previously. Sixty-three per cent of the respondents said that their jobs were more stressful than in the past. According to the National Association of Teachers in Further and Higher Education, eight out of ten lecturers at institutions of further education stated that their stress levels were unacceptable and one out of four had taken time off to deal with their stress. The report concluded that college lecturers were being driven to the verge of a nervous breakdown.[51]

In an important study of the growth of the British workplace stress epidemic, David Wainwright and Michael Calnan suggest that this development can be understood as the legacy of sociocultural changes – 'the heightened awareness of physical and mental vulnerability, the culture of victimhood, and the emergence of the therapeutic state – that account for experiences at work being interpreted through the medicalised prism of epidemic and disease'.[52] In particular, they draw attention to the point that changes in 'Britain's emotional script or ethno-psychology' mean that workplace problems are 'no longer seen as collective issues to be fought over through industrial action or political activity, but as individualised threats to the mental and physical health of the worker, to which therapeutic intervention is the proper response'.[53] Such problems are experienced in an isolated manner as risks to the individual.

The experience of job insecurity, anxiety about future prospects, problems of the emotion and the feeling of stress are not particularly unique responses to the conditions of our times. What is new is the medicalisation of these responses. The pathologising of stress and other workplace experiences is sanctioned by new cultural norms which inflate the sense of emotional injury and invite people to perceive themselves as ill. Through the institutionalisation of the therapeutic ethos in the workplace, estrangement from the process of work is experienced as being at risk of emotional damage. Human resource experts and management have become increasingly involved in the promotion of therapeutic techniques. Counselling for stress and other problems of the emotion has gradually become institutionalised in blue-chip companies.

Perceptions of risks are strongly influenced by cultural norms. With so much of life and everyday human encounters interpreted as risky and potentially victimising, it is not remarkable to find that the mere fact of feeling uncomfortable due to stress has been recast as a dangerous threatening condition. And once a particular condition is defined as potentially damaging, then it is bound to have a negative effect on people's health. Public institutions, health professionals and advocacy groups play an important role in constructing a therapeutic market place for promoting their ethos. Campaigns devoted to raising 'awareness' prompt people to reinterpret their problem through the discourse of therapy. Apparently objective surveys on levels of stress at the workplace are not merely designed to discover the facts, but also play a role in educating respondents about the dangers they face. Such research already assumes that stress has a negative effect on people and is oriented towards discovering what it already suspects. The pathologising of the stress response provides the idiom through which people are trained to make sense of their experiences. A survey charged with discovering the level of stress among staff at my university posed questions like 'have you recently felt constantly under strain'. Not surprisingly, people reported that they have, and the survey concluded that the 52 per cent of the respondents fell 'in a zone of potential psychological vulnerability'.[54] Other surveys invite people to report whether they face more stress at work today than in the past. Predictably, the majority of the respondents reply that the situation is getting worse.

Research into workplace stress contributes toward the amplifying perceptions of the problem. Professional intervention by therapists, lawyers and other experts also plays a crucial role in the framing of these perceptions. In many cases leaflets and pamphlets are distributed through advocacy groups into the workplace, which advise employees that they are probably suffering from stress or post-traumatic stress disorder. For example, a leaflet entitled 'Post Traumatic Stress Disorder and the Ambulance Service' distributed by the Association of Professional Ambulance Personnel and a firm of solicitors to ambulance workers in Liverpool informs people that they are 'potential stress victims' and they should think about contacting them if they think they are suffering from PTSD. Such intervention is at the very least likely to encourage people to associate their personal problem with stress. In many cases it will stimulate people to make sense of their existence through the prism of illness.

Although the current epidemic of workplace stress is shaped by cultural influences, it is as Wainwright and Calnan argue 'no less "real" for that'.[55] In a society where individuals are incited to regard themselves as at risk, relatively routine encounters are likely to be perceived as potentially damaging to the emotion. An ethnopsychology that continually lowers the threshold of acceptable distress and circumscribes the range of experiences with which individuals are expected to cope is likely to foster a climate where individuals are likely to interpret unpleasant events as threats to their health. For the self who is confronted with adversity at work, medical labels such as stress offer a personal narrative of meaning.

Ideas about emotional damage, stress, trauma and vulnerability are developed through a process of cultural interpretation of what constitutes an injury. Perceptions of emotional injury are a link to norms about how much distress individuals can be expected to cope with. As Farrell notes, 'a culture may make terror and loss heroically meaningful and so diminish its damage, but culture may contribute to psychic ruin'.[56] Contemporary culture finds it difficult to reconcile the individual to a loss. The absence of narratives of solidarity, responsibility and sacrifice deprive loss of any wider meaning. One of the clearest manifestations of society's aversion to loss is its aversion to risk-taking and dislike of risk. Therapeutic culture contributes to this response through continually inflating the damaging impact it has on the psyche of the individual. For the vulnerable self is by definition at risk.

7 Fragile identity
Hooked on self-esteem

The cultivation of vulnerability is inextricably bound up with the disorganisation of the sphere of informal relations. The dictates of emotion management encourage the distancing of the self from others. This distancing of the self from others coincides with the turn inward. One the most visible consequence of this inward orientation of the self is the growing significance attached to the question of self-identity. As this chapter argues, the question of identity is increasingly associated with feeling. In line with the dictates of emotional determinism, how one feels has come to define the self. These sentiments are systematically codified in the cultural myth of self-esteem. According to this myth, low self-esteem is the key problem facing society and high self-esteem provides the solution to it.

The inward turn

Ideas about the self are mediated through social experience. These ideas are continually subject to modification as society throws up new problems and challenges to the way that individuals make sense of their lives. Preoccupation with the self is a distinctly modern phenomenon. The emergence of a sense of self required the decline of status-based communities, where one's role was allocated according to custom. The rapid change and dislocation brought about through the development of industrial capitalism helped fuel a powerful process of individuation. Through the fragmentation of social experience, people's relationship to taken-for-granted communities declined. Forced to rely on their own individual resources, people developed a distinct sense of themselves. In such circumstances understanding the self became important. The quest for personal self-understanding through the act of self-reflection is one of the legacies of modernity.

During the past century, ideas about the self have undergone constant alteration. Current perceptions of human individuality have been influenced by the decline of wider shared systems of meanings and collective identities. As a result the question of individual identity has been increasingly perceived as an issue for personal choice and decision-making. This perspective is conveyed through therapeutic culture's orientation to the self. The therapeutic ethos also contributes to the construction of a distinct version of the self. So far we have dealt with one aspect of this construction – the assumption that powerlessness is one of the defining features of the self. There are other related features of the therapeutic self. One of the distinct themes of the therapeutic version of the self is its association with emotions. From the perspective of therapeutics, the self acquires meaning through the experience of the inner, emotional life. In contemporary imagination, the self lies within and through the individual's inner world. 'I am what my feelings are telling me', is how Winkle describes this emotionalisation of the self.[1]

The construction of the emotional self has helped to strengthen people's orientation towards their internal world. This psychological representation of self has become widely internalised and has led many to adopt the routine of self-monitoring. Through the internalisation of the therapeutic ethos the self becomes objectified as the 'real me'. The slightest swing in mood or alteration in feeling can and is often interpreted to have great significance. Relatively minor peculiarities of the self are regarded as characteristics of grave importance and become a 'matter of contemplation'.[2] The significance attributed to the feelings of the self reinforces and intensifies the historic tendency towards individualisation. The feelings of the self are private, personal matters that differentiate and distance people from each other. The emotionalisation of the self heightens the sense of individuation by shifting the focus inward.

Since the 1970s, the call to be in touch with yourself and to feel good about yourself has become a refrain that is regularly issued in a variety of institutional setting. That is why self-love is rarely seen as narcissistic, but as an instrument for raising awareness. The most striking manifestation of this narcissistic turn is the angel fad in the US. Numerous books and television programmes are devoted to stories about angels who watch over us. In line with society's narcissistic turn, each of us has our own internal angel to watch over us. As Ruth Shalit writing in *The New Republic* observes, the fascination with angels is driven by a spirituality that is entirely focused on the self. Whereas in the past, medieval angelology 'propelled people out of themselves, towards a stricter standard and a higher life', the modern variety is 'entirely, indulgently subjective'.[3] Angels are there to make our wish come true – above all they are there to flatter the self. The only responsibility recognised by the religion of feelings is to ourselves. Cultivating angels like the child inside us are means through which service to the self can be achieved. As the sociologist Thomas Luckmann noted, with the self as the object of worship, personal identity is redefined 'to mean "inner man"'.[4]

The emotional orientation towards the self does not simply foster an emphasis on individual identity. Individual identity is itself recast as inextricably linked to the inner person. It is a feelings-based identity apparently based on recognising the emotional signals that are transmitted from inside. However, feeling-based identities are fluid and ephemeral and difficult to capture. Luckmann has argued that 'since the "inner man" is, in effect, an undefinable entity, its presumed discovery involves a lifelong quest'. Gaining meaning from ambiguous feelings leads some individuals to adopt a career of self-monitoring. As Luckmann outlined, 'the individual, who is to find a source of "ultimate" significance in the subjective dimension of his biography embarks upon a process of self-realisation and self-expression that is, perhaps, not continuous – since it is immersed in the recurrent routines of everyday life – but certainly interminable'.[5]

Therapeutic culture attempts to resolve the tensions inherent in the process of individuation through, as Hewitt puts it, situating the self as 'the culturally created center of the person's essential being'.[6] The self is the real, authentic core of the person. Since how one feels defines the self, authenticity can only be understood through the language of emotions. However, this is a language that has become colonised by psychological and medical discourse. Fears of psychic injury influence our consciousness of the self-leading to its medicalisation. The self is 'increasingly measured by criteria of health and illness', argues Hewitt.[7] The most common way that therapeutic culture accounts for the health of the self is through the metaphor of self-esteem. A high level of self-esteem is symptomatic of a desirable state of mental and physical health, while a low level indicates that the self is ill and faces a crisis. As will be shown, therapeutic culture believes that through raising self-esteem both the self and society will flourish. Esteeming the self becomes an act of civic responsibility.

Cultivating the identity of estrangement

One of the distinct contributions of therapeutic culture is its transformation of the experience of estrangement from a problem into an object of veneration. In previous times, leading social thinkers regarded the alienation of the self from others as one of the defining problems of modern society.[8] It is true that since the rise of modernity there has been a growing tendency to place a greater value on that which distinguishes the self from others (the 'I' identity) than on that which binds people together (the 'We' identity). However, today the balance between the two forms of identity has tipped so much in favour of the celebration of the self that alienation from others is seen as an acceptable price to pay for the pursuit of self-understanding.

Although therapeutic culture frequently exhorts people to learn to communicate their emotions to others, it privileges the insights gained through self-reflection. As Swidler notes, from the perspective of therapeutics, self-discovery is logically prior to the forging of relationships. Its assumption is 'that individuals who have "gotten in touch with" their real selves, freed of the inauthentic residues of family pressures, social roles, or others' expectations, will be able to forge genuine bonds to others'.[9] Moreover, through the continual problematisation of interpersonal relations it elevates the self as the obvious focus for emotional investment. In previous times different religions and ideologies sought to tackle the problem of alienation and estrangement through offering a strategy for transcending isolation. Finding meaning through work, salvation, community, class or political commitment was represented as a strategy for reintegrating the individual into a wider web of meaning. In contrast, therapeutic culture opts for promoting an orientation to the self through issuing an invitation to self-love. This approach acquires a pure form in a 1970s bestselling American self-help book *How To be Your Own Best Friend*. The book advocated individuals to adopt a therapeutic orientation to themselves through loving themselves. It claimed that individual happiness required the construction of a self that was our best friend.[10] Although the authors of this self-help book tended to use the term 'best friend' metaphorically, they clearly implied that your most important relationship was with yourself rather than with others. With friendship decoupled from another person, the estrangement of the self from others is endowed with a potentially positive meaning. An extreme illustration of this trend was provided by Jennifer Hoes, a Dutch artist who has decided to marry herself. 'I want to celebrate with others how much I'm in love with myself', she told Haarlem's *Dagbald* newspaper. She declared that she will never divorce herself since she does not want to be emotionally dependent on another.[11]

The association of individual identity with the internal life of the person is often interpreted as a shift towards self-absorption and narcissism. And while this trend is clearly discernible in contemporary society, the private search for identity should be seen above all as an attempt to find meaning in a world where the self-relation to wider communities and networks is already tenuous. The ambiguous and fluid relationship of the self to external points of reference is the outcome of the indi-vidualising imperative of late modernity. Therapeutic culture mirrors this trend and it also provides a positive rendition of this development. Through a world-view that advocates the realisation of individual autonomy through the pursuit of self-expressions and self-realisation it legitimises the estrangement of people from one another. 'Be yourself' has become both a cultural obligation and a desired state of self-enlightenment. Indeed, self-autonomy is represented as the precondition for forging relationships. As Swidler notes, 'in the therapeutic view one must be an autonomous person in order to create valid ties to others'.[12]

Therapeutic culture does not merely reflect the process of individualisation – it also intensifies its development. The cultivation of individual autonomy does not necessarily contradict wider relationships and commitments. The realisation of individual autonomy can in principle be pursued through the assumption of individual responsibility for the life of a community of individuals. However, through shaping the sense of self through the language of emotions, individual autonomy is increasingly understood as the pursuit of what feels right for the self. And what feels right for the self often has an arbitrary and tangential relationship to the expectations of others and of wider society. As one observer notes, 'personal identity has been recast, primarily in terms of emotional need, and delinked from concepts such as class, creed or nationality'.[13]

There is little doubt that the orientation towards the self – one of the distinct features of therapeutic culture – serves to distance the individual from points of reference that are external to it. The potential tension between this orientation and the maintenance of links with others can have a serious impact even on the most intimate relations. From the standpoint of therapeutics, an intimate relationship or marriage should be 'evaluated how well it meets the needs of the married partners as individuals'.[14] Whilst the communication of individual needs can strengthen a relationship, the primary role allocated to individual self-interests contains a powerful potential for weakening the influence of any wider norms that bind people together in a relationship.

Through the emotionalisation of identity, the relationship of the self with wider external points of reference has dramatically altered. External constraints over the conduct of the self in everyday life – be it in the form of communal expectations, moral codes and taboos and social values – have diminished in significance. Most accounts of cultural developments concur that the past 40 years have recognised the steady expansion of the symbolic significance of the self. An important ethical shift has occurred and as Rice commented, 'the self, rather than society, has become by far the more important partner in the relationship between the two'. As a result the self enjoys an important moral status. Popular culture communicates the message that wider external demands are illegitimate if in some sense they thwart individual self-realisation. Therapeutics is fundamentally a self-referential ethos. Rice observes, that 'the self's overarching moral significance, expressed by the claim that every person has a right to autonomy from social and cultural proprieties, is psychotherapy's central organizing principle'.[15] The assumption that 'if it feels right . . .', it ought to be pursued is informed by an ethic that depicts self-expression as an end in itself. This perspective is conveyed through the cultural validation of the 'free agent' and the authority of the self. Whereas ideologies in the past demanded the denial of the self for the sake of a higher interest, therapeutic culture regards the affirmation of the self as the central element of a good life. Despite its rhetorical acknowledgement of community, therapeutics is not logically able to sustain a sense of commitment to anything that stands above the self.

The emotionalisation of the self has an important significance for the cultural understanding of identity. The association of the state of the self with its emotional needs is not confined to the constitution of individual identity. Increasingly, identities based on wider affiliations, such as that of nation, ethnicity or community, have been represented through the therapeutic language of feelings. The fact that even group identities appear to be influenced by the emotional needs of the self serves as testimony to the significance of therapeutic culture. Group identity is often represented through the emotional needs of its members by advocacy organisations pursuing the cause of victim groups, minorities and special interest lobbies.

Group causes are often justified on the ground that certain experiences have inflicted emotional damage on the people they represent. Historic misdeeds are held responsible for causing injury to the self today. It is frequently suggested that experiences, such as slavery and the Irish potato famine, have inflicted trauma on subsequent generations. It is often claimed that as a result of these experiences, people whose group has been historically victimised often suffer from low self-esteem. This argument is regularly advanced by the national campaign that aims to compensate Afro-Americans for what their ancestors had to endure. According to one supporter of this campaign, 'slavery fostered low self-esteem among blacks that has led to today's high teen-pregnancy and crime rates'.[16] This linkage between low-self esteem and group identity is pursued by a variety of interest groups, who argue that racism and discrimination causes target groups to feel bad about themselves. For example, it is argued that denigrating images of native Americans prohibits the development of the 'strong self-esteem needed to compete in society'.[17] In the United States, it is alleged that the low level of self-esteem of Hispanics and native Americans accounts for these groups' relatively poor performance in school. Low self-esteem is also held responsible for the reluctance of women university students to opt for 'hard' subjects, such as engineering.[18]

The proposition that certain groups suffer from a collective state of low self-esteem is grounded in the so-called damage theory of personality. According to this theory, the experience of racism and oppression permanently damage the psyches of the victim, consigning them to a permanent state of low self-esteem.[19] Gradually, the diagnosis that some experiences are damaging to the psyche and result in the lowering of self-esteem of certain groups has expanded beyond the confines of racism and oppression. Communities that are blighted by poverty and unemployment are often portrayed as suffering from a self-esteem deficit. President Bush's welfare-to-work partnership is designed to lead to 'more independence, more self-esteem, and more jobs and hope'.[20] The self-esteem deficit is often presented as a condition that transcends the individual and afflicts entire generations and communities. According to one account, schoolchildren who turn to drugs come from families 'with generations of lack of self-esteem'.[21] When a local railway station was closed down in Shildon, Co Durham, the manager of the local train museum observed that it represented a 'devastating blow to local self-esteem'.[22] 'Self-esteem seems to be a quality lacking in many sections of the European community', observes an advocate of community learning projects.[23]

The assumption that people's self-esteem is linked to group experience and identity is at first sight a puzzling one. The emotional state of the self is very much bound up with individual subjectivity. Indeed, as noted previously, the very orientation towards the self tends to distance individuals from wider networks and communities. Concern with the self or the level of a person's self-esteem tends to individualise problems. So how does this trend toward the individualisation of social experience reconcile itself with the identity of a group? Hewitt, in his important study of the 'myth' of self-esteem, believes that the 'answer may lie partly in the current ascendancy of feelings and emotional well-being in the culture as a whole'. Therapeutic culture does not merely influence individual behaviour. It also provides the cultural idiom through which groups can make sense of their predicament. The recasting of identity through the vocabulary of emotion influences individuals and groups alike. As Hewitt remarks, 'the myth of self-esteem draws into its orbit even those who might be suspicious of it, because discourse about emotions exerts a profound cultural gravity on the thoughts and words of everyone'.[24]

The impact of therapeutic ideals on the cultural understanding of the self is not confined to the sphere of individual identity. In a culture where nations heal, communities are traumatised and minorities suffer from a low level of self-esteem, important aspects of collective identities are understood through the prism of emotion. The influence of the therapeutic ethos on group identity indicates that what is at stake is not simply the individualisation of identity, but its recasting in an emotional form. Concern with the emotional self informs both individual and group identity. One of the distinct features of twenty-first-century society is its relentless preoccupation with the question of identity. Today's obsession with self-identity is the outcome of a variety of social developments. Elias has drawn attention to the 'greater impermanence of we-relationships'. Other sociologists have drawn attention to the weakening of institutionalised identities and of the wider social frameworks within which people formulate their identity. As a result, it is suggested that people are confronted with threats to both their social and their individual identities.[25] One response to these uncertainties is a constant quest for self-definition. Therapeutic culture directs this quest towards the realm of emotions since it is seen as the site where the real self can be found. As Lupton notes, 'emotional states are understood as a means of gaining an insight into the "true" self', since they have 'become the gold standard, revealing to one self how one is really responding to a phenomenon'.[26]

Ceaseless demand for identity

One indication of the powerful authority assigned to feeling is the way that ideas about the emotional self have come to influence the constitution of social identity. The tendency to represent social identity in terms of the emotions that affect the self is one of the distinct features of political discourse today. This development, which is symbolised by the motto 'the personal is political', has as its premise the conviction that the solutions to both individual and social problems have an important therapeutic dimension. Gloria Steinem's *Revolution from Within* offers a variant of feminist therapeutics that connects the low self-esteem of individual woman to the wider question of gender oppression. According to Steinem, steps designed to raise self-esteem would both empower the individual as well as women.[27]

The close connection between identity politics and the ascendancy of therapeutic culture has been widely noted in studies of American society. Indeed, some studies have gone so far as to present identity politics as the instrument through which preoccupation with feelings gained widespread social influence. 'The identity politics of the 1960s laid the ground for America's obsession with feelings in the 1970s', observes Moskowitz.[28] Whilst identity politics played an important role in the promotion of the politics of emotion, it itself was the product of cultural forces that were highly supportive of therapeutics. It is therefore more useful to conceptualise identity politics as the first movement to internalise the therapeutic ideal. Through identity politics the preoccupations of the self are converted into a wider group identity

The assimilation of feeling into group identity acquires a striking manifestation through the growing tendency to reinterpret the past in a therapeutic form. There is a long tradition of history being used to help forge a common identity.[29] History as the signifier of identity depends on the presentation of past experiences that are consequential for people today. The distinctive feature of today's therapeutic history is the way that it projects contemporary survivalist outlook back into the past. The representation of the Holocaust is paradigmatic in this respect. As we shall see, through the representation of the Holocaust, the survivor emerges as the central figure of history.

The shift of focus from the historical hero to the survivor of history mirrors the trend towards the emergence of a more passive form of subjectivity. During the past two centuries, the key motif in the rewriting of history was the desire to promote the unique greatness of a particular people or culture. National myths were about heroic deeds and glorious events. Such myths were not simply used as sentimental celebrations of the past. They were mobilised to construct a positive vision of the future. The myth of the American frontier promised a great destiny for that society. British, French and German national myths were mobilised to provide an optimistic representation of future possibilities. Today, the rewriting of history is driven by a very different impulse. The manipulation of collective memory makes no grand claims on the future. On the contrary, the historic memory serves as a monument to a people's historic suffering. In a perceptive contribution on this subject, Ian Buruma has drawn attention to the tendency of many minorities 'to define themselves as historic victims'.[30] This reorientation towards a preoccupation with past suffering provides a form of collective therapy that allows for a community of sentiment.

The therapeutic turn of history has encouraged victims of past wrong to frame their claims in the language of psychology. The psychiatrist Derek Summerville believes that contemporary ideas about emotional distress encourage the reinterpretation of the past along similar lines. 'Because many now believe that, for example, rape or other criminal violence, childhood sexual abuse, or even persistent bullying at school are all experiences that may have enduring or lifelong psychological effects, it seems unthinkable that torture or atrocity should not do this and more to almost all those exposed to them', writes Summerfield.[31] Similarly, it now seems unthinkable that violent and distressing episodes in the past should not continue to cause psychological damage to the descendants of the victims.

The Holocaust has become the icon for therapeutic history. The extreme and singular brutality of this event ensures that those who perished or suffered in the concentration camps are regarded with a reverence unmatched by any other groups of victims. It is worth noting that many of the direct survivors of the death camps talked very little in public about their terrible experience. As Summerville observes, 'those emerging from concentration camps in 1945 mostly sought to rebuild their social and work lives and to put the war behind them', and 'most did not seek, nor were offered, psychological help; post-war Europe and America did not see them as carrying a permanent psychological wound'.[32] The image of the psychologically scarred-for-life Holocaust victim is very much shaped by the cultural sensibility of the post-1960s era.

The stoic, self-contained response of Holocaust victims to their tragic circumstances in the 1940s stands in sharp contrast to the way some of their children and grandchildren, the so-called second and third generation survivors, have engaged with the experience. In recent years, some of the promoters of second-generation survivor groups have even criticised their parents for bottling up their emotions and refusing to embrace the identity of an emotionally damaged people.[33] In line with contemporary trends, Israeli identity has been recast around the Holocaust. Zionism, which had traditionally promoted an optimistic modernist vision of the pioneering new Jew, has in recent decades sought to forge community around an emotional connection with the Holocaust. The authority enjoyed by medicalised trauma discourse 'makes it well placed to confer legitimacy, whether to authenticate membership in a particular victim group, to enhance public recognition, or in compensation suits'.[34]

The appeal of the Holocaust as a formidable focus for survivalist identity formation has attracted the attention of competing groups of claimants for identity status. Gay activists have insisted that their suffering during the Holocaust should be recognised through the construction of monuments and memorials. Other activists representing gypsies and the disabled have also demanded that recognition should be accorded to their plight during this terrible experience. 'Sometimes it is as if everyone wants to compete with the Jewish tragedy', observes Buruma.[35] Certainly the language associated with Holocaust discourse – particularly the image of the traumatised survivor – has been appropriated by numerous activists determined to stake a claim to the status associated with emotional suffering. For instance, the Irish potato famine has been reinterpreted as an abusive experience that continues to traumatise people to this day. The emotional power of the Holocaust has been co-opted and transferred to other experiences, such as the African-American Holocaust, the Serbian Holocaust, the Bosnian Holocaust or the Rwandan Holocaust. In Germany, anti-abortion campaigners hold forth about a Holocaust of foetus and animal-rights activists denounce the Holocaust of seals in Canada. Frequently, this manipulation of the Holocaust turns the tragedy into a caricature and a cause of controversy. For example, many US Jews were angered when an animal rights organisation launched a campaign that compared the slaughter of livestock to the Holocaust. The exhibition called 'Holocaust on Your Plate' juxtaposed images of people in concentration camps with disturbing pictures of animals'.[36]

Historic injuries to the emotion are said to continue to damage subsequent generations. It is claimed that the children and grandchildren of Holocaust survivors ought to be considered just as much victims as their ancestors who had to directly confront the horrors of Nazi death camps. As a result, attention has shifted to the problems of the so-called second generation of Holocaust survivors. Some studies contend that children born to Holocaust survivors became the victims of their parent's own destructive experience. 'These children, now grown men and women, have sometimes been raised in a psychological atmosphere poisoned by the scarring that their survivor parents have brought to their child-rearing tasks', claims one authority.[37] According to proponents of this thesis, the second generation of survivors often grew up in a family atmosphere where they were stifled by overprotectiveness, shame and mistrust. It is suggested that the consequences of this parental trauma was to damage the emotional development of their children. As one writer on the subject argues, 'most members of the second generation whose voices have been heard feel that they have been damaged in some way through their parents' Holocaust experience'.[38]

The literature on the second generation provides useful insights into understanding the social construction of emotion-based identity. According to the accepted paradigm, the compulsive behaviour of concentration camps survivors has led to negative and stifling parenting styles, which in turn has had a damaging impact on their children. One of the most common claims made about camp survivors is that they sought to become parents in order to acquire a new identity for themselves. Parents often named their children after a lost favourite relative. It is claimed that children, who felt that they had been 'given the mission to be a link in the broken chain of families and to fill the emptiness in their parents' lives', often 'felt burdened and weighed down by such impossible expectations'. Descriptions of overprotective and demanding parents are recycled as the authors of a destructive family environment which has emotionally damaged their offspring's. Yet, severe dislocation, suffering and tragic loss leading to distinct overprotective parenting styles are by no means confined to any particular experience. Adults who have experienced the trials of war, hunger and death will invariably inflict their insecurities on their family. Whether such parental anxieties are particularly damaging for children is far from evident. The case of the second generation, with its redefinition of family life as a conduit for victimisation, says more about the therapeutic discourse of the post-1960s era than about the parenting skills of their fathers and mothers. The invention of the second generation may well be the outcome of a culture, which increasingly links individual identity to the emotional needs of the self.

It is worth noting that many who describe themselves as second generation survivors are involved in medicine, counselling, psychotherapy, social work and education and are therefore drawn towards expressing their identity through the vocabulary of therapy.[39] The activists in second generation survivor groups recognise the predominant role played by therapeutic professionals in this movement. The following advice to survivor groups by an activist illustrates this trend:

> Start your won 'Rap group' by just getting together on a weekly basis, or there is a good probability that one of your members may be a social worker, or a counsellor of some type. In my first group there was a clinical psychologist and a social worker.[40]

For second generation survivor activists, the past provides a medium through which the emotional needs of the self can gain meaning.

The fragile character of emotion-based identities dooms the self to a continuous quest for affirmation. The disorganisation of informal relations, the cultivation of the estrangement of people from each other and the weakening of external points of reference are trends that mutually reinforce one another to create a demand for cultivating a strong sense of self. The unprecedented concern with the emotional needs of the self has created a situation where it has acquired the status of a cultural fetish. Often the self is represented as having an existence in its own right. It is frequently treated as something that can be measured, quantified and changed through therapeutic techniques. This fetishisation of the self has acquired tremendous significance in relation to what is the most widely discussed fetish of therapeutic culture: the problem of self-esteem. It appears that self-esteem, which is defined as a 'person's unconditional appreciation of himself or herself', can be quantified as a thing in itself.[41] According to advocates of the therapeutic ethos, the measurement of how one feels about oneself provides an accurate insight into the behaviour of a person.

Self-esteem: a cultural myth for our times

The emotionalisation of the self can be seen through the importance that society attaches to the problem of self-esteem. The emotional needs of the self most often cited are, first, the need to feel good about oneself and, second, the need to be affirmed by others. How individuals feel about themselves is no longer seen as a personal matter. 'Few readers of this article will need convincing that self-esteem is not just a personal issue, you know it is a community issue', observes an author of a booklet on this subject written for therapeutic professionals.[42] It is claimed that low self-esteem is the cause of not only personal unhappiness, but also of most of the problems facing society.

Concern with self-esteem provides the single most powerful illustration of the impact of therapeutic culture on everyday life. On both sides of the Atlantic, self-esteem has acquired the cultural status of a taken-for-granted problem that afflicts the individual and society alike. Low self-esteem is invariably presented as an invisible disease that undermines people's ability to control their lives. When in a famous television interview the late Princess Diana informed the British public of her secret disease, bulimia, her audience knew what she meant when she stated that 'you inflict it upon yourself because your self-esteem is at a low ebb, and you don't think you're worthy or valuable'.[43] Diana's confession resonated with the common sense that perceives low self-esteem as the principal cause of individual and wider social problems. This point was echoed by Oprah Winfrey when she informed her audience that 'what we are trying to change in this one hour is what I think is the root of all the problems in the world – lack of self-esteem'.[44] When President Bush proclaimed 9 June 2002 as National Child's Day, he urged 'people to support and love all children' so that they 'can develop self-esteem and have a strong foundation for life'.[45]

Low self-esteem is now associated with virtually every ill that afflicts society. Nathaniel Branden, the influential author of *The Psychology of Self-Esteem*, remarked that 'I cannot think of a single psychological problem – from anxiety and depression, to fear of intimacy or of success, to spouse battery or child molestation that is not traceable to the problem of poor self-esteem'.[46] Policy-makers, media commentators and experts regularly demand that action should be taken to raise the self-esteem of schoolchildren, teenagers, parents, the elderly, the homeless, the mentally ill, delinquents, the unemployed, those suffering racism, lone parents, to name but a few of the groups experiencing this problem.

One of the most common ways of emphasising the negative consequence of a specific social issue is by outlining the damage it causes to self-esteem. Claim-makers frequently attempt to justify their concern with a problem by asserting its negative impact on self-esteem. In a statement of support for a British government initiative against domestic violence, Digby Jones, director general of the Confederation of British Industry, pointed out that this act 'can have a devastating impact on people' and that 'it can harm business as the victims often suffer from stress and low-esteem'.[47] According to a report published by the pharmaceutical company Pfizer, it is people's 'relationships and self-esteem' which is most affected by sexual health problems.[48] Antipoverty campaigners have shifted their focus from the broad structural picture to the impact of these conditions on self-esteem. One recently published study, *Hardship Britain: Being Poor in the 1990s*, is consciously promoted on the ground that it examines the 'experience of poverty and exclusion, and its impact on self-esteem and personal dignity'.[49]

Low self-esteem is not just represented as the consequence of problems such as poverty, racism or domestic violence, it is frequently depicted as a cause of virtually every form of social distress. Government agencies continually point to the self-esteem deficit as the direct source of social problems. 'Whilst there is no single route through which children become involved in prostitution, we know that the most common factors are vulnerability and low self-esteem', states a briefing document by the Department of Health for Wales.[50] According to Dr Christopher Cordess, a forensic psychiatrist, people who make malicious bomb hoax calls 'will be repeating offenders – men who have very little self-esteem'.[51] Lonnie Payne, Chair of the San Francisco AIDS Foundation, believes that self-esteem is a major factor in the spread of HIV. 'It is now absurd to ignore that feelings of self-loathing, isolation and worthlessness are core factors in HIV infection'.[52] According to John Kelly and Brian Karem, the authors of *Warning Signs – How to Read Early Signals of Low Self-Esteem, Addiction and Hidden Violence in Your Children*, low self-esteem is the root cause of the 'growing rate' of addiction, violence and depression amongst the 8 to 18-year-olds.[53] Researchers also claim that low self-esteem is associated with childhood obesity.[54]

Official and nonofficial public health advocates continually preach the virtues of raising self-esteem for the well-being of the individuals. Indeed, one of the ways that campaigners promote a particular issue is by linking it to its alleged benefits for self-esteem. Mission statements justify a bewildering variety of activities on the ground of raising self-esteem. To take a few examples, in 1993 the Ms. Foundation launched the Take Our Daughters to Work Day, in order to boost the confidence and self-esteem of girls.[55] In Britain, it is frequently claimed that single-sex schools and classes 'help promote girls' confidence and self-esteem'.[56] In America, President Bush has endorsed single-gender education on the same grounds. 'I've seen girls who had poor self-esteem, and you can see their self-esteem rise to heights that their parents couldn't believe could happen', states Pamela Smith, the founder of a single-sex education programme for African-American girls in Hartford.[57]

Everyone seemed to have jumped on the self-esteem bandwagon. Abstinence, the Better Choice, an Ohio-based advocacy group preaching abstinence, aims to build self-esteem through diverting teens from risky behaviours such as drinking and drug use in order to reduce premarital sex.[58] A major project promoting gardening for its therapeutic effects, by the charity Thrive, claims that one of the main benefits of this activity is that it 'increases self-esteem'.[59] The National Cycling Forum in its strategy document *Promoting Cycling: Improving Health* boasts that 'studies have shown that regular cyclists, compared with inactive people, have improved well-being, higher self-esteem and greater confidence in their ability to perform active tasks'.[60] Outdoor Education claims that guided experience of the outdoors 'increases self-confidence and self-esteem'.[61] The National Pyramid Trust aims to reach 'as many children as possible and to establish routine check of their emotional health needs', in order to help them build 'their self-esteem and resilience'.[62] The IPPR, one of Britain's leading think tanks, advocates business support for women from deprived areas because 'enterprise activity' can 'increase self-esteem'.[63] Groundwork, a charity devoted to environmental regeneration, claims that the 'process of identifying, planning and implementing improvements to the local environment offers an excellent opportunity to improve the self-confidence and self-esteem of young people'.[64] SureSlim, a commercial company helping people manage their weight, tells potential customers that the 'rewarding end product' for people who lose some weight is 'the boost in morale and self-esteem'.[65] The Communities United Project, which involves young people in football, aims to 'improve the self-esteem of adults by offering them the opportunity to get involved and run individual schemes'.[66] The Nationwide Foundation supports volunteering programmes that focus on 'raising the confidence and self-esteem of the volunteers themselves'.[67]

The sheer range of social evils attributed to the deficit of self-esteem indicates that it has become an all-purpose explanation for the problems of everyday life. There is now an almost automatic assumption that if you scratch the surface of a social or individual problem, a state of low self-esteem will be revealed. 'But why should anyone imagine that such diverse social issues and such complex types of human behaviour could be caused by just one factor: how good or bad one feels about oneself', asks Jennifer Cunningham, a community paediatrician from Glasgow.[68] It is not empirical reality but our therapeutic sensibility toward the emotion of the self that leads to the reduction of complex reality to the state of self-esteem. That one single factor can be held responsible for so many complicated social questions indicates that it is the forces of culture and not of scientific investigation that has led to the universalisation of the problem of self-esteem. As a result, the problem of self-esteem has acquired a free-floating character that can attach itself to any issue. Its ability to jump from one problem to the next suggests that the self-esteem deficit has become something of a folk myth that is transmitted through the conduit of our cultural imagination.

One of the attractive features of this folk myth is the claim that raising self-esteem works as a magic bullet that will solve the problems facing the individual and society. The British psychologist Terri Apter, a proponent of the miraculous effects of raising self-esteem, enthuses, 'new research confirms what has repeatedly been found to be true: self-esteem is a key to successful development and has a far greater impact on future success (and happiness) than intelligence or talent'.[69] State Senator John Vasconcellos of California, a leading voice of the self-esteem movement, regards self-esteem as the 'social vaccine safeguarding us all'.[70]

The self-esteem deficit is a cultural myth that is continually promoted by its advocates. That is why, especially in the United States, there are frequent references to the 'self-esteem movement'. Advocates of the problem of self-esteem regard their activities motivated by a just cause. So the promotion of this cultural myth can be seen as a cause, or more specifically it is a cause, that is constantly in search of arguments and validation. One of the most ambitious and widely publicised initiatives designed to scientifically validate the problem of self-esteem was the launching of the self-esteem task force by the California legislature in 1987. Typically, this task force not only sought to find empirical evidence to justify its concerns, but it was also charged with 'promoting public awareness' of programmes designed to build healthy self-esteem. Evidently, the aim of the task force was to prove what it already knew.

An inspection of the report of the California task force indicates that the problematisation of self-esteem is fuelled by a therapeutic sensibility that intuitively regards the emotional state of the self as the decisive influence on society. Indeed, contributors to the report openly acknowledged that their concern is intuitive, rather than an empirically grounded. In the key methodological chapter of the report, one of the main authors, Neil Smelser, remarked that 'as an intuitive matter – based on our own personal experiences and our observations of others – we know what it is to experience high self-esteem'. Smelser took the view that the aim of the task force is prove what 'we all know to be true' is also 'scientifically true'.[71] Smelser and his colleague feel more comfortable in the realm of intuition than of objectivity reality. He writes that 'we have a fairly firm grasp of what is meant by self-esteem, as revealed by our own introspection and observation of the behavior of others', but adds that 'it is hard to put that understanding into precise words'.[72] Smelser's problem is not surprising. As a taken-for-granted folk myth, self-esteem has a diffuse almost metaphorical character. Precisely because it is the product of therapeutic introspection, the problem is bound up with how one feels about oneself. So although we all know what it means, it means something different to most people.

Unfortunately for Smelser, what he suspects to be intuitively right is not backed up by empirical research. To his credit, Smelser acknowledged the failure of the California task force to find an association between low self-esteem and social problems. 'One of the disappointing aspects of every chapter in this volume' is 'how low the association between self-esteem and its consequences are in research to date', notes Smelser. Evidently, Smelser still believes that there is an association between the two, only it remains unproven. He remains convinced, despite the 'news most consistently reported', that 'the association between self-esteem and its expected consequences are mixed, insignificant, or absent'.[73]

Smelser's conviction that self-esteem is responsible for a multitude of social problems is not undermined by the failure of the task force to find evidence. He tries to come to terms with this failure by representing self-esteem as an elusive variable that cannot be pinned down by social research. He reports that the 'social-psychological variable of self-esteem is simultaneously one of the most central and one of the most elusive factors in understanding and explaining behaviors that constitute major social problems'. Through tautological reasoning, Smelser claims that the very fact self-esteem cannot be scientifically validated proves that it is elusive. It is elusive because it cannot be validated and it cannot be validated because it is elusive. 'The variable of self-esteem is elusive, however, because its precise role in the drama of self-realization is difficult to pinpoint scientifically', observes Smelser.[74] It never occurs to Smelser and the task force that the very premise of their crusade is based on a cultural myth. As far as they are concerned, their cause remains true – it merely needs proof. 'As scientific findings become more reliable, however, and as the involvement of self-esteem in the causes of social problems becomes better understood, policy interventions can profitably become correspondingly bolder', promises Smelser.[75]

The failure of the California task force to justify its crusade has been replicated on the other side of the Atlantic. Government-sponsored British advocacy research on the subject is forced to concede that that there is not even agreement on the meaning of the term 'self-esteem'.[76] One government publication notes that 'self-esteem has received more attention than almost any other concept as a barometer of coping and adaptation', before conceding that research is 'not robust enough to justify any substantive conclusions being drawn'.[77] Yet lack of consensus about the meaning of the term and the absence of empirical evidence that demonstrates the problem of self-esteem does not inhibit officials and advocacy groups from drawing very substantial conclusions about this subject.

To their credit, Smelser and his colleagues acknowledged their inability to find a significant correlation between the self-esteem deficit and social problems. Many other advocates of the self-esteem movements are far less scrupulous about acknowledging the lack of evidence for their claims. Indeed, the report of the California task force is often used as a positive endorsement for the self-esteem crusade. 'The two volume report presents an impressive range of research and recommendations', enthuses a British publication entitled *The Self-Esteem Directory*.[78]

The backlash against the myth

In recent years, there has been something of a backlash against some of the dubious policies designed to raise self-esteem. In particular, concern has been voiced about the preoccupation of parents and teachers with raising children's self-esteem. Numerous observers have claimed that American children are systematically flattered, fed on a diet of empty phrases and therefore become demotivated. This backlash against the myth has been fuelled by the apparent disorientation caused in American schools by the policy of raising children's self-esteem. Many American observers are concerned that the relentless pursuit of raising self-esteem has turned many children into self-centred and unbearably selfish brats.

Numerous commentators have observed that although American children appear to possess a high level of self-esteem they do rather poorly in school. Research carried out on US college students indicates that their self-esteem rose dramatically between 1968 and 1994. However, according Dr Jean Twenge of the Department of Psychology at San Diego University, during the same period that college students' self-esteem increased, their SAT scores declined. Other psychologists have questioned the alleged benefits of raising self-esteem on the ground that it appears to coincide with the deterioration of behaviour among young adults.[79]

But the growing disquiet about self-esteem took on real momentum following the school shootings at Columbine. It was claimed that the killers did not suffer from low esteem, as might have been assumed, but from an unhealthy streak of individualism. John Rosemond, a psychologist and author of numerous childcare manuals, argued that high self-esteem was linked to low self-control, which in turn can lead to violent behaviour.[80] Rosemond's argument was based on the findings of Dr Roy Baumeister, a social scientists based at Case Western University. Baumeister's research concluded that people with low self-esteem were not prone to aggressive responses. He found that acts of violence were far more likely to be associated with people who had a high opinion of themselves. 'Conceited, self-important individuals turn nasty towards those who puncture their bubbles of self-love', asserted Baumeiser.[81] Subsequently, the psychologists Laura Smith and Charles Elliot suggested that children with inappropriately enhanced self-esteem deal with disappointment by seeking a quick fix from drugs, violence and sex. In their book *Hollow Kids: Recapturing the Soul of a Generation Lost to the Self-Esteem Myth* they argue that 'it is time we stopped feeding empty praise into our children because it is making them into empty adolescents who are more self-absorbed and materialistic than previous generations'.[82]

Britain too has seen a minor backlash against the dogma of the self-esteem deficit. A survey of 15,000 children aged 14 and 15, conducted by the Schools Health Education Unit, found that contrary to conventional wisdom, 'youngsters with high self-esteem were more likely to take illicit drugs than those whose confidence was low'.[83] And a major study, carried out by Professor Nicholas Emler of the London School of Economics, dismissed as myth the idea that low self-esteem drives children towards antisocial behaviour. In a review of research published in scientific journals, the report concluded that it is confident children who are more likely to be racists, to bully others and to engage in drink driving and speeding. Emler concluded that the 'widespread belief in raising self-esteem as an all-purpose cure for social problems has created a huge market for self-help manuals and educational programmes that is threatening to become the psycho-therapeutic equivalent of snake oil'.[84]

The backlash against the self-esteem movement has been facilitated by the fact that the miraculous claims made on its behalf have no foundation in research. Yet, the backlash has appeared to have done little to undermine the influence of this cultural myth. One reason why the backlash has had such minimal impact may be due to the fact that it accepts the fundamental premise of its opponents, which is that how the self feels about itself has important implications for understanding society's problems. The idea that the state of one's self-esteem is a predictor of individual and social behaviour appears to influence both sides of the debate. Disagreement about whether it is low or high esteem that is the cause of problems still remains dominated by a preoccupation with the self. However, feelings about oneself are mediated through complex relationships and institutions. Nor are these feelings static. They alter in line with changing events and opportunities. The attempt to treat self-esteem as an independent variable that determines broad patterns of social behaviour requires a highly individualistic methodology that overlooks the broad cultural context within which people interact with one another. It appears that most parties to this debate accept the premise of this methodology.

Another reason why the absence of scientific affirmation does not act as a deterrent to the expansion of concern with self-esteem is because it works as a taken-for-granted common-sense cultural concept. Although its use is often ambiguous, it generally connotes the sense of feeling good about oneself. It is often used interchangeably with words such as self-respect and self-confidence. Since feeling happy and confident are desirable states of mind, the importance of self-esteem are unlikely to be seriously contested.

But the most important reason why the backlash against the promotion of self-esteem is unlikely to have a major impact is linked to the way that human subjectivity is represented today. As noted previously, therapeutic culture is founded on a feeble version of the subject, one that is characteristically defined by its vulnerability. Promoting self-esteem represents an attempt to help people come to terms with their emotional vulnerability. This reaction is particularly striking in relation to the preoccupation with the need to boost children's self-esteem. It is the fear that children are by definition emotionally vulnerable and therefore unable to deal with disappointment that has fed the idea that they need constant praise and acknowledgement of their efforts. As long as how the self feels is interpreted as the defining feature of individual identity, initiatives designed to make people feel good are likely to thrive.

An anti-intellectual emotional ethos

For the self-esteem movement, research and science have little importance other than to validate what it intuitively grasps. This orientation is reinforced by a stance which continually subordinates the act of reasoning to feeling. An anti-intellectual emotional stance seems integral to therapeutic culture today. It is not therapeutics as such, but its peculiarly strident celebration of emotionalism that lends it a strikingly anti-intellectual character. It is useful to recall that many of the leading innovators in the field of psychiatry and psychology took pains to distance themselves from emotionalism and regarded themselves as scientists. Freud did not valorise emotion – on the contrary, he sought to explore the consequences of irrational impulses and drives. Like many of his colleagues, he was concerned about the disruptive effects of irrationality on public life.

Today, an anti-intellectual emotional ethos appears to influence therapeutic culture. A recent survey of the counselling profession in Britain has noted that therapists do not engage in research and take a negative view towards it. The study concluded that 'there is a widespread anti-science, anti-research feeling in the therapeutic community'.[85] The authors of this study characterise counselling as an 'anti-intellectual movement' where 'feelings are more valued than thoughts and where there is little emphasis on "book learning"'. They also claim that 'research is invariably rejected in favour of emotionally held principles'.[86] The social psychologist Carol Tavris believes that 'the split between the research and practice wings of psychology' in the US has become so wide that 'many psychologists now speak glumly of the "science–practitioner gap"', although that is like saying there is an 'Arab–Israeli gap' in the Middle East. Tavris is concerned that the number of scientifically trained clinicians is shrinking and that many therapists 'fail to keep up with basic research on matters on which they are advising their clients'.[87]

The cultural shift from reasoning to emotionalism is most clearly expressed through the privileged status accorded to emotional skills in society. Self-esteem advocates argue that it is not intellectual abilities, but how you feel that really matters. According to one account, 'it is often our level of self-esteem rather than our intellectual abilities or academic achievements that determine our level of success and fulfilment in life'.[88] Therapeutic claim-makers frequently treat academic intelligence as less important than what is increasingly referred to as emotional intelligence. According to a media organisation training people for business, 'your emotional intelligence may be more important than your IQ'. This assertion is echoed by Dr Steven Stein, president of Multi-health Systems Inc., who reports that 'emotional intelligence is significantly and highly correlated with job performance, while cognitive intelligence has shown a very low and insignificant correlation with performance in the workplace'.[89]

Proponents of the idea of emotional literacy and of emotional intelligence develop the arguments of the self-esteem movement in relation to a wider cultural setting. Texts on emotional intelligence and emotional literacy tend to be lightweight, both theoretically and empirically. Most offer little more than homespun assertions in the language of psychobabble. Susie Orbach, who is probably the most subtle proponent of this concept, defines emotional literacy as the 'capacity to resonate with one another emotionally without being swamped, to emphathize without feeling impelled to make better, to register one's personal emotional responses in all their subtlety, so that there is space for those responses so often regarded because they are undramatic'.[90] This round-about way of describing what was once described as the quality of being sensitive is not in and of itself objectionable. It is the obsession with the domain of the emotion which gives this standpoint a dogmatic character.

Although self-help books on emotional literacy claim that emotion and reason are complementary, they one-sidedly privilege the former. Developing emotional literacy is imperative in Goleman's view, because 'of the two, emotional intelligence adds far more of the qualities that makes us more fully human'.[91] From this perspective, human beings are defined as above all emotional and consciousness is predicated upon understanding how you feel. This world-view implicitly rejects the view that human beings are defined by what they do – one of the key insights of Enlightenment thinking

The tension between reason and emotion goes back to debates in Greek philosophy and the advocacy of emotional intelligence can be seen as an ideal counterpoint to Plato's outlook. For Plato, the emphasis on emotion had the paradoxical effect of preventing people finding solutions to their hurt. 'We must learn not to hold our hurts and waste our time crying, like children who've bumped themselves, but to train our mind to banish grief by curing our hurts and rectifying our mistakes as soon as it can'.[92] Such a statement today would earn Plato the diagnosis of being in denial. And yet, throughout the modern era, self-control of emotion was seen as the foundation of a civilised society. Today, advocates of emotional intelligence would contend that Plato's unemotional exterior was merely a mask for his deep-seated malaise. Antidote, a UK-based organisation devoted to the promotion of emotional intelligence in public life, offers a distinctly anti-Platonic perspective. One Antidote psychologist argues for the extension of emotional literacy into politics, so 'that we can think of a citizenry who, as feminism has long argued, want to talk about politics and act politically in a coherent way, based on good information – and with feeling'.[93]

The promotion of emotional intelligence is symptomatic of a climate of intellectual pessimism. Suspicion towards reasoning and conventional learning has helped create a climate where so-called emotional skills can expect cultural support. 'Academic intelligence offers no preparation for the emotional turmoil of life', writes one devotee of emotionalism. Emotional education is presented as the answer to the problem of the contemporary individual.[94]

8 Conferring recognition
The quest for identity and the state

The contemporary world is characterised by the loss of a web of meaning through which people make sense about who they are and where they stand in relation to others. The British sociologist Ralph Fevre characterises the feeble sense of moral reasoning as the 'demoralization of western culture'.[1] Instead of a moral code that provides experience with meaning, we live in an age of 'values'. As Hunter notes, 'values are truths that have been deprived of their commanding character'. Values are oriented towards the individual self. 'Values are personal preferences, inclinations and choice', observes Hunter.[2] It is through values that therapeutic culture attempts to give meaning to the place of the self in society. According to Ulrich Beck, one of the key components of the therapeutically influenced value system is the 'principle of "duty to oneself"'.[3] Since values exist in a plural and individual form they cannot provide a moral grammar of meaning. The orientation towards values makes questions like 'who are we?' and 'what is our place in this world?' difficult to answer.

In an important exploration of our cultural fixation with trauma, the psychiatrist Patrick Bracken links it to the 'dread brought on by a struggle with meaning'.[4] He believes that as the 'meaningfulness of our lives is called into question', individuals respond to distress in an intensely individualised and traumatised fashion. Such a response of the vulnerable self 'stems from a wider cultural difficulty regarding a belief in an ordered and coherent world'.[5] From Bracken's perspective, the continuous search for a psychological diagnosis represents an attempt to find meaning in confusion.

A lack of clarity about who we are has been intensified by the disorganisation of the private sphere. This development has endowed the quest for recognition with a peculiar intensity. In the past, this quest was answered through the prism of a common culture, a shared view of the world, religion or political ideologies. Today, society appears to possess a diminished capacity to answer the question of who we are. This quest for meaning has led to an unprecedented concern with the question of identity. This preoccupation with identity has had a significant impact on popular culture, social and political life. This reorientation towards identity has had particularly powerful influence on the sphere of politics. As Jedediah Purdy, the American social commentator, remarked, 'identity politics, based on sex, sexuality, and, mostly, race and ethnicity, suggests that politics should work not so much to give people things, such as education and jobs, as to give them recognition'.[6] The growth of identity politics and the claim for recognition has had a significant influence on contemporary political discourse and policy-making. Nancy Fraser argues with force that 'questions of recognition are serving less to supplement, complicate and enrich redistributive struggles than to marginalize, eclipse and displace them'.[7]

This growing shift towards the politics of recognition constitutes the main subject of this chapter. This development is generally perceived as part of a wider turn away from social towards cultural issues. There is little doubt that over the past two decades the politicisation of identities and culture has had a significant impact on social life. However, a closer examination of this development suggests that it represents not just a turn toward culture in general, but towards one with an intense therapeutic sensibility. An orientation towards therapeutics underpins both the quest for recognition and the preoccupation with identity. Moscowitz believes that 'the identity politics of the 1960s laid the ground for America's obsession with feelings in the 1970s'. This point is echoed by Lowney who suggests that when movements for social justice felt thwarted or rejected 'they settled for constructing new collective identities'. She concludes that 'agendas switched from seeking dramatic social change to forging a new psychic acceptance of self'.[8] Moskowitz and Lowney are right to stress the close relationship between the growth of identity politics and the turn towards therapeutics. However, it is not so much the case that one led to another – rather both identity politics and the therapeutic turn represent responses to the demand for meaning.

The therapeutic imperative behind the expansion of the politics of recognition is often obscured by the fact that presentations of this subject tend to focus on conflicts of cultural identity. It is the controversies over multiculturalism, race and competing cultural identities that dominate the public imagination. So it is not surprising that the exploration of the struggles for recognition invariably associate it with the affirmation of cultural identities. One of the most important statements on the subject, Charles Taylor's essay on 'The Politics of Recognition', links the demand for recognition to the politics of multiculturalism.[9] Yet Taylor's own emphasis on the politics of recognition being driven by the 'goals of self-fulfilment and self-realisation' point not just simply to culture, but to the quest for identity in an intensely self-oriented form.[10] It is evident that the politics of recognition leads not only to valorisation of difference, but also to the privileging of therapeutic values. It represents therapeutic claims-making in the political sphere.

Since the end of the Cold War, the politics of recognition has been widely promoted as an enlightened alternative to previous norms of justice claims. One of the advantages claimed on its behalf is that it gives due recognition to the individual since it is directed 'at the particular qualities that characterise people in their personal difference'.[11] It is also argued that individual self-determination ought to be the basis for real democracy.[12] This focus on individual difference is underwritten by a premise, which regards self-affirmation as the fundamental need that society needs to address. Francis Fukuyama goes so far as to suggest that this quest for recognition is so profound that 'it is one of the chief motors of the entire human historical process'.[13] It is interesting to note that contemporary proponents of the politics of recognition have shifted the focus of this issue from the wider philosophical field (Hobbes and Machiavelli) to the sphere of intersubjective recognition. Its core assumption is that driven by a deep psychological need, the self becomes actualised through cultural identity. One of the most powerful advocate of this thesis, the German philosopher Alex Honneth, actually adopts Donald Winnicott's object-relations theory to promote a model where psychological damage is the central problem of injustice and inequality.[14] From this perspective the experience of exclusion above all refers to the sense of humiliation and shame that comes from not being recognised and affirmed. Thus, the focus of Honneth's concern is the psychological damage inflicted on people by a society that fails to encourage the development of their self-confidence, self-respect and self-esteem. 'The experience of being socially denigrated or humiliated endangers the identity of human beings, just as infection with disease endangers their physical life', writes Honneth.[15]

The association of the need for recognition with identity formation is not by itself a controversial point. However, this need is increasingly conceptualised as an individual right, thus encouraging an explosion of recognition claims. This demand for the right to be recognised also leads to the psychologisation of justice. 'The conviction that human beings have not only a deeply rooted need for recognition and acceptance, but also a fundamental right to it takes many forms, but appears, perhaps most vividly, in the commonly heard plea "accept me for who I am"', notes Hewitt.[16] The demand for the right to be esteemed unites both identity-based social movements and individuals concerned with their goal of self-realisation. That is why raising the collective self-esteem of a particular group is frequently put forward as one of the goals of social movements.

The politicisation of identity is often presented as part of a struggle to correct hitherto unrecognised wrongs and to allow people to express themselves through the life forms appropriate to their culture. Jurgen Habermas, a leading German social theorist, interprets these struggles as representing demands for the 'recognition of life forms and traditions which have been marginalized'.[17] However, this interpretation tends to read history backwards and overlooks the distinct features of contemporary recognition claims. It is not past wrongs, but the diminishing capacity of contemporary institutions – formal and informal – to confer and affirm identity that fuels the demand to be recognised. In turn, institutions have seized upon this demand in order to enhance their authority through providing recognition for a fragmented public. Traditional national identities have become highly problematic but public institutions have never been so busy offering recognition and respect to anyone who demands it through a bewildering variety of initiatives around the aim of 'inclusion'.

The demand for the right to be esteemed has troubled some of the theorists of recognition. Francis Fukuyama is concerned that the automatic granting of esteem avoids the making of moral choices about what deserves to be esteemed. He notes that the 'problem with the present-day self-esteem movement is that its members . . . are seldom willing to make choices concerning what should be esteemed'.[18]

Nancy Fraser argues that the view 'that everyone has an equal right to social esteem' renders 'meaningless the notion of esteem'.[19] However, once the right to self-realisation is accepted as a defining feature of a just society, it becomes difficult to place conditions on the automatic granting of esteem to every person regardless of their specific traits, accomplishments or contributions. As Lasch concludes, the therapeutic turn towards the demand for recognition has little to do with justice, but reflects a new relationship between self and society. 'Today men seek the kind of approval that applauds not their actions but their attributes', observes Lasch.[20] Approval thus becomes an act of affirmation of self rather than an evaluation of individual achievement.

Ironically, the institutionalisation of the right to recognition necessarily leads to emptying it of any moral content. Human struggles for recognition are mediated through specific historical and cultural forms. Such struggles often contain a creative dynamic of making history, enhancing self-consciousness, making moral choices, entering into dialogues and accomplishing the construction of identities organic to one's circumstances. Struggling for recognition involves a different process to gaining recognition on demand. In the former it involves an active engagement of construction, whilst in the latter it implies being acted upon by those conferring recognition. Such a right can never satisfy the craving to be recognised – it merely incites the individual for more assurances of respect. However, the very act of offering respect to those who crave it may make matters more complicated. As Richard Sennett suggests, the weak may quite rightly experience the extension of such respect as an empty gesture or worse still as ritual confirming their position of inferiority.[21]

The state of recognition

Numerous social theorists depict the struggles of new social movements for recognition as representing a significant challenge to the state.[22] However, the contemporary western state did not have to be press-ganged into absorbing the demand for recognition. On the contrary, it has swiftly embraced the therapeutic imperative and made it its own. In an important exploration of this development, Wendy Brown argues that it reflects a reorientation of state activities towards the provision of essential social repairs on a society 'stressed and torn by secularising and atomising effects of capitalism'.[23] Brown's concern with the 'steady slide of political into therapeutic discourse' is anticipated in Habermas' discussion of the colonisation of the life world. According to Habermas, the development of the welfare state leads to the steady growth of state intervention into the domain of private life. The fragmentation of social experience boosts the expansion of this trend. In a fragmented world, the provision of therapeutic assistance becomes a vehicle for social integration.[24] So instead of perceiving it as a threat, the state regards recognition claims as an opportunity to reinvent itself as the authoritative voice of affirmation.

The reorientation of the welfare state towards the repair of psychical injury and related therapeutic functions is not the main subject of our discussion. Suffice it to note that this development represents an attempt to confront the problem of legitimation faced by authorities throughout the western world. The internalisation of the therapeutic ethos in America has been well documented.[25] The institutionalisation of recognition and of the therapeutic ethos is also clearly demonstrated in the case of Britain. 'It is telling that technologies similar to those employed by counselling have now become part and parcel of the way in which the current British Government governs its people', notes Arnason.[26] Since the early 1980s when counselling emerged as a government policy directed at reintegrating the unemployed, therapeutic intervention has become a normal feature of social policy. These policies paralleled by the 'explosion of the therapy and counselling industry in Britain' have led to the colonisation of what David Smail calls the 'territory of ordinary social discourse'.[27] Moreover, the loss of credibility in the project of classical welfarism has encouraged the state to adopt a more individualised and therapeutic style of policy-making. Increasingly, policies are represented as 'supporting' and 'empowering', if not quite treating individuals.

Since the mid-1990s, policies are justified on the grounds that they 'support' a particular target group. Policy does not so much aim to 'solve' problems, but to support otherwise disempowered clients. This is particularly the case with policies that are designed to tackle social exclusion and encourage inclusion. The manner in which the language of social exclusion and inclusion is used conveys the impression that people suffer from disadvantage as a condition of their existence. Norman Fairclough's study of the language on New Labour suggests that social exclusion is conceptualised as a 'condition people are in, not something that is done to them'. Social exclusion is rarely presented as a process, but rather something like illness that people suffer from.[28] That is why the experience of social exclusion is frequently presented as a subjective one. 'Social exclusion is perceived and experienced "subjectively"', write the authors of a report for the Scottish Executive. In this report, the experience is presented as a form of social isolation that encompasses 'lack of contact with other people, a feeling of being trapped, low self-esteem and self-confidence, and feelings of insecurity, hopelessness and depression'.[29] The same point is echoed by the Library and Information Commission's report *Libraries: the Essence of Inclusion*. The report indicates that 'social exclusion is experienced subjectively and is therefore specific and relative to each individual, group or environment'.[30] From this perspective the erosion of civic solidarity and of informal networks is recast as essentially a psychological problem.

Of course, every social phenomenon is experienced subjectively. However, with the concept of exclusion, the psychological dimension acquires a decisive significance. The Library and Information Commission explicitly focuses on what it calls the 'psychology of exclusion'. It notes that 'individuals may become excluded through: experiencing or perceiving alienation; isolation; lack of identity; low self-confidence; low self-esteem; passivity; dependence; bewilderment; fear; anger; apathy; low aspirations; and hopelessness'.[31] Tackling this psychology of exclusion is not simply justified on the ground that it assists social integration, but also because managing this condition of psychological distress is increasingly interpreted as an integral part of the business of the state. This tendency for state policy to address the condition of suffering is supported by wider cultural norms, which as Brown notes regard 'suffering as the measure of social virtue'.[32] Thus inclusion, both at the level of policy-making and that of culture, represents an attempt to fulfil the demand for recognition and affirmation.

In its most extreme form, the ethos of inclusion subordinates social and cultural policies to the exigencies of recognition and the therapeutic ethos. Take the domain of culture. The Department for Culture Media and Sport (DCMS) has vigorously promoted the inclusion agenda by promoting projects that make people feel good about themselves. To this end, it has targeted museums, galleries, cultural organisations, such as the Arts Council and local cultural services, to adopt its therapeutic approach. Local organisations, interested in gaining funding, have quickly fallen in line. Thus the Director of Leisure and Cultural Services of Wigan Council promotes the benefits of sports, art and play on the grounds that these activities 'improve cognitive and social skills; reduce impulsiveness and risk-taking behaviours; raise self-esteem and self-confidence and improve education and employment prospects'.[33] Sport bodies requesting government funding now know that they need to flag up their commitment to social inclusion and advertise its therapeutic benefits. 'Sport is an ideal vehicle for improving self-esteem and helping people feel better about themselves', claims Sport Scotland.[34] The government has established a special team of advisors, called PAT (Policy Action Team), which specialises in policies that target social exclusion through raising the self-esteem of the excluded. It is worth noting that the Policy Action Team 10 social inclusion report to the DCMS acknowledged the potential for subordinating cultural services to demands of therapeutic recognition. 'We do not believe that every artist or sportsperson should be a social worker by another name, or that artistic or sporting excellence should take second place to community regeneration', it noted.[35] However, artistic excellence was conspicuously absent from the examples of best practice that the report promoted. One scheme praised by PAT 10 was a centre in Manchester, where people recovering from mental illness 'find that the arts are not merely a powerful antidote to loneliness, but also a significant means of self-fulfilment and of giving pleasure to others'.[36]

The DCMS has wholeheartedly embraced the spirit of therapeutic culture. A recent document published by the DCMS, *Centres for Social Change: Museums, Galleries and Archives for All*, demands that curators of museums and galleries take on board the objective of 'combating social exclusion'. It instructs curators that they have a duty to 'increase individuals' self-worth, value and motivation' and to raise 'self-esteem'.[37] This goal of transforming Britain's cultural institutions into centres for therapeutic engagement with excluded people is one of the clearest illustrations of the project to construct a public infrastructure for the cultivation of a therapeutic ethos.

Critics of the project of recasting social problems into that of exclusion sometimes interpret it as reflecting an agenda committed to moralising. This thesis is most persuasively argued by Ruth Levitas – who claims that the approach of the Social Exclusion Unit is 'about the pursuit of moral conformity and social order, presented as help'.[38] Whilst this thesis captures an important aspect of the process, it is important to note that the objective of conformity is rarely expressed in a morally literate form. Indeed, the reorientation from social, with a capital S, policy-making can be most accurately interpreted as part of a wider turn towards the therapeutic. Let us look at the experience so far.

The institutionalisation of therapeutic policy-making received a major boost in the 1980s under the conservative Thatcher and Major regimes. During the Thatcher era, many counsellors and therapists were astonished by the sudden demand for their services by the public sector. 'What is however both ironic and reassuring for those of us who have been in the counselling and guidance field for years, is the sudden appearance as part of the common core in both prevocational education-based courses and in youth training schemes (YTS), of such components variously labelled as counselling and guidance, reflecting upon experience, social and life skills, personal effectiveness and personal development', wrote a delighted proponent of the counselling movement in 1984.[39] Although therapeutic policy-making acquired momentum in the 1980s, it was under the Blair government that it came to exercise an important influence on the presentation of public policy. One of the principal underlying assumptions that informs New Labour policy-making is the importance of connecting with people's emotional needs and to offer measures that can boost the electorate's self-esteem. New Labour rhetoric is deeply embedded within the therapeutic discourse. Concepts like the 'Third Way', social inclusion and exclusion are directly wedded towards the objective of offering public recognition to the emotional needs of the British public. For example, according to Tony Blair, the problem of social exclusion is not so much about material poverty as about destructive influences that are 'damaging to self-esteem'.[40] Not surprisingly, almost every initiative promoted by the Blair government's Social Exclusion Unit (SEU) is designed to raise people's self-esteem.[41]

The SEU's therapeutic style draws heavily on the approach associated with John Vasconcellos, the state senator representing the Silicon Valley in California. Vasconcellos, one of the leading advocates of therapeutic politics regards self-esteem as a 'social vaccine safeguarding us all' from a variety of social ills. 'Our future well-being, economic as well as social, depends upon appreciating, incorporating everybody into our California family, as healthy growing responsible persons', notes Vasconcellos.[42] One American supporter of therapeutic governance claims that this approach is 'concerned with the development of new vocabulary in describing the relationship among citizens'.[43] In Britain, Californian self-actualising psychology is tempered by the legacy of the welfare state, leading to a synthesis which some of its supporters call 'positive welfare'. Writing in this vein, Anthony Giddens asserts that 'welfare is not in essence an economic concept, but a psychic one, concerning as it does well-being' and therefore 'welfare institutions must be concerned with fostering psychological, as well as economic benefits'. As an illustration of these psychological benefits, Giddens points to the provision of therapy: 'counselling, for example, might sometimes be more helpful than direct economic support'.[44] This shift of emphasis towards the affirmation of the self is not just a minor add-on to traditional welfare concerns but represents an attempt to forge a link with an intensely individualised and fragmented public.

The internalisation of the therapeutic imperative by the British state has a long history.[45] However, the importance of this trend was rarely acknowledged and was certainly not self-consciously promoted as an explicit political project. In recent years, however, therapeutic policies have assumed considerable significance as part of the New Labour project of modernising the welfare state. The political approach associated with this project, particularly its emphasis on the concept of social inclusion, is oriented towards establishing points contact with an individuated British public through the therapeutic management of social problems. One of the underlying features of this approach is the need for public authority to offer recognition and esteem to the individual self. Principally, inclusion is about offering recognition to otherwise misrecognised or invisible groups and individuals. It offers the right to esteem to all sections of society. Blair has defined his vision of a good society as one committed to the 'belief in the equal worth of all'. This recognition accorded to an individual's worth represents an important shift from the previous concept of social equality to that of the idea of 'equality of esteem'.[46] As a psychological/pseudo moral concept, equal worth has little in common with previous ideas about either equality of opportunity or equality of outcomes. It also has little in common with the distinction often drawn in moral philosophy between respect and esteem. According to Fraser, this distinction contrasts respect which is 'owed universally to every person in virtue of shared humanity and esteem, which is accorded differentially on the "basis of persons" specific traits, accomplishments, or contributions'.[47]

Although the concept of social inclusion is vague, and used to refer to a wide variety of problems, its central focus is to establish a series of linkages between formal institutions and the excluded. That is why policy statements across government departments continually adopt the rhetoric. In recent years there has been a systematic attempt to present policies in the sphere of sports, culture and arts from this perspective of inclusion. 'Sport is an ideal vehicle for improving self-esteem and helping people feel better about themselves', states a Sports Scotland statement on social inclusion. The government is also promoting policies that can turn public libraries and museums into institutions that can help raise the esteem of the excluded.[48] The Northern Ireland Executive has also adopted this approach. One of its recent consultation papers affirmed the need to help 'increase social inclusion and build self-esteem through participation in culture, arts and leisure activities'.[49]

Some of New Labour's most highly publicised initiatives – teenage pregnancy, employment schemes, parenting initiatives – prescribe the raising of self-esteem as its main objective. The June 2000 government-sponsored 'Body Image Summit' is paradigmatic in this respect. During the months preceding this event, government ministers spoke out on the alleged danger that the pressure to be thin posed for young women's self-esteem. According to Tessa Jowell, the then Minister for Women, young women are 'being held back from fulfilling their aspirations and reaching their potential because they lack confidence and self-esteem'.[50] According to recent government statements, low self-esteem is a common factor associated with child prostitution, homelessness, teenage pregnancy, drug abuse and a variety of antisocial and destructive behaviour. Consequently, social problems are increasingly presented as rooted in psychological pathologies that require therapeutic treatment. Even the hard-nosed Treasury has adopted this approach. One of its consultation documents, *Enterprise and Social Exclusion*, argues that local development policies will be marginal unless they help foster 'people's skills and self-esteem'. Other consultation papers argue that people can be 'removed from economic deprivation' through 'raising poor self-esteem'.[51]

The importance that government policy-makers attach to solving problems through raising people's self-esteem is driven by the conviction that some of the key problems facing people are rooted in a private sphere that characteristically fosters emotional havoc and which produces emotionally illiterate individuals who are unable to sustain thriving relationships. In extreme cases, the casualties of the private sphere are seen as part of the army of the socially excluded who go on to inflict there antisocial behaviour on others.

Emptying respect of its moral content

An important theme stressed by theorists across the political spectrum is the central role of the individual self and its demand for recognition and respect. The struggle for recognition by the individual is conceptualised as a transcendent need that shapes social and political life by a variety of influential thinkers. Francis Fukuyama depicts the struggle for recognition as the driving force of history. But at the same time, Fukuyama is troubled by the consequences of institutionalising recognition since it diminishes the ability of society to make moral judgements of individual action. 'Self-respect must be related to some degree of accomplishment, no matter how humble', he writes.[52] Others do not share Fukuyama's reservations about the automatic granting of esteem and respects to every individual. Charles Taylor contends that due recognition is a vital human need and that without the politics of equal recognition a democratic society is undermined.

The political elites of Anglo-American societies have seized upon the demand for recognition – either by accommodating to identity politics or to therapeutic ones – in an attempt to forge a new bond with an otherwise socially disengaged and estranged public.[53] That is why the British political class and its institutions have been drawn towards the role of affirming claims for recognition and acceptance by individual members of the public. Back in the early 1970s, Peter Berger and his collaborators anticipated this development in an interesting contribution, *On the Obsolescence of the Concept of Honour*. Berger claimed that the concept of honour had given way to that of dignity. He argued that whereas honour was linked to community, dignity related to the 'self as such' divested of all 'socially imposed roles and norms'. This shift to dignity of the self implied an identity that is 'essentially independent of institutional roles'. Berger concluded that as a result of this shift, the 'identity-defining power of institutions has been greatly weakened'.[54]

Berger's prognosis of the weakening of the 'identity-defining power of institutions' has been vindicated by the subsequent rise of identity politics and the crisis of legitimacy experienced by the institutions of the western state. However, it can be argued that the cultural preoccupation with individual dignity contains at least a provisional solution to the problem of legitimacy. Through refocusing the conduct of public affairs towards the objective of both managing and affirming individual subjectivity, the state has retained its power and authority to define identity. Although identity is now recast on an intensely individualised foundation, which inherently contradicts wider notions of community, the political class has found a new role for itself as managers of people's emotional anxieties. The ability of institutions to confer collective identities may have diminished, but it can still engage with an atomised public's preoccupation with recognition.

The colonisation of the private world by public authority is the inexorable logic of the institutionalisation of therapeutic politics. It is made possible by the dis-, organisation of the private sphere and the weakening of informal relations. The colonisation of the life world and the tendency towards the juridification of everyday life, first elaborated by Habermas, has developed new momentum with the reorganisation of the welfare state. As Habermas hinted, one of its consequences is the 'disintegration of life relations' and the consolidation of dependence on state services.[55] Through the juridification of the life world, recognition comes to be expressed through the legal form.

In many accounts, the growth of therapeutic culture is associated with the process of individuation, which is reflected in a rise towards individualism and a shift of focus towards a preoccupation with the self. As a description of a broad pattern, this interpretation serves to underline an important cultural trend, which is the privatisation of identity. However, terms such as individualism and the self are much too general to illuminate the question of just what kind of an individual and just what kind of a self is under discussion. Ideas about the constitution of the self are informed by social judgements and values that are both historically and culturally specific. Sennett reminds us that when Tocqueville coined the term 'individualism' in his *Democracy in America* in the nineteenth century, he argued that it consisted of love of family and friends, 'but indifference to any social relations beyond that intimate sphere'.[56] In contrast, today's individualism targets the sphere of intimate relations. In its therapeutic form, individualism encourages the distancing of self from friends, family members and other potential intimates.

It can also be argued that the concept of individualism is inappropriate for making sense of the present-day cultural demand for individual solutions. Contemporary culture's commitment to recognise and esteem the individual contains a profoundly anti-individualistic dynamic. Recognition, as cultural–political and state sanctioned right is consistent with the bureaucratic imperative of treating the individual according to an impersonal general formula. Despite its individualistic orientation, therapeutic intervention, such as counselling, often leads to the pursuit of the standardisation of people rather than encourage a self-determined individuality. Universal recognition overlooks individual differences and needs and fails to distinguish between achievement and failure and wisdom and ignorance. A real recognition of the individual requires that choices are made between knowledge and opinion and contributions that are worth esteeming as those that are not. Both the granting and the demand for universal esteem, serve to transform recognition to an empty ritual. Such formulaic reassurance cannot meet the existential quest for recognition. It can merely divert energy from constructive social engagement towards the quest for more institutional guarantees.

The very demand for the right to be esteemed posits a uniquely feeble version of the self. It places the individual in a permanent position of a supplicant, whose identity relies on a form of bureaucratic affirmation. The self is not so much affirmed or realised through the activities and relationships of the individual, but through the legal form. Wendy Brown describes the 'language of recognition' as the 'language of unfreedom'. Why? Because of 'its impulse to inscribe in the law and in other political registers its historical and present pain rather than conjure an imagined future of power to make itself'.[57] Here, autonomy, an essential component of human dignity, is exchanged for the quick fix of an institutionally affirmed identity.

Yet, many social commentators regard the politics of recognition as an assertion of progressive resistance or as a blow struck against the culture of deference. Influential voices within the field of sociology perceive the shift towards the self as containing the potential for a more aware subjectivity. Scott Lash and John Urry claim that contemporary trends produce 'not just a flattening, but a deepening of the self'.[58] The belief that the contemporary self is uniquely reflexive, aware and able to make conscious life defining choices is widely endorsed in present-day sociological theory.[59] But such positive accounts of the so-called reflexive self fail to account for the compulsive dependency of today's self on esteem and affirmation. According to contemporary culture, the self not only needs affirmation, it needs continuous affirmation. Moreover, the failure to affirm is increasingly interpreted as a slight or an injury to the self. 'Nonrecognition or misrecognition can inflict harm, can be a form of oppression, imprisoning someone in a false, distorted, and reduced mode of being', warns the philosopher Charles Taylor.[60] In cultural terms, the right to recognition means accepting people's account of their subjective states as valid. This reluctance to question people's account of themselves is reflected by the current climate of moral relativism. However, the very absence of a common moral grammar gives recognition to a superficial and provisional character. Recognition without dialogue and critical engagement represents a form of self-validation that tends to promote unstable and defensive identities. Ultimately it represents a new culture of deference. Not deference to traditional authority, but the institutional recogniser and ultimately the therapist.

Confusing recognition with a diagnosis

As noted previously, the belief that the defining feature of the self is its vulnerability informs Anglo-American culture's ethnopsychology. In this context, the provision of automatic recognition implies recognising the condition and experience of vulnerability. As Kenneth Gergen has noted, therapeutic culture offers 'invitations to infirmity'.[61] For the individual, the disclosure of vulnerability has the status of a moral statement that invites social and cultural affirmation. It encourages what Brown characterises as the 'establishment of suffering as the measure of social virtue'.[62] That is why it has become common for many people to define themselves through a psychological or medical diagnosis. Behind the cultural demand for recognition lurks this therapeutic imperative.

The growth of individuation, the erosion of social solidarity and community and the disorganisation of the private sphere has contributed to a sense of isolation which disposes many people to interpret emotional problems through the disease metaphor. Dr David Wainwright, in his fascinating study of work stress in Dover, argues that the medicalisation of stress is linked to the exhaustion of previous explanations of work-related problems. 'It is only since the prospect of overcoming problems at work through political or trade union activity has become so unthinkable, that the reduction of such problems to a biomedical idiom has occurred', he argues.[63] Since the 1980s, a more individuated workplace ethos has fostered a climate where problems are readily medicalised. At a time of existential insecurity, a medical diagnosis at least has the virtue of definition. A disease explains an individual's behaviour and it even helps confer a sense of identity. The medicalisation of everyday life allows individuals to make sense of their predicament and gain moral sympathy. Today, it also represents a socially sanctioned claim for recognition.

Recognition accorded through a diagnosis or through state policy represents a form of cultural flattery of passive subjectivity. The conviction that the individual requires ceaseless affirmation is underwritten by a concept of subjectivity, whose defining feature is vulnerability and dependence on professional or institutional affirmation. The model is the supplicant bereft of the aspiration to self-determination and autonomy. The demand to 'believe the child' or 'to believe the victim' or to 'believe the patient' both reifies experience and closes discussion. With the Macpherson Report's insistence that a racist crime is one that is subjectively perceived as such by the victim, the cultural flattery of passive subjectivity has been elevated to the level of public policy. The policy of believing narratives of the self is represented as supportive and respectful of the individual. However, it represents the subjection of external reality and truth to the dictates of sincerity as validation for social experience. However, this off-the-peg recognition is based on a perception of intense human fragility that accords the subject with a minimal level of resilience.

Therapeutic culture incites people to regard themselves as objects, rather than as subjects of their destiny. The promoters of the politics of recognition have implicitly adopted the vocation of reconciling the individual to a regime of low expectations. 'One poignant contribution that a psychotherapy viewpoint might make to political life is to help people face up to the inevitability of disappointment', advises one of the leading intellectual voices associated with therapeutic advocacy.[64] The politics of reconciling the individual to the inevitability of disappointment is underwritten by a culture that encourages its people to lower their expectations and acquire a diminished sense of themselves. Encouraging and reinforcing this perception of the self is the precondition for the continued flourishing of therapeutic culture.

Conclusion

Critical comments on the politics of recognition tend to raise concern about its particularist focus and potential for creating a 'self-righteous façade of legitimacy for the exclusion and domination of others'.[65] Others point to the tendency for recognition politics to reify identity and fear that it encourages 'separatism, intolerance and chauvinism'.[66] Experience has shown that such apprehensions are fully justified – the demand for recognition can never be entirely satisfied and each demand is a prelude to the next. Identities based on misrecognition become entrenched in the perpetuation of their condition of suffering. As Brown argues, 'politicized identity' becomes 'attached to its own exclusion' because 'it is premised on this exclusion for its very existence as identity'.[67] However, the tendency towards the institutionalisation of recognition also raises questions about the more fundamental problem of how we view human agency.

Formalising recognition through policy, public institutions and the law renders it an altogether different character. Interpersonal recognition mediated through institutions invariably leads to the marginalisation of informal networks through which people develop attachments and meanings towards each other. As David Smail observed in his indictment of the growth of therapy and counselling in the 1980s, the 'traditional "coping mechanisms" of family, neighbourhood and Church' were 'swept aside' by a 'professional network of counselling'.[68] Indeed, one of the characteristics of projects associated with the policy of inclusion is that it renders people's self-identity dependent on professionals and institutions. Its effect – unintentionally – is to alienate people from one another and to weaken their capacity to handle the difficulties and disappointments associated with the everyday struggle for recognition. At best, such 'policies' lead to the professionalisation of informal networks at worst to their marginalisation.

Yet it is not the formal recognition provided by the state or a counsellor or a therapist that serves to strengthen the identity of the self. Genuine recognition is specific and recognises a particular individual. This kind of recognition is usually transmitted through the network of informal relationships. Sadly, the politics of recognition tends to distract people from the sphere of informal relations – the one site where genuine recognition may be experienced. Instead, it provides the dubious benefit of a diagnosis.

9 Therapeutic claims-making and the demand for a diagnosis

The politics of recognition distracts people from developing themselves through their experiences and achievements. In particular it fosters a climate where instead of looking to an informal network of relationships for affirmation, people seek more formal forms of recognition. As noted in the previous chapter, through framing the demand for recognition in the language of therapeutics, it becomes easily confused with a diagnosis. As a result, the demand for a diagnosis has become a key motif in the making of claims in contemporary society.

How the self feels about itself, the state of its self-esteem and its emotion are matters that shape both individual and wider social relationship. Therapeutic culture does not merely provide society with a distinct narrative of the self; it also transmits ideas about how people should make sense of their circumstances and how they should respond to them. However, individuals do not simply internalise these ideas and act according to their dictates. People are not subject to the influence of therapeutic culture to the same degree. They are also exposed to a variety of influences and make sense or use therapeutic ethos pragmatically and in line with their experience. Nor are individuals mere recipients of cultural transmissions. People use culture and appropriate some – and by no means all – of its aspects.

In an important discussion of how culture is used, Ann Swidler observes that 'people vary greatly in how much culture they apply to their own lives'. But in the very act of using culture, people 'learn how to be, or become, particular kinds of persons'. Swidler claims that such 'self-forming' continually utilises the symbolic resources provided by the wider culture. 'Through experience with symbols, people learn desires, moods, habits of thought and feeling that no one could invent on her own', she observes.[1] These habits of thought and feeling influence the way individuals make sense of their experience. Culture provides people with ideas about what is expected of them and also about how they can expect to be treated. Through communicating a coherent version of the self, therapeutic culture provides people with ideas about what is expected of them and how they should assert their identity and interest. It frames the way people justify their actions, formulate their expectations and make claims on others and society. Through an exploration of therapeutic claims-making, important insights into how culture is used can be gained.

Therapeutic claims-making

Claims-making involves making statements about problems that deserve or ought to deserve the attention of society. A claim constitutes a warrant for recognition or some form of entitlement. Claims for injury draw on prevailing assumptions about vulnerability and resilience. As Joel Best, in his important analysis of claims-making, reports, 'how advocates describe a new social problem very much depends on how they (and their audiences – the public, the press, and policy-makers) are used to talking about, already familiar problems'.[2] As one would expect following the discussion in the previous chapters, problems and claims are frequently discussed through a medico-therapeutic vocabulary. Claim-makers focus on familiar therapeutic concerns – low self-esteem, trauma (especially PTSD), stress, depression, emotional damage or addiction – and draw upon the prevailing consensus regarding the harm of psychological injury.

The therapeutic ethos endows the claim of emotional injury with authority. As a result, numerous campaigns and crusades attempt to strengthen their cause by appealing to the public's concern with avoiding psychological damage. The New England Anti-Vivisection Society seeks to boost its campaign against animal experimentation by highlighting the trauma and psychological damage suffered by students involved in such procedures. Campaigners against the practice of male circumcision stress the psychological damage caused by this operation. Opponents of fundamentalist Christianity denounce it as 'psychologically damaging Christianity'.[3]

New claims of emotional pain build on pre-existing ones. 'Once a problem gains widespread recognition and acceptance, there is a tendency to piggyback new claims on to the old name, to expand the problem's domain', observes Best. According to Best, a good illustration of this process of domain expansion is the way that initial claims about PTSD were expanded to encompass a growing variety of new problems. The diagnosis of 'post-traumatic stress disorder' originated as a classification for Vietnam veterans' delayed psychological reaction to combat, but as Best points out, 'therapists soon began applying it to other "traumatic stresses", including rape, sexual abuse, crime victimization, natural disasters, work-related stress, UFO abduction and so on'.[4]

Concern with PTSD represents a resource that claim-makers can draw on to focus the public's attention to new claims. Take a leaflet distributed to group ambulance workers in Liverpool by a firm of personal injury lawyers. The leaflet, entitled 'Post-Traumatic Stress Disorder And The Ambulance Service', contends that emergency workers may be susceptible to a variant of PTSD known as 'prolonged duration stress disorder'. It states that unlike PTSD, this disorder does not require a 'trigger' event, since the problem is attributed to 'the cumulative effect of many stressful events'. The assertion that prolonged duration stress disorder 'has been plaguing the service for decades' is justified on the grounds that 'it is now accepted that emergency services staff are potential stress victims'.[5] Through drawing on previous concerns with PTSD, stress and the experience of victimisation, the authors of this leaflet seek to mobilise prevailing therapeutic sensibilities to mount a claim for compensation. In the same vein, a new diagnosis of 'post-traumatic slavery disorder' has been invented to attempt to link the historical episode of slavery to the contemporary experience of trauma.[6]

Since the invention of Vietnam syndrome, every military episode appears to construct its own syndrome. The numbers of newly invented syndromes – Gulf War syndrome, Mogadishu syndrome, Balkans syndrome, Kosovo syndrome, Chechen syndrome – seem to increase with every new military conflict. Although these syndromes are blamed on a wide variety of causes – some of which involves unknown toxic substances – they can be seen as an attempt to find a medico-therapeutic explanation for the pain, disorientation and shock associated with war. Feelings of displacement, estrangement and meaninglessness are transformed into symptoms, which are then described as a syndrome.

Take the recently reported Intifada syndrome. According to one account, a special 'rehabilitation village' has been set up to take care of former Israeli combat soldiers who 'suffer from a deep mental crisis'. It appears that some ex-soldiers have 'personal problems', have become addicted to hard drugs or have become suicidal or are 'generally emotionally distressed'. Such reactions, which constitute a range of emotional responses to war, can be understood as part of the moral dislocation caused by the inability to make sense of extraordinary events according to the prevailing web of meaning. In this case, an intense sense of meaninglessness shaped by social tension, the weakening of solidarity and of common belief is reinterpreted as a medical condition. The term 'syndrome' medicalises moral dislocation and renders it meaningful as pathology. The Intifada syndrome represents both a cry for help and a claim that Israeli combatants face extraordinary emotional damage in this conflict. For peace activists, the Intifada syndrome represents an acceptable therapeutic way of pressing their claim.[7]

Confusion, disorientation, disappointment, distress and other reactions often invite a therapeutic label. Intense experiences involving conflict, violence or war are habitually denuded of social and moral content and recast as damaging to the emotion. As Summerfield points out, victims of war are often expected to be vengeful because of their 'traumatisation' or 'brutalisation' and to promote new 'cycles of violence'.[8] The loss of certainty and of dislocation that accompanies wartime engagement with human misery and pain is often medicalised and given the diagnosis of a syndrome.

The authority of the victim

Veterans' syndromes, argues Downs, 'represents a new approach to the old problem of war trauma'. Through the term 'syndrome', morally shocking experiences can be internalised as psychological injuries that require therapeutic intervention. But syndromes also give expressions to what Downs characterises as a new world-view of 'victimisation'. This is an outlook which is based upon 'a condition in which the ethic of suffering replaces the ethic of achievement as the dominant intellectual and moral verity'.[9]

The consciousness of emotional vulnerability finds a powerful expression in the identity of the victim. Victim identity is fluid and subjective and can attach itself to virtually any contemporary claim. And since this identity provides one of the most legitimate routes to both recognition and claims-making, there is considerable incentive for people to embrace it. Claims based on emotional damage are increasingly seen as the acceptable way of demanding both resources and moral entitlements. Individual grievances at work are increasingly expressed through claims of suffering from bullying or harassment or discrimination. Trade union organisers, who in the past demanded higher wages on the grounds that their members needed more money, today feel far more comfortable mounting a case for compensating stressed-out workers victimised by management bullying. Demands for resources from public institutions are frequently couched in the vocabulary of 'special needs' or through petitioning for compensation. And, of course, the very success of victim claim-making encourages others to jump on the bandwagon.

Nor is the victim category restricted to those who suffer from crime or some other act of injustice. Virtually any misfortune can be assimilated into the perspective of victimisation. According to this convention, people who suffer from a physical or psychological problem are represented as victims of their condition. People do not so much have heart attacks; they are often portrayed as victims of heart attack. Alcoholics have been reinvented as victims of alcohol addiction. A multitude of new interest groups now claim that they are victims of addictive behaviour. Compulsive eaters, sex addicts, Internet addicts, shopping addicts, lottery addicts and junk food addicts are just some of the new group of victim addicts.

The tendency to depict addiction, syndromes and medical conditions as a variant of victimisation has stimulated the construction of an unprecedented number of new diseases. A growing number of distressing episodes has become medicalised and is now presented as grounds for special or differential consideration. This is the age of syndromes and disorders. Medical labels, such as post-traumatic stress disorder (PTSD), Gulf War syndrome, chronic fatigue syndrome and multiple personality disorder are being applied to a wide section of the population. Special interest groups have been set up to win public acceptance for the claim that their members are indeed suffering from a hitherto unacknowledged disease. They maintain that lack of recognition, especially by the medical profession, adds to the pain suffered by their members. Thus they often demand recognition for their cause on the basis that the refusal to accept their self-diagnosis will cause further distress. According to the ME Association, a UK-based advocacy group, the 'misunder-standings and prejudice which surrounds this illness have engendered a climate of disbelief which adds immeasurably to the distress and misery experienced by the sufferer'.[10] The corollary of this argument is that decent people have a moral duty not to offend victims by refusing to affirm their claims.

The mushrooming of new syndromes and physical conditions coincides with an increase in the number of people who are prepared to define themselves through a disease which afflicts them. According to the author of *Diseasing of America*, the number of people who 'seem eager to claim a disease for themselves' is on the increase. He suggests that 'having a disease is apparently so appealing that people stretch the criteria in order to include themselves, or perhaps even expand their behaviour to meet the criteria' designated for a disease.[11] As a result, people who suffer from shyness are sometimes prepared to describe their condition as that of social phobia or social anxiety disorder. As the numbers of Americans who describe themselves as shy increased between the 1970s and 1990s from 40 to nearly 50 per cent, the condition of social phobia is set to expand.[12]

Victim status is not confined to those individuals who have directly suffered from a particular grievance. Victim advocates argue for the recognition of what they regard as secondary or indirect victims. As Weed noted, 'crime victim activists have worked to expand the concept of victim to include the family and friends of the actual victim'.[13] Members of a family of the direct victim are often referred to as indirect victims. Victim advocates argue that family members and sometimes friends must be given access to therapeutic services and other resources. People who witness a crime or who are simply aware that something untoward has happened to someone they know are all potential indirect victims. The concept of the indirect victim allows for a tremendous inflation of the numbers who are entitled to claim victim support. Anyone who has witnessed something unpleasant or who has heard of such an experience becomes a suitable candidate for the status of indirect victim. This was the outlook that influenced the British government's law reform body, the Law Commission, when it recommended in March 1998 that people who suffer mental illness after witnessing or hearing of a relative's death, even on television or radio should have the right to compensation.[14]

The inclination to continually expand the experience of victimisation is paralleled by the augmentation of the moral dimension of victimisation. Moral entrepreneurs have a proclivity to frame their claim in a highly sensationalised discourse that alludes to terror and intense suffering. Even relatively ordinary incidents and mishaps are portrayed as scarring, damaging or traumatic. Specific instances of interpersonal conflict are interpreted as though they were part of a historical battle between good and evil. Feminists claim that violence against women should not be defined solely as a crime against an individual, rather it should be seen as a 'crime of misogyny, of hatred of women'. From this perspective, it makes sense for every woman to fear male violence and to regard themselves as a potential victim.[15]

One of the most overused metaphors adopted by moral entrepreneurs is that of the Holocaust. Through associating a specific experience of emotional injury to that of the Holocaust, advocates hope to convey a message of exceptional suffering. Writing in this vein, John Bradshaw observed that Adult Children of Alcoholics (ACOAs) are like Holocaust survivors.[16] Anti-abortion activists regularly claim that abortion is a Holocaust. And masculinist publications compare the position of American males under feminist rule to that of the Jews in Nazi Germany. The trivialisation of the Holocaust experience has been further developed through the widespread adoption of the survivor label. The casual use of the term 'survivor' by victim advocates reflects an attempt to gain moral authority through its association with the Holocaust experience. Initially, the term 'survivor syndrome' gained recognition in studies of survivors of the Second World War concentration camps and death camps, and the victims of the atomic bombings of Hiroshima and Nagasaki. As Donald Downs noted, gradually the term 'survival' and the representation of people as survivors have come to play 'pivotal roles in the development of research on the nature of trauma stemming from disaster, human cruelty and oppression'. He concluded that as 'knowledge of domestic violence, sexual assault, related forms of domination, and the effects of technological accidents gained currency through the interplay of research and politics, America began to define itself, at least in part, as a nation of "survivors"'.[17]

For moral entrepreneurs, the survivor concept represents more than just a moral claim to be treated on a par with those who suffered through the Holocaust. It also allows for a flattering representation of the emotional self for it suggests that despite the intense pain and suffering, these individuals have survived. This makes the survivor status all the more authoritative and remarkable.

A moral claim to the truth

Claim-makers who demand resources and entitlement are not simply driven by financial and material calculations. There is obviously an important monetary aspect that drives the so-called rights revolution and the explosion of litigation. The demand for compensation has become the rallying cry of an ever-growing section of society, who feel that they have been wronged or who believe that their special suffering entitles them to special treatment. However, therapeutic claims-making cannot be understood as simply the pursuit of financial reward. As noted previously, therapeutic culture influences people to interpret problems through the prism of illness. People are daily reminded of their emotional vulnerability. It is through claims-making that both the identity and the authority of the victim is asserted. Therapeutic culture confers moral privilege upon those possessing the status of the victim. In particular, victim advocates demand respect and recognition for their clients. That is why the claim of victimisation constitutes an invitation for moral recognition.

Individuals claiming compensation on account of victimisation often maintain that they are not motivated by financial calculation, but by the desire to gain public recognition for their predicament. Gary Owen, a British soldier who sued for compensation because he felt traumatised by the atrocities he saw while serving in Bosnia, stated that he was not concerned about money. Owen remarked, that 'all I want is for this never to happen again to anyone else'. Heather Mills, who won a sex discrimination case against the London Borough of Southwark, declared after her court victory that 'I can't tell you how much it meant to me to have the tribunal declare that I had been discriminated against'. She added, 'I knew that I had been the victim, but I needed others to know it'.[18] The gaining of public affirmation represents an important theme in the growth of litigation.

Indeed, one of the main complaints raised by victim advocates is that the suffering and difficulties experienced by their client is not sufficiently recognised. 'Raising awareness' is invariably one of the central aims of therapeutically oriented support groups. To achieve this objective it is essential that a particular condition or experience of suffering be publicly recognised and preferably given a name. Moral crusades against cult and ritualistic abuse are often thwarted by the lack of public credibility of their cause. One of their main complaints is that ritual abuse 'does not have a consensus definition' and is not 'classified as a separate crime category'. Campaigners contend that ritual abuse seems so unbelievable to those unfamiliar with the issue, that they detract from the credibility of the victims. As a result, their crusade seeks to gain public recognition of the prevalence of ritual abuse and campaigners demand that their version of events should be accepted by society.[19]

Recognition through the acceptance of their claim is particularly important to advocates of people who claim to suffer from a disputed syndrome or disease. In this case the validation of a particular claim of suffering requires an accepted label and diagnosis. The Fibromyalgia Association justifies its existence on the ground that those who suffered from this condition were ignored by society. According to the association's briefing paper, sufferers of fibromyalgia 'knew the severe pain, fatigue and various health problems they had been experiencing were real, but until recently there was no diagnosis'.[20] Gaining medical recognition for this condition became a crucial objective of the association. This objective was realised in the early 1990s, when the World Health Organization (WHO) incorporated fibro-myalgia into its International Classification of Diseases. The medicalisation of a condition through an officially designated label gives meaning to the victim existence. According to the Fibromyalgia Association, a common response of people diagnosed as victims of the disease is 'thank goodness, I thought I was going out of my mind imagining all these symptoms'.

The campaign to gain recognition for the diagnosis of fibromyalgia demonstrates that in contemporary times the demand for medicalisation comes from below. According to an important study of this search for symptom meaning, 'a key element in the process of medicalisation is the coming together of sufferers within self-help communities to translate their individual experiences of distress into shared expression of illness'.[21] This search for an illness identity is an important theme in contemporary claims-making. Indeed, for some people the search for a medical diagnosis has assumed the character of a crusade. In the European Union, an organisation entitled 'Rare Disorder Alliance' has been launched to gain prompt diagnosis for people suffering from rare disorders.[22] American chronic fatigue syndrome activists have reacted with fury against those who question this diagnosis, accusing them of an act comparable to Holocaust denial.[23]

An important study into the experiences of women claiming to suffer from repetitive strain injury stresses the significance that the claimants attached to gaining recognition for their plight. The authors of the study report that the 'issues which dominates many of the women's accounts of their illness is that of credibility'. The study describes the naming of their condition as repetitive strain injury as the initiation of a pilgrimage of pain, the seeking of external validation of their condition. 'Women spoke of their symptoms as if the diagnosis was a matter of faith rather than medicine, and their pilgrimage centred on finding other believers who may be able to offer help', observed the authors.[24] This search for sympathy and recognition and validation through a medical label motivates many of the illness groups that are mushrooming throughout society.

Through therapeutic culture, the ideals of nonjudgementalism, empathy and affirmation have been widely circulated. Consequently, believing and respecting an individual's account of their circumstances is increasingly represented as an obligation. 'Credibility means that as a human being and as a sick person one is taken seriously and that one's experiences are regarded as true', argue the authors of a study on women's experiences of living with fibromyalgia.[25] Validating an individual's interpretation of an illness is represented as by itself an empowering act. 'Diagnosis itself has the capacity to relieve anxiety and uncertainty on the personal level', argues Juanne Clarke in her study of the search for legitimacy by people suffering from chronic fatigue syndrome. According to Clarke, a diagnosis 'can be a resource for people even in the absence of available treatment', since it 'may open the door to various social, welfare, insurance and employment-related services'.[26]

Not surprisingly, there is considerable pressure on health professionals to recognise a variety of new diseases. As Clarke observes, 'some sufferers . . . [of chronic fatigue syndrome] . . . have organised themselves into support/advocacy groups to lobby for money to finance the discovery of diagnostic markers and treatments that would legitimise and indeed, medicalise the constellations of symptoms that they experience'.[27] This demand for a medical label is often promoted with a zeal comparable to previous movements driven by ideological fervour. Recently, questions raised about the appropriateness of the diagnosis of ME by a doctor led to an outburst of outrage. 'I don't care what my illness is called by health professionals', wrote one angry ME sufferer before demanding recognition that her affliction was real.[28] This demand for the right to a diagnosis is increasingly sanctioned through the institutionalisation of therapeutic ethos.

Under pressure from advocacy and parents' support groups, a growing number of British doctors now diagnose and treat hyperactivity in children. Those who promote 'awareness' of this illness claim that 'identification of the problem is useful in itself', because 'any harm done by labelling' is 'outweighed by the benefits to self-esteem'.[29] Medical labels are eagerly sought by some parents for their children. So hyperactive children are now 'considered to have an illness rather than to be disruptive, disobedient, overactive problem children'.[30] Parents are actually relieved when they 'discover' that their child has got some medical problem and is not responsible for his or her behaviour. 'I got my best Christmas present a few days before the big day this year', wrote a mother in *The Times*. She was referring to the wonderful news that her son was diagnosed as dyslexic and was therefore clearly not lazy, as she previously feared.[31] Until this diagnosis, school reports characterised the child as 'easily distracted' and 'occasionally disruptive'. As a victim of dyslexia the child will no longer be subject to official disapproval. Instead, the child can now expect recognition and moral support.

Henrietta Rose, who has written a book, *A Gift in Disguise*, about her difficult experience of bringing up a son with severe learning disability, is still disappointed that her son Tom was never diagnosed with a named condition. She claims that as a result she 'missed the opportunity to start mourning' the loss of her dreams and expectations.[32] This importance attached to recognition means that often parents look for a named condition, even when their children do not have a serious disability like Tom. A medical label eases the difficulty of dealing with problem behaviour. There is evidence in Britain that both teachers and parents collude in the popularisation of the learning disabled classification in schools.[33] At a time of existential insecurity, a medical diagnosis at least has the virtue of definition. A disease explains an individual's behaviour and it even helps confer a sense of identity. The medicalisation of everyday life allows individuals to make sense of their predicament and gain moral sympathy.

Individuals are often aware that it is their disease that defines them and they often display their addictions and syndromes in public as a statement of who they are. Although it may not confer approval on the addict or the diseased – a diagnosis at least provides them with moral recognition. As a result, alcoholism is no longer represented as moral weakness, but as a disease and victims of this condition are treated or helped rather than condemned. From the perspective of therapeutic culture, the identity of an alcoholic in recovery is one that can legitimately claim our moral support.

Since personal set-backs and disappointment are interpreted through a therapeutic vocabulary, there is a steady demand for a diagnosis that accounts for individual problems and failures. Adults are even prepared to embrace the learning disabled label. 'Some adults identified as learning disabled actually describe the LD label as a relief, not as something to be perceived negatively', notes an authoritative study on this subject. For these individuals, this diagnosis helps explain past failures and long years of problems in school. It also serves to boost the self-image of many who feared that they were 'just stupid'.[34] Labelling and self-labelling represents a demand to be taken seriously. That is why the medicalisation of social life appears to enjoy formidable moral authority.

Victim organisations assert that their clients have a privileged access to the truth. For example, the ME Association believes 'that the burden of proof of illness should not be borne by the sick and the disabled'. 'Believe the child', is the slogan of child protection activists. Victim advocates contend that it is wrong to question claims of child abuse, ritual abuse or rape. Their view is that victims' rights are synonymous with the right to be believed. Indeed, they often insist that those who subject such claims to critical inquiry are responsible for rewounding the victim. Consequently, insistence on evidence and the close interrogation of a claim is often rejected on the ground that it is likely to inflict further psychological damage on the victim.

The most symbolic manifestation of the privileged status enjoyed by victims is the widely held view that society has a responsibility to believe what they say. The right to be believed is based on the premise that those who are emotionally vulnerable need to be affirmed and validated. Any suspicion directed at their version of events is likely to inflict even more emotional pain on the victim. This approach is pursued with vigour in the domain of sex crimes. Advocates of victims of child abuse and rape claim that attempts by a defendant's lawyers to challenge a victim's version of events constitutes a form of emotional harassment. They claim that vulnerable witnesses require special protection from aggressive questioning. They also contend that the usual standards of evidence should not apply in such cases. One American prosecutor, Steve Chaney, informed a national symposium on child molestation that he was not asking the question 'was the child abused?', but rather 'can the child perform for us in the courtroom?' Chaney claimed that, whereas adult witnesses constantly lied, children tended to tell the truth and therefore his task was to create an environment where their story could be told.[35] Over the years this sentiment has been widely supported by American politicians, and gradually child witnesses have been removed from the courtroom. They are allowed to testify via short-circuit television. In some cases the courts have shown videotapes of social workers interviewing young infants. In others, parents, therapists and physicians have been allowed to present second-hand testimony about children's disclosures of abuse. According to Nathan and Snedeker, by the mid-1980s, 'the right of an accused to face-to-face confrontation with a complaining witness had been decimated for defendants in child sex-abuse cases'.[36] Typically, child witnesses are always referred to as victims and even civil liberties groups found it difficult to uphold the right of a defendant to a vigorous cross-examination of the evidence.

The proposition that children's evidence reflects the truth has been widely promoted by the child protection industry. This cavalier approach to evidence is well illustrated by Lucy Berliner, an American feminist social worker, in her comments on child abuse:

> A legal decision should never be confused with the truth. If we believe what children say we will be right 95–99 per cent of the time. If we want signs and symptoms as proof we will be right 70–80 per cent of the time. If we require medical evidence we will be right 20 per cent of the time and if we have to wait for a witness we will be right 1 per cent of the time.[37]

From this perspective, the demand for proof simply detracts from the transcendental truth of abuse. From a therapeutic perspective, even the manifest examples of false accusation are seen to contain some intrinsic truths. Thus according to one account, false accusations in child sexual abuse are rare, but 'when they occur it is nearly always a cry for help'. The authors add that it is 'clear that the children who make false allegations require help and support and as such these allegations should not be ignored'.[38] Such sympathy is rarely extended to the accused, and since allegations, even when they are false, 'should not be ignored', those at the receiving end cannot be entirely absolved of suspicion.

For victim activists, the obligation to believe the victim has the character of a moral imperative. They contend that victims have the right to be believed. Crusaders against satanic abuse disarm sceptics by insisting that probably the worst thing that can happen to the victim of sadistic ritual abuse is not to be believed. Patrick Casement seeks to guilt-trip sceptics along the following lines.

It may be that some accounts which are reputed to be of 'satanic' abuse are delusional, and the narrators may indeed be psychotic in some cases. But we must still face the awful fact that if some of these accounts are true, if we do not have the courage to see the truth that may be there . . . we may tacitly be allowing these practices to continue under the cover of secrecy, supported also by the almost universal refusal to believe that they could exist.[39]

From this standpoint, those who refuse to believe accusations of satanic abuse are themselves complicit in the act of victimisation.

The right to be believed, once confined to the relationship between therapist and patient, has been extended to a growing variety of encounters in society. This right represents an important moral claim on society. Not surprisingly, it creates an important moral incentive for the construction of the identity of vulnerability.

A claim for resources

As indicated previously, the state of vulnerability provides recognition and moral authority. Not surprisingly, it also constitutes a claim on resources and differential treatment. Rewarding the victim has become institutionalised through both public bodies and informal arrangements. With a clear financial incentive at stake, more and more people are describing an ever-expanding range of incidents as victimising. Since the feeling of being a victim is a highly subjective one, society finds it difficult to draw any clear definitions about what kind of encounters and incidents should be compensated. It is now common for people to claim damages for unspecific, hidden pain. People are now demanding compensation for feeling offended, for loss of self-confidence or self-esteem or for being traumatised. Many claimants insist that they have been emotionally scared for life. Others demand money for a traumatic event that happened in the distant past, of which they have only become aware recently.

One of the most extraordinary innovations of therapeutic culture has been the reclassification of existential psychological pain into a demand for financial compensation. The different manifestations of inner pain, which have historically haunted humankind, are now increasingly treated as symptoms of grave emotional injury. In the past, courts have been reluctant to take seriously claims for compensation on the grounds of psychological injury alone. It was felt that whereas physical injury could be understood if not measured, emotional distress was impossible to calculate. The negligent infliction of pure mental distress was not accepted as grounds for a suit. 'Unless the victim of negligence had been physically abused, she would have to take care of her own psychic injuries', concludes an author on the history of litigation.[40] Since the emergence of therapeutic culture, mental anguish and suffering have become legitimate claims for compensation. According to one American study, in recent years, between 30 and 40 per cent of awards in personal injury cases are attributable to psychological distress of one sort or another.[41] Psychological distress is open to such a wide interpretation that it can inflict individuals who were not directly victims of negligence, but merely witnesses to an event.

Claims based on a new generation of psychological injuries are on the rise, and seem set to continue to do so. Mental distress, trauma, stress and loss of confidence and self-esteem are increasingly presented as legitimate grounds for compensation. The American sociologist James Nolan argues that in the US personal injury cases are increasingly justified on the grounds of emotional damage. In California, between 1976 and 1986 there were ten times as many emotional as physical damage cases and subsequently this trend has become even more pronounced. Nolan contends that these figures reflect greater cultural sensitivity to the state of vulnerability and to the increase in the authority assigned to emotions.[42] A similar pattern is also evident in Britain.[43]

In recent years, it has become acceptable for British adults to sue their schools, foster homes and other institutions for the trauma they suffered during childhood. Many schools are being sued by former pupils who claim that they were bullied as far back as 15 years ago. Sebastian Sharp won £30,000 in an out-of-court settlement. He claimed that bullying had seriously affected his personality, making him anxious, depressed and suicidal.[44] There is considerable anecdotal evidence that schools and other public institutions are reluctant to fight such cases because of the expense and are therefore often prepared to make some kind of an informal financial settlement. This defensiveness on the part of public institutions has had the effect of encouraging even more litigation. Some students who have done poorly in their exams are arguing that their school has let them down and are therefore entitled to compensation.[45] And it is not just disappointed students who have jumped on this bandwagon. Soldiers, policemen and policewomen and other emergency services workers are now demanding compensation for incidents that in the past were considered a normal part of their duties. So an ex-soldier, who saw a friend killed by an IRA landmine 15 years ago, sued the Ministry of Defence. He claimed to be suffering from post-traumatic disorder and held the Army responsible for his failure to hold down a job and the break-up of his long-term relationship.[46] Through the medium of a diagnosis, failure in life has become an argument for compensation.

In 1998, a deputy head teacher, who claimed that a bullying headmistress drove him to a nervous breakdown, received £100,000 in an out-of-court settlement. The former deputy teacher claimed that he joined the school as a 'competent, confident person and ended up quite the opposite'. The main incident that seems to have contributed to his breakdown took place in December 1991, when he was asked to present a wrapped Christmas gift to a former teacher. It turned out to be a chocolate penis, which he was asked to hand over with the words: 'I hope you enjoy a nibble this Christmas'. Apparently the litigant was so embarrassed by this affair and suffered so much psychological pain that he felt he needed to quit the teaching profession. Many of the parents whose children attended the school, Sageston County Primary in Carew, were appalled by the wisdom of paying out £ 100,000 compensation for what they considered to be no more than 'light-hearted banter'.[47] However, what the parents overlooked was that therapeutic culture defines suffering in relation to how people claim to feel rather than what was done to them. From this perspective, only victims and their therapists know how much psychological pain they suffered. That is why claims for compensation that in the past would have been treated as eccentric are now taken so seriously.

Although the forces behind the litigation revolution are complex and cannot be reduced to a single cause, one significant influence has been the expanding definition of emotional vulnerability and the importance attached to psychological pain. Claiming resources for suffering emotional distress has become an alternative route to advance in the workplace in Britain and the United States. In the US, in particular, there has been a steady increase in workplace litigation. Individual litigants are claiming compensation for emotional distress, age discrimination and sexual harassment. Trade unions have opportunistically reoriented their activities away from collective action to suing employers for the emotional pain suffered by their members. Whereas in the past, trade unionists demanded higher wages and better conditions from their employers, these days they are far more likely to complain about workplace stress or victimisation. Wainwright and Calnan have described this process as the 'depoliticization of work stress'. They observe, 'rather than conceiving of the worker as an active social agent in a specific political and historical context, epidemiologists have constructed the "work stress victim" as a subject within medical discourse, i.e. as someone suffering a disease'.[48]

The reorientation of trade unions towards litigation illustrates the influence of therapeutic culture on claims-making. During the 1980s, union leaders found it increasingly difficult to find a role for themselves. The decline of collective solidarity and the loss of appeal of union activism had the effect of diminishing the influence of this movement. Union leaders found it difficult to promote their interest in the traditional language of trade unionism. Therapeutic advocacy not only helped improve the image of unions it also provided a language through which their demands could be formulated. Whereas industrial action is often perceived in negative terms, taking a boss to the courts is presented as a legitimate form of behaviour. In the US, there is now a thriving trade in self-help books, with titles like *Sue Your Boss*, which advise workers that there are 'vast sums' to be made from litigation.[49]

Trade union activists have been able to draw on a wider cultural consensus which defines stress as by definition harmful. This diseasing of stress by health activists and the therapy lobby has helped union activists gain widespread sympathy for their claim. In April 1996, an important legal precedent was set when John Walker, a senior social worker, received £175,000 compensation for the 'psychiatric damage to a normally robust personality'. The High Court ruled that an 'impossible workload' placed on Walker was the cause of his nervous breakdown. The refusal of his employer to reduce his workload or his stress convinced the judge of the legitimacy of Walker's claim. The case has set a precedent for other victims of a stressful working environment. Consequently, claims for compensation because of stress at work are on the increase. According to a TUC report published in September 1998, stress tops the list of cases which unions are taking to the courts.

In order to play an effective role as the advocate of the workplace victim, trade unionism has become a high profile advocate of therapeutic services. It spends little time agitating and organising, but devotes considerable resources to publicise its help-line for those facing management bullying. British unions now offer their members stress counselling and run workshops on how to cope with the demands of a busy workplace. Promoting a therapeutic ethos has given unions a new rationale for existence. Unions seem to find it easier to win compensation for a stressed-out member than to make significant gains through collective bargaining.

The diseasing of the workplace has been paralleled by the diseasing of childhood and schooling. The tendency to medicalise children's behaviour has helped create an atmosphere where parents continually insist that their child has special needs and therefore are entitled to differential treatment. The past two decades has seen a predictable rise in the variety of disabilities and syndromes which affect children. It is not just children's problem behaviour that is being pathologised, a growing number of schoolchildren are being classified as learning disabled. An important study by Louise Spear-Sweling and Robert Sternberg calls into question the manner in which poor readers have become reclassified as learning disabled (LD). They argue that the diseasing of poor class-room performance often has the unfortunate effect of intensifying 'the inclination toward lowered expectations on the part of parents and teachers, thereby decreasing the child's motivation even further'. Nevertheless, there are important incentives for parents and teachers to buy into the LD industry. One of the most effective ways for parents to get help for their children is to demand special treatment on account of their disability. Schools find it easier to attract funding for special education than for basic compensatory education programmes and are therefore often happy to classify children as LD.[50] New York City now spends one-fifth of its education budget – over $1 billion a year – on special education.[51]

In Britain, parents are increasingly demanding that their child should be categorised as having a special need. After registering their child as needing special need, a protracted process of negotiation ensues before statementing a student as entitled to special support. So for every child with a statement of special need there are many others who are still going through the four stages prior to statementing. The numbers of children with statements of special need has increased every year during this decade. It rose from 153,228 in 1991 to 232,995 in 1997.[52]

For its part, the learning disability lobby is fervently committed to both expanding the types of learning disorders, as well as the numbers of children afflicted by them. Some of the recently discovered learning disabilities include maths disability (dyscalculia), students having difficulties with spelling may well be suffering from dysgraphia and those who have difficulties with a second language may well be affected by foreign language disability. The symptoms usually associated with these disorders are normally ones which virtually everyone has experienced at one time or another. Some of the symptoms linked to dyscalculia or maths-learning disability are the inability to keep track of time, chronic lateness, difficulties with financial planning and budgeting, poor sense of direction or difficulty in remembering dance sequences.[53]

Advocacy groups frequently claim that 15 to 20 per cent of the American population have a learning disability. More and more adults and university students are claiming special treatment on the ground that they have a learning disability. In 1991, 8.8 per cent of US first-year college students reported some form of disability compared with 2.6 per cent in 1978. The numbers of students claiming to be disabled has continued to rise, as have the claims for special treatment. Learning disabled students writing university entrance exams SATs are often allowed to take 'non-standard SATs'. These are untimed or adjusted to meet a student's special needs. Eighteen thousand learning disabled examinees received special administration for the SAT in 1991–92. By 1996–97, that number had more than doubled to 40,000. According to researchers, the privilege of taking the SAT on an untimed basis raises students' scores by an average of 100 points.[54] Students with learning disability cannot only claim special dispensation from regular exam conditions. Such students have been exempted from taking prerequisite courses. And eligibility standards have been relaxed to compensate for the student's disability. Students claiming disability status have received extra time on exams, reduced course load, the services of professional note-takers and special accommodation on campus.

Therapeutic standards of accountability

The demand for a diagnosis represents a plea for a new form of accountability. In most circumstances society does not demand a strict absolute standard of accountability. It is generally recognised that there may be extenuating circumstances which could lighten the responsibility of an individual for a particular action. Legal concepts like contributory negligence express the widely held view that responsibility for a particular injurious act can be shared. However, the contemporary therapeutic ethos goes way beyond the notion of relative accountability to implicitly question the ethic of responsibility itself. Bad habits, antisocial and destructive behaviour tend to be portrayed as the outcome of dysfunctional parenting, family violence or of people's genes.

The attribution of responsibility and notions of accountability are strongly influenced by prevailing social and political norms. A heightened concern with the vulnerability of the self has significantly altered the norms of individual accountability. People who are instructed to believe that they cannot cope on their own are also not expected to behave with restraint and to be able to exercise self-control. And without some elementary conception of self-control, it becomes difficult to expect individuals to exercise responsibility for their behaviour. Therapeutic culture has accommodated to this feeble norm of responsibility by actually belittling the notion of self-control. The very idea of an addictive society – where practically everyone is a potential addict or an emotionally damaged survivor – represents a negation of the ability to exercise self-control. Therapeutic knowledge not only rejects, but is also hostile to, the aspiration for self-control. Kaminer points out that, 'self-control is not simply dismissed or ignored as a personal development goal; it is denigrated as a symptom of the disease of co-dependency'.[55] This sceptical, if not hostile, attitude towards self-control is the other side of the coin of powerlessness.

The new minimalist conception of self-control influences ideas about criminal and antisocial behaviour. Defence attorneys have always sought to portray the defendants as the helpless victims of forces beyond their control. However, more recently such arguments have become systematised into abuse and syndrome defences, where the prior episode of emotional injury diminishes the defendant's responsibility for his or her action. The defence of battered women's syndrome or battered children's syndrome are based on the presumption that a previously abused victim ought not to be held criminally responsible for killing an allegedly violent spouse or partner.[56]

The accommodation of legal practices to a minimalist conceptualisation of self-control is a testimony to the influence of therapeutic consciousness. In her excellent account of the emergence of victim defence strategies in the US, Saundra Westervelt draws attention to the way that changes in criminal law provides important clues about shifts in society's conceptualisation of problems. Any effective system of justice needs to possess some notion of free will and individual responsibility. Without such notions it is difficult to ascribe any conscious motive to an act and by implication to assign blame and responsibility. Westervelt contends that the American legal system still remains attached to the core values of responsibility and free will, but at the same time there has been an acceptance of the view that the victim should be treated according to different criteria. According to Westervelt, 'an analysis of the development and expansion of a defense based on victimization "tells the story" of a society that has accepted victimization as a new way of explaining and excusing misbehaviour'.[57]

Westervelt uses the concept of 'social victimization' to describe the premise of a new form of defence, which seeks to alleviate responsibility of those who have suffered injury as a 'result of social relations or conditions'. Social victimization refers to instances where individuals 'suffered physical abuse, neglect, socio-economic deprivation or discrimination'. In fact, successful social victimisation defence tactics relate to experiences that are not so much social as interpersonal. As Westervelt argues, 'in each case, the cause of the victimization is the action of another person', albeit influenced by the prevailing social environment.[58] Such tactics are most effective in situations where the defendant has been physically abused in the past. 'However, defendants claiming to be victims of more abstract forms of abuse, such as social deprivation, urban decay, or war trauma are rarely successful in reducing criminal responsibility', writes Westervelt.[59] The relative lack of recognition accorded to social injustice in comparison to interpersonal violence reflects the mood of suspicion towards the realm of informal relations discussed in Chapter 3.

Defence strategies based on the premise of social victimisation are concerned with the negative experiences of the defendant in the past. As a result of past abuse, the victim is diagnosed as suffering from a psychological condition, which then explains his or her violent behaviour. This approach has been most effective in cases where the defendant's action is presented as the outcome of battered women's syndrome. However, in recent years a strategy 'specifically designed to alleviate legal inequities in the treatment of battered women' has expanded to include men and children.[60] The expansion in the categories of legally blameless defendants has been limited by traditional principles of justice which rest on the premise of a degree of individual accountability. However, in other areas of social life, which are not subjected to the dictates of such legal principles, the notion of the blameless victim has expanded with far less restraint.

The notion of the blameless victim creates difficulties for any society that attempts to evaluate action on a commonly accepted principle of right and wrong. Once society calls into question the concept of self-control, then no-one, not even the victimiser, can be held responsible for their antisocial behaviour. This problem has led Sharon Lamb to argue against the notion of the blameless victim. She argues that if victims can be absolved of their action because of their previous experience of abuse, then so can the perpetrators of a crime. 'In excusing this kind of responsibility we would also be lending perpetrators a handy excuse', she writes.[61] Lamb raises important issues about the relationship between blaming and responsibility. Clearly, once a weak standard of accountability is applied to one section of society, it becomes difficult to apply a stronger version to another. There is also a logical inconsistency in absolving some people's action from any blame, but not those of others. Holding individuals to account is fraught with difficulties in a society, where powerlessness defines the human condition. And that is precisely the dilemma of a morality based on the diminished self. A morality that encourages the evasion of blame and responsibility cannot reconstitute itself as an effective system of accountability. Joel Best has suggested that one of the reasons why victim culture has spread so fast is because it has not threatened any vested interests. Victim culture is rarely able to hold anyone to account. Victim advocates demand that their clients receive sympathy and not blame. Winning support for the victim takes precedence over targeting the victimiser. 'Relatively few victims' movements generate well-organised opposition because relatively few specify their opponents', writes Best.[62]

The weakening of the standard of accountability has had a major influence on redefining the relationship between motive and behaviour. Individual responsibility cannot be attributed to many forms of negative behaviour. Consequently, we have the phenomenon of negative and antisocial acts committed by blameless individuals. But the distancing of the self from responsibility does not mean that society has ceased to blame. On the contrary! One of the major paradoxes of contemporary era is that precisely at a time when people are least likely to accept blame for their action they possess an intense sense of emotional injury. The victim feels entitled to reject responsibility for his or her predicament precisely because blame can be attributed to some external influence – toxic parents or a traumatic experience. So the more that a sense of responsibility is distanced from the self, the more common the practice of blaming.

However, in therapeutic culture the sociology of blaming lacks moral coherence. No external moral values are affirmed when victim advocates or therapeutic professionals advise their clients 'don't blame yourself' and by implication, invite them to blame someone else. In this context, blaming becomes a personal ritual with no wider social or moral focus. Consequently, the exhortation to free the self from blame does not have the capacity to create a moral community. Most likely, blaming in this form serves to distance the self from others. Blaming without a socially accepted norm of individual responsibility becomes an empty ritual, another acknowledgement of impotence. However, the cultural validation for blaming others continually fuels conflict between people.

Who can we blame?

The corollary of the therapist's reassurance that 'you are not to blame' is the lawyer's advice that 'it's not your fault'. The externalisation of responsibility from the self and the weakening of a commonly recognised standard of accountability provide a powerful impetus for the development of the pursuit of litigation. Most studies of the rising tide of litigation relate this phenomenon to the decline of authority. The growth of legal intervention in human relations 'appears to be a kind of replacement, a substitute for traditional authority' argues one leading text on the sociology of law.[63] Whilst new perceptions of authority may contribute to the emergence of new attitudes towards litigation, a much more important factor is the influence of the changing form of self-consciousness discussed previously.

American studies have pointed to an important shift from 'individualism emphasising self-sufficiency and personal responsibility' to 'rights-oriented individualism'. One study based on Sander County in Illinois sought to explain why the elderly were averse to suing for damages after an accident. The answer provided by the study was that the individualism of the elderly 'emphasised self-sufficiency rather than rights and remedies'.[64] This study pointed to an important shift in social attitude towards personal responsibility and expectations of entitlements from other people and institutions. However, the discourse of rights provides only a superficial insight into this process. What this process reflects is the redefinition of the relationship between individuals and the outcome of their action. The consciousness of powerlessness is experienced as a life shaped by individuals and forces external to the self. Consequently, misfortune and accident can be attributed to others, leading to the 'obvious' conclusion that one is entitled to compensation. The expansion of the right to compensation is proportional to the shrinking of the zone of individual autonomy.

Rights-oriented individualism refers to the tendency to look for solutions to problems from third-party sources, especially through the institution of the law. Many academic contributions on the sociology of law believe that rights-oriented individualism is a positive development. For example, Friedman claims that rights consciousness represents an aspiration for control and choice.[65] Such an interpretation of the development of the litigation revolution is based on an analysis of the relation between the individual and society which is insensitive to the development of diminished subjectivity. From the standpoint of our analysis, the term 'rights-oriented individualism' is actually a misnomer. Reliance on 'rights' represents a tendency to look for third-party institutional and professional solutions.

It represents the subordination of the self to new forms of therapeutic and professional authority. It is but a variant of the politics of recognition.

It is paradoxical that rights consciousness is presented as an exercise in citizen activism. Like therapy, litigation tends to promote the professionalisation of everyday life. From the outset, the litigant is thrown into a relationship of dependency on the lawyer, whose professional skills become decisive in the legal drama. All too often litigants discover that they become bit players who have little control over their lawyers and the proceedings in the court. The growth of litigation, at least in part, represents the failure of people to sort out problems for themselves. It is a sense of powerlessness which generates the demand for lawyers. This demand has also led to the growth of the legal profession in England and Wales, where the number of solicitors has increased from 33,864 in 1978 to 75,072 in 1998.[66]

The tendency to lean on the legal professional mirrors the development of dependency in the domain of therapy. But whereas therapy emphasises the blamelessness of the individual, legal advocates find someone else to blame for one's circumstances. Advocacy groups, consumers' organisations and legal activists are in the forefront of promoting the idea that there is no such thing as an accident for which you automatically bear responsibility. The legal profession in particular has become accomplished in cultivating this sentiment. A leaflet published by The Accident Line, an organisation launched to raise public awareness by the British Law Society, directly encourages people to look for someone to blame for their predicament.

IT WAS JUST AN ACCIDENT . . . OR WAS IT?

Even if you believe that your injury was just an accident, and that no one was to blame, it's still worth talking to a specialist solicitor. Many people who believed at first that their accident could not be blamed on anyone but themselves have gone on to make a successful claim.

The leaflet assures the reader that 'sometimes you don't even realise that someone or something else is to blame'. Educating people to discover that what they thought was their fault can actually be blamed on someone else seems to be the central mission of a new complaints industry. Encouraging blaming and complaining is increasingly presented as a service to the public. And the litigant is frequently depicted as an active citizen standing up for his or her rights.

Blaming involves externalising problems to sources outside the self. These days, even one's state of mind can be directly linked to actions precipitated by an external source. It merely requires that one's mental state is defined as a psychiatric illness and that this condition be attributed to another party's negligence. Since the meaning of psychiatric injury is continually expanded to incorporate a growing variety of unpleasant emotional experiences, the foundation for claims-making continues to grow. In recent years, the traditional dividing line between physical and psychiatric illness has become eroded. Consequently, people are now entitled to claim compensation for feeling offended, for the loss of self-confidence or self-esteem or for being traumatised, if they can prove that their condition was caused by someone else's negligence.

PTSD is now widely diagnosed to cover a range of emotionally upsetting events. Such events are routinely redefined as emotional trauma, worthy of the medical label PTSD. As one critic of this trend notes, PTSD has been diagnosed after a miner slipped down some stairs and landed on his buttocks 'without any resultant physical sequelae'. Tripping over an uneven pavement, being knocked down by a bicycle or receiving a trivial head injury as a result of merchandise falling from the shelf have all been linked to causing PTSD.[67] Hitherto, unexceptional human reactions, like the pain and trauma experienced by parents when the child they love dies, can now be recast as a psychiatric illness for which a 'negligent' hospital can be held responsible.[68] No doubt, hospitals and other large institutions can be insensitive in their handling of the bereaved. But to hold them responsible for the 'abnormal grief reaction' of the bereaved is to lose sight of the complex influences that shapes the reaction of the self. And if even the intense pain we feel over the loss of a child is the consequence of someone else's negligence, are there any feelings left for which we bear a measure of existential responsibility? The causes of a particular mental condition are complex and can rarely be reduced to a single event.[69] Unfortunately, blame-seeking is intolerant of complexity and believes that one's state of mind can be directly attributed to an external agent's negligence.

There is nothing objectionable about complaining or blaming as such. In contemporary society there are many issues and problems to complain about and all too many targets of worthwhile blame. Blaming only becomes a problem when the self becomes denuded of any sense of responsibility for one's predicament. We all live in circumstances over which we can exercise little control. But if we renounce the possibility of having some choice over the direction of our life then we risk diminishing the meaning of our humanity.

Final thoughts
Does it matter?

In the end, does it all matter? According to some accounts, the therapeutic turn represents a positive vision that promises to create a more enlightened society. Such sentiments are systematically transmitted through popular culture. The idea that we 'need support' and are vulnerable to various forms of emotional injury has become part of everyday common sense. Consequently, therapeutic activists positively welcome the reorientation of the state towards the management of individual psychology. Individuals who express concern about the potentially authoritarian implications of the state assuming the role of therapists are dismissed as naive or even as paranoid. Nikolas Rose, whose *Governing The Soul* provides the most comprehensive historical account of the British experience, views the therapeutic ethos and its institutionalisation in a relatively benign manner. Rose is critical of social analysts, such as Lasch and Sennett, for adopting a 'rather jaundiced view of the therapeutic culture of the self'. 'The paranoid visions of some social analysts, who see in the expansion of the therapeutic a kind of extension of state surveillance and regulation throughout the social body are profoundly misleading', he states.[1] According to Rose, the concern of the state with the management of subjectivity constitute 'therapies of freedom'. He argues,

> These technologies for the government of the soul operate not through the crushing of subjectivity in the interests of control and profit, but by seeking to align political, social, and institutional goals with individual pleasures and desires and with the happiness and fulfilment of the self. Their power lies in their capacity to offer means by which the regulation of selves – by others and by ourselves – can be made consonant with contemporary political principles, moral ideas and constitutional exigencies.[2]

This representation of state intervention in the internal life of people as essentially unobjectionable, even a desirable process, enjoys widespread intellectual support. From this perspective, the role of public authority and of the therapeutic professional is an empowering one. Without a hint of irony, Rose observed that 'empowerment has mutated from a term utilised by clients and advocates in the challenging of professional power to become part of the obligations of the responsible professional'.[3]

American advocates of therapeutic governance share Rose's positive assessment of the state management of subjectivity. According to Frank Scott, a professor in public administration at San Francisco State University, therapeutic governance is concerned with 'reuniting the self that modernism has sought to split apart'.[4] Supporters of therapeutic governance are not particularly concerned about the implications of assigning responsibility for 'reuniting the self' to the bureaucratic institutions of the state. The reorientation of the welfare state towards attending to the emotional needs of the public is also endorsed by some critics of traditional redistributionist social policy. They contend that in previous times policy was far too focused on the provision of economic goods. They advocate the case for a more emotional system of welfare on the ground that a 'holistic' approach is needed, one that meets 'the emotional, as well as physical need of human beings'.[5] This perspective resonates with the current tendency to reinterpret problems hitherto defined as principally social, as psychological in character. Thus the conviction that social inequalities are experienced through a 'psychosocial mechanism' that links poverty to individual health provides a boost to therapeutic policy-making. 'Emotions, health and distributive justice are therefore intimately related in the developed western world', argues one advocate of this approach.[6] There is a significant body of opinion within the field of British social policy that actually regards the assumption of the therapeutic role of the state as a long overdue reform. Paul Hoggett argues that the 'concept of "well-being" provides a core principle around which a new vision of positive welfare could be organized'. For Hoggett and his co-thinkers, 'well-being is defined essentially in mental-health terms'.[7]

The representation of therapeutic governance as essentially unproblematic and potentially even empowering is underwritten by a political culture that characteristically has a relatively weak sense of individual capacity. An outlook that regards the individual self as vulnerable and in need of support is happy to embrace the help offered by the therapeutic state. A feeble definition of individual subjectivity is the flip side of this new form of etatist intellectual outlook. It represents scepticism toward the ability of people to act as responsible citizens, without the support of professionals who knows best what is in their interest.

The representation of state policy as an instrument of empowerment recasts the relationship of dependence of the patient on the therapist in a disturbing institutional form. It is difficult to reconcile the view of an individual as someone whose emotional well-being is contingent on institutional support with the democratic vision of a citizen who holds the powers that be to account. The transformation of the citizen into a patient has the potential for altering the relationship between the people and the public institutions of society. As Vanessa Pupavac in her critique of *Therapeutic Governance* argues, the 'redrawing of the citizen and state relationship has been accompanied by the erosion of the social contract conceptualisation of the citizen as an autonomous rational subject'.[8] The new therapeutic social contract is underwritten by the paternalistic assumption that the vulnerable subject needs the management and 'support' of officialdom and the state.

Intolerance of dissident emotions

The ascendancy of therapeutic culture is often represented as one that is hospitable to the open display of emotions. However, as we argued previously, the promotion of emotionalism does not necessarily lead to a distinctly tolerant regime towards how people feel. In one sense, this response is not different to other cultures where some emotions are celebrated whilst others are stigmatised. As in previous times, not all forms of emotion enjoy cultural support today. The distinguishing feature of therapeutic culture is not an openness towards emotions, but the unusual interest it takes in the management of people's internal life. It transforms the private feelings of people into a subject matter for public policy-making and cultural concern. But at the same time it adopts a selective attitude towards what emotions can and what emotions cannot be displayed. The cultivation of certain emotional attitudes and the repression of others is systematically pursued by institutions and professionals devoted to the management of how people ought to feel.

Contemporary society lacks certainty about its beliefs. It finds it difficult to transmit a clear vision of a just world. In particular, there seems to be great hesitancy about offering people a clear system of meaning. It is this confusion about providing people with meaning that provides the therapeutic world-view with considerable opportunity to spread its influence. Today's cultural elite may lack confidence in telling people what to believe but it feels quite comfortable about instructing people how and what to feel.

The institutionalisation of therapeutics endows it with a potentially coercive dimension. Therapeutic authority acts on the premise that it alone knows what emotions are positive and negative. It acts on the assumption that it has the expert authority to train, educate and in some cases dictate how people should feel. In previous times, the orientation of public institutions was towards people's behaviour and beliefs. State intervention was directed towards cultivating and enforcing acceptable forms of conduct and beliefs. Today, these activities are also supplemented by an attempt to encourage conformity with key therapeutic values through the management of subjectivity. This approach extends the business of government from the public to the private and more disturbingly to the internal life of the individual.

Outwardly, the promotion of positive emotional behaviour appears to be a sensible and uncontroversial way of achieving desirable conduct. Who could possibly object to the following learning intention assigned to 6–8-year-old children in the English school curriculum, 'to recognise, name and deal with feelings in a positive way'?[9] But who decides what is a positive way of dealing with feelings? The child? The mother or father? The teacher, the psychologist? The official? And in any case, what is a positive way of dealing with feelings? And what right does the curriculum have to impose its version of dealing positively with feelings? Sometimes, children have very good reasons for dealing 'negatively' with emotional issues. Indeed, not naming feelings may be an appropriate way of dealing with individual circumstances. Encouraging teachers to step over the boundary that separates education from instructing pupils how to feel represents the expansion of therapeutics into the classroom.

The promotion of certain emotional styles always contains the implication that other responses are rendered inferior, if not illegitimate. In previous times, educators were charged with teaching children to behave well. Good conduct was associated with clearly defined public acts such as politeness, acts of honesty and altruism. The regime of therapeutic education is wedded to a form of behaviour modification that not only targets conduct, but also attempts to alter certain forms of feelings and emotions. Training a child how to feel is a far more intrusive and coercive process than educating a pupil how to behave. As one educational psychologist states, training children to become 'emotionally literate' is about 'reframing how we see ourselves'.[10] Yet, it may be possible that the self of a child that emotionally literate trainers want to reframe is a valid form of consciousness for the person concerned. Whether teachers and other professionals possess the wisdom and the authority to define what form of self-perception is appropriate for a child is a question that must disturb anyone who upholds the ideal of self-determination.

Previously we have discussed the hostility that therapeutic culture displays towards what it calls negative emotions, particularly anger and hate. Yet sometimes such emotions are far from negative – they represent an appropriate response to conditions that demand the manifestation of anger or hate. The crusade against anger and hatred may well be motivated by a genuine desire to minimise conflict and promote harmony. But instructing people to come to terms with their strong feelings may represent the demand for acquiescence and conformism. In some cases the demand to curb strong passion could mean pressurising people to tolerate appalling acts of injustice and oppression. As Derek Summerfield suggests, western therapeutic intervention in war-affected areas treats the emotional response of those suffering from violence as a disease that needs to be cured. 'The question is whether anger, hatred and a felt need for revenge in people who have been grievously wronged are necessarily bad things', he asks.[11] The diseasing of so-called negative emotions distract attention from the fact that maybe it is the conditions that gave rise to them that needs to be cured.

One of the most disturbing manifestations of therapeutic culture is the conviction that an individual's emotional state is not simply a personal matter, but a legitimate subject for public concern. This attitude is founded upon the belief that the state of emotion of the individual determines what happens in society. Emotional determinism influences the way that social problems are perceived. Emotional determinism is particularly powerful in relation to contemporary perception of childhood. According to this dogma, the problems experienced and caused by adults are rooted in the emotional world of the child. That is why public institutions feel that they have a warrant to shape and alter the feelings of a child. Consequently, a scheme launched in England targets children as young as 8 years in an effort to prevent them from becoming criminals. The scheme is based on 'research' carried out in the US which claims that 'aggression in 2-year-olds can manifest itself in criminal activity in adolescence'.[12]

It is not just children who are the targets of therapeutic activism. Once emotions are endowed with such formidable powers to determine the course of events, adults too become the focus of psychosocial intervention. For example, parents of children who want to play in the New Jersey Youth Hockey League have to attend its mandatory anger management programme. If they fail to attend these mandatory therapy sessions, their children will not be able to play in the league.[13] In many states, drivers convicted of an offence are forced to go and attend anger management programmes. The management of people's emotional state is gradually becoming an important sphere of public responsibility.

A demand for emotional conformity

The institutionalisation of the therapeutic ethos can also be interpreted as the constitution of a regime of social control. Experts are continually involved in designating what is and what is not an acceptable emotional response. The affirmation of certain forms of emotional behaviour goes hand in hand with the attempt to suppress others. This manipulation of people's feelings is frequently seen as the antidote to antisocial behaviour. In many states in the US, drivers accused of driving while intoxicated are required to undergo alcoholism treatment on the AA model as a condition for keeping their licences or avoiding a jail sentence. Prisoners who fail to come to terms with their emotions while undergoing therapeutic prison programmes are often penalised. Nolan cites the case of Arnie Hall, who failed his treatment programme at a maximum security correction facility near Austin, Texas, because he 'cut off his feelings and did not come to understand how his parents' treatment of him as a child helped explain his criminal activity'. At work, individuals who refuse to attend 'sensitivity training' courses often discover that they have put their career in jeopardy.[14] Nolan's concerns are echoed by Peele's critique of addiction treatments in the US. He is disturbed by the growing trend on the part of courts, employee assistance programmes and schools to force individuals to undergo treatment. 'People are then compelled in these programs to declare themselves addicts or alcoholics and to modify their behavior well beyond the punishments they might have been meted out had they simply been convicted', he points out.[15] In Britain, the early release of prisoners is conditional on attending courses in 'anger management, drug and alcohol addiction, or sex therapy'.[16]

Mandatory therapy is also forced on people whose behaviour scandalises prevailing social norms. So after John Rocker, a pitcher for the Atlanta Braves baseball team, used bigoted language during an interview, the Major League Baseball Commissioner decided to take action. However, before deciding what action to take, the Commissioner forced Rocker to attend a mandatory evaluation session with a psychiatrist.[17] Forcing convicted individuals into drug treatment therapy, couples counselling, parenting classes or anger management sessions is actively pursued by the American Drug Courts movement. Nolan points out that the concept of justice advocated through therapeutic jurisprudence 'allows the court to extend its authority into the lives of drug clients in unprecedented ways'.[18]

In Britain, corporate counselling has become a powerful instrument for maintaining managerial control. In some cases, managers have called in employees to an interview at which they were given the sack, asked to leave the premises immediately – and offered counselling.[19] PPP Healthcare employee assistance programmes offer a compulsory option for employers who want to force their employees to receive counselling. If employees refuse to participate in this programme, they can face disciplinary sanctions, including the sack.[20] The gradual expansion of mandatory counselling – 'we'll help you whether you like it or not' – indicates that the line between therapeutic intervention and policing has become blurred.

The phenomenon of mandatory counselling illustrates how the domain of feeling and emotion has been invaded by the therapeutic ethos. The very idea that how people feel about themselves and others is the business of government has helped to politicise the sphere of the emotion. Measures are enacted to help the emotional illiterate and to train those who deviate from the new therapeutic consensus to adopt an acceptable, emotionally correct form of behaviour. New, so-called 'hate crimes' are oriented towards policing unacceptable forms of individual thought on the ground of protecting the emotionally vulnerable target groups from prejudice. Such laws have little practical purpose since there already exist plenty of legal means for prosecuting different forms of violence and incitement to violence. Nevertheless, they serve an important symbolic role of indicating what forms of thoughts and emotions are acceptable and which ones are beyond the pale.

In Britain and the United States, free speech has been put to question by those who argue that since words hurt and can cause psychological damage, the victims should be protected from distress. Even art has come under scrutiny. Artists have faced censure and have been forced to close down their exhibitions on the grounds that their pictures offend sections of the public. It appears that the current climate of emotional correctness cannot tolerate the right to be offensive. Acts and words are often denounced for causing pain and offence. The statement 'I feel offended' is by implication a demand for censorship and an apology. Jonathan Rauch's account of contemporary attacks on free thought contends that the belief that people should be punished for holding offensive beliefs inexorably leads 'toward an inquisition'. He is particularly critical of the 'rapidly rising notion that hurtful words and ideas are a form of violence' leads to the 'criminalization of criticism'.[21] Critics like Rauch, who object to the attempt to protect the 'vulnerable' from offensive words, are invariably accused of letting down the victim. And in the name of protecting the victim, moral entrepreneurs demand an ever-increasing number of rules for regulating personal behaviour.

The growing elite consensus against offensive speech exemplifies how the politicisation of emotion can have such disturbingly authoritarian consequences as the marginalisation of nonconformist ideas. Throughout history, any idea worth its salt has been guaranteed to cause widespread offence. Everything from universal suffrage to organ transplants, from contraception to legalised divorce, was once considered an offence to standards of public decency. Each time, the pain caused to some people proved well worth it for the gains offered to humanity as a whole. The right to be offensive is always a prerequisite for public debate forwards. Today, this right is considered to be unacceptable because society has adopted a much more limited view of individual subjectivity. It is now widely assumed that people are too weak and vulnerable to get through the rigours of life without being protected from hurtful words or images. 'Hurtful' words are now likened to physical violence. A new language has been coined to describe this conflation of speech with violence, allowing people who have been offended by what somebody said to claim that they are actually victims of 'words that wound', 'assaultative speech', or even 'spirit murder'.

The politics of emotion is by definition arbitrary in its public impact. It is extremely difficult to objectively grasp concepts like intention, hate, emotional damage, trauma or an act of abuse. The elevation of feeling means that the subjective offence a victim claims to have suffered need have little to do with the objective actions of the offender. If you feel that someone's words or behaviour are offensive, that is enough to end the discussion, regardless of what was intended. After all, nobody can reasonably argue that you are not really offended, just as nobody can get inside your heart and check how upset you are.

The privileged moral status assigned to the victim is increasingly institutionalised in the Anglo-American system of justice. In Britain, in February 1999, the report of the Macpherson inquiry into the murder of the black teenager, Stephen Lawrence, fully endorsed the right of the victim to define whether a crime was racially motivated or not. The complexity of the question of motivation was resolved by Macpherson in the following terms, 'a racist incident is any incident which is perceived to be racist by the victim or any other person'.[22] The principle that an offence is in the eyes of the beholder – already informally established in numerous harassment codes – dictates the practices of a new emotionally charged system of justice.

The introduction of the victim's subjectivity into the domain of justice, indicates that the law is being used to send moral messages to correct attitudes. This symbolic use of the law to promote moral values is most consistently expressed in the construction of the concept of hate crime in the United States during the past 15 years. The concept of a hate crime is morally driven since it makes the transgressor's motive and character a salient issue. As Jacob and Potter's study of the construction of this crime points out, it is often suggested that hate crime victims suffer 'greater psychological and emotional injury than other victims'.[23] Although there is no empirical research which compares the emotional reaction of hate crime victims and ordinary crime victims, it fits in well with the reorientation of the legal system towards the institutionalisation of therapeutics. Minimising emotional pain has become an important motif in law-making. Concern with preventing such pain inspired victim activists in the United States to campaign for 'progressive censorship'. As Downs noted, victim politics in the 1980s created a climate where victim groups could demand 'laws against forms of expression that harmed their self-esteem and emotional security'.[24] For such campaigns, an offence to the emotion is so important that the right to free speech becomes negotiable.

The incorporation of the value of emotionalism into the system of justice is one of the most far-reaching innovations in the Anglo-American legal culture. This assimilation of victim's rights serves to reorient the character of justice. Campaigns for victim's rights aim to secure a status which places them in a privileged position relative to the defendant's rights. Victims' advocates demand an active role for their client in court proceedings. The acceptance of some of their demands – such as the use of victim impact statements undermines the possibility of maintaining an objective measure of criminal behaviour. As a result, criminal judgements now have a subjective component, since the victim is allowed at least indirectly to influence the outcome. Most states in the United States allow victims to testify about the emotional damage and physical harm inflicted on them by the defendant. In Britain, long-established safeguards which were elaborated to ensure fairness to the defendant have been weakened through the institutionalisation of a more victim-friendly system of justice.

It is clearly right that witnesses, complainants, victims and their families should be treated properly in the criminal process, and that they should be fully informed of developments. But the enhancement of the status of the victim in criminal proceedings has serious implications for a fair trial. This problem is strikingly manifest in the increasingly common indignation which witnesses express at being subjected to rigorous cross-examination: 'Who's on trial here?' Whilst the sense of outrage displayed by victims is understandable, its encouragement makes for bad justice. Wendy Kaminer, in her powerful critique of these trends, argues that 'to deny victims an opportunity to make these statements seems cruel; but to provide it is often inflammatory'. Kaminer is concerned that judges and juries 'swayed by particularly appealing, articulate victims may impose disproportion-ately harsh sentences on the defendants who wrong them'. And offenders lucky enough to 'choose especially resilient victims may be treated more leniently than defendants whose victims are easily traumatized'.[25] All this makes for arbitrary justice.

Kaminer's concerns are shared by the British legal academic John Fitzpatrick, who is worried that 'the more prominent the role of the victim (or their families)' in court proceedings, 'the higher the risk that emotion will upset the cool, measured consideration of the evidence which is crucial to fairness'.[26] And yet the introduction of emotion into proceedings that were once described as dispassionate is clearly in line with the wider social trends outlined above. Moreover, by giving voice to the emotional damage suffered by the victim, it is hoped that the demands of therapy will come to influence court proceedings. The victims' rights movement condemns what it sees as the dispassionate character of court proceedings and objects to its unresponsiveness to victims' rage, grief and emotion. As Sarat pointed out, 'by transforming courts into sites for the ritual of grieving', this movement 'seeks to make private experiences part of public discourse'. Kaminer has also drawn attention to this project of inserting emotion into the system of justice. She noted that from a victim's perspective, 'the trial, is in part, a therapeutic process' and warned,

> the victims rights movement partakes of the popular confusion of law and therapy and the substitution of feelings for facts. But if feelings are facts in a therapist's office, where subjective realities reign, feelings are prejudices in

a court of law, which strives for relatively objective decision-making. Justice is not a form of therapy, meaning that what is helpful to a particular victim, or defendant is not necessarily just and what is just may not be therapeutic.[27]

Kaminer's defence of objective justice is in part motivated by her apprehension of the potentially authoritarian consequences of emotionally correct law-making.

Critics like Fitzpatrick, Kaminer and Sarat have warned that the elevation of the victim in court proceedings and the institutionalisation of emotion into the system of justice represent the rehabilitation of the instinct of revenge. Sarat, in particular, argues that the 'demand for victims' rights and the insistence that we hear the voices of the victims are just the latest "style" in which vengeance has disguised itself'.[28] The encouragement of emotion within the system of justice represents a destructive institutional response to the demand for validating the voice of the victim. Whenever therapy and justice become confused, arbitrariness and the erosion of rights follow.

The new conservatism

Therapeutic culture is not responsible for all the trends discussed in the previous chapters. Its ascendancy was not so much the cause but the reflection of the changing form of subjectivity. However, therapeutics was not simply the beneficiary of the crisis of the modernist imagination, it also contributed to this process by distracting people from engaging with the wider social issues in favour of an inward turn to the self. For example, the turn away from the agenda of the social was influenced by a variety of historical experiences in the second half of the twentieth century. But the partial displacement of the idea of social causation by the recent rise of emotional determinism is a testimony to the influence of the therapeutic ethos over the society.

The authoritarian and coercive dimension of therapeutic culture rarely assumes an open and public form. Indeed, therapeutic authority seldom assumes an outwardly coercive form. It seeks to exercise control not through a system of punishment, but through cultivating a sense of vulnerability, powerlessness and dependence. The narrative of diminished subjectivity transmits a call for self-limitation. Through normalising the sick role and help-seeking, therapeutic culture promotes the virtue of dependence on professional authority. At the same time it discourages dependence on intimate and informal relations – an act which weakens the sense of belonging of the individual. Worse still, contemporary culture fosters a climate where people really do feel ill, insecure and emotionally damaged.

It is truly a regrettable state of affairs when so many of us seek solace and affirmation through a diagnosis. The transformation of illness into an identity is potentially a serious problem for public health. But most important of all it indicates that a regime of self-limitation has become institutionalised. It suggests that the fatalistic premise of the vulnerable self influences the behaviour of a significant section of society, at least some of the time. One of the clearest manifestations of this influence is the way it has succeeded in reversing the relationship between the individual and social experience. As noted in Chapter 6, the passive sense of self projected today does not so much take risks, as is at risk. In this scenario, the experimenting and transformative role of the individual is all but extinguished.

The passive narrative of the self promoted today acquires its apogee with the celebration of self-esteem. Advocates of this cause continually remind people of the virtue of the unconditional acceptance of the self. This static conservative view of the self represents a rejection of previous more ambitious calls for 'changing yourself', 'improving yourself' or for 'transcending the self'. The call for self-acceptance represents a round about way of avoiding change. This conservative orientation towards the future is clearly reflected within the role of therapy itself.

Although individual therapist's sometimes make extravagant claims about the effectiveness of their product, therapeutic culture is distinctly modest about the claims it makes. Therapies tend to be promoted on the grounds that they help people cope and come to terms with their condition. Such relatively modest claims stand in contrast to the way that therapy was promoted in the past. Throughout most of the twentieth century, therapy was advertised as both as cure and as an instrument for the construction of a happy society. It was promoted as a positive way of exploring and expanding the individual's personality.

From the perspective of today's therapeutic ethos, therapy is much more an instrument of survival than a means through which enlightenment can be gained. Individuals are not so much cured as placed in a state of recovery. They are far more likely to be instructed to acknowledge their problems than to transcend them. Therapy, like the wider culture of which it is a part, teaches people to know their place. In return it offers the dubious blessings of affirmation and recognition.

Notes

Introduction

1 See Patricia Leigh Brown 'Cinematography and chilling out? That's scouting', *New York Times* 13 May 2002 and 'Lavender calms stressed pupils', *BBC News Online* 14 May 2002.
2 See Hymowitz (2000) p. 96. Also see 'School phobia girl is excused lessons by GP'. *The Daily Telegraph* 5 June 2002.
3 See www.as.wvu.edu/carlsonprofessorship/Smelser 17 September 2002.
4 See Dr Moti Peleg 'A year after the assassination. A nation in post trauma', *Yediot Achronot* 29 November 1996.
5 'Getting McVeigh', *The Nation* 23 June 1997.
6 See Linenthal (2001) p. 96.
7 See Downs (1996) p. 25.
8 *The Oxford English Dictionary* (1989), vol. XIV, p. 920.
9 Citations obtained from Reuters' Factiva database.
10 See Hewitt (1998) p. 87.
11 Although this trend is far more developed in Anglo-American societies than elsewhere, its impact is evident throughout the western world. As Vanessa Pupavac has shown in a series of important contributions, therapeutic culture has become globalised. See Pupavac (2001).
12 See Real (1999).
13 'Study warns about rise in childhood trauma cases', press release, University of Alberta, 3 August 2000, www.ualberta.ca
14 'Martin Seligman forum on depression', 16 August 2002, http://abc.net.au/rn/talks/lm/stories/s648530.htm
15 See Catherine Scott 'Teaching in a culture of fear', Technology Colleges Trust, Vision 2020, Second International Online Conference, 13–26 October and 24 November–7 December 2002, www.cybertext.net.au/tct2002/disc_papers/staffing/pri../scott%20-%20printable.ht 'Ride gets rougher', *The Guardian* 15 May 2001 and 'Support sites', *The Guardian* 3 December 2002.
16 'Student stress', *The Site* September 2002, www.thesite.org/magazine/specials_mental_health/work.student_stress.html
17 'Confronting the social causes of psychological depression: too taboo?', *Radical Middle Newsletter* January/February 2001, p. 10.
18 'Primary pupils stressed by exams'. *The Guardian* 30 December 2002 and 'Entranced exams; pupils offered classes in self-hypnosis to help them relax before school tests', *Daily Mail* 17 October 2000.
19 See 'Looking back without anger', *BBC News Online* 21 November 1999.
20 'Counselling team helps school tots', *Hartlepool Mail* 6 June 2001 and 'Stress lessons for children at primary school', *The Daily Telegraph* 28 September 2000.

21   'Pupils to get therapy for big leap forward to secondary', *The Observer* 5 September 1999.
22   See 'Early warning system', *The Guardian* 21 July 1999.
23   See Furedi (2001), Chapter 10.
24   'Stress counsellors for England fans', *Evening Standard* 29 August 2001.
25   'Pet insurer offers grief counselling', *The Daily Telegraph* 3 May 2002.
26   See Donna Lafromboise, 'One of their own blasts therapists for shoddy work', *The Montreal Gazette* 11 January 1997.
27   See Karp (1996).
28   Cited in Horwitz (2002) p. 3.
29   Exact figures are hard to compile. The available evidence suggests that there are around 110,000 individuals working as full-time and part-time counsellors. There are also a far larger number of individuals working in the public sector – teachers, university lecturers, social workers, probation officers, law enforcement personnel, etc. – who practise their counselling skills as part of their job.
30   Totton, N. (1999) 'The baby and the bathwater: "professionalisation" in psychotherapy and counselling', *British Journal of Guidance and Counselling* 27(3) 88.
31   'Counselling is offered for the death of a council', *The Daily Telegraph* 25 October 1995.
32   Nolan (1998) pp. 9–12.
33   Nolan (1998) p. 8.
34   See Horwitz (2002) p. 4.
35   See Jennifer Cunningham, 'Counter the counselling culture', *LM* March 1999 p. 13.
36   Personal communication, Tony Watts, editor of *British Journal of Guidance and Counselling*. This figure includes: advice (540,000), advocacy (5,000), counselling (632,000), guidance (44,000), psychotherapy (5,500) and mediation (4,500).
37   Rose (1990) p. 2.
38   See 'A new growth industry emerges to cushion the blow as more people lose their jobs', *The Guardian* 19 January 1991.
39   See 'Taking the worry out of work', *The Daily Telegraph* 6 April 1999.
40   See 'The sharing and caring way to get to the top', *The Times* 6 January 2001.
41   Press release, 20 November 2000 DfEE news centre. Report findings of the Work–Life Balance Baseline Study.
42   Hedges (2002) pp. 3–5.
43   See Gutmann (2000) for a discussion of what she calls, 'The kinder, gentler military'.
44   See J. Rozenberg '2,000 sue MoD over psychiatric injuries of war', *The Daily Telegraph* 5 March 2002.
45   'Police "becoming soft"', *The Guardian* 16 June 1998.
46   Gergen (1990) p. 362.
47   Nolan (2001) p. 140.
48   Hunter (2000) p. 81.
49   See, for example, 'Managing grief after disaster', a National Center for PTSD Fact Sheet, by Katherine Shear, 26 October 2001.
50   Rand Health, 'After 9/11: stress and coping across America: research highlights', 15 November 2001, www.rand.org/health
51   For example, Yahoo constructed a 'Featured category: children and traumatic events'.
52   Abby Goodnough, 'Post-9/11 pain found to linger in young minds', *The New York Times* 2 May 2002.
53   See, for example, 'When nightmares won't go away', *Business Week* 18 March 2002.
54   Shankar Vedantam, 'After September 11, psychic wounds slow to heal', *Washington Post* 17 March 2002.
55   See 'Communities gear up for long-term effects of disaster', *Alcoholism & Drug Abuse Weekly* 37 (2001).

56 Stephanie Kriner, 'In New York, many still in shock', *DisasterRelief.org* 5 November 2001.

57 William Booth, '9/11 Trauma: studies find resilience, worry', *Washington Post* 7 September 2002.

58 Boscarino is cited in Sally Satel, 'New Yorkers don't need therapy', *The Wall Street Journal* 26 July 2002.

59 See Erica Goode, 'Program to cover psychiatric help for 9/11 families', *The New York Times* 21 August 2002.

60 Cited in Stephanie Kriner, 'In New York, many still in shock', *DisasterRelief.org* 5 November 2001.

61 'Nation's victim assistance organizations issue trauma recovery tips to Americans', MADD press release 12 September 2001.

62 National Association of School Psychologists, 'Memorials/activities/rituals following traumatic events. Suggestions for schools', September 2001, www.nasponline.org

63 'Q&A: helping adults, children cope with grief', *Washington Post* 24 September 2001.

64 Cited in Stephanie Kriner, 'In New York, many still in shock', *DisasterRelief.org* 5 November 2001.

65 Linenthal (2001) p. 4.

66 Linenthal (2001) p. 4 and 198–204.

67 'Tapping your resilience in the wake of terrorism: pointers for practitioners', October 2001, APA Online, www.apa.org/practice/practitionerhelp.html

68 Cited in 'For a shared expression of emotions, we turn to the arts', *Pittsburgh Post-Gazette* 11 November 2001. Attempt to give meaning through the medium of therapeutics and therapeutic influenced religion. Confessional television celebrity Oprah Winfrey gave clear expression to this outlook when she declared at an interfaith prayer service at Yankee Stadium that each victim of 9/11 instantly became an angel.

69 See Erica Goode, 'Program to cover psychiatric help for 9/11 families', *The New York Times* 21 August 2002.

70 Critics of this trend were conspicous by their lack of influence over events. Opposition was mainly restricted to a small number of mental health professionals and media commentators. See Sally Satel's 'New Yorkers don't need therapy', *The Wall Street Journal* 26 July 2002 – one of the few attempts to question therapeutic activism in the national media.

71 Mindy Hung, 'Note of caution sounded on trauma counselling', *MedscapeWire* 19 September 2001.

72 William Booth, '9/11 trauma: Studies find resilience, worry', *Washington Post* 7 September 2002.

73 See Bracken (2002) pp. 67–73.

74 See Moskowitz (2001), Rose (1990). Also see Herman's (1995) important study, *The Romance of American Psychology*.

75 Rieff (1966) p. 15.

76 'Therapy is new religion says Carey', *The Daily Telegraph* 1 August 2000.

77 See *The Guardian* 6 January 1996.

78 Sargeant (2000) p. 45.

79 Walter, T. (1999) *On Bereavement; The Culture of Grief*, Buckingham: Open University Press, p. 196.

80 Ibid.

81 Horwitz (2002) p. ix.

82 Ibid.

83 See 'Brash Britain breaks with its blushing habit', *The Sunday Times* 5 July 1998.

84 *The Guardian* 13 November 2000.

85 Ibid.

86 See *The Times* 5 November 1966.

87 McLean, I. and Johnes, M. (2000) *Aberfan: Government and Disasters*, Cardiff: Welsh Academic Press, pp. 104–6.
88 See *Daily Mail* 19 March 1999.
89 See, for example, '164 known dead in flood disaster', *The Times* 2 February 1953.
90 See 'Burial of flood victims: ceremony in valley of rocks', *The Times* 23 August 1952.
91 Cited in *The Times* 20 February 1953.
92 Ibid.
93 'Flooding and human health; the dangers posed are not always obvious', *British Medical Journal* 11 November 2000, p. 1167.
94 This research is discussed in *The Sunday Telegraph* 3 August 1997. On the writing of therapeutic history, see Frank Furedi, 'The "second generation" of Holocaust survivors', www.spiked-online.com 24 January 2002.
95 Bellah *et al.* (1996) p. 113.
96 See Berger and Luckmann (1967).
97 Hewitt (1998) p. 87.
98 See Swidler (2001) pp. 16 and 17.

1 The culture of emotionalism

 1 Smail (2001) p. ix.
 2 See Bracken (2002) p. 64.
 3 Ulrich Beck, 'Beyond status and class?' in Beck and Beck-Gernsheim (2002) p. 33.
 4 Ibid. p. 39.
 5 Smail (2001) p. ix.
 6 Bracken (2002) p. 179.
 7 Rice (1996) pp. 89–99.
 8 Moskowitz (2001) p. 2
 9 Lasch-Quinn (2002).
10 Joseph Rowntree Foundation (1999).
11 *The Guardian* 14 September 1999.
12 Cited in the *Times Educational Supplement* 25 July 1980.
13 See Paul Lashmar, 'Feel-bad factor', *New Statesman* 6 September 1995.
14 Ulrich Beck, 'Beyond status and class?' in Beck and Beck-Gernsheim (2002) p. 37.
15 Goleman (1996) pp. x–xi, 263–9.
16 See 'Attachment theory: a secure base for policy?', in Kraemer and Roberts (1996), pp. 36–7.
17 See *The Antidote Manifesto: Developing an Emotionally Literate Society*, London: Antidote, 2001, pp. 6 and 16.
18 Mark Brayne 'Journalists on the couch', *The Guardian* 5 August 2002.
19 Cited in Pupavac (2001), p. 7.
20 Ibid.
21 Post is cited in 'Saddam, tell me about your mum', *The Guardian* 14 November 2002. For a discussion of Saddam's pathology, see Con Coughlin 'Saddam: King of terror', *The Washington Post Online* 6 December 2002.
22 Bhutta, Z. (2002) 'Children of war: the real casualties of the Afghan conflict', *British Medical Journal* 324, 9 February 2002, p. 351.
23 Summerfield (2000) p. 426.
24 Kirby Farrell has characterised this development in the US as that of post-traumatic culture. See Farrell (1998).
25 See, for example, Madeleine Bunting 'Rewiring our brains', *The Guardian* 13 November 2000.
26 Cited in Summerfield (1999) p. 1451.
27 See 'Negative emotions can make life a misery', Better Health Channel, 23 August 2002, www.betterhealth.vic

28 Barbara l. Fredrickson (2000) 'Cultivating positive emotions to optimize health and well-being', *Prevention and Treatment* 3, March, p. 2.
29 Wilks (1998).
30 Dr Thomas Yarnell 'Release negative emotions', Dr Yarnell's self-help solutions store, http://members.aol.com/tototmnow/page3/ August 2002.
31 Wilson Schaeff (1990).
32 Langford (1999).
33 Mark Sichel and Alicia Cervini 'The alcohologenic parent', Psyber Square, www.psybersquare.com/recovery_alcohologenic.html August 2002.
34 See John Bradshaw audio archives, www.bradshawcassetts.com/archives.html
35 Irvine (1997) p. 352.
36 Irvine (1997) p. 351.
37 Ibid. p. 361.
38 Hochschild (1994) p. 3.
39 See 'Profile: university counselling service', University of Dundee Press Office, Contact, www.dundee.ac.uk/pressoffice/contact/2000/decjan/counselling.htm (2000).
40 Kaminer (1993) p. 36.
41 David Overton, 'Why counselling is not sought in deteriorating relationships: the effect of denial', *British Journal of Guidance and Counselling*, 1994 (22): 3.
42 V. Seidler, 'Men, sex and relationships' and 'Postscript, men therapy and politics', in Seidler (1992), pp. 1, 2 and 245.
43 D. Kindlon and M. Thompson 'Fighting inner turmoil', *The Times* 15 June 1999.
44 Ibid.
45 See *The Guardian* 25 April 1996 and Horrocks (1994) p. 17.
46 MacInnes (1998) p. 57
47 See Lyng (1990) p. 872 and Stanko and Hobdell (1993).
48 Kaplan and Marks (1995) p. 207.
49 The cultivation of help seeking in relation to child rearing is discussed in Furedi (2001), Chapter 10.
50 See Linenthal (2001) pp. 89–96.
51 Anne Karpf, 'Farmers' grief leaves us all bereft', *The Guardian* 12 April 2001.
52 Lowney (1999) p. 18.
53 See S. Moore, 'The Windsors still don't understand us', *The Independent* 3 September 1997 and interview with A Scott Berg, *The New York Times* 5 August 1998.
54 Hochschild (1983) p. 22.
55 Metstovic (1997) p. 65.
56 See notice on www.Amazon.com
57 Lowney (1999) p. 19.
58 See Wendy Kaminer, 'I spy', *The American Prospect* 11 (18), 2000.
59 Cited in *The Guardian* 17 February 1997.
60 Cited in *Independent on Sunday* 16 October 1994.
61 Peele (1995).
62 Calcutt (1998) pp. 26–7.
63 See *New York Times Magazine* 12 May 1996.
64 Peele (1995) p. 83.
65 See *The Guardian* 19 October 1998.
66 See Laura Miller 'My syndrome myself', *Salon Magazine* 24 June 1998.

2 The politics of emotion

1 See Tessa Mayes 'Restraint or revelation? Free speech and privacy in a confessional age', spiked on-line, 22 October 2002.
2 Jonathan Freedland 'Now Brown is one of us', *The Guardian* 9 January 2002.
3 Cited in Furedi (1992).

4 Hobson (1988) p. 4, Laski (1932) p. 43.
5 Perham (1962) p. 114.
6 Hobson (1901) p. 9.
7 Le Bon (1990) p. 110.
8 Lippman (1922) p. 75 and Paget (1929) 'Sudden changes in group opinion', *Social Forces* 7(3): 439.
9 Schumpeter (1951) p. 264.
10 Lipset (1963) p. 114.
11 Eysenck (1960) p. 137.
12 Bell (1964) p. 375.
13 See Madeleine Bunting 'We are the people', *The Guardian* 17 February 2003.
14 See Mackenzie and Labiner (2002).
15 See Cloud (1998) pp. 94, 97.
16 See, for example, Jim McGuigan (2000) 'British identity and the people's princess', *Sociological Review*, February.
17 Ian Robertson, 'Big boys don't cry', *British Medical Journal* 15 June 1996, p. 1547.
18 See Park (1999) 'The politics of emotional literacy', *Renewal* 17(1): 52.
19 See *The Antidote Manifesto: Developing an Emotionally Literate Society* (2001) London: Antidote.
20 Samuels (2001) pp. 2, 202 and 203.
21 See Barry Richards, 'Introduction', paper given at the 'Conclusions' seminar in the 'Affect, Ethics and Citizenship Series', 8 May 2000, Department of Cultural Studies, University of East London.
22 Bell (1964).
23 Lasch (1979) p. 43.
24 See 'The United States of Apathy?' *BBC News* 11 January 2000.
25 See Seth Gitell, 'Apathy at the polls', *The Boston Phoenix* 4 December 2002.
26 Mackenzie and Labiner (2001) pp. 2–3.
27 Curtice, J. and Jowell, R. 'The sceptical electorate', in *British Social Attitudes, The 12th Report* (1995) pp. 141 and 148.
28 Findings of the poll published in *The Guardian* 8 June 1999.
29 'Politics a "turn-off" for under 45s', *BBC News* 28 February 2002.
30 See Alice Thomson, 'Politics doesn't have to be like the Big Brother House', *The Daily Telegraph* 4 December 2002.
31 Melucci (1989) p. 49.
32 See Madeleine Bunting, 'No politics, we're British', *The Guardian* 15 May 2000.
33 Clare Garner, 'Church turns to Diana to boost attendance', *The Independent* 20 February 1998.
34 'TV boss backs BBC political review', *BBC News* 5 February 2002.
35 Nolan (1998) p. 45.
36 Wendy Kaminer, 'Jesus and the Politicians', *Free Inquiry Magazine* 20 (2), 29 June 2002.
37 Sarah Womack, 'MPs "need help to fight depression"', *The Daily Telegraph* 14 November 2001.
38 See John Sutherland, 'Politicians, dry your eyes', *The Guardian* 30 April 2001.
39 See *The Guardian* 21 June 1999.
40 Cited in 'In Sickness and in health?' *Wall Street Journal* 4 August 1999.
41 See Nolan (1998) pp. 275–6.
42 See 'Crying if he wants to', transcript of Online Newshour, 10 July 1996. www.pbs.org/newshour/essays/fleming_7–10.html
43 David Skinner, 'Matters of the heart', *Salon* 20 September 2000, www.salon.com
44 Steven Thomma, 'Faced with this crisis, Bush must tap a reserve of emotional discipline and maturity', *Knight Ridder Newspapers* 21 September 2001.
45 *The Telegraph* 25 October 1996.

46 'Assured of her place in history', *The Irish Times* 12 October 1999. I would like to thank Dr Chris Gilligan for drawing my attention to this report.
47 See Altheide (2002) p. 108.
48 Nolan (1998) p. 237.
49 See Fraser P. Seitel, 'Rudy Giuliani's crisis communications leadership', *O'Dwyer's PR Daily* 17 September 2001, www.ODWYERPR.com
50 Jonathan Freedland, 'Inching towards peace', *The Guardian* 10 November 1999.
51 Rose (1990) pp. 1–2.
52 Arnason, A. (2000) 'Biography, bereavement story', *Mortality* 5 (2): 194.
53 Cited in *The Times* 4 August 1999.
54 See *The Guardian* 23 September 1998.
55 See DfEE (2000) *Sex and Relationship Guidance* and Scottish Executive (2000) *Educating the Whole Child: Personal and Social Development in Primary Schools and the Primary Stages of Special Schools.*
56 See the discussion in *Antidote*, August 2000.
57 For a discussion of this project, see *Time Out* 25 October 2000.
58 See 'The real life class', *The Guardian* 11 April 2000.
59 'New Deal – so play your hand right', *The Observer* 13 September 1998.
60 See *The Daily Record* 7 September 1999.
61 *The Guardian* 8 August 2001.
62 *Supporting Families: A Consultation Document* (1999) London, p. 30.
63 This point is elaborated in Furedi (2001) Chapter 11.
64 See 'Draft Speech for the Home Secretary – Launch of the Lords and Commons Family and Child Protection Group's report "Family Matters"', 23 July 1998.
65 See Home Office 'The Crime And Disorder Act. Guidance Document: Parenting Order', 2 June 2000.
66 See 'Social exclusion: keeping the doors open', *The Guardian* 21 July 1999.
67 Home Office, Research Development and Statistics Directorate (1998) *An Evaluation of the Prison Sex Offender Treatment Programme*, London.
68 'Straw plan to tag more ex-inmates', *The Guardian* 27 January 2000.
69 See Nolan (2001).
70 See *The Irish Times* 1 July 1998.

3 Targeting privacy and informal relations

1 Altheide (2002) p. 108.
2 See *The Independent* 13 October 1991.
3 E. Wurtzel 'Memoirs are made of this', *The Guardian* 27 October 1998.
4 See Oates' comments in *The New York Times* 28 August 1988.
5 See M. Kakutani, 'Critic's Notebook: Biography becomes a blood sport', *The New York Times* 20 May 1994.
6 Freud (1985) p. 151.
7 Leading social theorists, like Jurgen Habermas, were critical of what they saw as the sham of privacy and wrote of the 'pseudo-privacy' of family life, but did not question the right to privacy as such. See, for example, the discussion in A. Wolfe 'Public and private in theory and practice', in Weintraub and Kumar (1997).
8 MacKinnon (1989) p. 168.
9 Strauss *et al.* (1980) p. 3.
10 Bob Franklin, 'The case for children's rights: a progress report', in Franklin (1995) p. 4.
11 Furedi (2002).
12 See 'Survey of parents on abuse', www.Childabuse.com 2001.
13 This is paticularly the case within the discipline of the sociology of the family. For an exceptional counterpoint to this trend, see the articles, particularly those of Jean Cohen and Jean Bethke Elshtain, in Weintraub and Kumar (1997).

14 See Lafontaine (1990) and R. Sapford, 'Endnote: Public and Private' in Muncie *et al.* (1993).
15 Archard (1993) p. 92.
16 Ibid. p. 125.
17 Irvine (1999) p. 20.
18 Arendt (2000) p. 200.
19 A. Samuels, 'Therapists with attitude', in Samuels (2001).
20 See Moskowitz (2001) p. 7.
21 Nolan (1998) p. 165.
22 Janov (1993) p. 284. See J. Cunniham, 'Primal therapies – stillborn theories', in Felthan (forthcoming) for an excellent critique of these therapies.
23 Wilson Schaef (1989) pp. 43, 105.
24 Bauman (2000) p. 67.
25 Parsons (1964) p. 317.
26 Jacoby (1975) p. 142. Jacoby's critique of the radical therapy movement provides valuable insights into the consolidation of the antifamily consensus.
27 See Smith (1995) p. 23. According to Smith, Gloria Steinem's *Revolution from Within* and Patti Davis's *The Way I See It* are illustrative of this trend.
28 Forward (1990) pp. 5–6.
29 See Braiker (2001).
30 Isaacs (1999).
31 Frost (2003).
32 Deepak Chopra, 'Ten Keys to Happiness', www.sppiritwalk.org/chopra10keys.htm (2002).
33 Treacher in Richards (1989) pp. 131–46.
34 Lowney (1999) p. 23.
35 See Dian Katz, 'Relationships: fireworks or fizzle', *Lesbian News* July 1999, p. 24.
36 Nancy Joy Carroll (1998) *The Love Handbook for Singles*, available through www.carrollconsulting.cc/lovehandbook.html
37 See Oliver James, 'Addicted to order', *The Sunday Times Magazine* 18 January 1998.
38 Wilson Schaef (1990) p. 31.
39 'General mental health issues: co-dependency', www.nmha.org/infoctr/factsheets/43.cfm (1997).
40 Ibid.
41 See 'Compulsive helping', www.promis.co.uk/?view=chelp (2002).
42 See http://joy2meu.com/Relationship.html (2001).
43 Cited in Treacher, op. cit. p. 145.
44 See 'Teenagers warned of sex trauma', *BBC News Online* 2 June 1999.
45 Levine and Troiden (1988) p. 357.
46 Lasch (1979) p. 103.
47 Treacher op. cit. p. 145.
48 See Craib (1994), Chapter 2, for a discussion of this process.
49 See 'Valentine sweet-talk could mask a violent monster, abuse charity warns', *The Independent* 9 February 1998.
50 D. Finkelhor, 'The victimization of children and youth' in Davis *et al.* (1997) pp. 89 and 91.
51 On average five to six children are killed by strangers and four by their siblings per year in Britain. See 'At home and so at risk', *The Times*, 16 March 1998.
52 See 'Childhood sibling abuse common, but most adults don't remember it that way, study finds', press release issued by the American Psychological Association, Washington, DC, August 8, 1997.
53 See Sibling Abuse Survivors' Information and Advocacy Network, www.sasian.org (2000).
54 See review on www.qwi.net/-tbkkpt/justine.htm

55 Bellah *et al.* (1996) p. 127.
56 Ibid.
57 Lasch (1979) p. 62.
58 See 'Help shape a manifesto for an emotionally literate society', *Antidote* August 2000 8, p. 2.

4 How did we get here?

1 Wootton (1959) p. 17.
2 Szasz (1963).
3 Berger (1965) pp. 26–8.
4 Halmos (1973), originally published in 1965.
5 See Moscovici (1961) and Luckmann (1967).
6 See Berger (1965), Lasch (1979), Lasch (1984), Rieff (1966), Sennett (1976).
7 See Paul Heelas 'Introduction: Detraditionalization and its rivals', in Heelas *et al.* (1996) p. 2.
8 Rieff (1966) p. 22.
9 North (1972) p. 26.
10 Giddens (1991).
11 See Giddens (1995), especially Chapter 5.
12 Gellner (1993) pp. 62–3.
13 Gellner (1993) p. 33.
14 See Furedi (1992) p. 91–3.
15 'The values of the psychotherapeutic ideology appear to be gaining ground', commented North in 1972. At the time, that was as far as he was prepared to go, since the influence of this ideology was far from dominant over social life. North (1972) p. 57.
16 Rieff (1966) pp. 18–19.
17 Rieff (1966) p. 15.
18 Walter (1999) p. 196.
19 Hunter (2000) p. 82.
20 Wootton (1959) pp. 338–9.
21 North (1972) p. 52.
22 Berger (1965) p. 39.
23 Nolan (1998) p. 18.
24 See Max Weber, 'Science as a vocation', in Gerth and Wright Mills (1977) p. 139.
25 Lupton (1998) p. 170. James Nolan, in his exploration of the rise of the therapeutic state, also takes the view that the process of rationalisation not only undermined traditional moralities but also prepared the 'cultural soil for a more widespread concern with emotions'.
26 Nolan (1998) p. 301.
27 See 'Therapy is new religion says Carey', *The Daily Telegraph* 1 August 2000. Also see website of the American Association of Pastoral Counsellors, www.aapc.org
28 See Bell (1964), Fukuyama (1992), Furedi (1992).
29 Halmos (1973) pp. 8, 24.
30 Lasch (1979) p. 43.
31 Cloud (1998) p. xiv.
32 Cloud (1998) p. xiii.
33 Cloud (1998) p. 13.
34 Heelas (1991).
35 Russell (1991) p. 347.
36 See Joanna Moncrieff (1997) 'Psychiatric imperialism: the medicalisation of modern living', *Soundings* 6, reprinted on www.critpsynet.freeuk.com/sound.htm
37 Dineen (1999) p. 238.
38 See Cushman (1995) and Herman (1995).

39 See Lippmann (1934) for a classic elitist orientation towards public opinion.
40 According to one study such policies included 'assisting the individual to manage stress and enhance his or her self-esteem, acquire new identities and goals in order to inject some new purpose into their lives'. See Hayes and Nutman (1981) p. 114.
41 See Chapter 9.
42 Conrad (1992) p. 216.
43 See Furedi (1999) for a discussion of this trend.
44 Cloud (1998) p. xii.
45 Lupton (1998) p. 171.
46 Moskowitz (2001) p. 179.
47 Parsons (1965) p. 115.
48 Parsons (1965) p. 317.
49 See Chapter 8.
50 Parsons (1978) pp. 77–8.
51 See Peter Miller, 'Psychotherapy of work and unemployment', in Miller and Rose (1986) p. 152.
52 Woolfolk (2001) p. 27.
53 Parsons (1965) pp. 323–4.
54 Parsons (1978) p. 76.
55 Showalter (1997) p. 19.
56 See Soderberg, S, Lundman, B, and Norberg A. (1999) 'Struggling for dignity: the meaning of women's experiences of living with fibromyalgia', *Qualitative Health Research* 9 (5): 584; and Zebrack B. (2000) 'Cancer survivor identity and quality of life', *Cancer Practice* 8 (5): 241.
57 See Fox (1977) p. 15.
58 Wolfe (1998) p. 54.
59 Lasch (1977) p. 389.
60 Cited in Dineen (1999) p. 233.
61 For example, see the discussion in Chriss (1999) pp. 4–5.
62 As James Chriss remarked, 'this perception of a lack of guidance and insight among the average citizen sets the stage for the encroachment of "experts" into virtually all walks of life'. Chriss (1999) p. 5.
63 Berger (1965) p. 27.
64 Summerfield (2001).
65 Dineen (1993) p. 244.
66 Chriss (1999) p. 6.
67 Dineen (1999) p. 250.
68 Lasch (1979) p. 383.
69 Hochschild (1983) p. 192.
70 Smail (2001).
71 See Wolf (2001) p. 185.
72 See Clarke (2000) p. 74.
73 How this process informs the parent and child relationship is discussed in Furedi (2001).
74 Rice (1996) pp. 78–9.
75 Bellah *et al.* (1996) p. 127.
76 Herman (1995) p. 262.
77 Cited in Dineen (1999) p. 7.
78 Lasch (1977) p. 389.
79 Jacoby (1975) pp. 134, 142.
80 Rice (1996) p. 36.
81 See Moskowitz (2001) p. 282.
82 Moskowitz (2001) p. 282. See also Herman (1995).
83 Ann Swidler, 'Love and marriage' in Bellah (1996) p. 98.
84 Gergen (1990) p. 360.

5 The diminished self

1 See Smail (1996) p. 36.
2 Sharp (2001) p. 3.
3 See Illouz (1997) p. 206.
4 See Giddens (1991).
5 Russell (1999) p. 347.
6 Heelas claims that such optimistic accounts of the self 'smack of a pelagian like leap of faith'. See Heelas (1991) p. 43.
7 Russell (1999) p. 348.
8 Gergen (1990) p. 360.
9 University of Bath Counselling Service: 'Help for common problems', www.bath. ac.uk/counselling/cshelp.htm 3 September 2001.
10 'Hereditary peers "need counselling on job loss"', *The Daily Telegraph* 6 April 1999.
11 'Sporting stars find times hard after the cheering stops', *Independent on Sunday* 22 October 2000.
12 Nancy Silcox 'Finding their way; campus counsellors see almost 25% increase in mentally ill students', in *The Record.com* 12 April 2002.
13 See Gutmann (2000) p. 57.
14 'Transition counselling needed following exposure to combat *situations*, Yale researcher recommends', Press release, 22 January 2002, EurekAlert, www.eurekalert.org/pub_releases/2002–02/yu-tcn012202.php
15 See 'Stand by your sickbeds', *The Guardian* 14 August 2002.
16 'SAS men seek help to stem wave of suicides', *The Sunday Times* 5 August 2001.
17 Kates (1999).
18 See, for example, a report of a study published in the *British Journal of Psychiatry* that claimed that one in three ambulance workers suffer from mental health problems. *The Daily Telegraph* 4 January 2001.
19 'Mental disorders key health problems in US military' *Reuters Health* 20 September 2002.
20 See 'Stress', 9 July 1998 on web page created by jpmock@ix.netcom.com
21 See *The Guardian* 1 November 1996.
22 'Surge in mental disorders predicted' *BBC News* 9 January 2001.
23 'One in four gays suffers mental illness over sexuality', *The Guardian* 16 November 2001.
24 'Caregiving impacts emotional health of the giver', *Women's Health Weekly* 25 March 2000.
25 'Housework "makes you depressed", say scientist', *The Daily Telegraph* 30 September 2002.
26 'Stress makes 25% of GPs want to quit the NHS', *The Guardian* 18 October 2001.
27 'Pupils "stressed out" over school', *BBC News* 18 September 2002.
28 Cited in Mark Satin, 'Confronting the social causes of psychological depression: too taboo', *Radical Middle Newsletter*, January–February 2001, www.radicalmiddle.com
29 Cited by Erica Goode, 'More in college seek help for psychological problems', *The New York Times* 3 February 2003.
30 See www.surgeongeneral.gov/library/mentalhealth 1999.
31 See Secretary of State for Health (1998) *Our Healthier Nation* (Department of Health: London).
32 Sarah Stewart-Brown (1998) 'Emotional wellbeing and its relation to health', *British Medical Journal* 317, p. 7173.
33 Micheal G. Conner, 'About domestic violence against men', 21 September 2002, www.crisiscounseling.com/AbuseViolence/Domestic ViolenceMen.htm
34 Richard Mayou and Andrew Farmer (2002) 'Trauma', *British Medical Journal* 325, pp. 426, 429.

35 See Beck, R. and Franke, D. (1996) 'The rehabilitation of victims of natural disasters', *Journal of Rehabilitation* 62 (4).
36 'Flooding and human health; the dangers posed are not always obvious', *British Medical Journal* 321, 2000, p. 1167.
37 Nigel Hawkes, 'Floods sap health and confidence', *The Times* 15 October 2001.
38 See Furedi (2001).
39 See Frances Rickford, 'Early warning system', *The Guardian* 21 July 1999.
40 'Children suffer stress over their "love lives"', *The Guardian* 28 October 2000.
41 See Hough and Mayhew (1983).
42 *The Times* 10 March 1998.
43 See Hewitt (1998).
44 Summerfield, D. (2001) 'The invention of post-traumatic disorder and the social usefulness of a psychiatric category', *British Medical Journal* 322, 13 January.
45 Craig and Greenslade (1998) pp. 5–7.
46 See Wainwright and Calnan (2000) p. 232.
47 Lasch (1984) p. 59.
48 See Craib (1994) p. 158.
49 'Depression and violence', press release of the American Psychological Association, 3 September 1998.
50 Diocese of Oxford (1996) pp. 5–6.
51 'An accused priest speaks out', *The Boston Globe* 9 January 2002.
52 Marilyn Elias, 'Is homosexuality to blame for church scandal?', *USA Today* 15 July 2002.
53 *Pastoral Care Today, Practice, Problems and Priorities in Churches Today*. An interim report from a major survey initiated by CWR/Waverley Christian Counselling in Association with the Evagelical Alliance conducted by the Centre for Ministry Studies, University of Wales, Bangor (2000) (CWR, Farnham, Surrey), pp. 10 and 12.
54 See 'Wounded heroes', ACF News source, 28 September 2002, www.acfnewsource.org/cgi-bin
55 See www.kairosinstitute.org
56 See BALM website.
57 *PA News* 26 July 1998.
58 Cited in *The Guardian* 21 June 1996.
59 See Downs (1996) p. 3.
60 Studies cited in Furedi (1997) p. 86.
61 Rice (1996) p. 103.
62 Rice (1996) p. 104.
63 Rice (1996) pp. 110–11.
64 For a discussion of the politics of memory, see Hacking (1995) Chapter 15.
65 Susan Krygsvel 'The codependent self construct; an ethnopsychological perspective', 1995, p. 12, www.sfu.ca/~wwwpsyb/issues/1995/spring/krygsvels.htm
66 See Carol Tavris, 'Mind games: psychological warfare between therapists and scientists', *Chronicle of Higher Education* 28 February 2003.
67 See Rind and Tromovitch (1997) p. 253.
68 Hacking (1995) p. 60.
69 See 'Introduction' in Viano (1990) p. xviii.
70 Peele (1995) p. 29.
71 See 'Lottery addict children', *Daily Mail* 21 February 1998.
72 Cited in 'Hooked on the exercise high', *The Guardian* 24 October 2000.
73 Downs (1996) p. 5.
74 Conrad and Schneider (1980) p. vii.
75 Kasl (1990) p. 378.
76 See 'Action on addiction' press pack, October 1997.
77 Davis Kasl (1990) p. 175.

78 'Introduction', Viano (1990) p. xviii.
79 See Helen Wilkinson, 'Addicts anonymous', *The Observer* 12 December 1998, and Oliver James, 'Addicted to order', *The Sunday Times Magazine* 18 January 1998.
80 Nolan (1998) p. 8.
81 See Giddens (1995) especially Chapter 5.
82 Rice (1996) p. 105.
83 Lowney (1999) p. 99.
84 Wilson Schaef (1990) p. 38.

6 The self at risk

1   Herman (1994) p. 33.
2   Ibid.
3   Linenthal (2001) p. 92.
4   Bracken (2002) p. 81.
5   Vanessa Pupavac (2002) 'Traumatising children: war and trauma risk management', Paper given at The Society for The Study of Social Problems, 52nd Annual Meeting, Chicago, p. 10.
6   Summerfield (1996) p. 25.
7   'Center for the Study of Traumatic Stress, Executive Summary', www.usuhs.mil/psy/traumaticstress/center_body.htm
8   Richard Gist and S. Joseph Woodall, 'There are no simple solutions to complex problems: the rise and fall of critical incident stress debriefing as a response to occupational stress in the fire service', in Gist and Lubin (1999) p. 213.
9   'IFRC: community-based psychological suppprt', *Reuters Foundation Alert* 20 July 2001.
10 See Wessely, S.J., Bisson and Rose, S. 'A systematic review of brief psycho-logocal interventions ('debriefing') for the treatment of immediate trauma-related symptoms and the prevention of post-traumatic stress disorder', in Oakely-Browne *et al.* (2000).
11 See Vanessa Pupavac, 'Therapy against politics', paper presented at the Commonwealth Institute, London, 1 February 2001.
12 Lasch (1984) p. 57.
13 Giddens (1991) p. 193.
14 Ulrich Beck, 'The ambivalent social structure', in Beck and Beck-Gernsheim (2002) p. 48
15 R. Holton, 'Problems of crisis and normalcy in the contemporary world', in Alexander and Sztompka (1990) p. 39.
16 'Hurricane season: USF professors can share research on risks, trauma, evacuation', University of South Florida press release: 2 May 2002.
17 Kai Erikson, 'Toxic reckoning: business faces a new kind of fear', *Harvard Business Review* January–February 1990, p. 123.
18 See Peter Greste, 'Trauma hits quake victims', *BBC News* 14 February 2001.
19 'Handling of crisis left broken men scarred for life', *Western Mail* 2 October 2002.
20 See Furedi (2002).
21 Beck (1992) p. 49
22 See Furedi (1992) pp. 204–9.
23 'Introduction' to Alexander and Sztompka (1990) p. 24.
24 See Furedi (2002) Chapter 2 for a discussion of this issue.
25 Zizek (2000) p. 38.
26 Thoits (1989) p. 322
27 Dave Robinson (2002) 'Cancer clusters: findings vs feelings', American Council on Science and Health: New York, p. 12.
28 Agency for Substances and Disease Registry (1995) 'Report of the Expert Panel

Workshop on the Psychological Responses to Hazardous Substances – Executive Summary, US Department of Health and Human Services: Atlanta, Georgia, p. 2.

29 Vyner (1987).
30 Edelstein (1988) p. 52.
31 Bartolomew and Wessely (2002).
32 Burgess (2003) forthcoming.
33 Paul Slovic, 'Public perception of risk', *Journal of Environmental Health* 59 (9), 1997, p. 24.
34 Brauner (1996) pp. 28, 30.
35 Ivan Beale 'Human fear of new technology. Can the judiciary grasp the biopsychosocial model?' Transcript of address to the 6th New Zealand Health Psychology Conference, Okororire, New Zealand, February 1999.
36 Report of the IEMPG
37 Bulcroft *et al.* (2000) p. 63.
38 See the NSPCC's 'Protecting children from abuse: a guide for everyone involved in children's sport', London.
39 See 'Child protection guidelines and procedures, Wirral Area Child Protection Committee', 1997.
40 IDS (1999) p. 5.
41 Okami (1992) p. 116.
42 Okami (1992) p. 117.
43 See the claim made by a survey of 331 professionals in *Personnel Today* August 1999.
44 These reports cited in Frank Furedi, 'Bullying: the British contribution to the construction of a social problem', in Best (2001).
45 Thompson, R. (1999) 'Workplace violence experts see lessons from littleton', HR News online (June 14) pp. 1–4.
46 Cited in ibid.
47 O'Neill (1996).
48 Ibid.
49 Julia Kaminski, 'Low blows in the name of high performance: bullying triggers stress', *The Independent on Sunday* 29 May 1994.
50 See cases cited in O'Neill (1996).
51 Cited in ibid.
52 Wainwright and Calnan (2002) p. 161.
53 Ibid.
54 ICAS (1998) 'University of Kent at Canterbury, levels of stress among campus staff, survey report and recommendations', ICAS: London.
55 Wainwright and Calnan (2002) p. 161.
56 Farrell (1998) p. 13.

7 Fragile identity: hooked on self-esteem

1 Winkle (2001) p. 6.
2 Ibid.
3 See Ruth Shalit, 'Quality wings', *The New Republic* 20 July 1998.
4 Luckmann (1967) p. 110.
5 Luckmann (1967).
6 Hewitt (1998) p. 138.
7 Ibid. p. 138.
8 For a review of the philosophical discussion of alienation, see Meszaros (1972).
9 Swidler (2001) p. 143.
10 Newman and Berkowitz (1971).
11 See story filed in *Ananova* 14 February 2003.
12 Swidler (2001) p. 144.

13 See Madeleine Bunting (2001) 'From socialism to Starbucks: the decline of politics and the consumption of our inner self', *Renewal* 9 (2 & 3): 5.
14 Swidler (2001) p. 17.
15 Rice (1996) p. 30.
16 'Orlando group hoping to pique concern for slavery reparations', *The Orlando Sentinel* 21 July 2002.
17 'Racism poses Indians' biggest challenge, speaker says', *United Methodist News Service* 2 August 2000.
18 For a critical view of this approach, see Dinesh D'Souza 'Education's self-esteem hoax', *The Christian Science Monitor* 24 October 2002.
19 For a discussion of 'damage' theory, see Moskowitz (2001) pp. 180–93.
20 See *The White House Bulletin* 27 February 2002.
21 See comments of Jane Lovey to the Annual Conference of the Professional Association of Teachers in Rebecca Smithers 'Young "see law change as green light for cannabis"', *The Guardian* 31 July 2002.
22 Cited in 'End of the line – getting up steam to defend the birthplace of railways', *The Daily Telegraph* 29 March 1993.
23 Janice Dolley (1995) 'Developing self-esteem through building on skills', *Adult Learning* 6(10): 294.
24 See Hewitt (1998) p. 96.
25 See Elias (1999). For a helpful overview of this discussion, see Russell (1999).
26 Lupton (1998) p. 89.
27 Steinem (1992).
28 Moskowitz (2001) p. 218.
29 See the discussion in Furedi (1992).
30 Buruma, 'The joys and perils of victimhood', *The New York Review of Books* 8 April 1999.
31 See Summerfield, D. (1996) 'The psychological legacy of war and atrocity: the question of long-term and transgenerational effects and the need for a broad view', *The Journal of Nervous and Mental Disease* 184(1): 375.
32 Summerfield (1996) p. 375.
33 See Williams (1993).
34 Summerville (1996) pp. 375–6.
35 Buruma 'The joys and perils of victimhood', *The New York Review of Books* 8 April 1999.
36 '"Holocaust on a plate" angers US Jews', *The Guardian* 2 March 2003.
37 Chodoff (1997) p. 155.
38 Bloomfield (1997) p. 288.
39 Ibid pp. 286, 288. The key role of counselling and therapy is noted by the author.
40 http:www.geocities.com/Athens/Delphi/7279/ 'Association of Second Generation Holocaust organizations', August 1997.
41 The *Cambridge International Dictionary of English* (2002) defines self-esteem as the 'belief and confidence in your own ability and value'. See www.dictionary.cambridge.org/define.asp?key=selfesteem*1+0
42 Gael Lindenfield 'The self-esteem building citizen', in Alexander (1997) p. 16.
43 See 'The Diana Interview', *The Guardian* 21 November 1995.
44 Cited in Moscowitz (2001) p. 7.
45 'President proclaims June 9 National Child's Day'.
46 Cited in Dineen (1999) p. 154.
47 See Michael White 'Drive against domestic violence', *The Guardian* 27 May 2002.
48 Pfizer 'New survey reveals importance of sexual health to relationship and self-esteem but finds many refuse to speak to their doctors', press release, 10 April 2001.
49 Cohen, R., Coxall, J., Craig, G. and Sadiq-Sangster, A. (1992) *Hardship Britain: Being poor in the 1990s*, London: CPAG.

50 Department of Health and National Assembly for Wales (2000) 'Safeguarding children involved in prostitution'.
51 Cited in 'The power and fantasies of a 999 hoaxer', *The Daily Telegraph* 21 February 1991.
52 'Racism homophobia. which do you prefer?, www.sfaf.org/aboutsfaf/outreach/april00/commentary_bbe.html (April 2000).
53 See 'Authors reveal "Warning Signs"; low self-esteem can lead to problems for children', *The Boston Herald* 14 July 2002.
54 'Self-esteem related to childhood obesity', in Brown University Child and Adolescent Behavior Letter 16 (3).
55 'Daughters . . . and sons', *Chicago Tribune* 26 April 2002.
56 BBC News On Line, 'Education, why girls do well', 12 August 1999.
57 'Hartford could be model for initiative', *The Hartford Courant* 20 May 2002.
58 'Abstinence finds core of support', *Akron Beacon Journal* 17 February 2002.
59 Loughborough University, 'Could gardening help people's health and well-being to grow?', press release, 13 March 2002.
60 See National Cycling Forum, 'Promoting cycling; improving health', April 1999, p. 2.
61 See Community Education website homepage, www.w-isles.gov.uk/commed/web06.htm
62 See NPT statement on www.nptrust.org.uk
63 Institute for Public Policy Research, 'Sisters are doing it for themselves – because they have to', press release, 25 October 2002.
64 Tony Hurley and Graham Dunxbury 'Engaging disaffected young people in environmental regeneration', January 2002. See www.groundwork.org.uk/policy/rep
65 See 'Our aim', SureSlim UK Research, 22 March 2001. www.sureslimspain.com
66 Adam Woolf, 'Football scheme boosts community's self esteem', *The Guardian* 1 June 2001.
67 See statement on home page of www.nationwidefoundation.org.uk
68 See J. Cunnigham, 'Self-esteem. Is confidence building the key to success', lecture given at the Royal Society for the Encouragement of Arts, 13 July 2000.
69 Terri Apter, 'Confidence tricks', *The Guardian* 27 September 2000.
70 See John Vasconcellos, 'Visions and writings', *San Francisco Chronicle* 21 January 1993.
71 See N. Smelser 'Self-esteem and social problems', in Mecca, A., Smelser, N. and Vasconcellos, J. (1989) pp. 7–8.
72 Ibid., p. 9.
73 Smelser adds that 'this nonrelationship holds between self-esteem and teenage pregnancy, self-esteem and child abuse, self-esteem and most cases of alcohol and drug abuse'. Ibid. p. 15.
74 Ibid. p. 18.
75 Ibid, p. 23.
76 Dennison, C. and Coleman, J. (2000) 'Young people and gender: a review of research', a report submitted to the Women's Unit, Cabinet Office and the Family Policy Unit, Home Office, London: Women's Unit, p. 74.
77 Ibid., p. 78.
78 Alexander (1997) p. 5.
79 'Self-esteem of college students increases dramatically over 25-year period but benefits to society unclear, says expert', *Ascribe Newswire* 15 October 2001.
80 See 'Author offers new take on self-esteem', *The Wichita Eagle* 19 April 2001.
81 Baumeister, R.F. (2001) 'Violent pride', *Scientific American* 284(4) 102.
82 Cited in F. Furedi 'Can self-esteem be bad for your child' *The Times* 7 January 2002.
83 See Jason Burke 'Confident kids likely to try drugs', *The Observer* 11 February 2001.
84 Cited in 'Low self-esteem not as damaging as claimed', *PA News* 28 November 2001.
85 Williams and Irving (1999) p. 367.

86 Ibid.
87 See Carol Tavris, 'Mind games: psychological warfare between therapists and scientists', *The Chronicle of Higher Education* 28 February 2003.
88 See Alex Yellowlees, 'Self-esteem and mental health', in Alexander (1997) p. 14.
89 See 'Why your emotional intelligence may be more important than your IQ', www.media-associates.co.nz/fie.html 2001 and 'Emotional intelligence (EQ) more important than IQ for work success', press release of the BarOn Emotional Quotient Inventory, http://gwmi.imi/eqhtml/articles-eq-iq-work-success.shtml 2001.
90 S. Orbach 'People in distress' in Franklin (1997) p. 96.
91 Ibid. p. 45. For my understanding of the psychological theory that underpins the concept of emotional intelligence, I am indebted to conversations I have had with Dr Jenny Cuningham.
92 Plato (1995) p. 388.
93 A. Samuels 'Therapists with attitude', www.ed.uius.edu, 21 March 1997.
94 See A. McCluskey 'Emotional intelligence', 7 July 1997, www.e-news.connected.org

8 Conferring recognition: the quest for identity and the state

1 Fevre (2000).
2 Hunter (2000) pp. xiii, 76.
3 Beck (2001) p. 38.
4 Bracken (2002) p. 2.
5 Bracken (2002) pp. 14, 207.
6 Purdy (1999) p. 64.
7 Fraser (2000) p. 108.
8 Moskowitz (2001) p. 218 and Lowney (1999) p. 23.
9 See Taylor, 'The Politics of Recognition' in Gutmann (1992).
10 Ibid. p. 30.
11 See Honneth (1995) p. 122.
12 See 'Zombie Categories: Interview with Ulrich Beck', in Beck and Beck-Gernsheim (2002) p. 208.
13 Fukuyama (1995) pp. 6–7.
14 See Honneth (1995).
15 Honneth (1995) p. 135.
16 Hewitt (1998) p. 29.
17 Habermas (1993) p. 129.
18 Fukuyama (1992) p. 303.
19 Fraser (1998) p. 24.
20 Lasch (1979) p. 116.
21 Sennett (2003).
22 See, for example, Habermas (1981).
23 Brown (1995) p. 17.
24 See Habermas (1987) pp. 355–64.
25 See Nolan (1998), also see Moscowitz (2001).
26 Arnason, A. (2000) 'Biography, bereavement story', *Mortality* 5 (2): 194.
27 Smail (2001).
28 Fairclough (2000) pp. 54–5.
29 William O'Connor and Jane Lewis 'Experiences of social exclusion in Scotland', *Scottish Executive, Central Research Unit*, Research Programme Research Findings No. 73 (1999).
30 Library and Information Commission, *Libraries: The Essence of Inclusion*, 2000.
31 Ibid.
32 Brown (1995) p. 70.
33 See 'Realising the potential for cultural services', 17 December 2001, Wigan Council.

34 See 'Social Inclusion' web page of Sport Scotland.
35 *Building on PAT 10 – Progress Report on Social Inclusion*, February 2001, p. 5.
36 Ibid. p. 22.
37 Department of Culture, Media and Sports, *Centres for Social Change: Museums, Galleries and Archives for All*.
38 See R. Levitas, 'Government more concerned with conformity than poverty', *The Guardian* 23 March 2001.
39 See Jones (1984) p. 11.
40 Tony Blair 'Speech at Stockwell Park School, Lambeth, December 1997'.
41 It is worth noting that a recently published government commissioned report acknowledges that there is no agreed definition of the term self-esteem nor is there any British research that can be used to justify self-esteem raising policies. See Dennison and Coleman (2000).
42 John Vasconcellos, 'The time is ripe: are we?', *San Francisco Chronicle* 21 January 1995.
43 Frank E. Scott, 'Reconsidering a therapeutic role for the state: anti-modernist governance and the reunification of the self', http://online.sfsu.edu/~fscott.scottf2000apsa.htm (2000).
44 Giddens (1998) p. 117.
45 Although different in form, it is arguable that the therapeutic state in Britain is as developed as in the United States. For a discussion of the therapeutic state in the US, see Nolan (1998).
46 See 'Prime Ministers speech to the Global Ethics Foundation, Tubingen University, Germany, 2000, see at http://www.number-10.gov.uk/default.asp?PageId=1881
47 Fraser (1998) footnote 32.
48 Sports Scotland (2000) *Social Inclusion*.
49 Northern Ireland Executive (2000) *Investing For Health*, Belfast, p. 55.
50 See Cabinet Office press release, 20 June 2000, 'Pressure to be thin affecting young women's self-esteem: body image summit', 21 June 2000.
51 See National Strategy for Neighbourhood Renewal: Policy Action Team 3 (1999) *Enterprise and Social Exclusion*, (HM Treasury: London) and Northern Ireland Executive (2000) *Investing for Health*, Belfast, p. 55.
52 Fukuyama (1992) p. 302.
53 The role of therapeutic politics in relation to the attempt to tackle the crisis of political legitimacy is well argued by Nolan (1998). For the parallel development of this trend, in Britain, see Furedi (2001) Chapter 7.
54 See Berger, Berger and Kellner (1973) pp. 81–3.
55 Habermas (1987) pp. 364 and 369.
56 Sennett (2003) p. 197.
57 Brown (1995) p. 66.
58 See Lash and Urry (1994) p. 31.
59 See, for example, Giddens (1998).
60 Taylor, op. cit. p. 25.
61 Gergen (1990) p. 356.
62 Brown (1995).
63 Wainwright (1999) p. 26.
64 Samuels (2001) p. 3.
65 See Alexander and Pia Lara (1996) p. 136.
66 Fraser (2000) p. 112.
67 Brown (1995) p. 73.
68 Smail (2001).

9 Therapeutic claims-making and the demand for a diagnosis

1 See Swidler (2001) pp. 46 and 71.
2 Best (1999) p. 164.
3 See NEAVS 'Student Concerns' 2000, www.neavs.org/esec/studeent_concerns_index.htm and Circumcision Resource Centre 'Psychological Impact of Circumcision on Men' www.circumcision.org/impact.htm and 'Christianity in Transition' Dwapara Press, news release, 1 November 1997.
4 Best (1999) pp. 168–9.
5 'Post-traumatic stress disorder and the ambulance service', leaflet published by the Association of Professional Ambulance Personnel, Liverpool, 1999.
6 See 'Theory links slavery, stress disorder', *Boston Globe* 12 November 2002.
7 Eitan Rabin, '"What have I done!" – a hundred soldiers treated for "Intifada Syndrome"', *Jewish Voice For Peace* 5 November 2002. www.jewishvoiceforpeace.org/resources/jpn2.htm
8 Derek Summerfield, 'Effects of war: moral knowledge, revenge, reconciliartion, and medicalised concepts of "recovery".' *British Medical Journal* 325, 9 November 2002, p. 1105.
9 Downs (1996) pp. 19, 32, 50.
10 Myalgic Encephalomyeltis Association home page, 'The Role of the ME Association', p. 1.
11 Peele (1995) p. 135.
12 See Margaret Talbot, 'The shyness syndrome: bashfulness is the latest trait to become a pathology', *New York Times* 24 June 2001.
13 Weed (1995) p. 34.
14 *The Times* 10 March 1998.
15 See INFOLINK, www.ncvc.org, National Victim Center, 'Hate crime – the violence of prejudice'.
16 Cited in Kaminer (1993) p. 27.
17 Downs (1996) p. 49.
18 See *The Guardian* 9 October 1997 and *The Observer* 14 December 1997.
19 See 'Ritualistic Abuse Task Force', *Believe The Children Newsletter* Winter 1990, p. 1.
20 'Who are We', Home page of Fibromyalgia Association UK.
21 Barker, K. (2002) 'Self-help literature and the making of an illness identity: the case of fibromyalgia syndrome', *Social Problems* 49 (3): 295.
22 See the website of this organisation; www.eurodis.org
23 'Chronic Disability Payments', 23 December 1998.
24 Reid, Ewan and Lowy (1991) pp. 609 and 611.
25 Soderberg, S., Lundman, B. and Norberg, A. (1999) 'Struggling for dignity: the meaning of women's experiences of living with fibromyalgia', *Qualitative Health Research* 9 (5): 583.
26 Clarke, J.N. (2000) 'The search for legitimacy and the "expertization" of the lay person: the case of chronic fatigue syndrome', *Social Work in Health Care* 30 (3): 89.
27 Ibid. p. 74.
28 See letter page in *The Guardian* 8 February 2002.
29 Taylor, E. and Hemsley, R. 'Treating hyperkinetic disorders in childhood', *British Medical Journal* 6 April 1995.
30 Conrad (1975) p. 18.
31 *The Times* 26 December 1997.
32 Cited in *The Guardian* 30 September 1998.
33 Interviews with teachers, January 1998.
34 Ibid. p. 3.
35 Cited in Nathan and Snedekert (1990) pp. 200–1.

36 Ibid. p. 207.
37 Cited in G. Taylor, 'Challenges from the margin' in Clarke (1993) p. 132.
38 Anthony and Watkeys (1991) p. 120.
39 P. Casement 'The wish not to know' in Sinason (1994) p. 24.
40 Huber (1988) p. 117.
41 Ibid., p. 121.
42 Nolan (1998) pp. 50 and 66.
43 See Furedi (1999a).
44 *The Guardian* 16 November 1996.
45 *The Guardian* 3 December 1996.
46 See *The Mail on Sunday* 19 April 1998.
47 For an account of this case and the local reaction to it, see *The Guardian* 17 July 1998.
48 Wainwright and Calnan (2002) p. 43.
49 Cited in Olson (1992) p. 9.
50 Spear-Swerling and Sternberg (1996) p. 37.
51 Peele (1995) p. 130.
52 See the DFEE green paper, *Excellence for all Children – Meeting Special Educational Needs*, October 1997.
53 'Dyscalculia symptoms' by R. Newman, www.dyscalculia.org/dss/html, Dyslexia and Dyscalculia Support Services of Shiawassee County, 27 October 1997, p. 1.
54 See R. Shalit, 'Defining disability down', *The New Republic* 25 August 1997.
55 Kaminer (1995) p. 16.
56 This issue is discussed in Wilson (1997).
57 Westervelt (1998) pp. 8–10.
58 Ibid. p. 13.
59 Ibid. p. 9.
60 Ibid. pp. 116–23.
61 Lamb (1996) p. 184.
62 Best (1997) p. 17.
63 Friedman (1990) p. 17.
64 See Engle (1984).
65 See Friedman (1990) pp. 2–3, 10.
66 See Furedi (1999b) p. 28.
67 Field (1999) p. 152.
68 A recent report by the Law Commission takes a very different view on this matter. It described a court decision which dismissed the claim for damages for 'abnormal grief reaction' as 'harsh' and 'arbitrary'. See Law Commission (1998) p. 35.
69 See a useful exploration of this subject in Hotopf and Wessely (1997) p. 2.

Final thoughts: does it matter?

1 Rose (1990) p. 257.
2 Ibid.
3 Rose added that 'behavioural techniques are no longer viewed as coercive and heteronomous incursions upon subjectivity of the individual, but are widely deployed by doctors, clinical psychologists and psychiatric nurses, as well as social workers and many others, as a means for the re-empowering of the disempowered self'. See Rose, N. (1996) 'Psychiatry as a political science: advanced liberalism and the administration of risk', *History of the Human Sciences* 9 (2).
4 See Frank E. Scott, 'Reconsidering a therapeutic role for the state: anti-modernist governance and the reunification of the self', http://online.sfsu.edu/~fscott/scottf 2000apsa.htm 2000, p. 8.
5 See Hoggett, P. in Lewis, G., Gewirtz, S. and Clarke, J. (2000) (eds) *Rethinking Social Policy* London: Sage. p. 144.

6 See Williams, S.J. (1998) '"Capitalising" on emotions? Rethinking the inequalities in health debate', *Sociology* 32 (1): 132–3.

7 See Hoggett P. in Lewis *et al.* (2000) 'Social policy and the emotions' p. 145.

8 Pupavac (2001) p. 3.

9 Cited in *The Guardian* 10 September 2002.

10 See Joyce Jerry, 'Emotional literacy', www.getting-on.co.uk/toolkit/emotiona.html

11 Summerfield (2002) 'Effects of war: moral knowledge, revenge, reconciliation, and medicalised concepts of "recovery"', *British Medical Journal* 325, 9 November, p. 1105.

12 See P. Johnston, 'Children of eight to be targeted as future criminals', *The Daily Telegraph* 24 October 2002.

13 'On the Baseline', *Columbia Chronicle Online* 9 December 2002.

14 Nolan (1998) pp. 292–94.

15 Peele (1995) p. 221.

16 See A. Travis, 'Straw plan to tag more ex-inmates', *The Guardian* 27 January 2000.

17 For a discussion of this incident, see Sally Satel, 'Baseball is off its rocker', *The Wall Street Journal* 1 January 2000.

18 See Nolan (2001) pp. 202–3.

19 See B. Charlton, 'Corporate counselling', *LM* 18 March 1999, p. 15.

20 See 'See our shrink – or you're fired', *The Observer* 20 June 1999.

21 Rauch (1993) pp. 26–8.

22 Cited in *The Guardian* 25 February 1999.

23 Jacobs and Potter (1998) p. 82.

24 Downs (1996) pp. 24–8.

25 See Kaminer (1995) p. 85.

26 See J. Fitzpatrick, 'The Macpherson Report in the dock', *LM* April 1999, p. 9.

27 Sarat (1997) p. 164 and Kaminer (1995) p. 84.

28 Sarat (1997) p. 171

Bibliography

Books

Alexander, J.C. and Sztompka, P. (eds) (1990) *Rethinking Progress*, Boston: Unwin Hyman.

Alexander, T. (ed.) (1997) *The Self-Esteem Directory*, Dover: Smallwood Publishing.

Altheide, D.L. (2002) *Creating Fear: News and the Construction of Crisis*, New York: Aldine de Gruyter.

Archard, D. (1993) *Children's Rights and Childhood*, London: Routledge.

Arendt, H. (2000) 'The public and the private realm', in P. Baehr (ed.) *The Portable Hannah Arendt*, London: Penguin.

Baglow, R. (1994) *The Crisis of the Self in the Age of Information*, New York: Routledge.

Bauman, Z. (2000) *Liquid Modernity*, Cambridge: Polity Press.

Beck, U. (1992) *Risk Society: Towards a New Modernity*, London: Sage.

Beck, U. and Beck-Gernsheim, E. (2002) *Individualization*, London: Sage.

Bell, D. (1964) *The End of Ideology: On the Exhaustion of Political Ideas in the Fifties*, New York: The Free Press.

Bellah, R., Madsen, R., Sullivan, W. *et al.* (1996) *Habits of the Heart: Individualism and Commitment in American Life*, Berkeley: University of California Press.

Berger, P. and Luckmann, T. (1967) *The Social Construction of Reality*, Harmondsworth: Penguin.

Berger, P., Berger, G. and Kellner, H. (1973) *The Homeless Mind*, Harmonsworth: Pelican.

Best, J. (1999) *Random Violence: How We Talk About New Crimes and New Victims*, Berkeley: University of California Press.

Best, J. (ed.) (2001) *How Claims Spread: Cross National Diffusion of Social Problems*, New York: Aldine de Gruyter.

Bracken, P. (2002) *Trauma: Culture, Meaning and Philosophy*, London: Whurr Publishers.

Braiker, H. (2001) *Lethal Lovers and Poisonous People: How to Protect Your Relationships That Make You Sick*, iUniverse, Inc.

Brauner, C. (1996) *Electrosmog – A Phantom Risk*, Zurich: Swiss Re.

Britton, F. (2000) *Active Citizenship; A Teaching Toolkit*, London: Hodder & Stoughton.

Brown, W. (1995) *States of Injury: Power and Freedom in Late Modernity*, Princeton: Princeton University Press.

Burchell, B.J., Dat, D., Hudson, M., Lapido, D, Mankelow, R, Nolan, J., Reed, H. (1999) *Job Insecurity and Work Intensification*, York: Joseph Rowntree Foundation.

Burgess, A. (2003) *Panics Over Cell Phones*, New York: Cambridge University Press.

Cancian, F. (1987) *Love in America: Gender and Self-Development*, Cambridge: Cambridge University Press.

Chriss, J.J. (1999) (ed.) *Counselling and the Therapeutic State*, New York: Aldine de Gruyter.

Clarke, J. (ed.) *A Crisis in Care/Challenges to Social Work*, London: Sage.

Clarke, J. ed. (1993) *A Crisis in Care? Challenges to Social Work?* London: Sage.

Cloud, D.L. (1998) *Control and Consolation in American Culture and Politics: Rhetoric of Therapy*, Thousand Oaks, CA: Sage.

Conrad, P. and Schneider, J.W. (1980) *Deviance and Medicalization: From Badness To Sickness*, St. Louis: C.V. Mosby.

Craib, I. (1994) *The Importance of Disappointment*, London: Routledge.

Craig, P. and Greenslade, M. (1998) *First Findings from the Disability Follow-Up to the Family Resources Survey*, London: DSS Social Research Branch.

Cushman, P. (1995) *Constructing the Self, Constructing America: A Cultural History of Psychotherapy*, Reading: Addison-Wesley.

Dennison, C. and Coleman, J. (2000) 'Young people and gender: a review of research', a report submitted to the Women's Unit, Cabinet Office and the Family Policy Unit, Home Office, London: Women's Unit.

Davis, R. Lurgio, A., and Skogan, W. (eds) (1997) *Victims of Crime*, London: Sage.

Dineen, T. (1999) *Manufacturing Victims: What the Psychology Industry is Doing to People*, Toronto: Robert Davies Publishers.

Downs, D.A. (1996) *More Than Victims: Battered Women, the Syndrome Society, and the Law*, Chicago: The University of Chicago Press.

Edelstein, M.R. (1998) *Contaminated Communities: The Social and Psychological Impact of Residential Toxic Exposure*, Boulder, CO: Westview Press.

Eisner, D.A. (2000) *The Death of Psychotherapy: From Freud to Alien Abduction*, Westport: Prager.

Elias, N. (1999) *The Society of Individuals*, Oxford: Blackwell.

Emler, N. (2001) *Self-Esteem: The Costs and Causes of Low Self-Worth*, York: YPS.

Eysenck, H.J. (1960) *The Psychology of Politics*, New York: Praeger.

Fairclough, N. (2000) *New Labour, New Language?* London: Routledge.

Farrell, K. (1998) *Post Traumatic Culture: Injury and Interpretation in the Nineties*, Baltimore: Johns Hopkins University Press.

Fevre, R.W. (2000) *The Demoralization of Western Culture: Social Theory and the Dilemmas of Modern Living*, London: Continuum.

Forward, S. (1990) *Toxic Parents: Overcoming the Legacy of Parental Abuse*, London: Bantam Press.

Franklin, B. (1995) *A Handbook of Children's Rights*, London: Routledge.

Franklin, J (ed.) (1997) *The Politics of Risk Society*, Cambridge: Polity Press.

Freud, S. (1985) *Leonardo Da Vinci and a Memory of his Childhood*, London: Pelican.

Friedman, L.M. (1990) *The Republic of Choice: Law, Authority, and Culture*, Cambridge, MA: Harvard University Press.

Fraser, N. (1998) *Social Justice in the Age of Identity Politics: Redistribution, Recognition and Participation, The Tanner Lectures on Human Values*, Salt Lake City: University of Utah Press.

Frost, P. (2003) *Toxic Emotions at Work*, Cambridge, MA: Harvard Business School Press.

Frye, M. (1992) *Willful Virgin: Essays in Feminism, 1976–1992*, Freedom, CA: Crossing Press.

Fukuyama, F. (1992) *The End of History and the Last Man*, London: Hamish Hamilton.
Fukuyama, F. (1995) *Trust: The Social Virtues and The Creation of Prosperity*, London: Hamish Hamilton.
Furedi, F. (1992) *Mythical Past, Elusive Future: History and Society in an Anxious Age*, London: Pluto Press.
Furedi, F. (1997) *Culture of Fear: Risk Taking and the Morality of Low Expectation*, London: Cassell.
Furedi, F. (1999) *Courting Mistrust: The Hidden Growth of a Culture of Litigation in Britain*, London: Centre for Policy Studies.
Furedi, F. (2001) *Paranoid Parenting*, London: Allen Lane.
Furedi, F. (2002) *Culture of Fear: Risk Taking and the Morality of Low Expectation*, 2nd edn, London: Continuum Press.
Gates Jr., H.L., Griffin, A.P., Lively, D.E. *et al.* (1994) *Speaking of Race: Speaking of Sex; Hate Speech, Civil Rights, and Civil Liberties*, New York: New York University Press.
Gellner, E. (1993) *The Psychoanalytic Movement; The Cunning of Unreason*, London: Fontana Press.
Gerth, H.H. and Wright Mills, C. (eds.) (1977) *From Max Weber: Essays in Sociology*, London: Routledge and Kegan Paul.
Giddens, A. (1991) *Modernity and Self-Identity: Self and Society in the late Modern Age*, Cambridge: Polity Press.
Giddens, A. (1995) *The Transformation of Intimacy: Sexuality, Love and Eroticism in Modern Societies*, Oxford: Polity Press.
Giddens, A. (1998) *Third Way: The Renewal of Social Democracy*, Oxford: Polity Press.
Gist, R. and Lubin, B. (1999) *Response to Disaster: Psychosocial, Community and Ecological Approaches*, Philadelphia: Brunner/Mazel.
Goleman, D. (1996) *Emotional Intelligence; Why It Can matter More Than IQ*, London: Bloomsbury.
Gutmann, A. (1992) *Multiculturalism and 'The Politics of Recognition'*, Princeton: Princeton University Press.
Gutmann, S. (2000) *The Kinder, Gentler Military: How Political Correctness Affects Our Ability To Win Wars*, San Franscisco: Encounter.
Habermas, J. (1987) *The Theory of Communicative Action, Vol. 2. Lifeworld and System: A Critique of Functionalist Reason*, Cambridge: Polity Press.
Hacking, I. (1995) *Rewriting the Soul: Multiple Personality and the Sciences of Memory*, Princeton: Princeton University Press.
Hanmer, J. and Maynard, M. (eds) (1987) *Women, Violence and Social Control*, London: Macmillan Press.
Hayes, J. and Nutman, P. (1981) *Understanding the Unemployed: The Psychological Effects of Unemployment*, London: Tavistock Publications.
Halmos, P. (1973) *The Faith of the Counsellors*, London: Constable.
Hedges, C. (2002) *War Is A Force That Gives Us Meaning*, Oxford: Public Affairs Limited.
Heelas, P. (1991) 'Reforming the self: enterprise and the characters of Thatcherism', in Keat, R. and Abercrombie, N. (eds), *Enterprise Culture*, London: Routledge.
Heelas, P., Lash, S. and Morris, P. (eds.) (1996) *Detraditionalization: Critical Reflections on Authority and Identity*, Oxford: Blackwell.
Herman, E. (1995) *The Romance of American Psychology:Political Culture in the Age of Experts*, Berkeley: University of California Press.
Herman, J.L. (1994) *Trauma and Recovery: From Domestic Abuse To Political Terror*, London: Pandora.

Hewitt, J. (1998) *The Myth of Self-Esteem; Finding Happiness and Solving Problems in America*, New York: St. Martin's Press.

Himmelfarb, G. (1995) *The De-moralization of Society: From Victorian Values to Modern Values*, London: IEA.

Hobson, J.A. (1988) *Imperialism: A Study*, London: Unwin Hyman.

Hobson, J.A. (1901) *The Psychology of Jingoism*, London: Grant Richards.

Hochschild, A.R. (1983) *The Managed Heart: The Commercialization of Human Feeling*, Berkeley: University of California Press.

Hoggett, P. (2000) *Emotional Life and the Politics of Welfare*, Basingstoke: Macmillan Press.

Honneth, A. (1995) *The Fragmented World of The Social: Essays in Social and Political Philosophy*, Albany: State University of New York Press.

Horrocks, R. (1994) *Masculinity in Crisis*, London: Macmillan.

Hough, M. and Mayhew, P. (1983) *The British Crime Survey: The First Report*, London: HMSO.

Horwitz, A.V. (1982) *The Social Control of Mental Illness*, Orlando: Academic Press.

Horwitz, A.V. (2002) *Creating Mental Illness*, Chicago: The University of Chicago Press.

Huber, P.W. (1988) *Liability. The Legal Revolution and Its Consequences*, New York: Basic Books.

Hughes, R. (1993) *Culture of Complaint*, London: The Harvill Press.

Hunter, J.D. (2000) *The Death of Character: Moral Education in an Age Without Good or Evil*, New York: Basic Books.

Hymowitz, K. (2000) *Ready or Not: What Happens When We Treat Children as Small Adults*, San Francisco: Encounter Books.

IDS (1999) *IDS Studies: Personnel Policy and Practice, Harassment Policies*, London: IDS.

Illouz, E. (1997) *Consuming the Romantic Utopia: Love and the Cultural Contradictions of Capitalism*, Berkeley: University of California Press.

Irvine, L. (1999) *Codependent Forevermore: The Invention of Self in a Twelve Step Group*, London: The University of Chicago Press.

Isaacs, F. (1999) *Toxic Friends/True Friends*, Chicago: William Morrow.

Jacobs, J.B. and Potter, K. (1998) *Hate Crimes: Criminal Law and Identity Politics*, New York: Oxford University Press.

Jacoby, R. (1975) *Social Amnesia: A Critique of Conformist Psychology from Adler to Laing*, Hassocks: The Harvester Press.

Janov, A. (1993) *The New Primal Scream: Primal Therapy Twenty Years On*, London: Abacus.

Jenkins, P. (1992) *Intimate Enemies, Moral Panics in Contemporary Great Britain*, New York: Aldine de Gruyter.

Jenkins, P. (1996) *Pedophiles and Priests*, New York: Oxford University Press.

Jenkins, R. (1996) *Social Identity*, London: Routledge.

Jeffreys, S. (1990) *Anticlimax: A Feminist Perspective on the Sexual Revolution*, London: Women's Press.

Jones, A. (1984) *Counselling Adolescents: School and After*, London: Kogan Page.

Jowell, R., Curtice, J., Park, A. *et al.* (eds) (1995) *British Social Attitudes, The 12th Report*, Dartmouth: SCPR.

Kaminer, W. (1993) *I'm Dysfunctional, You're Dysfunctional: The Recovery Movement and Other Self-Help Fashions*, Reading, MA: Addison-Wesley.

Kaminer, W. (1995) *It's All The Rage, Crime and Culture*, Reading, MA: Addison-Wesley.

Kaminer, W. (1996) *True Love Waits: Essays And Criticism*, Reading, MA: Addison-Wesley.

Kasl, D.C. (1990) *Women, Sex and Addiction – A Search For Love And Power*, Minneapolis: Mandarin.

Kates, A.R. (1999) *CopShock, Surviving Posttraumatic Stress Disorder (PTSD)*, Cortaro, AZ: Holbrook Street Press.

Karp, D. (1996) *Speaking of Sadness: Depression, Disconnecting and the Meaning of Illness*, New York: Oxford University Press.

Kinchin, D. (2001) *Post-Traumatic Stress Disorder: The Invisible Injury*, Didcot, Oxfordshire: Success Unlimited.

Kraemer, S. and Roberts, J. (eds.) (1996) *The Politics of Attachment: Towards a Secure Society*, London: Free Association Books.

LaFontaine, J. (1994) *Extent and Nature of Organized Ritual Abuse*, London: Department of Health.

Lamb, S. (1996) *The Trouble with Blame: Victims, Perpetrators, and Responsibility*, Cambridge, MA: Harvard University Press.

Langford, W. (1999) *Revolution of the Heart*, London: Routledge.

Lasch, C. (1979) *The Culture of Narcissism: American Life in an Age of Diminishing Expectations*, New York: Warner Books.

Lasch, C. (1984) *The Minimal Self: Psychic Survival in Troubled Times*, New York: W.W. Norton.

Lasch-Quinn, E. (2001) *Race Experts: How Racial Etiquette, Sensitivity Training, and New Age Therapy Hijacked the Civil Rights Revolution*, New York: W.W. Norton.

Lash, S. and Urry, J. (1994) *Economies of Signs and Space*, London: Sage.

Laski, H.J. (1932) *Nationalism and the Future of Civilization*, London: Watts.

Law Commission (1998) *Liability For Psychiatric Illness*, London: The Stationery Office.

Le Bon, G. (1990) (reprint) *The Crowd: The Study of the Popular Mind*, London: Norman and Berg.

Lewis, G., Gewirtz, S. and Clarke, J. (eds) (2000) *Rethinking Social Policy*, London: Sage.

Linenthal, E.T. (2001) *The Unfinished Bombing: Oklahoma City in American Memory*, New York: Oxford University Press.

Lippman, W. (1922) *Public Opinion*, New York: Macmillan.

Lippman, W. (1934) *Public Opinion*, 4th edn, New York: Macmillan.

Lipset, M. (1963) *Political Man: The Social Basis of Politics*, New York: Anchor Books.

Lowney, K.S. (1999) *Baring Our Souls: TV Talk Shows and the Religion of Recovery*, New York: Aldine de Gruyter.

Luckmann, T. (1967) *The Invisible Religion: The Problem of Religion in Modern Society*, New York: Macmillan.

Lupton, D. (1998) *The Emotional Self: A Sociocultural Exploration*, London: Sage.

MacInnes, J. (1998) *The End of Masculinity: The Confusion of Sexual Genesis and Sexual Difference in Modern Society*, Buckingham: Open University Press.

Mackenzie, G. and Labiner, J. (2002) *Opportunity Lost: The Decline of Trust and Confidence in Government After September 11*, Washington, DC: Center For Public Service.

MacKinnon, C. (1989) *Toward a Feminist Theory of the State*, Cambridge, MA: Harvard University Press.

Maguire, M. and Pointing, J. (1988) *Victims of Crime: A New Deal?* Milton Keynes: Open University Press.

Maguire, M., Morgan, R. and Reiner, R. (eds) (1997) *The Oxford Handbook of Criminology*, Oxford: Clarendon Press.

Martin, L.H., Gutman, H. and Hutton, P.H. (eds) (1988) *Technologies of the Self: A Seminar with Michel Foucault* London: Tavistock Publications.

McLean, I. and Johnes, M. (2000) *Aberfan: Government and Disasters*, Cardiff: Welsh Academic Press.

Mecca, A., Smelser, N. and Vasconellos, J. (eds) (1989) *The Social Importance of Esteem*, Berkeley: University of California Press.

Melucci, A. (1989) *Nomads of the Present: Social Movements and Individual Needs in Contemporary Society*, London: Hutchinson Radius.

Mestrovic, S.G. (1997) *Postemotional Society*, London: Sage.

Meszaros, I. (1972) *Marx's Theory of Alienation*, London: Merlin Press.

Miller, G. and Holstein, J.A. (1993) *Constructionist Controversies: Issues in Social Problems Theory*, New York: Aldine de Gruyter.

Miller, P. and Rose, N. (eds) (1986) *The Power of Psychiatry*, Cambridge: Polity Press.

Morgan, J. and Zedner, L. (1992) *Child Victims: Crime Impact and Criminal Justice*, Oxford: Clarendon Press.

Moscovici, S. (1961) *La Psychoanalyse – Son Image et Son Public*, Paris: Presses Universitaires de France.

Moskowitz, E. (2001) *In Therapy We Trust: America's Obsession with Self-Fulfillment*, Baltimore: Johns Hopkins University Press.

Muncie, J., Wetherell, M., Dallos, R. and Cochrane, A. (eds) (1993) *Understanding the Family*, London: Sage.

Nathan, D. and Snedeker, M. (1995) *Satan's Silence: Ritual Abuse and the Making of a Modern American Witch Hunt*, New York: Basic Books.

Newman, M. and Berkowitz, B. (1971) *How To Be Your Own Best Friend*, New York: Ballantine.

Nolan, J.L. (1998) *The Therapeutic State: Justifying Government at Century's End*, New York: New York University Press.

Nolan, J. (2001) *Reinventing Justice: The American Drug Court Movement*, Princeton: Princeton University Press.

North, M. (1972) *The Secular Priests*, London: George Allen & Unwin.

Oakely-Browne, R., Churchill, R., Gill, D. *et al.* (eds) (2000) *Depression, Anxiety and Neurosis Module of the Cochrane Database of Systematic Reviews*, Oxford: The Cochrane Library, Issue 3. Oxford Update Software.

Olson, W. (1992) *The Excuse Factory: How Employment Law is Paralyzing the American Workplace*, New York: Free Press.

O'Neill, J. (1995) *The Poverty of Postmodernism*, London: Routledge.

O'Neill, R. (1996) 'Stress at work: trade union action at the workplace' (unpublished report), London: TUC.

Oxford English Dictionary (1989) 2nd edn, vol. XIV, Oxford: Clarendon Press.

Parsons, T. (1965) *Social Structure and Personality*, New York: Free Press.

Parsons, T. (1978) *Action Theory and The Human Condition*, New York: Free Press.

Patai, D. and Koertege, N. (1994) *Professing Feminism: Cautionary Tales from the Strange World of Women's Studies*, New York: Basic Books.

Pearson, G. (1979) *The Deviant Imagination: Psychiatry, Social Work and Social Change*, London: Macmillan.

Peele, S. (1995) *Diseasing of America: How We Allowed Recovery Zealots and the*

Treatment Industry to Convince Us We Are Out of Control, New York: Lexington Books.

Pendergrast, M. (1995) *Victims of Memory: Incest Accusations and Shattered Lives*, Hinesburg, VT: Upper Access.

Perham, P. (1962) *The Colonial Reckoning*, London: BBC.

Plato (1955) *The Republic*, Harmondsworth: Penguin.

Polsky, A.J. (1991) *The Rise of the Therapeutic State*, Princeton: Princeton University Press.

Purdy, J. (1999) *For Common Things: Irony, Trust, And Commitment in America Today*, New York: Alfred A. Knopf.

Rauch, J. (1993) *Kind Inquisitors: The New Attacks on Free Thought*, Chicago: The University of Chicago Press.

Real, T. (1999) *I Don't Want To Talk About It: Overcoming the Secret Legacy of Male Depression*, New York: Fireside Books.

Rice, J.S. (1996) *A Disease of One's Own: Psychotherapy, Addiction, and the Emergence of Co-Dependency*, New Brunswick, NJ: Transaction.

Richards, B. (ed.) (1989) *The Crises of the Self: Further Essays on Psychoanalysis and Politics*, London: Free Association Books.

Rieff, P. (1966) *The Triumph of the Therapeutic: Uses of Faith After Freud*, London: Chatto and Windus.

Rock, P. (1998) *After Homicide: Practical and Political Response To Bereavement*, Oxford: Clarendon Press.

Rose, N. (1990) *Governing the Soul: The Shaping of the Private Self*, London: Routledge.

Rosenblum, N. (ed.) (1989) *Liberalism and the Moral Life*, Cambridge, MA: Harvard University Press.

Rustin, M. (2001) *Reason and Unreason: Psychoanalysis, Science and Politics*, Middletown, CT: Wesleyan University Press.

Sargeant, K.M. (2000) *Seeker Churches: Promoting Religion in a Nontraditional Way*, New Brunswick, NJ: Rutgers University Press.

Samuels, A. (2001) *Politics on the Couch: Citizenship and the Internal Life*, London: Profile Books.

Schumpeter, J. (1951) *Capitalism, Socialism and Democracy*, London: Allen and Unwin.

Seidler, V. (ed.) (1992) *Men, Sex and Relationships*, London: Routledge.

Sennett, R. (1976) *The Fall of Public Man*, New York: Knopf.

Sennett, R. (2003) *Respect; The Formation of Character In an Age of Inequality*, New York: W.W. Norton.

Sennett, R. and Cobb, J. (1993) *The Hidden Injuries of Class*, New York: W.W. Norton.

Sharp, P. (2001) *Nurturing Emotional Literacy: A Practical Guide for Teachers, Parents and Those in the Caring Professions*, London: David Fulton.

Showalter, E. (1997) *Hystories: Hysterical Epidemic and Modern Culture*, London: Picador.

Sinason, V. (ed.) *Treating Survivors of Satanist Abuse*, London: Routledge.

Sinason, V. (ed). (1994) *Treating Survivors of Satanist Abuse*, London: Routledge.

Smail, D. (1996) *How to Survive Without Psychotherapy*, London: Constable.

Smail, D. (2001) *The Origins of Unhappiness: A New Understanding of Personal Distress*, London: Robinson.

Smith S. (1995) *Survivor Psychology*, Boca Raton, FL: Upton Books.

Spear-Swerling, L. and Sternberg, R.J. (1996) *Off Track: When Poor Readers Become 'Learning Disabled'*, Boulder, CO: Westview Press.

Steinem, G. (1992) *Revolution From Within: A Book of Self-Esteem*, Boston: Little, Brown and Company.

Strauss, M.A., Gelles, R.J. and Steinmetz, S.K. (1980) *Behind Closed Doors, Violence in the American Family*, New York: Anchor Books.

Strauss, L. (1991) *On Tyranny*, New York: The Free Press.

Summerfield, D. (1996) *The Impact of War and Atrocity on Civilian Populations: Basic Principles for NGO Interventions and a Critique of Psychosocial Trauma Projects*, London: ODI.

Sumner, C. (1994) *The Sociology of Deviance: An Obituary*, Buckingham: Open University Press.

Swidler, A. (2001) *Talk of Love: How Culture Matters*, Chicago: The University of Chicago Press.

Szasz, T. (1963) *Law, Liberty and Psychiatry*, New York: Macmillan.

Szasz, T. (1984) *The Therapeutic State; Psychiatry in the Mirror of Current Events*, Buffalo: Prometheus Books.

Totton, N. (2000) *Psychotherapy and Politics*, London: Sage.

Treacher, A. (1989) 'Be your own person, dependence/independence, 1950–1985', in B. Richards (ed.) *The Crises of the Self: Further Essays on Psychoanalysis and Politics*, London: Free Association Books.

Turner, B.S. (1995) *Medical Power and Social Knowledge* London: Sage.

Viano, E.C. (1990) *The Victimology Handbook: Research Findings, Treatment, and Policy*, New York: Garland Publishing.

Vyner, H. (1987) *Invisible Trauma: The Psychosocial Effects of Invisible Environmental Contaminants*, Lexington, MA: Lexington Books.

Wainwright D. (1999) *Understanding Work Stress: Report of a Qualitative Study in Dover*, Canterbury: Centre for Health Services Studies, University of Kent at Canterbury.

Wainwright, D. and Calnan, M. (2002) *Work Stress: The Making of a Modern Epidemic*, Buckingham: Open University Press.

Walter, T. (1999) *On Bereavement: The Culture of Grief*, Buckingham: Open University Press.

Weed, F.J. (1995) *Certainty of Justice: Reform in the Crime Victim Movement*, New York: Aldine de Gruyter.

Weintraub, J. and Kumar, K. (eds) (1997) *Public and Private in Thought and Practice: Perspectives on a Grand Dichotomy*, Chicago: The University of Chicago Press.

Wells, C. (1995) *Negotiating Tragedy: Law and Disasters*, London: Sweet & Maxwell.

Westervelt, S.D. (1998) *Shifting The Blame: How Victimization Became a Criminal Defense*, New Brunswick, NJ: Rutgers University Press.

Williams, S.S. (1993) 'Impact of the holocaust of survivors and their children', found on http://libra.netmasterllc.com/jameschell/causes/cpshpsyc.htm

Wilson, J.Q. (1997) *Moral Judgment: Does the Abuse Excuse Threaten Our Legal System?* New York: Basic Books.

Wilks, F. (1998) *Intelligent Emotion: How to Succeed Through Transforming your Feelings*, London: Heinemann.

Wilson Schaef, A. (1987) *When Society Becomes An Addict*, San Francisco: Harper and Row.

Wilson Schaef, A. (1990) *Escape from Intimacy: The Pseudo Relationship Addictions*, New York: Harper.

Wolf, N. (2001) *Misconceptions, Truths, Lies and the Unexpected on the Journey to Motherhood*, London: Chatto and Windus.

Wolfe, A. (1998) *One Nation, After All: What Middle-Class Americans Really Think About*, New York: Viking.

Wootton, B. (1959) *Social Science and Social Pathology*, London: Allen and Unwin.

Zizek, S. (2000) *The Ticklish Subject: The Absent Centre of Political Ontology*, London: Verso.

Articles and papers

Alexander, J. and Pia Lara, M. (1996) 'Honneth's new critical theory of recognition', *New Left Review*, November–December.

Albee, G.W. (1990) 'The futility of psychotherapy', *The Journal of Mind and Behavior* 11 (3–4).

Anthony, G. and Watkeys, J. (1991) 'False allegations in child sexual abuse: the pattern of referral in an area where reporting is not mandatory', *Children and Society* 5 (2), 120.

Arnason, A. (2000) 'Biography, bereavement story', *Mortality* 5 (2).

Azhar, M. and Varma, S. (1995) 'Response of clomipramine in sexual addiction', *European Psychiatry* 10 (5).

Baker, L.(1995) 'Food addiction deserves to be taken just as seriously as alcoholism', *Addiction Letter*, July.

Baron, L., Reznikoff, M. and Glenwich, D.S. (1993) 'Narcissism, interpersonal adjustment, and coping in children of Holocaust survivors', *The Journal of Psychology* 127.

Bartholomew, R.E. and Wessely, S. (2002) 'The protean nature of mass sociogenic illness; from possessed nuns to chemical and biological terrorism fears', *British Journal of Psychiatry* 46 (2).

Bellamy, R.(1997) 'Compensation neurosis – financial reward for illness as nocebo', *Clinical Orthopaedics and Related Research* 336.

Berger, P. (1965) 'Towards a sociological understanding of psychoanalysis', *Social Research* 32 (1).

Best, J. (1997) 'Victimization and the victim industry', *Society* 34 (4).

Bloomfield, I. (1997) 'Effects of the Holocaust on the second generation', *Counselling* 8 (4).

Brown, J.D. 'The professional ex-: an alternative for exiting the deviant career', *The Sociological Quarterly* 32 (2).

Bulcroft, R., Bulcroft, K., Bradely, K. and Simpson, C. (2000) 'The management and production of risk in romantic relationships: a postmodern paradox', *Journal of Family History* 25 (1).

Chodoff, P. (1997) 'The Holocaust and its effect on survivors: an overview', *Political Psychology* 18 (1).

Clark, D. (1991) 'Guidance, counselling, therapy: responses to "marital problems" 1950–90', *The Sociological Review* 39.

Clarke, J. (2000) 'The search for legitimacy and the "expertization" of the lay person: the case of chronic fatigue syndrome', *Social Work in Health Care* 30 (3).

Conrad, P. (1975) 'The discovery of hyperkinesis: notes on the medicalization of deviant behavior', *Social Problems* 23.

Conrad, P. (1992) 'Medicalization and social control', *Annual Review of Sociology* 18.

Conrad, P. and Potter, D. (2000) 'From hyperactive children to ADHD adults: observations of the expansion of medical categories', *Social Problems* 47 (4).

Cruikshank, B. (1993) 'Revolutions within: self-government and self-esteem', *Economy and Society* 22 (3).

Dworkin, R.W. (2001) 'The medicalization of unhappiness', *The Public Interest* 144.

Engle, D.M. (1984) 'The oven bird's song: insiders, outsiders, and personal injuries in an American community', *Law and Society Review* 18.

Field, L.H. (1999) 'Post-traumatic stress disorder: a reappraisal', *Journal of the Royal Society of Medicine* 92, January.

Fox, C.R. (1977) 'The medicalization and demedicalization of American society', *Daedalus* 106 (1).

Fraser, N. (2000) 'Rethinking recognition', *New Left Review*, May–June.

Gagne , P. (1996) 'Identity, strategy, and feminist politics: clemency for battered women who kill', *Social Problems* 43 (1).

Gergen, K.J. (1990) 'Therapeutic professions and the diffusion of deficit', *The Journal of Mind and Behavior* 11 (3–4).

Habermas, J. (1981) 'New social movements', *Telos* 49.

Habermas, J. (1993) 'Struggles for recognition in constitutional states', *European Journal of Philosophy* 1 (2).

Hacking, I. (1991) 'The making and molding of child abuse', *Critical Inquiry* 17.

Hollway, W. and Jefferson, T. (1996) 'PC or not PC: sexual harassment and the question of ambivalence', *Human Relations*, 49 (3).

Hochschild, A.R. (1994) 'The commercial spirit of intimate life and the abduction of feminism: signs from women's advice books', *Theory, Culture and Society* 11.

Hotopf, M. and Wessely, S. (1997) 'Stress in the workplace: unfinished business', *Journal of Psychosomatic Research* 43 (1).

Irvine, l. (1997) 'Reconsidering the American emotional culture: co-dependency and emotion management', *The European Journal of Social Sciences* 10 (4).

Kaplan, M. and Marks, G. (1995) 'Appraisal of health risks: the roles of masculinity, femininity, and sex', *Sociology of Health and Illness* 17 (2).

Levine, M.P. and Troiden, R.R. (1988) 'The myth of sexual compulsivity', *Journal of Sex Research* 25 (3).

Lyng, S. (1990) 'Edgework: a social psychology of voluntary risk taking', *American Journal of Sociology* 95 (4).

McShane, M.D. and Williams, F.P. (1992) 'Radical victimology: a critique of the concept of victim in traditional victimology', *Crime and Delinquency* 38 (2).

McLeod, J. (1994) 'Issues in the organisation of counselling; learning from NMGC', *British Journal of Guidance and Counselling* 22 (2).

Miller, P. and Rose, N. (1994) 'On therapeutic authority: psychoanalytical expertise under advanced liberalism', *History of the Human Sciences* 7 (3).

Okami, P.(1992) '"Child perpetrators of sexual abuse", the emergence of a problematic deviant category', *The Journal of Sex Research* 29 (1).

Park, J. (1999) 'Politics of emotional literacy', *Renewal* 7 (1).

Pupavac, V. (2001) 'Therapeutic governance: psychosocial intervention and trauma risk management', unpublished paper, London.

Reid, J., Ewan, C. and Lowy, E. (1991) 'Pilgrimage of pain: the illness experiences of women with repetition strain injury and the search for credibility', *Social Science Medicine* 32 (5).

Richards, G. (1995) '"To know our fellow men to do them good": American psychology's enduring moral project', *History of the Human Sciences* 8 (3).

Richards, G. (2000) 'Psychology and the churches in Britain 1919–39: symptoms of conversion', *History of the Human Sciences* 13 (2).

Rind, B. and Tromovitch (1997) 'A meta-analytic review of findings from national samples on psychological correlates of child sexual abuse', *The Journal of Sex Research* 34 (3).

Rock, P. (1998) 'Murdererd, victims and "Survivors"; the social construction of deviance', *The British Journal of Criminology* 38 (2).

Rose, N. (1996) 'Psychiatry as a political science: advanced liberalism and the administration of risk', *History of the Human Sciences* 9 (2).

Russell, J. (1999) 'Counselling and the social construction of self', *British Journal of Guidance and Counselling* 27 (3).

Sarat, A. (1997) 'Vengeance, victims and the identities of law', *Social and Legal Studies*.

Scott, F.E. (2000) 'Reconsidering a therapeutic role for the state: anti-modernist governance and the reunification of the self', http://online.sfsu.edu/-fscott/scottapsa.htm

Stanko, E. and Hobdell, K. (1993) 'Assault on men: masculinity and male victimisation', *British Journal of Criminology* 33(3).

Summerfield, D. (1996) 'The psychological legacy of war and atrocity: the question of long-term and transgenerational effects and the need for a broad view', *J Nerv Ment Dis* 184.

Summerfield, D. (1999) ' A critique of seven assumptions behind psychological trauma programmes in war-affected areas', *Social Science and Medicine* 48.

Summerfield, D. (2000) 'Childhood, war, refugeedom and 'trauma': three core questions for mental health professionals', *Transcultural Psychiatry* 37(3).

Summerfield, D. (2001) 'The invention of post-traumatic disorder and the social usefulness of a psychiatric category', *British Medical Journal* 322, 13 January.

Thoits, P.A. (1989) 'The sociology of emotions', *American Review of Sociology* 15.

Wainwright, D. and Calnan, M. (2000) 'Rethinking the work stress "epidemic"', *European Journal of Public Health* 10 (3).

Williams, D.I. and Irving, J.A. (1999) 'Why are therapists indifferent to research?', *British Journal of Guidance and Counselling* 27 (3).

Winkle, H. (2001) 'A postmodern culture of grief? On individualization of mourning in Germany', *Mortality* 6 (1).

Woolfolk, A. (2002) 'The denial of character', *Society* 39 (3).

Index